YOUR CHILD
HAS A
DISABILITY

YOUR CHILD HAS A DISABILITY

A Complete Sourcebook of Daily and Medical Care

MARK L. BATSHAW, M.D.
Physician in Chief, Children's Seashore House

LITTLE, BROWN AND COMPANY

Boston   New York   Toronto   London

First Edition

Edited by Lisa Bain

Permissions to reprint previously copyright material appear on page
334.

Library of Congress Cataloging-in-Publication Data

Batshaw, Mark L., 1945–
  Your child has a disability : a complete sourcebook of daily and
medical care / Mark L. Batshaw. — 1st ed.
      p.   cm.
  Includes bibliographical references and index.
  ISBN 0-316-08368-2
  1. Developmentally disabled children—Medical care.
2. Developmentally disabled children—Care. 3. Developmentally
disabled children—Education. 4. Developmentally disabled children—
Legal status, laws, etc. I. Title.
  [DNLM: 1. Child Care. 2. Child Development Disorders.
3. Handicapped. 4. Nervous System Diseases—in infancy & childhood.
WS 340 B334y]
  RJ506.D47B37   1991
  649'.15—dc20
  DNLM/DLC   91-10580

10   9   8   7   6   5

RRD-VA

Published simultaneous.*y* in Canada by
Little, Brown & Company (Canada) Limited

Printed in the United States of America

In loving memory of my mother, Rachel Levitt, medical social worker and teacher of a learning-disabled child.

Contents

Author's Note

I would like to initially acknowledge four professionals who have helped turn my ideas into the reality of this book. The first is Lisa Bain, a medical writer without peer, who edited this book. She is the author of her own book on Attention Deficit Hyperactivity Disorder. She worked to turn the chapters that I and my collaborators wrote into easily understandable, well-organized and well-written literature. If you find the book appealing to read, it is Lisa that you have to thank. A book such as *Your Child Has a Disability* is best understood with illustrations to explain some of the medical complexities. A medical illustrator is indispensable and we had one of the best, Lynn Reynolds. Lynn was given the ideas that needed illustration and brought them to fruition in the beautiful figures that grace this book. I also wish to acknowledge Margi Ide, the medical photographer at Children's Hospital of Philadelphia, who produced the wonderful photographs in the text. Finally, I wish to credit my assistant, Margaret Rose, who organized this endeavor and kept it and me on track, as she does with all my professional activities.

I would also like to acknowledge the many friends and professionals who have reviewed and offered comments on this manuscript. These include Alan Crocker, Carolyn Morris, John Sladky, Bob Clancy, Susan Phillips, Peggy Monahan, Virginia Stallings, Mark Helpin, Joe Piven, Elaine Zackai, Beverly Emanuel, Susan Folstein, and Symme Trachtenberg.

Throughout the manuscript I have alternated between feminine and masculine pronouns in order to avoid favoritism. The names in the case vignettes have been changed to maintain confidentiality, and often represent the combined characteristics of several patients I have treated.

Preface

All parents expect their children to be brighter, prettier, happier, and more successful than themselves. In fact, we want our children to be perfect in every way. We conceived them, love them, and feel responsible for them; we see them as extensions of ourselves. When something goes wrong and our hopes are dashed, we have to deal with a wide range of unpleasant emotions, including depression, anger, anxiety, and embarrassment.

Some disabling conditions, such as Down syndrome, are evident at birth, while other disorders may not become apparent until later in childhood. Whatever your child's disability, it will necessitate some change in your attitudes and expectations. It may require that you learn new skills, administer medicines, and give various types of therapy. Initially, you won't feel you can cope; but you *will*, because your child needs you.

This book will answer many of your questions about your child's disability. It is divided into five sections. The first section deals with getting the diagnosis. Here we talk about the initial feelings you may have experienced when you first learned that your child had a disability. We also discuss steps you can take that will help you find the right doctor to care for your child.

The second section attempts to answer the question "Why my child?" These chapters describe the causes and other medical aspects of various disabling conditions and the value of genetic counseling.

The third section gives practical information about the various developmental disabilities: mental retardation, chromosomal abnormalities including Down syndrome, seizure disorders, cerebral palsy, hearing and communication disorders, blindness, autism, spina bifida, and muscular dystrophy.

The fourth section describes approaches to therapy, including behavior management techniques, nutrition and dentistry, physical therapy, occupational therapy, and the use of medications.

The final section is titled "Growing Up with a Disability." Chapters in this section explore educational issues as well as other problems you may encounter in the future. What will happen to your child as he or she grows up? What financial problems might you face and how can you deal with them? What are your legal rights? What will your child do when you are no longer around to care for her?

Each chapter begins with an introductory section that summarizes what will be discussed. This is followed by one or more vignettes about children I or my colleagues at the Children's Seashore House, a regional hospital for the care of children with special needs, have treated, and ends with some answers to commonly asked questions. Selected readings are listed at the end of the book.

This guide is intended to answer the question "How do I cope with my exceptional child?" It is the result of requests by parents who have read my textbook, *Children with Handicaps: A Medical Primer*, that I write a "Dr. Spock" for them. *Your Child Has a Disability* is derived from questions that patients and their parents have asked me and based on the assumption that knowledge adds to confidence and competency. While it will provide you with a little medical background, the book will primarily assure you that your own good common sense can be relied upon.

It is my belief that your child's problems can be managed effectively and that you and your entire family can live happily together. It is my hope that this book can help you achieve that goal.

Mark L. Batshaw, M.D.

I Getting the Diagnosis

1 YOUR CHILD HAS A DISABILITY

When you first learn that your child has a disability, you may experience profound grief, mixed with anger, denial, and guilt. In addition to coping with the loss of the normal child you expected, you must deal with the feelings of your family and friends. To act effectively, you need to understand your child's diagnosis and formulate a plan of action. You need concerned professionals who will work with you on a long-term basis. You need the support and knowledge of other parents who have gone through a similar experience. Most of all you need the love and acceptance of your family. Working together, your family will survive and eventually emerge whole. You *can* do it! When you first learn your child has a disability, you are starting at square one, but you will end up as an expert, capable of teaching others.

FIRST FEELINGS

You have a child with a disability. Maybe the realization has come only recently. Maybe you still haven't fully accepted it. As time passes, you will develop an understanding of your child's problem and proceed with the day-to-day process of meeting his or her needs. But at the same time, you must sort through your feelings of grief, anger, guilt, and despair. All parents react differently, depending on their individual personalities, their support systems, other life experiences, and the type and severity of their child's disability. But no one will deny the profound impact a disabled child has on the family.

Years ago you might not have been told your child had a disability until the doctor decided you were "ready." Although you might have suspected a problem, and even questioned your doctor, months or even years might have passed before you were told of your child's diagnosis. Doctors who withheld information from parents often did so with the best of intentions, hoping to prepare the parent and cushion the shock. "He will grow out of it" was a frequently used phrase. But instead of relieving anxiety, the withholding of information often led parents later to feel guilty that they could have done more had they known sooner. Today, parents expect straight talk, not evasion. They want as much information as possible about their child's condition, and they expect truthful answers to their questions and in terms they can understand. This consumerism has led most doctors to inform parents of the diagnosis as soon as it is made.

Yet, not all disabilities are easily diagnosed. While a child with Down syndrome can be identified on the first day of life, the effects of prematurity on development may not be evident for months or years. In some cases, the diagnosis of a developmental disability may be made only after a long period of concern about slow development. Generally speaking, the more severely affected your child is, the sooner a diagnosis can be made.

No matter when the diagnosis is actually made, and no matter how much you may have anticipated it, it usually comes as a shock. Initially, your jumbled feelings may leave you feeling numb and unable to comprehend the enormity of the situation. But once the numbness begins to subside, it often gives way to profound grief — grief over the loss of the normal child you had expected and pain at the realization that you instead have an "imperfect" child.

The dreams and hopes you have for the child you conceived are shattered when a severe disability is diagnosed. After all, to some extent most of us view our children as extensions and reflections of ourselves. Although we may openly admit to having only simple goals for them, we privately harbor great expectations and ambitions — that they will be more intelligent, more beautiful, happier, and more successful than we are. We find it difficult to imagine that a child with disabilities can provide the joy and fulfillment we had anticipated.

Parents may grieve for months or years, just as at the death of a loved one. Some parents say the grief never really ends, although it comes and goes as the child grows and changes.

During this time of pain and confusion, the family and friends you rely on for understanding and emotional support are often dealing with their own grief, leaving you feeling alone and isolated. Your spouse is probably also numbed by the knowledge, your children unable to understand what is happening, and your parents dealing not only with the grief for their grandchild but their sadness for you as well. Kind and well-meaning friends may stay away out of embarrassment, or simply because they don't know what to do. And even when you have loving support, no one can really penetrate your grief.

This grief is usually mixed with other feelings — denial, frustration, depression, guilt, and anger, to name a few.

Denial

The initial shock of the diagnosis may lead to the response "This can't be true. There must be some mistake." Denial can lead you down many frustrating paths — searching for the doctor or other professional who will give you a different diagnosis or who will promise a miracle cure. Denial can also prevent you from obtaining the proper therapy or medication, and it can leave you feeling frustrated at your child's lack of progress. Finally, outward denial of something you inwardly believe can damage your own emotional health.

Depression

Denial is often accompanied by depression, including the physical symptoms of insomnia, loss of appetite, and restlessness. You may feel profoundly sad, unable to get up in the morning to face the day. Things that previously gave you pleasure no longer make you happy. Jokes are not funny, sexual feelings disappear. You just try to make it to the end of each day.

Hopelessness and Helplessness

Many parents say they feel hopeless and helpless; hopeless at what the future offers and helpless to do anything about it. Tied up with these are feelings of failure: "I could not (or did not) protect my child from being disabled and I cannot help him now. I failed in my most basic job as a parent."

In addition, particularly with severely disabled children, you may feel helpless to satisfy even your child's most basic needs — food and love. Physical disabilities may make feeding difficult and cuddling nearly impossible. The parent who provides the day-to-day care of the child may feel some sense of satisfaction from the comforts she is able to provide, but the other parent may feel especially helpless.

At the same time, you may feel hopeless about your own future. Everyone has heard inspiring stories of mothers or fathers who abandoned their own goals so they could devote their entire lives to their disabled children. Such selflessness is certainly admirable, and has no doubt enriched the lives of some people, but for others it can be stifling and destructive.

Anger and Guilt

At some point, and perhaps frequently, many parents feel angry and search for someone or something to blame. Your anger may be directed at doctors — "What did they do (or not do) that caused this handicap?"; at your spouse — "Why do I have to do all the work?"; at friends with normal children; or even at your child. Often the anger is directed at God or at the whole world — "Why me? Why my child?" Finally, the finger-pointing may be self-directed — "What did I do to deserve this?"

Anger like this often breeds guilt, particularly when the anger is directed at your child. Even if you love your child unquestioningly, you will at some times feel angry — either because of something your child has done, such as making a huge mess, or because of the general chaos inflicted upon the entire family. You may worry that your child will be forever stigmatized, and that you too will carry this stigma. You may even wonder how you will ever love this child who seems like a stranger in many ways. You may feel ashamed of your baby. All of these feelings may lead to a sense of guilt and damaged self-esteem.

Guilt arises from other sources as well. Mothers may ask themselves, "What did I do during my pregnancy that might have caused this? Maybe I shouldn't have taken that trip, or that medication." Both parents may wonder if the disability came from their side of the family. When there is no clear explanation for the disability, guilt feelings may be severe and long lasting.

The insensitivity of others may also contribute to the problem. This may even be true of the professional who is trying to make a diagnosis or offering genetic counseling. People may ask you if you drank liquor or took any medications during your pregnancy. You may interpret such questions as "Was it your fault?" and "What can *I* do so this won't happen to any of my children?"

Of course, sometimes there is a clear reason for the disability, such as prematurity, difficult or prolonged labor and delivery, or illness in the newborn period. But even when you know the answers, you may still wonder how it could have been avoided. Even when you *know* that you did not cause the problem, you may say to yourself, "Maybe this wouldn't have happened if only I had . . ."

Guilt feelings may be further complicated by fears that you are ignoring the needs of your other children who are not disabled. The child with special needs places such a drain on time and energy that you may have little left for the other children.

Bargaining

Some parents avoid facing these feelings altogether — either by distancing themselves physically and emotionally or by intellectualizing the problem. A parent who is not engaged in the daily care of the child may have more difficulty confronting his own feelings and may retreat into a wealth of technical data, reading and gathering as much information as possible. By diverting all of his energy into the technical side of the child's problem, this parent avoids dealing with his own feelings.

Later, a period of bargaining with God, fate, or doctors may follow. Parents may change doctors or seek out help from a variety of professionals. Even parents who normally are practical and rational may find themselves thinking, "If I try this unconventional treatment, maybe he will get better," or "I'll never ask for anything again if only God will make my child whole." Parents at this time are extremely vulnerable to quacks and frauds. Even though you may see that an unconventional treatment method lacks promise, you may be tempted to reach for any thread of hope.

EFFECTS ON SIBLINGS

Brothers and sisters of children with disabilities share many of the same emotions you feel — guilt, grief, and anger. Some of this arises from misunderstanding and fear. For instance, an older sibling may think she caused the handicap by wishing harm on the new baby, whom she viewed as an intruder. Or she may fear that she could "catch" the disability, as she could catch the flu. She may also wonder, "Why did this happen to him and not to me?"

Your other children may also feel resentful and jealous of the attention given to the sister or brother who has a disability, and they may feel guilty about having these feelings. In fact, you may occasionally ignore the needs of your nonhandicapped children, reasoning that they don't need the attention as much as your affected child does. To complicate matters, your other children may hide their feelings and needs from you in an effort to protect you from additional worries. They don't want to be a "burden."

Having a brother or sister with a disability can create many conflicts for your other children. While they may feel loving and protective toward their sibling, they may also feel embarrassed. When friends laugh or make fun of the handicap, the unaffected sibling is torn between wanting to defend his brother or sister and wanting to "fit in" with his friends. He may become isolated; an "outcast." As a result, he may deny he even has a sibling with special needs.

Despite these problems, having a disabled sibling can have its positive aspects. Studies have shown that most brothers and sisters of children with disabilities develop good relationships with their family, friends, and the disabled child. They learn at an early age to be responsible, caring people. The idealism and selflessness they develop often lead them, as adults, into helping professions.

EFFECTS ON GRANDPARENTS

The birth of a child with a disability has an effect on grandparents, too. They grieve not only for their grandchild, but for you, their child, as well. And, because they don't live with the child every day, they may continue to deny the disability long after you have accepted it. Your parents may try to persuade you to deny the presence of a disability and may be unable to appreciate the difficulties involved in raising a disabled child. Some grandparents blame the parents in some way for the disability (especially the parent that is not their child). They may have rigid and old-fashioned ideas about medical care and institutionalization that make it difficult for them to support decisions that differ from their own beliefs.

Yet despite all these difficulties, grandparents can be a source of support, love, and acceptance that binds the whole family together. They are, after all, your (or your spouse's) parents — and they can give you the unconditional love that only parents can give. Many grandparents can also provide respite care, sound advice, and financial support.

ADJUSTING

During the first months of adjustment, the task of caring for your disabled child may seem overwhelming. Caring for any child consumes a parent's time and energy, but is ordinarily balanced by the rewards of witnessing the baby's rapid growth and development. When the child develops slowly, however, or if he is frequently ill or has physical disabilities, the pleasure of parenting may be nonexistent or overshadowed by anxiety, worry, and sadness.

You are always watching for signs of a problem that might further complicate your child's life and your own. You worry, "Will I recognize the first signs of a problem?," fearing that if you wait too long before seeking help, your child may become more disabled. You think to yourself,

"How can I protect my child when I was not able to make him whole to begin with?"

To add to your anxiety, your baby may be fussy and difficult to comfort, handle, or feed, making it hard for you to know whether he is ill or just bad tempered. Should you call your doctor, or wait and see if the condition resolves itself? There is no simple solution to this problem. In the beginning there will be many false alarms, but with time you will come to know your child better and you will feel more confident in trusting your instincts. You will develop a sort of "sixth" sense after the child's first few months of life.

In fact, it is uncommon for parents to miss a significant medical problem in their disabled child. More likely, you might miss a problem in one of your other children, simply because you may be less attentive to that child.

You may also worry about money. Will you be able to support your child and afford all of the needed treatments — the therapy sessions, the necessary equipment, special schooling, and so on? You may find that the added financial burden prevents you from buying a home, going on vacations, or providing special opportunities for your other children. You may feel angry about your unchosen responsibility.

The pressures from so many directions can strain your marriage to the breaking point. In fact, the incidence of divorce is higher for parents of special-needs children than for the general population. You may be unable to understand and accept your spouse's reactions to these difficulties. Everyone deals with feelings in a different way, and you may want to talk while your spouse may prefer to keep things inside. If your spouse is denying the disability, you may find it especially difficult to discuss your feelings. If you are feeling extremely angry, your spouse may distance himself from you further.

Be kind to one another. Realize that your anger is directed against the unfairness of life and not against each other. Don't turn away from each other in pain. Talk, hold each other, plan for the future. Allow yourself to express your feelings and forgive yourself for the thoughts that seem unacceptable to you. Encourage your spouse to do the same.

If you do not have strong spousal support of if you are a single parent, involve extended family members or close friends. Single parents as well as parents with strong marriages can benefit from professional counseling during this difficult time. Counseling services from a social worker, psychologist, or psychiatrist may be available through private practitioners, family and children's social service agencies, and from medical centers. Ask your doctor for a referral. Most agencies and medical centers work on a sliding scale of fees based on income. Many of these services are also covered under major medical policies.

Try not to let the presence of your child's disability dominate all aspects of your life. It is virtually impossible to be a good parent twenty-four hours a day. Take time for yourself. Get a baby-sitter so you can go out some nights, find respite care so you can spend a weekend away. Finding a baby-sitter can be difficult and take much perseverance, but is absolutely necessary for your own mental health. Try engaging your child's therapists, teachers, or aides. Depending on the disability, names of caregivers may also be available through local organizations such as the Association of Retarded Citizens or the United Cerebral Palsy Association.

Go out and do things for yourself and for your other children. When you feel better about yourself, you will be a more effective parent.

REACHING OUT

Many parents find that their feelings of helplessness or inadequacy subside somewhat when they take action. Find something you can do to help your child. For instance, you might enroll him in an infant stimulation program, seek out the proper toys, or arrange for him to get special types of therapy. Infant stimulation programs are run, without cost to you, by publicly funded agencies and public school systems (see chapter 20). If indicated, you may want to combine this with private occupational, physical, and/or speech therapy (see chapters 11, 17, and 18).

Become involved in parents' groups. Knowing that you are not alone can be comforting, and you may find helpful suggestions in the experiences of other parents. Hospitals, social service agencies, and parents' organizations may offer special-needs groups for parents of children with certain disabilities, for instance premature babies, or children with cerebral palsy or Down syndrome.

Your personal involvement can reach beyond the needs of your own child. As you become familiar with services available to children with disabilities, you may find a new target for your anger. In many states, programs are inadequate. Political activism to improve local and federal support for children with disabilities, or involvement in self-help organizations (such as the Association for Retarded Citizens), can give you a new sense of direction and satisfaction. However, it is important that your interests remain multidimensional and not solely focused on activism to the exclusion of other activities.

ACCEPTANCE

After months or even years of emotional upheaval, most parents eventually come to terms with their child's disability. Unfortunately, acceptance may not come to both parents at the same time. When views of the child are very different, communication between parents may become strained. One parent may never emerge from a state of denial or grief, lessening his or her ability to cope.

Even once acceptance has occurred, certain events or periods in your child's life may rekindle the sense of pain and loss. These times include school entrance, when your child is placed in a special education program; middle adolescence, when children normally start dating; late adolescence, when other children leave home, go to college, or start a job; and young adulthood, when children enter into marriage and parenthood. At these junctures in life, you may again need to come to terms with your feelings of anger and sadness.

When acceptance has been achieved by both parents, family life can begin to take on a sense of normality. Of course, your family will never be "normal" in the sense that you imagined before the birth or diagnosis of your child with a disability, but you will begin to enjoy the simple pleasures of family life that had been buried under grief, anger, and guilt. As one mother explained, "Our child's disability is no longer the main theme in our lives." You may even develop a deeper sense of appreciation for people and things around you.

You will also begin to see your child's disability with a wider perspective. You will no longer feel constantly overwhelmed, but in better control and able to manage. And you may see progress in your child that, while it may lag far behind the norm, will fill you with the same sense of pride you felt when your other children reached developmental milestones.

SOME QUESTIONS ANSWERED

I'm afraid of my baby. What should I do?

Having a child with major medical problems is frightening. It is natural for you to worry about whether you are feeding him enough or if you are hurting him. You should make sure you understand instructions about caring for your child before you take him home from the hospital. All states have early intervention programs that start in infancy and are provided at no cost. Usually, a physical or occupational therapist will work with your child and train you. If there are severe medical problems, a public health nurse may be able to visit you regularly at home. The more you learn, the more confident you will feel in caring for your child. By the time he is a year old, you probably will feel quite safe and secure.

What do I tell our family, friends, and neighbors?

It is better to take the mystery out of the situation. Tell them briefly what is wrong and what is being done about it. Concealing your child's diagnosis only leads to rumors and future embarrassment and discomfort. Your family and friends can be an enormous source of support to you, but not if you keep them at a distance. If they seem remote or uncomfortable at first, remember that you too may have felt uncomfortable around a person with a disability before you had your child.

Although you may be fortunate in having supportive relatives and friends, you may find yourself extra-sensitive and easily offended by remarks made by strangers, friends, and family members. With time you will learn to respond appropriately to such awkward situations. You do not have to give an explanation to everyone who makes a well-intentioned but insensitive remark. If someone is genuinely interested and helpful, you may want to give a short explanation, but if they are simply prying, give them a dirty look!

What do I tell her sister and brother?

This depends on the age of your unaffected children. Young children require only simple explanations; be sure to be clear and specific. For example, if your child is mentally retarded, you might say: "Your sister cannot learn things as quickly as most children can, and we will all need to help her." If a young child wants more information, he or she will ask.

As your children grow older and become more capable of understanding, you can tell them more. Be frank and forthright. There are many books written for children that describe various disabling conditions. You may want to read these to your child as a focus for your discussions.

Older children will need a fuller and more accurate description of their brother's or sister's disability. Don't hold things back; it only leaves them guessing at the truth. In trying to protect them, you may actually convey the message that you don't trust them, which can intensify their feelings of insecurity. Or they may interpret your withholding of information as proof that you think the disability is something too horrible to think about or to discuss. They may think you are angry with them, or that they are to blame for causing this disability. They may fear they will catch it. Truth will help to allay these fears and will bring you closer together.

2

FINDING A DOCTOR
Pediatric Care

Your child will receive services from a number of health-care professionals. But it is usually the pediatrician who provides overall management, arranging for different types of treatment and monitoring your child's progress. So it's important that you find the right pediatrician, one who will be willing to spend more time than usual with you, and show sensitivity to your child's special needs. Even if their child gets specialized care from a multidisciplinary medical facility, most parents depend on a community pediatrician for routine care.

How do you select the best pediatrician for your child? Many parents choose a pediatrician before their baby is born — usually with no idea that their child will have a disability. Sometimes parents have developed a relationship with the pediatrician who cares for their older children. But the birth of a disabled child presents special challenges for a pediatrician, and it marks a good time to reassess earlier choices.

First, you must feel assured that your pediatrician has excellent medical skills. Any physician can call himself a pediatrician, but only one who has completed

three years of formal pediatric training after medical school and has passed an examination administered by the American Board of Pediatrics is a Fellow of the American Academy of Pediatrics (FAAP). Make sure the pediatrician you choose has passed this exam.

Second, try to assess other aspects of the physician and his or her practice that are important for your child's situation. Many knowledgeable pediatricians do not enjoy working with disabled children, or they may be so busy that they can't give your child adequate attention. Depending upon your own and your child's needs, you may prefer an older doctor with years of experience; or you may choose a doctor recently graduated from medical school who may be more knowledgeable about the latest techniques and approaches to specific problems.

You can obtain recommendations about good pediatricians from a number of places. Parents of other disabled children are one good source, as are organizations concerned with your child's specific disabilities. These groups often can provide a list of pediatricians in your area who have a special interest in developmentally disabled children. You can also contact the state chapter of the American Academy of Pediatrics, which has a list of pediatricians belonging to the subspecialty section of Disabilities. Such pediatricians may also be members of the American Academy for Cerebral Palsy and Developmental Medicine or the Society for Developmental Pediatrics. These physicians work specifically with children who have developmental problems. Finally, many children's hospitals have child-development treatment programs and maintain lists of interested pediatricians.

If you already have a pediatrician for your other children, you may want to schedule a consultation to discuss whether he or she feels comfortable taking care of your newly diagnosed disabled child. Most physicians will be candid and refer you to a colleague with a specific interest in handicapped children if they don't have the time or inclination to treat your child.

If you are already going to a pediatrician and find he doesn't suit your needs, explain your concerns to him. If you still feel dissatisfied, or if he is unresponsive or insensitive to your concerns, find someone else and don't feel guilty. It will be best for both of you if you change doctors rather than allowing yourself to become angry or feel desperate. However, if your doctor is the one to tell you that your child has a disability, you may be inappropriately angry with him because of the bad news. Please remember not to "kill the messenger." Also, if you are looking for another doctor just because the physician has not found a cause or cure for your child's disability, reconsider your decision to change doctors. Remember that there usually are no quick answers.

A complicating factor in your selection of a doctor is the revolution currently going on in health-care delivery systems.

Health Maintenance Organizations (HMOs), a form of prepaid health insurance, are becoming increasingly popular with both employers and employees because they offer a lower-cost alternative to Blue Cross or other third-party-payor programs. However, if you belong to an HMO, you relinquish the freedom to choose any doctor — you must go to a doctor within the health plan and you cannot seek specialist consultation without prior approval. Further, you may not be able to receive compensation for rehabilitation services. A second type of health care delivery system, a Preferred Provider Organization (PPO), is a somewhat more costly alternative. In a PPO you have more freedom choosing a physician as long as he or she accepts this prepaid health plan.

These systems contrast with the traditional, and more expensive, fee-for-service medical care, which allows you to go to the doctor or hospital of your choice, with payment provided either by you or by an insurance plan such as Blue Cross/Blue Shield.

Make sure you understand the limitations imposed by your insurance policy. Read the small print on the contracts or get help from your agent. This information will help you make an informed choice regarding your selection of a health-care provider. In some cases, you may have to balance expense against the quality of services offered.

TAKING YOUR CHILD'S HISTORY

Once you have made your choice, your child is ready to have an examination. How will this visit differ from those you have experienced with your other children? In many respects, the examination will be the same, although usually more detailed. The exact form of the exam will depend on the type and severity of your child's problems. Expect fairly personal questions.

To begin the evaluation, the pediatrician may ask if you have any particular concerns. Take this opportunity to guide the doctor toward problems that might be troubling you, for example, "Why doesn't he talk?" or "When will he start walking?"

The doctor will then take an extensive history of your pregnancy, delivery, and your child's problems. He may begin by asking questions about your pregnancy. Did you have spotting? Did you have high blood pressure, diabetes, asthma, thyroid problems, or other chronic diseases? Were you receiving medications? You may be asked if you drank, smoked, or took drugs during the pregnancy. Don't be offended by these questions; they often give the physician clues about the nature of your child's problems. For example, women with diabetes are at increased risk for having children with malformations, and anticonvulsant medications are known to increase the risk of developmental disabilities. Chapter 3 discusses some of the known associations between medications and illnesses and disabilities. Most disabilities are not linked to diseases or to medications taken during pregnancy. Nevertheless, many mothers fear that they did something wrong during pregnancy that affected their child. Your first appointment is a good time to bring up your fears and have the doctor comment.

Remember, the questions asked are not meant to place blame; rather, they may provide pieces of the puzzle that will help the doctor know what to look for and lead him to an accurate diagnosis. They may also allow the doctor to rule out genetic disease, which, if present, increases your risk of having a second affected child.

Next, the pediatrician will ask whether your labor was prolonged or the delivery difficult, if there was premature rupture of membranes, if a cesarean section was needed, and whether the afterbirth looked normal. Sometimes difficult deliveries result in oxygen deprivation in the baby, which can lead to disabilities. Questions about the newborn period will also be asked to determine if your child appeared normal at birth. Were there any physical abnormalities? Information about your child's height, weight, and head size in the newborn period may indicate whether he grew normally during the pregnancy. Low birth weight suggests that the placenta, or afterbirth, was not functioning properly and that the child did not get adequate nourishment or oxygen before birth. Decreased head size often indicates the presence of prenatal brain damage.

Questions will also be asked about problems during the newborn period. Did your baby have yellow jaundice? Did he require oxygen? Were there seizures or problems with low blood sugar? Were there infections? What the doctor is looking for is whether there were complications that may have caused brain damage. You may not know the answers to all these questions, but the hospital record can fill in many of the blanks. You have the right to see and obtain a copy of that record. (We will cover the interpretation of medical records later in this chapter.)

The next questions concern what happened after your baby came home. Did he suck well after the first week? Many normal babies have a weak suck during the first few days of life, but infants who are overly sleepy or have a persistently weak sucking reflex or a weak cry may have a developmental disability. Was he "too good" a baby — quiet even when left alone for a prolonged period of time? Was his muscle tone stiff, floppy, or normal? Abnormalities in tone often signal that some type of brain damage occurred prior to, during, or shortly after birth. If everything was normal in infancy, the cause of the disability probably occurred sometime later in life.

The history-taking will then move on to your child's past hospitalizations, evaluations, illnesses, accidents, allergies, immunizations, and medications. Have there been side effects to certain medications? Your own records and copies of records from past medical examinations can help provide the information.

Next, the doctor will take a detailed developmental history. When did your child sit up, roll over, walk? When did he coo, babble, say his first word? How old was he when he transferred objects from hand to hand, fed himself, dressed himself? (Normal developmental milestones are discussed in detail in chapter 5.) Your baby book may help you answer these questions. But don't get flustered if you didn't write everything down or if you have trouble remembering. You aren't being graded as a parent by how many milestones you can remember. It is simply a way of determining when development became abnormal. It also allows the doctor to determine if the rate of development has changed over time. Your doctor might ask, "Is your child smarter now than he was last year, and by how much?" or "At what age level does your child seem to be functioning?" Parents are often surprised to find that after all the testing is done, their initial guess at their child's level of functioning usually turns out to be quite accurate.

For older children, a school history will be taken. How long has your child been attending his present school? Is he in a special-education class? Are you satisfied with that placement? Is your child happy at school? Have you seen his IEP (individual education plan) for the year?

The doctor will then scrutinize your child's behavior. How long is his attention span? Is he distractible, noncompliant, or hyperactive? Are there sleeping problems? Is he aggressive, impulsive, fearful, or destructive? Does he follow directions? Does he have temper tantrums, show attention-seeking behavior, have episodes of lying or stealing? Does he rock back and forth, suck his thumb, grind his teeth, bang his head, or have other self-stimulatory or self-injurious behavior? How does he get along with other children? Has he been treated by using behavioral therapy or stimulant medications? With these questions, the doctor is attempting to determine the extent of behavioral problems and the steps that have been taken to correct them.

Last, a family history will be taken to probe for genetic-based disorders. The doctor will want to know if other members of your family have had similar problems and if you and your spouse were related prior to marriage. Some genetic disorders that cause developmental disabilities are more likely to occur in families in which relatives have intermarried. Recognition of a genetic basis for your child's disability can have implications for future pregnancies (see chapter 4) and may also affect how your child is treated. For example, some developmental disabilities are caused by genetic defects in the production of certain enzymes, as in the case of phenylketonuria (PKU); modification of diet can improve outcome in these cases.

THE PHYSICAL EXAMINATION

The physician will now examine your child. During the interview, he has been observing your child and developing some preliminary impressions. For instance, is this child overactive or, on the other hand, uninterested in her environment? Does she have an unusual facial appearance? Is her muscle tone abnormally increased or decreased? Is she reacting to sights and sounds around her?

The examination often begins with the head and ends with the toes, but this sequence varies from one physician to another. We will cover some of the main features of the exam. The physician or nurse may measure your child's height, weight, and the circumference of his head. By plotting these data on a chart, the physician can determine if your child's physical growth is normal. Many children with mental retardation are smaller than normal.

She will examine the eyes. She may shine a light into your child's eyes to see if the pupils (the dark center) constrict and if the child can follow the light normally. Next, she uses an ophthalmoscope, a magnifying lens with a light source, to look through the pupil into the back of the eye. She can see the retina (the photographic film of the eye), the optic nerve, and the blood vessels in the eye, and can determine if there is a physical reason for any visual loss.

She will examine hearing by observing whether your child responds to crinkling paper or whispering, or whether your child will turn toward a loud noise. The physician will also examine your child's ears with an otoscope, another magnifying light source. Scarring of the eardrum or fluid collection behind the membrane may indicate a middle ear infection.

She will listen to heart and lung sounds with a stethoscope placed against the chest. The doctor will then feel your child's abdomen. Tenderness might indi-cate an intestinal problem. She may also detect liver or spleen enlargement, which can be present in children with certain neurological disorders.

Your doctor will examine the arms and legs to see whether the limbs move normally and whether the muscle tone is normal. By watching your child walk, by testing his strength, and by moving the limbs around, the doctor will answer several questions: Does the child walk or crawl normally? Are there any muscle contractures or spasticity? Are there unusual movements of the arms or legs?

The neurologic examination continues by testing tendon reflexes by lightly tapping against tendons at the elbow, wrist, knee, and ankle with a rubber reflex hammer. Normally the tapping elicits a slight jerking of the limb; no response or a very strong jerk is abnormal.

The doctor will next test the function of the cranial nerves. The doctor will also check for the presence of primitive reflexes that are found in newborns. Normally these reflexes disappear before one year of age, but they persist in children with cerebral palsy.

Testing

After he has given your child a physical examination, the doctor may decide to do medical tests that will further assess the disability. We will describe some of the more commonly used tests, but keep in mind that different tests are appropriate for different disabilities and, in some cases, no medical tests at all may be needed. Some of the most common tests are the EEG, CT or MRI scan, chromosomal analysis, and metabolic screen. Depending on the complexity of the test, results will take anywhere from one day to one month to become available. You should call your doctor to be counseled regarding the test results. Don't just assume the results are normal if you haven't heard from your doctor. They could have been lost or forgotten! You will also have less anxiety once you know the tests are normal.

The EEG or electroencephalogram, often called the brain wave test, looks for seizure activity in the brain. It is not a test for mental retardation. Often, the child is given a sedative before the test so that she will lie still and perhaps fall asleep. (This test is described in more detail in chapter 8.)

The CT or computed tomographic scan is a technique in which multiple X-ray images are assembled by a computer into cross-sectional views of the brain. Another test called MRI, or magnetic resonance imaging, produces more precise images of the brain and doesn't use X-rays. Both tests can show if the brain is normal in size or shrunken, and if there is enlargement of the ventricles suggesting hydrocephalus (see chapter 14). Most children with mental retardation, however, will have either normal scans or images that show nothing more than mild shrinkage of brain tissue.

A chromosomal analysis is a blood test to study the number and structure of the chromosomes in your child's cells. This test is usually reserved for children who are born with multiple malformations or who may have Fragile X syndrome (see chapter 7). The chromosome study requires about a teaspoon of blood. The test results are available in about three weeks.

A metabolic screen may be done on blood or urine. Its purpose is to detect inborn errors of metabolism, which indicate a child born with a defective or absent enzyme that is needed to detoxify waste products in the body (see chapter 16). The diseases that result — examples include phenylketonuria, hypothyroidism, and ma-

ple syrup urine disease — can cause mental retardation.

READING A MEDICAL REPORT

After all this questioning, examining, and testing, your doctor will write up a report. Like any other technical area, medicine has its own specialized language. This makes doctor's records as difficult to understand as lawyer's contracts! The following is a sample medical history of a child with a developmental delay, along with an accompanying translation. You may find it helpful in interpreting what you read in your own child's records. It is crucial, however, that you sit down with your doctor and go over your child's record so that you understand the important points.

A Medical History

CHIEF COMPLAINT: John is an eleven-month-old white male referred by his pediatrician for evaluation of developmental delay.

PAST HISTORY. John was the 2.5 kg product of a thirty-four-week gestation born to a thirty-year-old gravida 2, para 0 mother by spontaneous vertex delivery after an eight-hour labor. The pregnancy was complicated by intermittent spotting and pre-eclampsia. Fetal activity was normal. Five-minute Apgar score was 4.

TRANSLATION: John weighed 5½ pounds when he was born six weeks before his due date. (The normal pregnancy is forty weeks.) His mother had two previous pregnancies (gravida 2) but this was to be her first live born child (para 0); the other children were miscarried. She was delivered normally, with the baby's head coming out first from the birth canal (spontaneous vertex delivery). The mother had high blood pressure and protein in her urine during the pregnancy (pre-eclampsia). The fetus kicked and moved about normally (normal fetal activity). However, at birth the baby was not active and had trouble breathing. This accounts for the low Apgar score (4 out of 10), which measures activity of the newborn baby minutes after birth.

In the neonatal period the child's course was complicated by RDS and he required mechanical ventilation for five days. Jaundice was also evident with a peak level of 12 mg/dl which required phototherapy. At seven days of age he developed lethargy and refused feedings. He was found to be septic with beta Streptococcus cultured from the blood and required intravenous antibiotics for fourteen days. Ultrasound of his head revealed a grade 3 intraventricular hemorrhage. This resolved over two weeks. He was discharged home at one month of age, feeding well and showing interest in his environment. However, he was noted to have increased tone in his lower extremities.

TRANSLATION: In the first day after birth (neonatal period), he developed a breathing disorder common to premature infants called respiratory distress syndrome, or RDS. Treatment involved placing a tube down the windpipe and using a ventilator to keep the lungs expanded and filled with air (mechanical ventilation). Within days the lungs started to produce the chemical necessary to keep the lungs expanded and the baby was able to be taken off the ventilator. His liver was also immature, resulting in a buildup of the yellow pigment bilirubin in his blood. This turned his skin and the whites of his eyes yellow (jaundice). His bilirubin level of 12 was quite high for a premature baby, who normally would have levels of about 1 to

2. Because high levels of bilirubin can cause brain damage, he was placed under fluorescent lights (phototherapy) in order to break down the bilirubin pigment. He also had blood poisoning (sepsis); the bacteria Streptococcus had infected his body. Fortunately, this organism was responsive to the antibiotic penicillin, which was given into a vein (intravenous) in his forearm.

The major concern at the time of discharge was that an ultrasound of his head showed some blood in the ventricles or reservoirs of the brain (intraventricular hemorrhage). This hemorrhage may have resulted from the sepsis or from lack of oxygen due to the RDS. Although repeat ultrasounds demonstrated that the blood gradually disappeared over a two-week period, this placed the baby at risk for having cerebral palsy and swelling of the ventricles (hydrocephalus).

DEVELOPMENTAL HISTORY: Expressive language: John cooed at four months, babbled at five months, produced a non-specific da-da at seven months. Receptive language: social smile four months, understood "no" and played gesture games at ten months. Gross-motor skills: held head up three months, sat with support at eight months. Does not sit alone, crawl, or pull to stand. Fine-motor skills: unfisted at six months, transferred objects seven months, pincer grasp at 10 months. Mother feels most skills are at a seven- to eight-month level.

TRANSLATION: Language skills are developing normally while there is a delay in motor skills (see chapter 5).

PHYSICAL EXAM: Height 71 cm (10 percentile), Weight 11 kg (50 percentile), Head circumference 50 cm (greater than

95 percentile). John's appearance is of an attractive child with a large head, who seemed happy and attentive.

HEENT: no focus of infection. Anterior fontanel open. Intermittent left esotropia. Fixes and follows visually.

Chest: lungs clear

CVS: heart sounds and rhythm normal without murmurs

Abdomen: soft without organomegaly

Genitalia: normal male with testes bilaterally descended.

Extremities: feet held in equinus position. Tone increased in lower extremities with clasp-knife spasticity. Achilles tendon could not be dorsiflexed to a neutral position.

CNS examination: Cranial nerves are intact. Reflexes are 4+ in the lower extremities and 2+ in the upper extremities. Babinski sign was present bilaterally. The only persisting primitive reflex was the positive support.

TRANSLATION: At eleven months of age when he was referred to us, his height and weight were within the normal range for age, but his head circumference was very large. This suggested the possibility of hydrocephalus. His soft-spot (anterior fontanel) was normally soft, indicating that the brain was not under excessive pressure. There was no evidence of infection in the head, eyes, ears, nose, or throat (HEENT). The eyes were crossed (esotropia), which is common in children with cerebral palsy. Listening with the stethoscope to the chest revealed no abnormalities in the lungs.

The cardiovascular system (CVS) showed no heart murmur or other abnormality. The abdominal exam did not reveal an enlargement in the kidneys, spleen, or liver (no organomegaly). The baby's penis and testes were normal in size, and the testes were in the sack (descended). The arms

moved normally and had normal tone and reflexes. However, his feet were held pointed downward (equinus) and the ankles (Achilles tendon) could not be flexed to a normal walking (neutral) position. His legs were spastic, with increased tone that suddenly gave way like a boy-scout knife blade (clasped-knife). When the tendon below the kneecap was tapped lightly, the leg jerked briskly (4+ reflex). When the bottom of the foot was stroked, the big toe moved upward (Babinski sign) rather than flexing downward, as is normal at that age. All primitive reflexes should have been gone by eleven months, but in John, the positive support reflex was still present, meaning that he held his legs stiff when his feet were bounced on the floor.

DEVELOPMENTAL TESTING: Cognition: expressive and receptive language were judged to be at the nine- to ten-month level as he was able to say an inappropriate "mama," oriented toward a bell, and exhibited understanding of gestures and "no." His problem-solving skills were also at the nine- to ten-month range, including pincer grasp. Motor: gross-motor skills, however, were delayed and felt to be in the six-month range. He was able to roll over and sit with support.

TRANSLATION: The developmental examination showed that his gross-motor skills (sitting and walking) were delayed but that his cognitive (intellectual) skills were near appropriate for his age. This indicates that the damage does not appear to have affected his intelligence. His legs were more affected than his arms.

DIAGNOSES:

1. Cerebral palsy — mild spastic diplegia
2. No significant cognitive delay
3. Rule out hydrocephalus

DISPOSITION:

1. Evaluation by Physical Therapy, Occupational Therapy.
2. Referral to infant stimulation program with physical therapy.
3. CT scan scheduled for evaluation of suspected hydrocephalus.
4. Return to clinic three months.

TRANSLATION: All signs are consistent with cerebral palsy. That the signs were present in the legs (*lower extremities*) more than the arms provides the diagnosis of *spastic diplegia* (spastic cerebral palsy affecting primarily the legs). This is the most common form of cerebral palsy occurring in premature infants. It probably resulted from lack of oxygen and decreased blood pressure, leading to a hemorrhage into the brain and subsequent damage to the part of the brain that controls leg movement.

As mentioned earlier, his intellectual ability does not appear impaired. However, John may be at risk for further brain damage if he has developed hydrocephalus. If a CT scan confirms hydrocephalus, John will probably undergo surgery to have a drainage tube or *ventricular-peritoneal shunt* placed. This will divert the accumulating ventricular fluid into the abdominal cavity where it can be absorbed (see chapter 14). We will also refer him to an infant stimulation program where he will receive an appropriate educational experience and he will be evaluated by occupational and physical therapists for other types of treatment. He will come back for reevaluations at three-month intervals to make sure he is making progress and that there are no new problems.

SOME QUESTIONS ANSWERED

Will my doctor get angry if I question what he is doing?

If your doctor yells at you when you ask questions, consider getting another doctor! Doctors with busy practices may not schedule sufficient time for long explanations during a routine visit, but you can make an appointment for a longer consultation during which he can take the time necessary to answer all your questions.

What if I want to refuse to have a test done on my child?

A physician cannot perform any test on your child without your approval. In fact, for certain tests you have to sign a written consent form. Do not be afraid to decline a test if you are worried that your child may not benefit from it or that it may be painful to him. State your reason for refusing. Your doctor may be able to provide information that will allay your fears, or he may agree with you. In any event, you will have made an informed decision.

How often should my child be examined?

That depends on your child's medical problems. In some cases once every six to twelve months may be sufficient. In other instances, such as a child who has many seizures, biweekly or monthly visits may be necessary. However, at least once a year your child should be reexamined to see how he is doing, to adjust medications, and to determine if there are any new therapies that should be started. Generally, children are seen less frequently as they grow older.

II Why My Child?

3

WHY MY CHILD?
Causes of Disabling Conditions

Every parent of a disabled child asks, at one time or another, "Why my child?" For some, an answer will help them choose therapy, find a support group of parents who have children with similar disorders, or make decisions about having other children. But for many parents, there will be no answers. When no explanation for the handicap can be found, parents may expend much emotional energy, and a great deal of money, searching for a diagnosis. Lacking a cause, they find themselves uncertain about the long-term prognosis and the possibility of future children being affected. Sometimes the long search for a cause can take precious time away from the search for solutions.

In general, the more severe the disability, the more likely there is to be a diagnosable cause. Conversely, the majority of mild disabilities remain mysteries. In this chapter, we will discuss some of the many causes of developmental disabilities. You may find clues that will help you answer your questions, or you may decide that your energy would be better spent elsewhere.

The causes of developmental disabilities can be divided into those that occur before

birth (prenatally), during birth (perinatally), or after birth (postnatally). We will discuss each in turn.

PRENATAL CAUSES OF DEVELOPMENTAL DISABILITIES

Most severe developmental disabilities occur before birth, either as a result of a genetic disorder, exposure to damaging substances in the environment, infection of the mother, or for as yet unknown reasons. With so many opportunities for things to go wrong, one might wonder not that there are so many disabled children, but that there are so few. It is important to understand that although there are many causes of disabilities, each is so rare that the total number of affected children is small. About 95 percent of all children are born healthy.

Genetic Causes

The most common genetically transmitted developmental disabilities are the chromosomal disorders Down syndrome and Fragile X syndrome (see chapter 7). The second type of inherited disorder involves defects in single genes inside a chromosome and causes diseases such as phe-nylketonuria (chapter 16) and muscular dystrophy (chapter 14). Finally there can be interactions between heredity and environment as in spina bifida (chapter 14).

Radiation

Other forms of prenatally induced brain damage have an environmental basis. Environmental agents include radiation and drugs. The most extreme example of radiation damage occurred in pregnant women who survived the atomic bomb blasts in Hiroshima and Nagasaki. A large percentage of these women gave birth to babies who had small heads and were severely mentally retarded. These women received massive doses of irradiation. In contrast, diagnostic medical X-rays expose a woman to minute doses. Nevertheless, since we do not know what dose of radiation is safe for the fetus, doctors generally avoid exposing women to medical X-rays, especially during their first three months of pregnancy, when the baby's organs are being formed.

Medications

Likewise, some drugs given to women in the first three months of pregnancy can adversely affect the fetus. A number of medications have been associated with fetal malformations. The most disastrous example occurred in the late 1950s when thalidomide, an antinausea medication, was introduced in Europe. Hundreds of infants were born with short, flipperlike limbs before the link with thalidomide was established. In recent years, other medications have been shown to damage the fetus. Dilantin, a commonly used seizure-control medication, produces malformations of the face, arms, and legs, and mental retardation in about 10 percent of infants whose mothers take it during the first three months of pregnancy. Use of de-

pakene, a new seizure medication, has been linked to an increased incidence of spina bifida. Accutane (also called Retin A or isotretinoin), a vitamin A preparation used to treat acne, has resulted in the birth of a number of infants with facial and brain malformations. Although there has been concern about other drugs, such as aspirin, the medications mentioned here are the principal ones in general use that have been conclusively shown to cause fetal malformations. However, it is suggested that you avoid taking any medication during your pregnancy other than that which is essential to your health. Such decisions should be made in consultation with your doctor.

Alcohol

The drug most commonly associated with fetal malformations is not one of these medications; it's alcohol. Approximately one-third of babies born to alcoholic women are mentally retarded and may have deformed limbs, small heads, and heart defects. The degree of malformation depends on the amount of alcohol consumed, when it was consumed during the pregnancy, and whether the drinking occurred in binges. No one has yet identified a "safe" drinking level; even moderate or occasional drinking may place the fetus at some risk. Until more is known, most doctors recommend that you abstain from drinking, especially during the early months of pregnancy.

At this time, there is no concrete evidence that marijuana, cocaine, hallucinogens, or even heroin causes fetal malformations. However, some drugs of abuse, especially heroin and cocaine, may lead to a serious withdrawal state in the baby's first week of life, characterized by episodes of low blood sugar and seizures. Cigarette smoking also has not been proven to cause fetal malformations. However, if you smoke one to two packs per day, your baby is likely to be one to two pounds underweight at birth. Low birth weight predisposes the baby to a whole host of problems.

Viral Infections

Illnesses in pregnant women, especially viral infections, can also affect the fetus, causing brain damage and other disabilities. In years past the most common virus at fault was rubella, or German measles. This illness causes only a low-grade fever and rash in the mother, but can severely affect the fetus. Approximately one-half of mothers infected with the rubella virus during the first three months of pregnancy bear babies who are vision impaired, deaf, and usually mentally retarded. Until 1969 when a vaccine became available, epidemics occurred regularly at eight-year intervals. Fortunately, since that time the congenital rubella syndrome has become very rare. Women are now routinely given a blood test before they become pregnant to determine if they are protected against the rubella virus. If they are not protected, they are vaccinated and told to avoid becoming pregnant for two months. It is comforting to note that even women who became pregnant within weeks of their vaccination have had normal babies.

Unfortunately there are no vaccines for the other common viral illnesses that can damage the fetus, including cytomegalovirus (called CMV or CID), herpes, and AIDS. CMV infections are often asymptomatic in the mother, but may infect the fetus, causing malformations and mental retardation. Some research suggests that 10 percent of all babies with small heads (microcephaly) may have been affected by CMV infection of the mother during early pregnancy. Later in pregnancy, CMV infection may cause hearing loss in affected children, but not mental retardation. Fortunately, only a small fraction (perhaps one in one hundred) of fetuses exposed to CMV develop abnormalities. However, the high incidence of this infection in the general population has led to the search for a vaccine.

Herpes can infect the fetus causing congenital malformations during the first months of pregnancy only if the mother develops a severe infection, shown by high fever and a rash. Cold sores and vaginal infections do not affect the fetus. However, a baby born to a mother with active vaginal herpes is at about a 50 percent risk for contracting herpes during passage through the infected birth canal. The systemic infection that can result in the infant can be life-threatening and can cause mental retardation. Babies born to mothers with vaginal herpes are delivered by cesarean section in order to prevent infection. Women treated for their herpes infection have a less than 5 percent risk of infecting their babies via vaginal delivery.

Chicken pox may also harm the fetus during the first three months of pregnancy, although the abnormalities are less severe and less common than with rubella, CMV, or herpes. Limb or facial abnormalities and, less frequently, brain damage may result. A vaccine for chicken pox is now being tested.

The most recent concern for fetal damage is congenital acquired immune deficiency syndrome, or AIDS. AIDS is a fatal viral disease that damages the body's immune system, leaving the affected individual at the mercy of infections. The disease is transmitted sexually or through the blood. Hemophiliacs and others who receive blood transfusions are also at some increased risk. Women who become pregnant while carrying the HIV virus can pass on the disease to their baby. If this occurs during early pregnancy, the baby may develop AIDS.

Maternal Illness

Unlike the specific viral infections mentioned above, other viral and bacterial infections, such as influenza, strep throat, or urinary-tract infections, do not damage the fetus. Thus, you shouldn't be worried if you have a cold or fever during pregnancy. Also remember that after the first three months of pregnancy, malformations are unlikely to occur. However, there are other illnesses in the mother that can affect the baby. The most common of these is diabetes. Fetuses of diabetic mothers are at risk for a number of abnormalities, including spina bifida, heart problems, and malformations of the legs. Good control of the diabetes has shown to reduce markedly the risk to the fetus.

Placenta Praevia and Toxemia

There are also other maternal problems that develop late in pregnancy and place the fetus at risk for brain damage. Such complications include placenta praevia and toxemia. In placenta praevia, the placenta, or afterbirth, overlies the cervix, the entry from the womb into the vagina. When the cervix opens prior to delivery, the placenta may tear, leading to hemorrhage. This requires emergency delivery, usually by cesarean section. Fortunately, ultrasound can detect placenta praevia before the onset of labor. Then an elective C-section may be performed to avoid tearing the placenta.

Toxemia, or pregnancy-induced hypertension, is a disorder most commonly found in pregnant teenagers and in women over the age of thirty-five. Its symptoms are high blood pressure, edema (swelling), and the presence of protein in the urine. If left untreated, toxemia often leads to premature delivery, brain damage, or stillbirth caused by a lack of adequate oxygen. Treatment of toxemia includes bed rest and medications to control the mother's high blood pressure. But sometimes premature delivery is unavoidable.

PERINATAL PROBLEMS

Labor and delivery present a new set of potential problems for the baby. A number of complications can arise during the birthing process that may deprive the baby of oxygen. This, in turn, can cause brain damage. These complications, which are mostly avoidable if the baby is delivered by C-section, include nonprogressive labor, cord prolapse, breech presentation, twinning, and cephalo-pelvic disproportion.

Nonprogressive Labor and Cord Prolapse

In cephalo-pelvic disproportion, the baby's head is too large to make it through the mother's pelvic opening. This leads to a nonprogressive labor, in which the baby fails to move adequately through the birth canal. This stresses the baby's oxygen supply and places the child at risk for brain damage. The obstetrician will then perform a C-section.

In cord prolapse, the umbilical cord, through which the baby receives fresh blood from the mother, gets trapped below the head of the infant and is compressed during the labor contractions. This restricts the blood flow to the baby and may lead to brain damage. The treatment again is a C-section.

Breech Presentation and Twins

Breech (backside first) presentation is a problem because the baby may not move as smoothly through the birth canal as he would in a normal, head-first presentation.

The baby's head may get stuck or undergo excessive pressure during a breech delivery. Again, blood flow to the brain may be compromised.

Twin births are also risky, especially for the second baby born. The labor may last longer than usual, and the second twin is often breech, complicating the delivery.

The Apgar Score

Problems during labor and delivery are often detected by low Apgar scores. The Apgar score is a screening tool used by birth attendants to assess the baby's condition. Developed by the pioneering anesthesiologist Virginia Apgar, it is used to measure the infant's neurologic condition one and five minutes after birth. Five characteristics are scored: breathing rate, heart rate, skin color, muscle tone, and gagging reflex. Each is given a score of 0, 1, or 2; these scores are then added together to get the final score, with the maximum being 10. Scores of 6 or more at five minutes after birth suggest that the child has not suffered ill effects; over 97 percent of these children develop normally. Apgar scores below 5, although not diagnostic of brain damage, indicate an increased risk of cerebral palsy and mental retardation. However, even with the increased risk, over 80 percent of these children develop normally.

There is some new evidence suggesting that physicians may be blaming too many cases of developmental disabilities on the effects of labor and delivery. A study by the National Institutes of Health showed that over half of the children with difficult births actually had preexisting brain damage that made them more likely to suffer birth injury. Thus, while birth trauma may appear to have caused birth defects, the difficult birth may, in fact, have been the result of a problem that began early in pregnancy.

POSTNATAL CAUSES OF DEVELOPMENTAL DISABILITIES

Over 99 percent of children who are normal at birth will not develop serious developmental disabilities. (We are excluding learning disabilities and hyperactivity, which are much more common but less severe developmental disabilities.) However, there are certain conditions that occur during infancy and childhood that may lead to brain damage. These problems fall into four categories: metabolic disturbances, infections, toxins, and accidents.

Metabolic Disturbances

The newborn infant is at a greater risk for developing a severe illness than is an older child. The infant must emerge from the protected environment of the womb into the outside world, where he has to fend for himself. There are a number of metabolic changes that must be made shortly after birth. For example, the baby must begin to regulate his own blood sugar level. If the blood sugar level drops very low, a condition called hypoglycemia, the infant may have seizures. To prevent this from occurring, extra sugar can be given either from a bottle or through an intravenous injection. Although most children with hypoglycemia recover completely, severe and long-lasting hypoglycemia can result in brain damage.

The newborn baby's liver must also start functioning to rid the body of toxins such as bilirubin, the yellow pigment released when fetal blood cells break down. If the baby's liver cannot keep up with the bilirubin released, the excess bilirubin circulates in his blood, causing the skin and whites of his eyes to take on a yellowish cast, called jaundice. Mild jaundice is common and not dangerous. However, when bilirubin levels get very high, the toxin can accumulate in the brain, damage the nerve cells, and lead to cerebral palsy. In order to prevent damage, the infant may be placed under fluorescent lights that help to break down the bilirubin into harmless by-products. If bilirubin levels rise despite fluorescent light therapy, an exchange blood transfusion may be needed.

Infections

At birth, the baby has an immature immune system and is therefore unable to mount an adequate defense against infection. She is able to fight off some infections because of protection passed on from her mother. But when this line of defense is breached, bacteria and viruses that would be handled easily in later childhood can cause a life-threatening illness. Blood poisoning (sepsis) and spinal meningitis (infection of the spinal cord) are two examples of infections that can cause severe illness and subsequent brain damage.

Prematurity

Premature infants represent about 2 percent of all births. Many of the problems we have already mentioned are an even greater threat to the premature infant, who is born too early and too small. A baby born at full term has been in the womb for forty weeks. When an infant is delivered before thirty-seven weeks, she is considered to be premature. These infants weigh less than 5½ pounds, sometimes as little as 1½ pounds (about 600 grams). They have more difficulty adapting to the environment outside the womb because their body organs are immature. Further, they may suffer a number of biochemical and physical disturbances that place them at increased risk for brain damage. Among these problems are respiratory distress syndrome (RDS) and periodic breathing or apnea.

Approximately 20 percent of all prema-

ture infants develop respiratory distress syndrome, sometimes called hyaline membrane disease. The more premature the baby, the greater the likelihood of developing the disorder. While less than 10 percent of all babies born between thirty-four and thirty-six weeks gestation develop RDS, over 60 percent of babies born before thirty-two weeks gestation (seven months) are affected.

RDS occurs in a premature baby because her immature lungs lack a chemical substance called surfactant, which allows the tiny air sacs to expand and contract easily with each breath. In the absence of surfactant, each breath is like blowing up a stiff, new balloon, and the baby shortly becomes exhausted and unable to breathe. Typically, these babies are placed on mechanical breathing machines, called ventilators, that keep their lungs filled with the proper mixture of air and oxygen. Within a few weeks, the lungs have usually matured enough for the baby to breathe unassisted. As long as she has received adequate oxygen during this time, she should be protected against brain damage. Unfortunately, an unexpected complication linked to oxygen therapy has been the development of retinopathy of prematurity, an eye disorder that can lead to vision impairment or blindness (see chapter 13).

Another problem for the premature infant is an immature central nervous system, which controls, among other things, his breathing rate. Not only does the infant have difficulty moving air into the lungs, he often stops breathing for short periods of time (ten to twenty seconds). This is called apnea. The more premature the infant, the more serious is the problem. Infants who have suffered brain damage because of other newborn complications are most likely to have apnea. A drug related to caffeine has been found to be helpful in stimulating respiration in these infants.

Over the past twenty years, advances in the care of premature infants have been phenomenal. In 1960, less than 30 percent of the infants who weighed three pounds at birth, and less than 10 percent of those who weighed two pounds, lived beyond the newborn period. Of those who survived, more than three-quarters were mentally retarded and/or had cerebral palsy. Fewer than 10 percent of these infants developed normally. Now, about 70 percent of the infants who weigh three pounds are surviving, as well as about half of the infants who weigh two pounds. Even some infants who weigh less than two pounds are surviving. Premature infants weighing two to three pounds at birth have a 75 percent chance of developing normally, and infants weighing one to two pounds at birth have about a 50 percent chance.

Lead Poisoning

Later in childhood, toxins and accidents replace infections and metabolic problems as the major causes of developmental disabilities. The most common toxin, lead, is a major problem in older homes, especially in inner cities. Prior to 1945, paint contained lead. But when lead was found to be toxic to the nervous system, laws were passed prohibiting lead-based paint. However, the walls in older homes, although repainted, may have undercoats containing lead. Flaking wall plaster in these homes can pose a serious problem for infants and children who like to put nonfood items into their mouths. Even minute amounts of lead can cause lead poisoning.

Mild forms of lead poisoning result in developmental delay, especially in the area of language. Severe poisoning can lead to seizures and coma. If the lead poisoning is discovered at an early stage, treatment can prevent brain damage. The treatment uses medications that bind to the lead and eliminate it in the urine. Of course, this must be combined with a program to prevent further ingestion of lead-containing paint. This means the child must be taught not to eat nonfood items, and the lead-containing paint must be removed from the home. With this in mind, programs have been set up in many inner cities to help identify and treat affected children.

Accidents

The most common injury causing brain damage in children results from motor vehicle accidents. The relatively soft bony covering of a child's brain is no match for a dashboard, window, or car bumper. However, child injury and death in automobile accidents is largely preventable by seating children in the back seat, using effective car seats for young children and seat restraints for older children, and by adult supervision and teaching street safety.

4 WHAT ABOUT OUR NEXT CHILD?
Genetic Counseling

Henry and Janice, both twenty-four years old, were devastated when their firstborn son, David, was born with Down syndrome, a disorder they thought was limited to babies born to older couples.

Nancy and her husband Richard are both twenty-eight years old. Last year, their four-year-old son Jason died of Tay-Sachs disease, a progressive and uniformly fatal disease of the nervous system.

Susan and Jack have two children, eight-year-old Marc and four-year-old Joseph. Joseph developed slowly compared to his older brother. Susan's brother had also shown this pattern as a child and was diagnosed as having Fragile X syndrome.

Though these couples have borne children with different disorders, they have something in common — the diseases are heritable, that is, they were passed down to the children through their parents' genes. The couples share another characteristic as well. All of them want to have another child, but they know they are at risk for passing on the same disorder to their future offspring. In order to understand their risks and options, they sought the services of a genetic clinic.

In this chapter, we will discuss the basic rules of genetic inheritance and some common genetically inherited disorders. Then we will explain how a geneticist or genetic counselor can help guide you to clarify your own situation, and how prenatal diagnostic techniques can provide some answers. First, we will explain some facts about genes and chromosomes, and how they affect the growth and development of a fetus.

ABOUT CHROMOSOMES AND GENES

Our bodies are made up of cells. All cells, with the exception of red blood cells, have a center, or nucleus, that contains the chromosomes. Chromosomes are made up of a material called DNA (deoxyribonucleic acid). Humans have forty-six chromosomes, arranged into twenty-three pairs. One chromosome in each pair was contributed by the mother, one by the father. Chromosomes can be thought of as the blueprint for development — they store all the instructions that the body needs to develop properly.

Chromosomes store the information in units called genes. Each chromosome contains one to two thousand genes; all together, human beings possess some fifty thousand to one hundred thousand genes. Each gene resides on a specific position on one of the twenty-three pairs of chromosomes. The genes code both for physical traits, such as hair or eye color, and for hormones and enzymes necessary to control biochemical reactions in the body.

Genetic disorders can be broadly classified into two groups: those that are caused by chromosomal abnormalities and those that are caused by abnormalities in individual genes. First we will discuss chromosomal abnormalities.

CHROMOSOMAL ABNORMALITIES

In order to explain how chromosomal abnormalities arise, we must first briefly describe the normal process of fertilization.

We have stated that each human cell contains forty-six chromosomes. But sperm and egg cells are exceptions to this rule. The mature female egg and male sperm each contain only twenty-three chromosomes, one of each pair. At the time of fertilization, the egg and sperm come together to reestablish the forty-six chromosomes that are needed to form the human embryo.

Among the twenty-three pairs of chromosomes is one pair that determines the sex of the baby. These two chromosomes are called the sex chromosomes; the other twenty-two pairs are called autosomal chromosomes. Sex chromosomes are referred to as the X and Y chromosomes because of their physical resemblance to those letters of the alphabet. Males have one X and one Y chromosome, while females have two X chromosomes. Remember that the fertil-

ized egg receives one chromosome of each pair from the mother's egg and one from the father's sperm. Since the mother has only X chromosomes, all her eggs will have one X chromosome to contribute. But the father has an X and a Y, so his sperm will have either the X chromosome or the Y chromosome. When a Y-containing sperm fertilizes the X-containing egg, a male will develop. When an X-containing sperm unites with an X-containing egg, the result is a female. It is, therefore, the father's sperm that establishes the sex of a baby.

Chromosomal abnormalities arise because of mistakes that occur when the egg and sperm cells are formed. At their earliest stages of development, the immature egg and sperm cells actually do contain forty-six chromosomes, or twenty-three pairs. But as they mature, these cells undergo a reductive division (meiosis) that splits the paired chromosomes into separate cells, each with only one of the pair (Figure 4.1). Sometimes, however, the division proceeds unequally, resulting in cells with either twenty-two or twenty-four chromosomes. The cell with too few chromosomes dies, because it lacks necessary information for development. But the cell with twenty-four chromosomes can go on to be fertilized, resulting in an embryo with forty-seven rather than forty-six chromosomes; the embryo has three copies of one of the chromosomes rather than two.

This condition, called trisomy, most commonly occurs with chromosome number twenty-one, resulting in Down syndrome (see chapter 7), but it also occurs with other chromosomes, including the sex chromosomes. Trisomic conditions lead to numerous abnormalities, including mental retardation, heart defects, and unusual facial appearance.

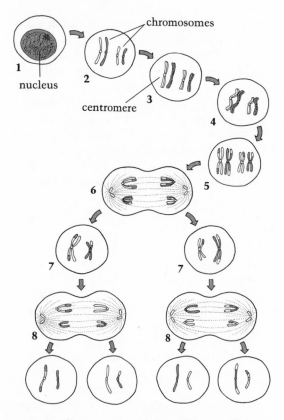

Figure 4.1. *Meiosis. (1) Between divisions, chromosomes appear as strands in the cell nucleus. (2) At
the beginning of meiosis the chromosomes shorten
and fatten, forming pairs. Each pair consists of
one chromosome from the mother (shaded) and
one from the father (unshaded). For simplicity
only two pairs of the twenty-three chromosomes
in each cell are shown. (3) Each chromosome du-
plicates, with its double held together at the centromere. (4-5) Crossing over of information occurs
between the pairs of chromosomes so each chromosome now contains genetic information from
both mother and father. (6) Fibers attached to the
centromere pull one of the paired chromosomes to
each half of the dividing cell. (7) The two resultant cells still have double the number of chromosomes normally found in the sperm and egg. (8) A
second division occurs, resulting in four daughter
cells, each with the normal number of chromosomes. It is during the complex process of meiosis
that mistakes in division leading to Down syndrome and other chromosomal abnormalities are
most likely to occur.*

SINGLE GENE DISORDERS

The second type of genetic disorder arises
when mistakes within individual genes are
present. In this situation, the message of a
gene is scrambled or lost, and incorrect developmental or biochemical instructions
are given. Profound changes in normal development may occur.

As we said earlier, we inherit our genes
from either our mother or our father. Thus,
the mistake is also inheritable. When a
baby is born with a gene disorder, either he
inherited it from one (or both) of his parents, or it occurred as a random mishap
during development. Either way, the mistake is now a part of that baby's genetic
blueprint.

In order to understand how genetic diseases are passed from generation to generation, we must understand certain basic
concepts of heredity. We have already discussed the first two points: that chromosomes are composed of genes and that half
of your genes come from your mother and
half from your father. The third important
concept is that there are dominant, or
strong, genes that block the action of
weaker, or recessive, genes.

Let us look at the example of eye color.
You inherit genes for eye color from both
parents. It is known that genes for brown
eyes are dominant and genes for blue eyes
are recessive. Therefore, if you get a gene
for brown eyes from your mother, and a
gene for blue eyes from your father, you
will have brown eyes. In order to have blue
eyes, you must have inherited recessive
blue eye genes from both parents. In other
words, a recessive gene can only be expressed if an individual inherits two of
them — one from his mother and one from
his father — but a dominant gene, such as
brown eyes, will be expressed if the person
receives only one gene of this type, either

from the mother or father. This is why there are more people with brown eyes than blue eyes. It is also why two brown-eyed parents can have a blue-eyed child, if both parents had one brown-eye and one blue-eye gene.

In single gene disorders, such as Tay-Sachs disease and muscular dystrophy, one gene within a chromosome is defective, and it is this single error that causes all of the problems. One of three types of inheritance patterns can result: autosomal recessive, autosomal dominant, or sex-linked. Additionally, in some disorders such as cleft palate, environmental factors may influence gene expression. This situation is called multifactorial inheritance; that is, genes plus environment.

AUTOSOMAL-RECESSIVE DISORDERS

An autosomal disorder means that the defect occurs in a gene on one of the twenty-two pairs of nonsex chromosomes. At the beginning of the chapter we introduced Nancy and Richard, who lost a child to Tay-Sachs disease, an autosomal-recessive disorder. This disease results from a deficiency of one specific enzyme whose production is controlled by a gene on chromosome fifteen. Normally, this enzyme, called hexosaminidase A, enables the body to dispose of a toxic product from the nerve cells in the brain. In Tay-Sachs disease, the enzyme is defective, leading to an accumulation of toxic material and eventually resulting in death. There is no treatment for Tay-Sachs disease.

When Nancy and Richard went for genetic counseling, they were told that any baby they conceived had a one-in-four chance of inheriting Tay-Sachs disease. The counselor explained that their first baby, Jason, had received two recessive genes for the Tay-Sachs enzyme, and that

this meant that both Nancy and Richard were carriers, that is, each of them had one normal dominant gene and one Tay-Sachs recessive gene. Their offspring could thus inherit either two normal genes, one normal and one Tay-Sachs gene, or two Tay-Sachs genes (Figure 4.2). The baby would be affected only if he received two Tay-Sachs genes, which, according to the laws of probability, had a one-in-four chance of occurring with each pregnancy.

The counselor told them that a test could be performed while Nancy was pregnant to determine whether the child did, indeed, have Tay-Sachs disease. During the fourth month of Nancy's second pregnancy, she underwent the prenatal diagnostic technique amniocentesis. The Tay-Sachs enzyme activity of Nancy's fetus was measured. Three weeks later, Nancy and Richard learned that their baby, a boy, had normal enzyme activity, meaning that he did not have the disease. Now six years old, their son, Steven, is healthy and normal.

Tay-Sachs disease is a recessive disorder, and therefore a child must inherit two abnormal genes — one from each parent — in order to have the disease. If the child inherits only one gene, either from the mother or father, he will appear normal and is called a carrier. A carrier is an individual who is not affected by the disorder, but who carries a defective gene that can be passed on to the next generation.

Because Tay-Sachs is fatal in childhood, it may seem surprising that it and other fatal recessive disorders continue to be passed on from one generation to the next. The explanation is that carriers pass on the abnormal gene to future generations. As noted above, when two carriers have children, there is a one-out-of-four chance with each pregnancy that the child will inherit

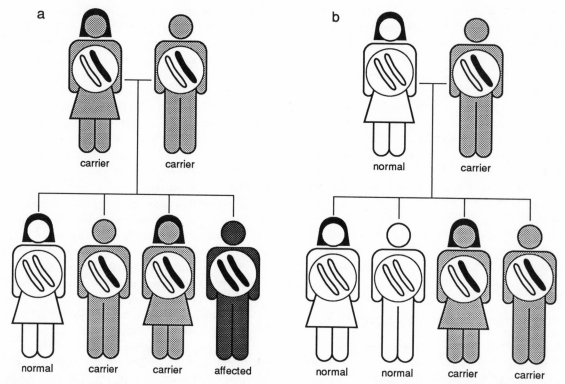

Figure 4.2. *Inheritance of autosomal recessive disorder:* (a) *if two unaffected carriers marry, for each pregnancy there is a one-in-four (25 percent) chance the child will be normal, a one-in-two (50 percent) chance the child will be an unaffected carrier, and a one-in-four risk the child will be affected;* (b) *if a carrier and a normal person marry, for each pregnancy there is a 50 percent chance the child will be normal and a 50 percent chance the child will be a carrier. No children will be affected.*

abnormal genes from both parents and be affected. There is a three-out-of-four chance the child will either inherit one abnormal gene and be a carrier or inherit no abnormal genes and be normal. Boys and girls are equally likely to inherit an autosomal-recessive disease.

Remember that the one-out-of-four chance of the disease occurring is a statistical risk. This does not mean that if a family already has one affected child, the next three children will all be unaffected. Each new pregnancy carries the same one-in-four risk. It is as if you had a pair of dice and were throwing them over and

over again. Two carrier parents could have four children and by chance all four might be affected, all four could be normal, or there might be any other combination between these extremes.

It is important to reemphasize that a recessive disorder can appear only if two carriers have children. If a carrier marries a noncarrier, they will *always* produce unaffected children, because all the children will inherit a normal gene from the unaffected parent. However, their children will all have a one-in-two chance of being carriers of the defective gene. Siblings of affected children should not be at a signifi-

TABLE 4.1   Examples of Diseases Inherited as Autosomal Recessives

Abetalipoproteinemia	Dysautonomia	Methylmalonic aciduria
Acrodermatitis enteropathica	Farber disease	Mucolipidoses
Adrenal hyperplasia	Friedrich ataxia	Mucopolysaccharidoses (except
Agammaglobulinemia	Fructose intolerance	MPS II)
Agenesis of corpus callosum	Fucosidosis	Myasthenia gravis
Albinism	Galactosemia	Niemann-Pick disease
Alexander disease	Gaucher's disease	Ornithinemia
Argininemia	Generalized gangliosidosis	Osteogenesis imperfecta
Argininosuccinic aciduria	Glutaric acidemia	Osteopetrosis
Arthrogryposis multiplex congenita	Glycogen storage diseases	Phenylketonuria
Ataxia telangiectasia	(except Type VIII)	Pituitary dwarfism
Batten's disease	Hallermann-Streiff syndrome	Prader-Willi syndrome
Carbamylphosphate synthetase	Hallervorden-Spatz disease	Progeria
deficiency	Histiocytosis	Refsum disease
Cerebral gigantism	Homocystinuria	Retinitis pigmentosa
Chrondrodysplasia punctata	Isovaleric acidemia	Sickle-cell anemia
Citrullinemia	Krabbe disease	Smith-Lemli-Opitz syndrome
Combined immune deficiency	Lactase deficiency	Tay-Sachs disease
Congenital hypothyroidism	Laurence-Moon-Biedel syndrome	Thalassemia
Cystic fibrosis	Mannosidosis	Tyrosinemia
Cystinosis	Maple syrup urine disease	Wilson's disease
Cystinuria	Metachromatic leukodystrophy	Zellweger's syndrome
Dibasic aminoaciduria		

cant risk for having affected children themselves unless they themselves carry the gene *and* they marry another carrier of the disease.

Other examples of autosomal recessive disorders include phenylketonuria, cystic fibrosis, Hurler's syndrome, and dystonia (see Table 4.1).

AUTOSOMAL-DOMINANT DISORDERS

The inheritance pattern for autosomal-dominant disorders is quite different from that of autosomal-recessive disorders. Again, the defect occurs on one of the non-sex, or autosomal, chromosomes. But in this case, an individual needs to inherit only one abnormal gene in order to develop the disease; the disease gene is dominant over the normal gene. This contrasts with autosomal-recessive disorders, in which the disease gene is recessive to the normal

TABLE 4.2   Examples of Disorders Inherited as Autosomal Dominants

Achondroplasia	Neurofibromatosis
Acromegaly	Pituitary dwarfism
Amyotrophic lateral	Polycystic kidneys
sclerosis (Lou Gehrig's disease)	Polyposis
	Porphyria
Calcification of basal	Psoriasis
ganglia	Retinitis pigmentosa
Huntington chorea	Spastic paraparesis
Crouzon craniofacial	Spinocerebellar ataxia
dysostosis	Spondyloepiphyseal
Torsion dystonia	dysplasia
Ectodermal dysplasia	Sturge-Weber syndrome
Ehlers-Danlos syndrome	Syndactyly
Hyperlipidemia	Treacher-Collins syndrome
Myotonic dystrophy	drome

gene and thus will be expressed only if the individual has two abnormal genes.

The risk of passing on a disorder to one's children also differs between dominant and recessive diseases. In autosomal-dominant disorders, offspring will have a one-in-two chance of inheriting the abnormal gene from the affected parent and thus developing the disease (Figure 4.3). The unaffected parent does not contribute to this inheritance pattern. As in the case of recessive disorders, males and females are equally likely to be affected.

One example of an autosomal-dominant disorder is achondroplasia, a form of dwarfism. An achondroplastic parent has a 50

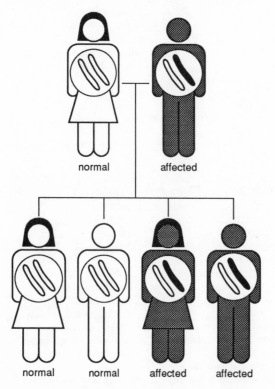

Figure 4.3. *Inheritance of autosomal dominant disorders: If an affected person marries a normal person, each pregnancy carries a 50 percent risk of the child being affected and a 50 percent chance of being normal. However, about half of dominantly inherited disorders represent new mutations in which neither parent is affected. In these cases, there is no increased risk of recurrence in subsequent children.*

percent chance of giving birth to a child with the disorder.

There is another important difference in the inheritance of dominant and recessive disorders. Recessive disorders can be traced back to carrier parents and grandparents. But in half of the individuals who have autosomal-dominant disorders, the disease results from a new mutation — that is, a spontaneous change in the DNA structure of a gene. The mutation occurs for the first time within the affected individual and is not inherited from a parent. Therefore, siblings of the affected child are not at risk for developing the disease. However the affected individual can pass the disease on to his or her children.

SEX-LINKED DISORDERS

Autosomal-recessive and autosomal-dominant disorders involve genes located on the twenty-two pairs of nonsex chromosomes. Those diseases involving genes that are located on the sex chromosomes are called sex-linked disorders. Most sex-linked disorders are recessive. To this point, no diseases have been found to be associated with the Y chromosome, but many have been found to involve the female, or X, chromosome. As in the case of autosomal-recessive disorders, a woman with one normal and one abnormal gene on the X chromosomes is a carrier. However, if a male has the abnormal gene on his X chromosome, he will be affected because he has no second X chromosome to provide the normal gene. Offspring of the carrier woman will have a one-in-two chance of inheriting the abnormal gene (Figure 4.4). If the offspring are girls, they will inherit the normal gene from their father (assuming he is unaffected), and be carriers. Boys who inherit the abnormal gene from their mother, however, will be

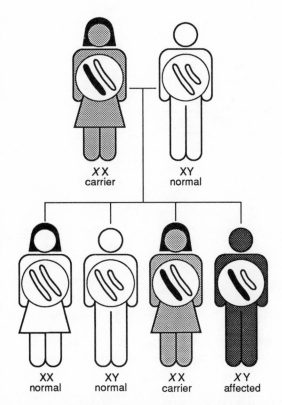

XX
carrier

XY
normal

XX
normal

XY
normal

XX
carrier

XY
affected

Figure 4.4. *Inheritance of sex-linked disorders: If a carrier woman marries an unaffected man, each pregnancy resulting in a male child carries a 50 percent risk that he will be affected, and each pregnancy resulting in a female child carries a 50 percent risk that she will be a carrier (usually unaffected).*

affected, because they lack the compensating normal gene. As a result of this inheritance pattern, boys are much more frequently affected by sex-linked disorders than are girls.

Color-blindness and baldness are examples of mild sex-linked disorders. But there are also more serious sex-linked conditions, including the bleeding disease, hemophilia. A mother can carry the gene for hemophilia but not be affected. Her male children, however, have a one-in-two chance of being hemophiliacs. Her female children have a one-in-two chance of carrying the abnormal gene, but are usually not affected.

Some historians believe that the Russian Revolution hinged on hemophilia because of its fateful occurrence in Czar Alexander's only son and heir, Alexis. The family tree of Alexandra (Alix), Alexis's mother, helps illustrate the inheritance of hemophilia from mother to son (Figure 4.5). The family tree begins with Alexandra's maternal grandmother, Queen Victoria of England, who was a carrier of the hemophilia gene. Two of Victoria's three daughters were carriers of the gene. These women passed on the disease to their sons and the carrier state to their daughters, one of whom was Alix. She in turn passed this disease on to her son, Alexis.

In this family tree, note the frequency of the disease in sons (approximately 50 percent) and the frequency of the carrier state in daughters (about 50 percent). Although the statistical relationship is present in this large family, remember that a carrier mother could by chance have three normal sons or three affected ones in a row. Each time a pregnancy occurs, it is as if a coin is being tossed: heads, a normal son, tails, an affected one. The same is true for the daughters: heads, the girl is normal; tails, she is a carrier.

Recently a sex-linked form of mental retardation has been identified. It is called the Fragile X syndrome because the lower end of the X chromosome is fragile and breaks (see chapter 7). Susan and Jack's son Joseph, whom we introduced at the beginning of the chapter, had this syndrome. Generally, affected boys are mentally retarded. Although most carrier women are unaffected, about 10 percent have a mild form of the disorder, manifested as learning disabilities.

Other examples of sex-linked disorders

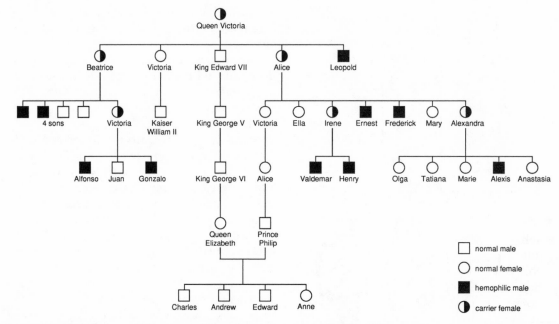

Figure 4.5. *Family tree of Czarina Alexandra and Prince Alexis of Russia, illustrating the pattern of inheritance of the sex linked disorder hemophilia. Approximately half of the women were carriers and half of the men were affected.*

include the following progressive neurological disorders: Menkes syndrome, Lesch-Nyhan syndrome, adrenal leukodystrophy, and muscular dystrophy (Table 4.3).

TABLE 4.3 Examples of Disorders Inherited as Sex-Linked Disorders

Adrenal leukodystrophy	Aqueductal stenosis, X-linked
Fragile X syndrome	
Lesch-Nyhan syndrome	Ichthyosis
Muscular dystrophy	Incontinentia pigmenti
Hemophilia	Leber optic atrophy
Combined immunodeficiency	Lowe syndrome
	MPS II
Colorblindness	Ornithive transcarbamy-lase deficiency
Aicardi syndrome	
Glucose-6-phosphate dehydrogenase	Pelizaeus-Merzbacher disease
Chronic granulomatous disease	

MULTIFACTORIAL INHERITANCE

Many traits are not determined solely by genes, but rather from the interaction of heredity and environment. Height and weight are traits inherited in this manner. Short parents, for example, have a greater-than-average chance of having short children, but environmental factors such as improved nutrition can influence the height of a child. This explains why children of Japanese ancestry who came to live in the United States and ate a higher-protein diet grew to be significantly taller than their parents.

Because many factors interact to produce a characteristic such as height or weight, the individual contributions of heredity and the environment are rarely clear-cut. Many diseases are also known to have both genetic and environmental components. These disorders include cancer, heart disease, high blood pressure, and diabetes. Examples of birth defects that come from this interaction include spina bifida, pyloric stenosis, clubfoot, cleft lip, and cleft palate. In these situations, a fetus may inherit the tendency to develop the disease or defect, but other factors, such as viral infections or drugs, are required in order for the disease to appear.

GENETIC COUNSELING

The three families described at the beginning of the chapter all sought genetic counseling because they wanted to add to their families and yet knew that their future children were at risk. Other families who have not had an affected child may seek counseling because of a background of genetic disease in their family or because of advanced maternal age. Whatever the reason, the first few steps are the same.

First, you should contact a genetics clinic. Such facilities are usually found at university hospitals and other large medical centers. See the booklet *Comprehensive Clinical Genetic Services Centers*, obtainable from the U.S. Department of Health and Human Services (DHHS Pub #HRS-D-MC 86-1) for a list of these centers. They are generally staffed by a genetic counselor, a geneticist, and an obstetrician.

Your first meeting is usually with a genetic counselor, who has a master's degree in genetic counseling and is very knowledgeable about genetic risks and prenatal diagnosis. She will take a thorough family history and construct a family tree. The family tree helps to identify the inheritance pattern of a particular disorder, and from this the counselor and the physician-geneticist are able to calculate your risk of having an affected child in the future. If there is a prenatal diagnostic test that can identify if your fetus has the disease, they

will describe it to you and explain its risks. The counselor will also explain your options for avoiding the birth of an affected child, including adoption, artificial insemination, and terminating an affected pregnancy.

Even if termination of pregnancy is not an option for you, you may wish to know whether you are carrying an affected child. Many parents find that knowing a diagnosis permits them to prepare emotionally and materially for the new baby. And if the baby is unaffected, months of uncertainty and emotional stress can be avoided.

Remember, however, that not all genetic diseases can be diagnosed prenatally, and that prenatal diagnosis need only be undertaken if you have an increased risk for a particular disorder. Furthermore, no test is 100 percent accurate. Though the frequency of errors is very low, you should ask about the specific error rates for the disorder that is being tested in your baby. There is no comprehensive screening test that will check your baby for all genetic diseases. Prenatal diagnosis can detect only what is being tested for; one has to know the suspected diagnosis before specific tests can be performed.

Genetic counseling can be useful even if a prenatal diagnostic test is not available. If there are other affected members in your family and the disease has a known pattern of inheritance, the geneticist can calculate a specific risk figure for your future pregnancies. If a specific risk figure isn't available, more general risk figures may be given. For example, if a couple has had one child severely retarded from undiagnosed cause, the calculated risk of recurrence is 3 percent. This knowledge, even if inexact, may help you plan for the future. In planning future pregnancies, some families are willing to accept a 25 percent risk of occurrence; others will not accept a 1 percent risk.

PRENATAL DIAGNOSIS

The most common reason for seeking prenatal diagnosis is to detect chromosomal abnormalities, especially Down syndrome. Women between the ages of twenty and twenty-five have a 1-in-2000 risk of bearing a child with Down syndrome; but by age forty-five, women can anticipate Down syndrome in one out of thirty-two births. As a result of this increasing risk, pregnant women over thirty-five years of age are routinely offered prenatal diagnosis. Women who previously have had one child with Down syndrome are also offered prenatal diagnosis regardless of their age. They usually have a 1-in-100 risk of bearing another child with Down syndrome.

Prenatal diagnosis is also used to detect gene disorders. A recently compiled list of genetically inherited diseases catalogues over thirty-nine hundred disorders, of which more than three hundred can be diagnosed prenatally. These include muscular dystrophy, Fragile X syndrome, Tay-Sachs disease, phenylketonuria (PKU), and sickle cell anemia. In order to decide if prenatal diagnosis would be appropriate for you, it is important to know which genetic disorder you "carry" and if this disorder can be diagnosed prenatally. Besides chromosomal and single gene disorders, certain multifactorial disorders such as spina bifida can also be detected prenatally.

PRENATAL DIAGNOSTIC TECHNIQUES

When we hear the term prenatal diagnosis, most of us think of amniocentesis. There are, however, other common diagnostic procedures, including chorionic villus bi-

opsy and ultrasound scanning. Each is described below.

Amniocentesis is relatively safe and painless, and the results are usually conclusive. The procedure is done on an outpatient basis between fourteen and sixteen weeks into the pregnancy, at which time about eight ounces of amniotic fluid surround the fetus. Under a local anesthetic and using ultrasound guidance, the obstetrician inserts a needle just below the mother's navel. It passes through the uterine wall and placenta and enters the amniotic fluid sac, which holds the fetus. About an ounce of fluid is withdrawn into a syringe for analysis. Withdrawal of this small amount of fluid does not harm the baby.

The amniotic fluid is primarily composed of fetal urine and fetal skin cells shed into the fluid. Both the fluid and the cells may be studied. For example, to diagnose spina bifida, the fluid is tested for high levels of a substance called alpha fetoprotein. To diagnose chromosomal disorders, such as Down syndrome, the fetal cells are grown for about two weeks until they are sufficient in quantity to obtain a good sample of chromosomes. Then the number and structure of the chromosomes can be studied under a microscope. Chromosomes can also be used to determine sex in disorders that are sex-linked, aiding in genetic counseling. In enzyme deficiencies such as Tay-Sachs disease, these same cells are tested for the deficient enzyme. Recently, geneticists have also developed methods to study the DNA of the cells to seek out individual defective genes. So far, this method has been used to detect phenylketonuria, cystic fibrosis, and muscular dystrophy, but tests for other disorders are on the horizon.

You might fear that the needle used in

amniocentesis will mark or puncture your baby, but this is most unlikely. There is the rare complication, about one in four hundred, of miscarrying the fetus as a result of amniocentesis. If this occurs, it usually happens within a day or two of the procedure. There is an even smaller risk of bleeding or of the mother's uterus becoming infected.

Chorionic villus biopsy, which is also called chorionic sampling, is a newer method of prenatal diagnosis. This procedure is performed much earlier in the pregnancy, at about eight to ten weeks, before the mother looks noticeably pregnant and before she has begun to feel any movement from the fetus. With this procedure, any uncertainty over the health of the fetus exists for a much shorter period of time. If the mother chooses to terminate the pregnancy, she can do so early, when there is much less risk to her health and somewhat less of an emotional bond to the baby.

Chorionic villus biopsy is a painless outpatient procedure that is most commonly performed in a manner similar to a normal pelvic examination. Under ultrasound direction, a thin, hollow, and pliable plastic tube is threaded through the vagina and into the uterus. Small pieces of the placenta, called villi, are clipped off and recovered for examination. Because the placenta belongs to the fetus, it has the same genetic makeup. Yet, the placenta is separate and tissue is not being removed from the fetus itself. In addition, the amount of tissue removed is quite small. The risk of miscarriage is not much different from amniocentesis, and this technique is likely to become the procedure of choice in most cases in the future.

Ultrasound, or sonography, uses high-frequency sound waves to produce an image of the fetus on a video screen. This technique is similar to the use of sonar to detect submarines. It is painless and, as far as we know, involves no risk to the mother or fetus. An externally applied probe is moved over the mother's abdomen until a clear image of a part of the fetus is visualized. A skilled operator can actually see the fetus moving and can detect the presence of twins. Additionally, the fetal spine can be seen, aiding in the diagnosis of spina bifida. Head size also can be measured. Finally, fetal sex can be determined with good accuracy from around twenty-four weeks gestation by detecting the presence of a penis. Besides its diagnostic uses, ultrasound aids in the correct placement of the needle during amniocentesis and in the manipulation of the sampling tube in chorionic villus biopsies.

SCREENING FOR GENETIC DISEASES

Until recently it was not possible to offer genetic counseling to parents until they or another family member had already produced a child with a genetic disease. Today, however, it is possible to screen couples before conception for two autosomal-recessive disorders, Tay-Sachs disease and sickle-cell anemia.

Tay-Sachs disease, a progressive neurologic disorder, most commonly occurs in Jewish families of Eastern European ancestry. Sickle-cell anemia, a severe form of anemia, occurs primarily in black families. Screening tests are restricted to these two populations. In Tay-Sachs disease, the affected child develops normally in the first six months of life but then loses motor and language skills. These children generally die in early childhood and there is no effective treatment. In Tay-Sachs disease, the defective enzyme can be measured in the blood of the parents. A carrier parent has the gene for both the normal and the defective enzyme. Likewise, in sickle-cell anemia, carrier parents have the gene for both sickled and normal hemoglobin. In both of these situations, the carrier parents are unaffected because they possess near normal enzyme or hemoglobin. However, if each member of a couple is screened and each is found to be a carrier, they are advised that each pregnancy carries a one-in-four risk of producing an affected child. They will also be told that an affected child can be detected through prenatal diagnosis. Because these are recessive disorders, the couple can be reassured that there is no risk of their having an affected child if only one, or neither, is found to be a carrier.

Blood tests to determine carriers are not presently available for other single gene diseases. There is, however, a blood-screening test available to pregnant women that can help detect spina bifida and Down syndrome in the fetus. The test measures amounts of alpha fetoprotein (AFP), a substance that is normally produced by the fetus and is found in the bloodstream of pregnant women (see chapter 7).

SOME QUESTIONS ANSWERED

Does my child have a genetically inherited disorder?

If your child has a developmental disability, there are certain situations that make it either more or less likely that the disorder has a genetic basis. For example, meningitis can cause brain damage in an infant, yet this is not a genetic cause of disability and the risk of recurrence in future children is no greater than in the general population. Similarly, if your child's disability was caused by head injury, there is no indication of a genetic cause.

On the other hand, if a close member of your family has had a similar disorder, an inherited disorder is strongly suggested. ("Close family members" include mother, father, brothers, sisters, aunts, uncles, or first cousins.) A disability in more distant relatives usually is not an indication of an inherited disorder. The risk of genetic disease is higher in autosomal-recessive disorders if you and your husband were related prior to marriage — if you were first or second cousins, for example.

Certain signs and symptoms in a child also suggest a genetic disease. If your child's appearance is different from other family members, and he has unusual physical features, such as an odd-looking face or hands, this may suggest a chromosomal disorder. A progressive worsening of a child's condition, rather than a stable or improving situation, may also indicate an inherited disorder. You should ask your doctor about these possibilities and he may refer you to a genetic specialist for further counseling or tests.

Should I consider terminating the pregnancy if the baby is affected?

At this time, there are very few diseases for which prenatal therapy is available. Therefore, when we consider prenatal diagnosis, we are also discussing the possibility of terminating a pregnancy in which the fetus is found to have an abnormality. Clearly, this will not be acceptable to some families. However, in other families it may represent the only way in which parents would consider having future children, because they would not otherwise risk the birth of a second affected child. In these instances, prenatal diagnosis can be viewed as giving the chance of life to children who would not otherwise have been conceived. Obviously, the ideal situation would be to identify affected fetuses and then treat them prenatally. However, at present, this simply is not possible, and for some diseases it may never be a possibility.

If you are carrying an affected child, the decision whether or not to terminate a pregnancy is for you to make, using your doctor as a consultant. In the event that you would not consider a therapeutic abortion, but are at high risk for recurrence in future children, you may wish to consider other alternatives, such as artificial insemination or adoption.

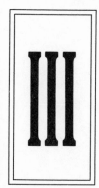

III Developmental Disabilities

5 THE DEVELOPMENT OF A YOUNG CHILD

Now that we have considered the possible causes of your child's disability, let us turn to the issue of development. A human baby at birth may seem totally helpless but in fact is considerably more mature and requires less parental care than newborn animals of some species. A baby kangaroo, for example, is born while still technically a fetus and must spend further months incubated in its mother's pouch. At the other extreme is the newly hatched turtle, which immediately goes out on its own to forage for food. Somewhere in between these two extremes are human babies. They are totally dependent on their parents to bring them food and take care of their most basic needs. But unlike baby kangaroos, they can suck, see, and hear.

Humans also have the longest period of "nesting" before they are able to live apart from their parents. This period of dependence varies with the skills and abilities of the individual; in children with disabilities, it may last a lifetime.

The normal development of a child can be thought of as a path, or a series of steps. Intelligence and motor development progress along similar paths, with simple skills preceding more complex ones. Generally, children with disabilities will not progress as quickly nor as far as unaffected children.

THE DEVELOPMENT OF THE NERVOUS SYSTEM

The brain of an infant has the same basic structure as an adult brain (Figure 5.1). It also has the same number of nerve cells, but these cells are immature, resembling bare saplings. By late childhood, they will have developed intricate branches, called processes, that make them look more like grown trees (Figure 5.2). Our ability to think arises from this network of cells and processes that intertwine and exchange information. The growth of these processes causes the total size of the brain to double in the first year of life and triple by the second year. The normal adult brain weight of about one pound is reached at approximately six years of age.

During the first six months of life, the nerve-cell processes not only grow in size and complexity, but they also develop an insulating sheath that permits more rapid conduction of nerve impulses and the ready exchange of information between muscles, sensory organs such as the eyes, and the brain. As a result, a six-month-old

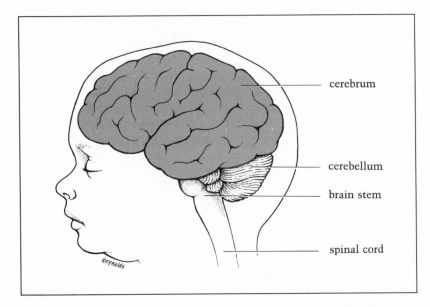

Figure 5.1. *Horizontal view of a child's brain showing the major structures.*

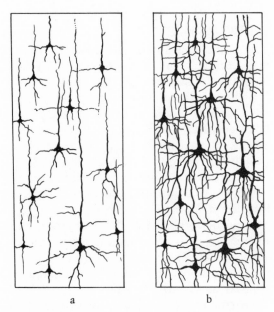

Figure 5.2. *Growth of nerve cells in the brain. There is an increase both in the number of cells and in the complexity of their projections. (a) section of the brain from a newborn infant and (b) from a six-year-old child.*

can perform complex voluntary activities such as crawling, grasping objects, and babbling.

The Newborn

Until recently, popular thinking held that newborns had poor eyesight, were unable to distinguish colors, and were incapable of learning. Recently, however, it has become apparent that we did not fully appreciate the newborn's learning capabilities. Newborns can see with about 20/100 acuity; that is, seeing clearly at a twenty-foot distance an object that a person with perfect 20/20 vision can see at one hundred feet. He can fix his gaze on his mother's face only minutes after birth. And newborns have color vision and show a preference for brightly colored objects. Newborns can also learn; in fact, they can learn before birth. Studies have shown that if a particular musical recording is played a number of times in the presence of the mother during the final weeks of pregnancy, her newborn baby will suck on a bottle in order to hear this same recording. But he will not suck in order to hear other music. Furthermore, a newborn infant will suck in order to hear a recording of his or her mother's voice, but will not do so to hear the voice of another woman. In other words, the baby has already learned preferences and has developed memory. We should not be surprised to find that newborns start out with such capacities; birth is a rather arbitrary time in the development of a person. Development starts during fetal life, and new skills are gained throughout life.

Despite his intellectual gifts, the newborn is restricted in motor skills by primitive reflexes that he cannot control. Many of these reflexes are protective. He "roots," or turns his head in response to a touch on the cheek, in order to find his mother's nipple. His sucking reflex allows him to grasp onto the nipple and draw milk from it. Other reflexes, however, may limit his adaptability to the world around him. For example, if his neck is jostled, he has no choice but to shoot out his hands as if in surprise; this is called the Moro response. Imagine how difficult it would be to work or play if your hands shot out whenever your neck was jostled! If a newborn baby's head is turned to one side, the arm and leg on that side will extend while the limbs on the other side will automatically flex; this is called the asymmetrical tonic neck, or fencer's reflex. This action interferes with sitting when it persists beyond the first six months of life.

It is important to remember that both physical and neurological development proceed in an orderly fashion. Yet, that progression is more like a series of steps or rungs of a ladder than a smooth curve. One step must be reached before going on to the next one. A disabled child may follow an unusual pattern of development with certain steps missed and the rate slower than normal.

DEVELOPMENT DOES NOT FOLLOW A SMOOTH CURVE: THE THEORY OF PIAGET

Since children do gain skills through a series of steps, they may seem to rest on a plateau for some time and then suddenly hurdle to a new level. One of the first to appreciate this pattern was the Swiss psychologist Jean Piaget. Piaget's theory is particularly useful in explaining developmental disabilities. He divided development into four stages of progressively increasing complexity of thought. Piaget noted that prior to eighteen months of age, in the period he called the sensorimotor stage, a child is not capable of solving problems. For instance, if the child loses something, he will dismiss it immediately from his thoughts or become upset and cry. If he cannot see the object, he believes it has actually ceased to exist. Around eighteen months, the child is suddenly able to conceptualize the problem. He realizes the object has fallen and will search for it around his immediate area, knowing that it is somewhere, even if he cannot see it. If it is beyond his reach, he may use a stick to retrieve it. Further, the child is now able to coordinate his activities to reach goals. He can formulate a plan to attack his problem. However, his discoveries are made through trial and error, and the successes are not generalized to similar situations in the future; in other words, he forgets what he has learned. Therefore, although a twenty-month-old may finally figure out how to use a doorknob after many attempts, he may not remember his solution the next day. He will instead follow the same process of trial and error to solve the same problem.

By two years of age the child can use language to control his environment and help solve problems. Piaget called this time the preoperational stage of development. The child can describe what he did today and can sing a song. He will also ask "what" and "why" questions. Objects within his world can be described: a ball is round, a box is square. Thus, objects can be classified as to their purpose. Opposites, such as small and large, fast and slow, are understood. The world can now be divided into subunits and understood more easily. But there are limits at this stage as well. The child is still not able to perform abstract reasoning. If water is poured from a wide glass to a narrow one, he believes there is more water in the narrow glass. He also does not understand concepts such as death or honesty.

It is during the third stage, called the period of concrete operations, that the elementary school student, six to twelve years old, learns to see complex interrelationships, permitting the study of academic subjects. The child is able to classify objects in sequential order according to size, weight, or time sequence. Panels of a cartoon can be mixed up and put back in the correct order to form a story. At this stage, the child learns to solve simple arithmetic problems and read well. He can also participate in debates, clearly stating his position and appreciating someone else's opinion. However, he still has difficulty dealing with hypothetical situations and abstract concepts involved in the study of science and higher mathematics.

According to Piaget, the final developmental period, the stage of formal operations, begins at around twelve years of age and continues throughout the remainder of one's life. Using imagination, the person is now able to project into the future and set up long-range goals. The individual is more sensitive to the needs of others, and can also understand abstract concepts, isolate a problem, review it systematically, and test out the possible solutions. This permits the study of algebra, physics, philosophy, and other higher-level subjects. The adolescent is no longer gullible; he no longer believes fanciful stories.

In sum, Piaget says that intellectual development involves the addition of increasingly complex and abstract concepts at each step up the developmental ladder. An adult who did not have the capacity to progress through all the Piaget stages will be limited in his or her ability to function in the world. This person is mentally retarded. The degree of severity of the mental retardation can be viewed in light of these developmental stages. In very general terms, a mildly retarded person will pass through all but the final, formal operations, stage; moderately retarded individuals will be arrested at the preoperations, or second, stage; and the severely/profoundly retarded child will not emerge from the sensorimotor stage.

BRAIN DEVELOPMENT AND LEARNING

Piaget also suggested that there must be a particular level of brain maturation and development in order for a person to perform certain intellectual tasks. If the necessary neurological organization has not been attained, no amount of practice will produce the intellectual skill. Therefore, although one can teach a severely retarded child to memorize the words associated with pictures in a book, she is not actually reading because the words do not carry meaning for her. However, if she is neurologically ready to learn a new skill, education will make a big difference. Without education, a child will not usually start to read or learn arithmetic on her own.

While intellectual skills require practice as well as neurologic maturation, motor skills will appear spontaneously when the child's nervous system has reached the proper level of development. You may have heard that children must learn to crawl before they can walk. It's not true. Ancient American Indians routinely strapped their infants to papooses or cradle boards during the first year of life, depriving them of the opportunity to roll over, sit, or crawl. Yet when these children were released from the boards at around one year of age, they walked within a matter of days. They walked not as the result of practicing more primitive modes of movement but because their brain had developed the proper circuitry for this skill. In sum, in order to move from one rung to the next up the developmental ladder, brain growth must take place.

JENNIFER AND LISA

To illustrate the development of a young child, let us consider two children: a mentally retarded child and her unaffected sister. Stacey and Philip have two children, Lisa, age six years, and Jennifer, age nine months. During her first months of life, Jennifer seemed to develop much more slowly than Lisa. At six months she had not rolled over, a skill Lisa had mastered by four months. Jennifer also didn't coo or make baby noises. She didn't smile until four months of age, while Lisa had done this at six weeks. At first Stacey and Philip thought they must have forgotten when Lisa reached these developmental levels. So they found her baby book and compared milestones; they had not been mistaken. Jennifer's other skills were similarly delayed when compared to Lisa.

Philip and Stacey were concerned but tried to put aside their fears. However, at Thanksgiving, when Jennifer was eleven months old, the extended family came together, including two cousins who were

the same age as Jennifer. The cousins were saying words and walking with help, while Jennifer had just learned to sit and babble. Stacey and Philip decided they should see their doctor about their fears. Their family doctor was equally concerned and sent them to a pediatric developmental specialist, who examined Jennifer extensively and confirmed that she was significantly delayed for her age. At twelve months she was functioning at a six-month level, or progressing at about half the normal rate. They were told that if this continued, Jennifer would be mildly to moderately mentally retarded. A follow-up appointment was scheduled for six months, and Jennifer was started in an infant stimulation program. When reevaluated at eighteen months and later at twenty-four months, Jennifer was still traveling at half speed. At this time the diagnosis of moderate mental retardation was made (see chapter 6).

NORMAL DEVELOPMENT

We will now explore normal developmental milestones using Jennifer's sister, Lisa, as our guide. Lisa has progressed in a fairly average fashion. It is important to understand that there is significant variation in the normal development of children. For example, sitting may develop anywhere from five to eight months. Also keep in mind that a mild delay in one aspect of development may not necessarily indicate a problem. However, a serious delay in even one area may indicate a developmental disability. A delay in speech may result from a hearing or vision deficit; a delay in motor skills may indicate cerebral palsy. Delays in all areas are found in children who are mentally retarded.

With this background, we will discuss the different developmental milestones Lisa passed through between birth and six years of age. In order to help you follow the sequence of development, Tables 5.1 and 5.2 list important milestones from birth to six years. We divide development into four areas: gross-motor skills, for instance running and walking; fine-motor skills, such as holding a block or pencil; social-adaptive abilities; and language. Remember that a mentally retarded child usually follows the same sequence of development as a normal child, but at a slower rate.

The First Six Months

Babies experience especially rapid development during the first six months of life. At birth, Lisa's abilities were limited to motor skills, like moving her head from side to side and sucking; and social skills, such as responding to sounds, looking at her mother, and crying. By two months Lisa demonstrated good head control (motor development) and could follow a mobile as it turned (visual development). Socially, she smiled and started to anticipate her feedings, actively kicking and gurgling at the sight of her bottle or her mother's breast. Her main communication skill was cooing.

Lisa developed many new skills between four and six months. She rolled over from her back to her stomach and made swimming movements at four months. By six months she could sit briefly, with support, and a month later she required no support at all. By four months her hands remained open much of the time rather than being clenched as they had been before. She developed other fine-motor skills as well, including reaching, grasping, and shaking objects such as rattles. At six months, she could transfer objects from one hand to the other and feed herself a cookie placed in her clutches. She also helped hold her bottle. Her social skills included having a belly laugh by four months and enjoying a game of "peekaboo" and "so-big" at six months. She could discriminate between her parents and other adults by four months, and at six months she could understand tones of voice and whether her parents were angry or happy. In the area of language development, she produced different sounds for different needs by four months, and at six months her sounds became distinguishable as vowels and consonants; she babbled "ba."

Six to Twelve Months

By eight months of age, Lisa began crawling on her knees, and could explore her world. She also enjoyed bouncing on her toes. At ten months, her gross-motor skills included standing with support and crawling with expertise and daring. Finally, at twelve months, Lisa began cruising — walking around furniture — and shortly thereafter she walked without any support.

At eight months her fine-motor development involved exploration of objects; she grabbed, twisted, smelled, tasted, and finally threw them. By ten months Lisa could feed herself some finger foods. At twelve months she enjoyed putting objects into containers and turning the pages of a book.

Lisa's social development also progressed. At ten months she played many interactive games such as "pat-a-cake" and waving "bye-bye." At twelve months she began to take turns while playing with other children.

At eight months she babbled all the time. Some of the sounds were "ma" and "da," although they were not specifically said to her parents Philip or Stacey. Lisa also understood the tone of voice when Stacey said, "No," although she did not always obey. By ten months, "mama" and "dada" were said specifically to get her

TABLE 5.1   Selected Developmental Milestones, Birth to 2 Years

Age	Gross Motor	Fine Motor	Language	Social Adaptive
birth	moves head to side dominated by primitive reflexes	fixates on a face	cries	sleeps most of the time
1 month	head lags	follows 90° visually clenched fists	quiets to noise	sleeps 14+ hours
2 months	better head control lifts chin off mattress	follows 180°		smiles anticipates feeding
3 months	primitive reflexes less prominent lifts chest off bed	follows 360° hands mostly unfisted swipes at objects	cooing sounds more vocalizations	differentiates parents chortles pulls at clothing
4 months	rolls from back to stomach swimming movements	grabs objects hands held in midline shakes rattle	produces different sounds for different needs	belly laughs
5 months	rolls from stomach to back		babbles — "razzes" turns toward voice	frolics when played with
6 months	sits briefly with support creeps	raking grasp transfers objects holds bottle	imitates sounds makes consonant sounds differentiates "friendly" and "angry" voices	searches for lost object smiles at mirror
7 months	bounces when standing sits without support	feeds self a cookie drinks from cup	imitates noises responds to name	
8 months		rings a bell	understands "no" nonspecific "mama"	throws objects
9 months	crawls	explores objects	recognizes familiar words	mouths all objects
10 months	stands with support		specific "dada"	waves "bye" pat-a-cake
11 months	cruises around objects	pincer grasp	follows gesture command	
12 months	takes first step	puts objects in container turns pages	2 or 3 specific words	takes turns
13 months	stoops to pick up object climbs sits down from standing dances to music	points with fingers looks for lost toy puts cube in cup stacks rings	3 or 4 words in addition to "mama" and "dada" looks toward named object ("Where's the ball?") responds to name obeys "give it to me"	trial and error used to solve problems plays responsive games demands attention separation anxiety temper tantrums fights sleep
14 months	climbs stairs on hands and knees	cooperates in dressing	brings coat to indicate desire to go outside names all family members	indicates preferences in food likes an audience fear of strangers and the dark can play by self

TABLE 5.1   Selected Development Milestones, Birth to 2 Years (*continued*)

Age	Gross Motor	Fine Motor	Language	Social Adaptive

15 months	in constant motion	marks with pencil
		spoon feeds
		builds tower with
		  blocks
		opens boxes
		puts peg in pegboard
		pats textured objects
		pushes toy cars
			jargons
			follows 1-step com-
			  mand without
			  gesture
			4 to 6 words
			1 or 2 body parts
				gives kisses
				imitates chores
				negativistic
				indicates when wet

16 months	sits on chair	turns pages of book
		likes push-pull toys
			enjoys explanation of
			  pictures in book
			points to simple pic-
			  tures
				hunts for missing
				  parent
				plays in sandbox

17 months	stands on one foot hold-
	  ing on
				exploratory behavior
				demands personal
				  attention
				afraid of large animals
				enjoys baths
				plays hide-and-seek

18 months	runs stiffly
	tries to climb out of
	  crib
		handedness is
		  determined
		scribbles
		takes off clothes
		puts pellet in bottle and
		  pours it
		unzips
			follows 2-step
			  commands
			points to one picture in
			  book
			10 words — uses "no"
			  mostly
				constantly plays with
				  toys
				uses stick to reach
				  toy — inventive
				  solutions
				readiness to being toilet
				  trained
				only puts food in
				  mouth

19 months	kicks ball	builds 3- or 4-block
		  tower
		flushes toilet
			10 to 15 words
			likes to be read to
				likes rocking horse
				enjoys swings
				pulls wagon with toys
				  inside

20 months	jumps	throws ball
		puts lid on box
			labels actions: "up" =
			  pick me up
			questions "what's
			  that?"
				possessive about toys
				fear of water (bath)
				puts on shoes
				washes hands
				plays with pounding
				  bench
				imaginary play — "tea
				  party"

21 months	walks up steps holding
	  railing
		folds paper	uses word combinations
			echolalia
			uses pronoun "I"
				likes bugs and other
				  small objects

22 months		puts pop-it beads
		  together
		unwraps packages
			listens to stories
			repeats nursery rhymes
				starting to cooperate,
				  but tests limits

23 months	walks up and down
	  steps alone, both feet
	  on each step
	runs all the time
		likes to fill and empty
		  water glasses
			asks for food and drinks	"reads" book to self
				easily frustrated

24 months	walks backward	matches objects
		draws horizontal lines
		turns on water faucet
			associates names with
			  familiar objects
			up to 50 words
			distinguishes one vs.
			  many
			communicates feeling
			  using words and
			  gestures
			verbalizes toileting
			  needs
				still doesn't share
				not cooperative
				avoids bedtime
				parallel play

parents' attention. At twelve months, she developed a few meaningful words, understood only by Philip and Stacey. Lisa began to follow simple commands accompanied by a gesture. For example, if Lisa was holding a rattle and Stacey pointed and said, "Give it to me," Lisa handed the rattle to her. As is usually the case, her understanding of language was ahead of her ability to express her own thoughts.

Twelve to Twenty-four Months

Lisa's second year of life was spent refining the skills that had started to appear in the first twelve months. Walking became more efficient. She no longer marched in a bowlegged fashion with her arms extended, like a tightrope artist. By thirteen months she could stoop to pick up objects and wiggle her fanny to music. By fifteen months Lisa climbed stairs on her hands and knees. She started to run, could stand briefly on one foot, and kick a beach ball at eighteen months. At twenty months she could jump, and at two years she tentatively climbed steps and walked backward.

There were great changes in her fine-motor skills during this same period. She started stacking rings at thirteen months. By fifteen months she would mark with a crayon, build block towers, open boxes, put pegs in a pegboard, and push toy cars. She also began to feed herself with a spoon and aid in dressing herself. She was clearly right-handed by eighteen months and began to scribble. Improvements in her dexterity allowed Lisa to pluck up a bead, place it in a bottle, and then dump it out. She was also an expert at undressing, sometimes performing this skill when her mother least expected it! At twenty-two months she enjoyed playing with pop-together beads and unwrapping presents. At two years Lisa was able to draw vertical

and horizontal lines and could turn on the water faucets.

Social skills similarly improved. At thirteen months Lisa started to solve problems such as taking a lid off a box to get an object inside. At the same time, she developed anxieties, first of separation from her parents, then of strangers, and later of the dark. Although Lisa was able to amuse herself briefly, she preferred an audience for her antics. She gave kisses and imitated household chores, but she was also quite negativistic. "No" was her favorite word. Between fifteen and eighteen months there was an increase in her exploratory behavior. She could find novel solutions to problems, such as using a stick to get an object that was beyond her reach. Lisa enjoyed watching *Sesame Street*, playing in a sandbox, and playing "hide and seek." Yet at this same time her fears intensified, especially of large animals and later of baths.

Eighteen to twenty-one months was a time of increasing independence. She washed herself and tried to get dressed. She even showed some interest in controlling her bowels, although she did not become toilet trained until three years of age. Lisa's achievements included riding a rocking horse, pounding pegs into a workbench, playing on a swing, and pulling a wagon filled with toys. Imaginary games also appeared; she held tea parties and "talked" on the telephone. She became increasingly interested in the neighborhood children, though she played tentatively and alongside, rather than with, other children. By two years, she started to interact but not to share; "mine" was her most frequently used word. She was constantly testing limits, trying to discover how far she could try her parents' patience.

It was perhaps language that showed the most startling changes during this second year of life. At thirteen months Lisa had three or four words in addition to "mama" and "dada." By fifteen months she started to "jargon," that is, to use sounds that simulate words but do not carry meaning. She knew the names of all her family members, including Blackie the cat. Additionally, Lisa used nonlanguage communication, such as bringing Stacey her coat to indicate she wanted to go outside. At eighteen months her jargon became interspersed with real words and her vocabulary grew to ten words. Between eighteen and twenty-one months, Lisa's vocabulary expanded to twenty to thirty words. She also labeled actions; for example, "up" meant "pick up a cup"; "on" meant "turn on the lights." She began to question: "What's that?" By twenty-one months she used the pronoun "I" and started saying a few word combinations such as "go out" and "want cookie." Lisa also echoed the last few words spoken to her by her mother. Between twenty-one and twenty-four months, her vocabulary expanded to more than fifty words, and included a number of two-word phrases. She asked for specific foods, repeated nursery rhymes, and began to verbalize her need to go to the bathroom.

Her understanding of language increased even more during this time. At thirteen months she turned to look at an object when Stacey said, "See the ball." She also obeyed simple commands, without an accompanying gesture. Stacey could now say "give it to me" without pointing. By sixteen months Lisa could identify an object represented by a picture and enjoyed having Stacey read her a story about the picture. She also learned to point to her nose and to her belly button. At eighteen months she could follow some two-step directions, such as "close the door and then sit down." By nineteen months she enjoyed having Stacey read complete stories to her. At twenty-one months she was ready for "touch me" books such as *Pat the Bunny*. Finally, at two years, Lisa distinguished the concept of one from many and other complex ideas such as big and little.

The Preschool Years — Two to Six

Lisa's motor skills became more coordinated and complex during the preschool years, although between two and three years she was still somewhat clumsy (Table 5.2). This awkwardness, combined with an absence of fear and marked exploratory behavior, made her accident prone. She had many scrapes and bruises, and on one occasion required five stitches. Her coordination improved between three and four years. She learned to kick a ball, hop, climb a jungle gym, and ride a tricycle. Between four and five years she could do somersaults and jump from heights. She delighted in showing off all her skills, sometimes to the distress of Philip and Stacey. By six years she skipped, threw a ball, rode a bicycle, and danced.

Her fine-motor skills improved along with gross-motor functioning. Between two and three years, Lisa learned to unscrew lids, turn doorknobs, feed herself with a fork, pour drinks, and partially dress herself. Improved eye-hand coordination allowed her to draw straight lines and circles and solve simple puzzles. Between three and four years, she learned to draw a cross, finger paint, work with Play-Doh, and cut with scissors. Her dressing abilities improved and she was able to zipper, button, and put her shoes on the right feet. By five years she could draw a recognizable stick figure of a person as well as copy some letters and understand number concepts. By six she started to print her name, and sort objects by size, color, and shape. She could also tie her shoes. She had the readiness

TABLE 5.2   Selected Developmental Milestones, 2 to 6 Years

Age (years)	Gross Motor	Fine Motor	Language	Social Adaptive
2–2 ½	accident prone	turns doorknobs adult grip on crayon unscrews lids draws vertical lines tower of 5 cubes	2-word phrases uses own name points to and names many pictures sings parts of songs	constant motion noncompliant — "no"

2 ½–3	runs well
	alternate feet walk-
	  ing up stairs
		improved hand-
		  finger
		  coordination
		solves 6- to 12-piece
		  puzzle
		feeds self
		takes off shoes and
		  socks
		draws a circle
			learns 50
			  words/month
			3- or 4-word
			  sentences
			gives full name
			understands concept
			  of "one"
			follows 3-step direc-
			  tions
				bossy, moody
				helps around the
				  house
				plays with others

3–3 ½	stands on one foot
	walks straight line
	  and backward
	catches and kicks
	  large ball
	rides tricycle
	controls bowel and
	  bladder during
	  daytime
		copies a cross
		strings beads
		fingerpaints and
		  Play-Doh
		matches colors
		pours juice
		undresses self
		zippers
			approximately 900
			  words
			repeats 3 digits
			asks "how? why?"
			prepositional com-
			  mands (put the
			  ball under the
			  cup)
			describes actions in
			  pictures
			uses plurals and
			  pronouns
			watches Sesame
			  Street
				attached to mother
				nightmares
				improved attention
				doll play

3 ½–4	hops
	climbs jungle gym
		cuts with scissors
		uses fork and spoon
		shoes on correct feet
			4- or 5-word
			  sentences
			likes stories and
			  rhyming
			counts to 3
			recalls events in re-
			  cent past
				shares
				develops playmates
				phobias
				thumbsucking
				sibling rivalry

4–5	somersaults
	jumps from height
		draws primitive pic-
		  ture of face
		copies some letters
			names nickel, dime,
			  and penny
			knows gender
			enjoys jokes
				prefers children to
				  adults
				imaginary playmates
				sensitivity to praise
				likes sandbox
				enjoys construction
				  toys
				dresses up as adult
				washes self and
				  brushes teeth

5–6	skips
	climbs, slides,
	  swings
	catches ball
	bicycle with training
	  wheels
	dances
		distinguishes right
		  from left hand
		draws recognizable
		  picture of person
		copies triangle
		copies many letters
		prints name
		sorts objects by size
			speech fluent
			knows address and
			  birthday
			sings songs, tells
			  stories
			knows size
			  differences
			can explain what is
			  troubling him
				Oedipal complex
				independent
				  behavior
				fear of death
				imaginative play
				can amuse herself

skills and fine-motor coordination necessary for first grade.

Social skills also improved. Between two and three years of age, Lisa had a changeable personality, as is typical of this period called the "terrible twos." At times she was moody, bossy, and noncompliant. Yet, at other times she was delightful. She helped around the house and played quietly with other children. Between three and four years of age, she showed an improved attention span and the ability to develop friendships with other children. By five years Lisa began to prefer the company of children her own age to adults, but at the same time she longed for applause from her parents. She was more adult in caring for herself; she could wash her hands and brush her teeth. By six years she was capable of imaginative and independent play.

The evolution of Lisa's language led to the expression of more and more complex ideas. Between two and three years, she used short phrases and sang fragments of songs. When asked, she would tell you her name. She learned new words at the rate of about fifty per month, and her understanding of language kept pace. She identified pictures in a book and followed complex three-step directions. Between three and four years, she asked her mother "how does this work?" and "why is this?" questions, from dawn to dusk. She described actions performed in a picture, used plurals and pronouns, and could answer questions about the recent past, such as "What did you do today in nursery school?" Her sentence structure became more complex, containing four or five words, and her vocabulary numbered well over a thousand words. Lisa could also perform tasks involving prepositions — for example, "Place the block under the cup." By five years she enjoyed jokes, and could differentiate pen-

nies from quarters. By six years she had mastered over two thousand words. Her speech was now fluent and grammatically correct. She told stories, and knew her address. When upset, she could even tell her mother what was troubling her instead of crying inconsolably.

As Lisa's development demonstrates, an infant is born with some intellectual abilities and much potential. The final outcome depends both on the child's intelligence and on the training she receives. Development involves a sequence of steps leading to higher and more complex levels of understanding. Until brain maturation has reached a point where a certain skill is capable of being learned, no amount of practice will result in the development of this skill. However, intellectual skills can benefit from education and practice if the proper neurological circuitry is in place.

SOME QUESTIONS ANSWERED

How exact are developmental milestones?

In Tables 5.1 and 5.2 we have listed the average age at which various skills are attained. However, there is a wide range of variability, and there are gender and racial differences. Girls tend to reach language milestones somewhat earlier than boys, and black children tend to walk before white children. There are also familial influences; in some families children start to talk or walk earlier or later than usual.

Should I believe my doctor when he says, "Your child will grow out of it"?

Many children who have mild delays in their development will catch up over time. So the words "he/she will grow out of it" may be appropriate. However, if you are still worried or if your child has not "grown out of it" after six months or a year, request a second opinion from a specialist who works with developmentally disabled children. Depending upon your child's problem, the evaluation may include one or more of the following evaluations: formal IQ testing, a neurological examination, special education, physical therapy, occupational therapy, vision, hearing, and language evaluations. This comprehensive assessment should either ease your mind that the problem is not serious or direct you toward appropriate therapy to help your child. Don't wait a long time to do this. If you have concerns, make certain that you receive answers that make sense to you.

Does the term "developmental delay" mean mentally retarded?

Physicians use the term *developmental delay* to describe a young child who is slow in developing but has the potential to catch up. This contrasts with mental retardation, which implies a permanent slowness in development. We often use the words *developmental delay* to describe a premature infant or a child who has suffered a prolonged illness and, as a result, is delayed in developing. This term is not appropriate for a child older than two to three years of age, however, because by then the child has usually declared himself as being normal, having a sensory deficit, or being mentally retarded. Unfortunately, the term *developmental delay* is often used by professionals long after it has become clear that the child is mentally retarded. It then becomes a way of delaying the "truth" which is painful to both parent and professional.

Do infant stimulation programs help the development of children with disabilities?

These programs can be very helpful. Generally, when your child is between the ages of three months and two years, a trained teacher will work with him weekly for about an hour. The teacher will evaluate your child's abilities and make suggestions to you about what skills are evolving and how to help your child learn these new skills. She may also suggest appropriate play activities (see chapter 20).

How important is play to the development of my child?

Play is a young child's work. It is through playing with objects, games, and other children that your child learns about the world and its interrelationships. Thus, it is important for you to have toys available that are at your child's developmental level. For example, your child will not be interested in playing with cars at twelve months, but may become very interested when he reaches a two-year-old developmental level. Some good developmental games are listed in the book *Let's Play to Learn*. Remember to have your child play at his developmental level, *not* his chronological age level.

How much time should I spend teaching my child?

You are always teaching your child, even if it is done informally. When you talk to your two-year-old at the breakfast table, describing the eggs or juice, you are giving her information. When you take a walk and talk about the leaves on the trees, you are teaching her about the world around you. If you set up a game between two children, you are educating them about sharing and taking turns. Your teaching rarely has to be formally organized; formal teaching can be left to the school or your child's teacher or therapist.

6 | MENTAL RETARDATION

In the preceding chapter we followed the development of a normal child, showing how motor, visual-perceptual, and language skills increase in a step-wise fashion. Most mentally retarded children also follow this pattern, developing skills in a similar sequence but progressing more slowly and not reaching the same level. How slowly a mentally retarded child will progress and what level she will eventually reach varies tremendously depending on the degree of impairment.

Consider the following three children: Linda suffered brain damage as a result of a traumatic birth; she is severely retarded. Sandy, a child with Down syndrome, is moderately retarded. Billy is mildly retarded, the cause unknown. In the following descriptions of the development of these children, the age at which an average child achieves the specific milestones is referred to in parentheses.

LINDA

Linda was a full-term baby. During her mother's labor, Linda's heart rate dropped from the normal 160 beats per minute to 40 beats per minute. Her doctors, noting

fetal distress, performed an emergency cesarean section. At birth, Linda did not breathe spontaneously and required oxygen therapy. Within two hours she started to have convulsions, which were treated with anticonvulsant medication. During her hospitalization, Linda did not suck well, and her cry was weak and high pitched. At three weeks of age, she was sent home but was very irritable, frequently crying for no apparent reason and arching her back. She showed little interest in her surroundings.

Because of her difficult birth and problems in the first few months of life, the pediatrician closely monitored Linda's developmental milestones. At six months Linda could not roll over (four months) or even hold up her head (two months). She lacked the fine-motor control necessary to hold her hands open (three months). She couldn't follow objects with her eyes (two months), although she was able to fix her gaze on her mother's face (birth to one month). She did not smile (two months) or make baby noises (three months). In sum, her skills at six months were below a two-month level.

The pediatrician told Linda's parents

that her development would continue to be very delayed, but that it was too early to estimate the extent of her impairment. However, even though her ultimate level of functioning could not be accurately predicted, he said that she would undoubtedly require special education, and would most likely be unable to live independently as an adult. Linda's parents had difficulty accepting the diagnosis, especially since they were not given a specific prognosis and could not, therefore, plan for their daughter's future. Although they were told to "take it one day at a time," they were haunted by uncertainty. As time went on, they came gradually to accept the fact that Linda would be very severely affected. Linda was enrolled in an infant stimulation program and a special-education teacher started coming into the home each week to provide therapy.

Linda continued to develop very slowly. At two years of age most of her skills were at a six-month level. She was able to roll over (four months), sit with support (six months), grasp objects (four months), and transfer them from one hand to the other (six months). She laughed (four months) and smiled at her image in the mirror (six months), and had begun to babble (six months). At three years of age Linda entered a special-education class for the severely handicapped. Now six, Linda has continued to make slow progress. Her present abilities place her at an eighteen-month level. Formal psychological testing revealed an IQ of 25. With this level of functioning, Linda's parents can hope that as an adult she will be able to communicate to some degree, manage some self-care skills, and participate in a group-activities program. However, she will always need to live at home or in a group home or institution (see chapter 21).

SANDY

Sandy was the fourth child born to Susan, aged thirty-nine, and George, aged forty-one. Sandy's birth occurred before prenatal diagnosis was available. At birth, Sandy's doctors noted that she had oriental features, low muscle tone, and a heart murmur. The doctors told Susan and George that Sandy appeared to have Down syndrome, a diagnosis that was confirmed when chromosome studies revealed the presence of an extra number 21 chromosome (see chapter 7). Sandy's parents were devastated; they knew that children with Down syndrome are mentally retarded. However, because they had received a firm diagnosis, they were able to contact other families who had children with Down syndrome. The support they received from these other parents helped them accept the situation and plan for the future.

Sandy was a happy baby and fed well, but her development proceeded slowly, at a little less than half speed. She sat without support at twelve months (seven months) and walked at twenty months (twelve months), rode a tricycle at five years (three years) and first rode a bicycle at ten years (six years). Language was also delayed: She babbled at twelve months (six months), had two or three specific words at twenty-eight months (twelve months), and did not speak in short sentences until six years (two and a half years). Formal testing revealed an IQ of 45 at five years of age. She has been in a self-contained class for moderately retarded children in the public school system since that time. As an adult, Sandy should be able to care for herself, do errands, and work in a sheltered workshop. She will probably live at home or in a group home.

BILLY

Billy had a normal delivery and seemed a perfectly healthy baby. During his first few years of life, his development seemed normal, although, in retrospect, his parents realized that he reached milestones somewhat later than did his two older brothers. At age three he entered nursery school and was found to be significantly slower than the other children in his class. He was unable to ride a tricycle (three years) or even walk up steps (two and a half years). He had difficulty unscrewing lids of jars and building block towers (two to two and a half years). He spoke only in two-word phrases (two to two and a half years), and could not follow complex commands (two and a half to three years). He did not play well with other children (two and a half to three years).

At his nursery school teacher's suggestion, Billy's parents had him evaluated by a developmental pediatrician and a clinical psychologist. Formal psychological testing revealed an IQ score of 60 and a mental age slightly under two years. Although Billy's parents had thought of him as "slow," it took them several years before they could accept the words "mentally retarded." By the time he entered first grade, his limitations had become more evident. He lacked the readiness skills needed for academics and was moved into a special-education program for the mildly retarded. He has done well and can be expected to be self-sufficient and eventually to live in a group home or even independently.

The case histories of these children illustrate a number of points. First, the degree of severity usually determines how early a diagnosis can be made; very severe disabilities are usually apparent shortly after birth, while a mild impairment may not be iden-

tified for several years. Second, the diagnosis becomes clearer if the child has been followed by a pediatrician for years and if development has followed a constant but significantly delayed rate. Third, no matter how certain the diagnosis, it is always difficult to accept. Finally, having a specific diagnosis, for example Down syndrome, helps families cope, as it allows the pediatrician to discuss prognosis as it relates to a large group of children with the same disorder.

WHAT DOES THE TERM MENTAL RETARDATION MEAN?

The definition of mental retardation has three components:

1. The IQ score of a mentally retarded child is below 70.
2. Mental retardation is a nonprogressive disorder evident during childhood.
3. A mentally retarded individual has an impaired ability to adapt to his or her environment. We will discuss each of these characteristics.

IQ Score

The diagnosis of mental retardation relies on a measure of intelligence called the intelligence quotient, or IQ. The quotient refers to a computed mental age divided by the child's chronological age and multiplied by 100. The average IQ score is 100. For example, a twenty-four-month-old girl with the mental age of twenty-four months has an IQ of 100 (24 divided by 24 and multiplied by 100 equals 100). Linda, who at six years of age had a mental age of eighteen months, has an IQ of 25 (18 months divided by 72 months and multiplied by 100 equals 25). The mental age can be measured using various psychological tests of language, reasoning, visual-perceptual, and mathematical skills.

Mental retardation means that the IQ score falls well below average. Statistically speaking, thirty points below average, or an IQ below 70, signifies mental retardation. Each additional fifteen points below IQ 70 is defined as a more severe form of retardation. Thus, a person with an IQ between 55 and 69 is said to be mildly mentally retarded, an IQ of 40 to 54 is the range of moderate mental retardation, and 25 to 39 is the range for severe mental retardation (Table 6.1). Scores below 25 fall into the range of profound mental retardation. Keeping these ranges in mind for our three previous examples, Linda would be classified as severely retarded (IQ 25); Sandy, moderately retarded (IQ 45); and Billy, mildly retarded (IQ 60).

A Nonprogressive Disorder of Childhood

The term *mental retardation* applies only to children who have developmental delays as a result of an injury or disorder that existed prior to age eighteen. The following example illustrates this concept: A serious car accident leaves two victims, a father and his three-year-old son, both brain damaged and with severe intellectual deficits. The child is labeled mentally retarded, while the father is said to have an "organic brain syndrome." Mental retardation implies that the damage occurred while the brain was still actively growing.

Mental retardation also implies that the brain damage is not progressive. The child above will not become any more brain damaged as he grows up. In contrast, some progressive nervous-system disorders such as Tay-Sachs disease continue to worsen as the child grows.

Impaired Adaptive Abilities

A low IQ score has more than statistical significance; it implies an impairment of a person's ability to adapt and interact with his environment. For school-aged children, that means having difficulty learning in school and participating in group activities. Adults with poor adaptive skills are less likely to hold a job, handle financial matters, succeed in marriage, or abide by conventional social mores.

THE SPECTRUM OF DEVELOPMENTAL DISABILITIES

Another problem, especially limiting the adaptability of severely and profoundly retarded individuals, is that mental retardation may not be the only developmental disability; it may be just one manifestation of a more complex syndrome. While a mildly retarded child is unlikely to have other problems, children with more severe forms of retardation have an increased frequency of seizure disorders, cerebral palsy, speech and hearing problems, and vision impairments. Thus your child may be further limited by these other disabilities, which will be discussed in later chapters. It is important to remember that your child should be tested for other disabilities so that appropriate treatment can be provided.

TABLE 6.1   IQ Scores and Degree of Retardation

IQ	Degree of retardation
85–115	Normal intelligence
70–84	Borderline normal intelligence
55–69	Mild mental retardation
40–54	Moderate mental retardation
25–39	Severe mental retardation
< 25	Profound mental retardation

EARLY CLUES TO MENTAL RETARDATION

As mentioned earlier, mental retardation may be diagnosed as early as the first day of life or as late as school age, with more severely affected children generally being diagnosed earlier. Sometimes a baby's appearance may lead to an early diagnosis, for example, in children born with very small heads (microcephaly), or in those with facial characteristics typical of Down syndrome or with physical deformities suggestive of other genetic syndromes. In addition, children who are very premature, weighing less than three pounds, are at some increased risk for being retarded.

In addition to the above conditions, some other less-obvious traits may alert a pediatrician to check for mental retardation, such as a baby who is very irritable and inconsolable or alternately "too good," lying without complaint for hours. Difficult feeding times may indicate that the baby does not suck well, another indication of developmental delay. An abnormally high-pitched and strident cry, little recognition of parents even at three or four months of age, or a lack of reaction to sound or an inability to follow objects visually may also indicate mental retardation. There may also be abnormalities in muscle tone, the baby being either very floppy or spastic.

As described earlier, a delay in reaching certain developmental milestones may also alert parents or the pediatrician to a problem. These milestones include smiling at two months, babbling at six months, sitting without support at seven months, saying single words at twelve months, and walking by fifteen months. Significant delays in reaching these milestones suggest a developmentally delayed child. The presence of these delays indicates a high-risk infant who should be followed closely.

IQ TESTING

There are many tests available that give IQ scores. Some of these are group tests given together with achievement tests to all schoolchildren as a way of screening for learning disabilities. The Otis-Lennon is an example of a group IQ test administered in first, third, and fifth grades in many school systems. Scores from this test are compared to an achievement test, such as the Iowa or California Achievement Test, to determine if there is a significant discrepancy between a child's potential (measured by the IQ score on the Otis-Lennon) and his or her achievement in school (measured by the Iowa or California test). The group IQ test gives only an approximation of your child's abilities. Language skills and other cognitive abilities are not tested, resulting in an IQ score that may differ by ten points or more from a score obtained using individual tests. A child who may have a significant developmental delay should be given an individual IQ test rather than a group test.

There are different psychological tests for children of various ages. We will describe the three most commonly used tests: the Bayley Scales of Infant Development, the Stanford-Binet Intelligence Scale, and the Wechsler Intelligence Scales. Each takes about two hours, during which time a clinical psychologist will evaluate your child's abilities in different areas of intelligence: motor skills, visual-perceptual skills, reasoning and language abilities.

The Bayley Scales

The Bayley Scales are used for infants and toddlers from two months to two and a half years of age. Parents usually stay in the room with the child during the test. The child is expected to play with various objects or perform certain tasks. For example, a six-month-old is expected to reach for two blocks, transfer them from hand to hand, and bang them together. At twelve months the child should be able to place a round peg in a pegboard. An eighteen-month-old's tasks include imitating a crayon stroke and pointing to body parts on a doll. At two years the child is asked to solve three-piece puzzles, and at two and a half to follow prepositional commands such as "put the doll under the chair."

Language skills are the single best predictor of intelligence. Because language does not emerge as a major skill until about eighteen months of age, the Bayley Scales are primarily based on the observation of visual-motor skills and therefore have limited predictive value. Any testing performed with children under two years of age is not as accurate as are tests given later in childhood, when the child has a greater repertoire of behaviors that can be sampled. Over half of infants tested before two years of age will have adult IQ scores that differ by more than ten points from their Bayley Scales.

Despite these limitations, the Bayley Scales are a good predictor of intelligence for moderately to severely retarded infants, in whom the level of performance differs significantly from normal. These children will show a severe delay not just in one area of intelligence, but in all areas. However, for children with mild mental retardation, errors in diagnosis are not infrequent. A normal infant may be misdiagnosed as being delayed, or a mildly retarded child may be diagnosed as having normal development.

Stanford-Binet Scale

Beginning at two and a half years of age, the Stanford-Binet Intelligence Scale is often used. In this and other psychological tests given to older children, your child is examined without your presence, as you may distract her or unintentionally "help" her answer the questions. You may be able to watch the testing through a one-way mirror, without being observed by your child.

In contrast to the Bayley Scales, the Stanford-Binet Scale relies heavily on verbal responses to questions. For example, a two-and-a-half-year-old is presented with a group of pictures and is asked to name the objects shown. The quality and quantity of words your child puts together into phrases gives the examiner an assessment of spontaneous language. At three and a half years, your child is asked to "tell about the pictures," and is also asked questions that require more complex reasoning, discriminating *similar* versus *different* objects. At four years of age, your child is asked relational questions such as if "brother is a boy; sister is a . . ." At five years, your child is given incomplete drawings and is asked to describe what is missing. The expectation is that expressive and receptive language will increase in complexity as the child grows. Nonlanguage reasoning skills are also measured using puzzles and crayons.

Wechsler Scales

Although the Stanford-Binet test can be used throughout childhood, the most commonly used tests after four and a half years of age are the Wechsler series of intelligence scales. The WPPSI (Wechsler Preschool and Primary Scale of Intelligence) is used from the ages four and a half to six years. The WISC–R (Wechsler Intelligence

Scale for Children–Revised) is used for children aged six to sixteen years. The WAIS (Wechsler Adult Intelligence Scale) is given to adolescents and adults.

Similar to the Stanford-Binet, the Wechsler scales test both language abilities and visual-perceptual (eye-hand or perfor-mance) skills. The tests are divided into six verbal and six performance subtests, none of which requires reading or spelling. The verbal subtests include information, comprehension, arithmetic, similarities, vocabulary, and digit span. The perfor-mance subtests include picture comple-tion, picture arrangement, block design, object assembly, coding, and mazes. Verbal and performance subscales are generally equally low in children who are mentally retarded.

Although these are the most commonly used psychological tests, many other tests are also available. Some are particularly useful in testing children with hearing or vision deficits. For example, the Leiter test is used with deaf children or those with a significant communication disorder. It does

not depend on language but rather on non-verbal reasoning abilities. With blind chil-dren, only the verbal portion of the Wechsler test is used. Some tests focus on adaptability or social functioning rather than reasoning, such as the Vineland test of social maturity.

CATEGORIES OF MENTAL RETARDATION

When the IQ score is less than 70, espe-cially if this is a replication of an earlier test and the child is over two years of age, the term *mental retardation* is used to de-scribe the child's intellectual functioning. We will now examine the different grada-tions of mental retardation (Figure 6.1).

Mild Mental Retardation (IQ 55–69)

In the United States, there are over seven million mentally retarded citizens out of a total population of 248 million. Approximately 90 percent of these people fall into the range of mild mental retarda-tion. Usually the cause of mild mental re-

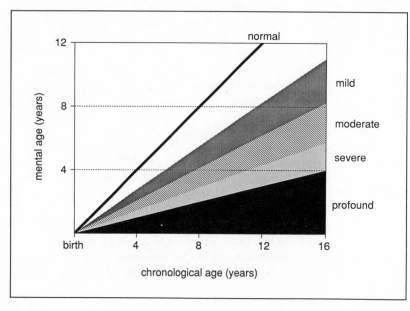

Figure 6.1. *The effect of var-ious degrees of mental re-tardation on mental age as compared to chronological age. Sixteen years is consid-ered the end of brain matu-ration. Thus, for example, a young adult with mild mental retardation would be expected to function at an eight- to eleven-year (third to fifth grade) level.*

tardation is unknown. Early identification has proven difficult, since motor skills are often normal and developmental milestones may be reached on, or near, schedule. Only when the child enters kindergarten or first grade do impairments become evident. Once the problem is recognized, the child should undergo a complete psychological and educational evaluation in school or at a developmental center so that the proper diagnosis can be made. After completion of the evaluation, he or she will be assigned to a special-education program that is usually in a neighborhood school.

The prognosis for mildly mentally retarded people generally follows this pattern: By age twenty-one, they should have completed school and achieved approximately third- to sixth-grade skills, reading and understanding arithmetic well enough to meet their everyday needs. Their life span is normal. They usually work in semiskilled, unskilled, or domestic occupations: About 15 to 20 percent work in skilled occupations, particularly when the economy is thriving.

Unfortunately, impaired adaptive abilities lead to an increased incidence of emotional problems. Thus, families should continue to provide support to this individual throughout life, even though he or she may be living independently. Although mildly retarded individuals can bear children, the additional stress on a couple, who may already be having both emotional and financial difficulties, can make parenthood especially difficult. The risk of child abuse is increased in this population. These people should be encouraged to use contraception and to limit their family size if they choose to have children. If possible, the retarded person's family should be involved in these life decisions. However, the couple has the legal right to make their own choices. Parents can suggest, but not force their ideas on the couple.

Moderate Mental Retardation (IQ 40–54)

Moderately retarded people account for approximately 7 percent of the mentally retarded population, numbering about half a million. There is more likely to be an identifiable cause for the disability in this group than in the mildly retarded (see chapter 3). Unlike the mildly retarded child, these children clearly develop slowly throughout infancy and early childhood. By two years of age their delayed development of speech and motor skills has usually led to a diagnosis and formal psychological testing. A special-education program should be started in the preschool years and continued in special-education classes throughout elementary and secondary school.

By the end of schooling, moderately retarded people will have academic skills between a four- to eight-year level. They will not be functional readers or writers, and their arithmetic skills will be rudimentary. However, they may have a "survival" vocabulary that permits them to identify familiar signs and phrases. They should also be able to write their names. Often unable to make change, they can, however, return with change of "one dime and one quarter" if given this specific instruction. They can have a moderate degree of independence: they can clean up around the house, make simple meals, clothe and wash themselves. They will also form lasting friendships and interact with others cooperatively.

However, they are not able to function without supervision, even as adults. These individuals are at risk for promiscuous sexual contacts. They need to be taught to protect themselves from unwanted advances and practice appropriate behavior in social situations.

Moderately retarded individuals will also tend to have behavioral problems that need to be managed. Self-stimulatory behavior may include masturbation, rocking, head-banging, biting, and finger play. Hyperactivity, distractibility, aggressive behavior, and emotional disturbances are also common. Behavior-modification therapy can be very helpful in treating some of these problems (see chapter 15). This involves rewarding appropriate behavior and ignoring or punishing inappropriate behavior.

Severe (IQ 25–39) and Profound (IQ Less Than 25) Mental Retardation

Severely and profoundly retarded individuals make up the remaining 3 percent of the retarded population and account for virtually all of the institutionalized mentally retarded individuals in the United States. As a result of the deinstitutionalization movement of the 1970s and 1980s, most of these individuals are now cared for at home and attend special programs in the public school system. This is the group most likely to have a known cause for their disability and to show other developmental disabilities in addition to mental retardation. The educational programs for these children focus on improving self-care skills and providing therapy for the accompanying disabilities.

As adults, severely retarded people are capable of some self-care skills: They may be able to talk in brief phrases, understand simple instructions, and pay attention for short periods of time. However, they will not be able to live independently outside of a home or institutional setting.

Profoundly retarded adults have an even smaller repertoire of behaviors than do severely retarded people. They usually func-

tion below a two-year-old level. Some may learn to feed themselves, put on clothing, wash their hands, and use a toilet. If not affected by cerebral palsy, their motor skills could include climbing, hopping, and throwing a ball. Communication abilities may involve a simple vocabulary that carries meaning or, if nonverbal, they may use gestures or signs. They may also follow simple commands like "Give it to me." Social interactions in simple games such as playing house and dancing to music are likely.

In contrast to mildly to severely retarded people who have normal life spans, profoundly retarded individuals with multiple disabilities often have shortened life expectancy, living an average of twenty-five years. Twenty years ago the life span was only about half this. Deaths usually occurred from respiratory and other infections, and from malnutrition. With improved nutrition, increased antibiotic use, more exercise, and increased home care, it is likely that longevity will increase further.

TREATMENT OF MENTAL RETARDATION: AN HISTORICAL PERSPECTIVE

The history of approaches to treating the mentally retarded has been cyclical. They have been at times tolerated and at other times shunned. The Romans simply discarded mentally retarded children by throwing them into the Tiber River. In the middle ages, the mentally retarded fared better. In accordance with superstitions and fear of the supernatural, they were regarded as messengers of God. This attitude was reversed during the eighteenth-century "Age of Reason," when the retarded were considered agents of the devil. And throughout time, up until the twentieth century, there persisted confusion between mental retardation and mental illness.

Conditions for the mentally retarded first began to improve at the beginning of the nineteenth century. In 1801 Jean Marc Gaspard Itard (1774–1838) reported to the French Academy of Sciences his study of the Wild Boy of Aveyron, a retarded child who had been left to die in the forest and had been raised by wolves. When found at the age of nine, the boy was thought to be profoundly retarded. Itard's efforts resulted in marked improvements in the child's functioning. This was the first evidence that a retarded child could learn.

Edouard Onesimus Seguin (1812–1880) followed up on Itard's observations by developing a teaching curriculum for the mentally retarded. He set up residential educational institutions that used the modern techniques of behavior modification and sensory-motor training. Between 1850 and 1875, a large number of these institutions were built. These schools, with excellent teachers and an intricate curriculum, fueled optimism that mental retardation could be cured if only the right environment was provided. Environment was, in fact, seen as the cause of most cases of mental retardation.

But by 1900 it became evident that although the mentally retarded could be taught many things, they remained retarded. The realization that a cure wasn't possible led to a period of profound pessimism that was to stall progress in the field for fifty years. Between 1900 and 1950, the size of institutions for the mentally retarded grew and the quality of care declined. These facilities simply became warehouses for the retarded.

It was also at this time that mild mental retardation was first recognized as a distinct entity. The term *mental retardation* was previously used to refer only to moderately to severely retarded individuals, but at the turn of the century, it was realized that some slow learners were actually "mildly" retarded. Rather than leading to new educational and treatment approaches, however, this recognition resulted in the stigmatization of the mildly mentally retarded. In fact, many of the social ills of the time were laid at the feet of the mildly retarded, who were considered likely to engage in criminal behavior.

Things started to change again in the mid-1930s with the discovery of phenylketonuria (PKU). It became apparent that environment was not always the problem and that there were genetic causes of mental retardation. This trend was accentuated with the discovery in 1959 by Jerome LeJeune of the presence of an extra chromosome in people with Down syndrome. No longer considered a social evil, mental retardation was placed back in the realm of a medical/educational problem.

The modern era in care began with the administration of President John F. Kennedy and the development of the University Affiliated Facilities, which trained therapists and provided federally funded services for the developmentally disabled. This was followed by public movements to deinstitutionalize the retarded, develop group homes, and credit the achievements of the retarded with such programs as the Special Olympics. Finally, the passage in 1975 of Public Law 94-142, the Education for All Handicapped Children Act, dictated quality public education for all disabled children. More recently, Public Law 99-457 mandates infant stimulation programs for high-risk infants (see chapter 20). There has never before been a time when the retarded have been provided as many services or have been as well accepted into the community.

PRESENT TREATMENT OF MENTAL RETARDATION

Unfortunately, mental retardation has no cure; quick fixes and magic potions are bound to fail. But there are many things that can be done to help your child reach his or her potential. Multidisciplinary therapy, in which several different specialists work together with you and your child for a prolonged period of time, has proven particularly effective. This therapy is directed at a number of aspects of your child's life: education, social and recreational activities, behavior and emotional problems, and associated deficits. Each of these is discussed in detail in later chapters. Here, we will summarize some of the approaches to give you a general background.

Education (also see chapter 20)

As with a child of normal intelligence, the life of a mentally retarded child revolves around school. The educational rights of a developmentally disabled child are enumerated in the Education for All Handicapped Children Act of 1975, which provides for the free, appropriate public education, in the least-restricted environment, for all children who require special education and related services. Related services covered by this federal legislation include physical therapy, occupational therapy, speech and language therapy, and psychological counseling.

Most retarded children are placed in special-education classes in neighborhood schools. Those with mild mental retardation may be mainstreamed with unaffected children for home room, art, music, and gym and are separated only for academics. Children with moderate mental retardation usually attend entirely self-contained classes in either neighborhood or special-education schools. Finally, those with more severe deficits are generally placed in special programs serving the entire school district.

There has been much furor about the issue of "mainstreaming," the process of placing disabled children in regular classrooms. It seems clear that it is valuable for "normal" children to come in contact with disabled children. Studies show that the general population is more accepting of people with disabilities if exposed to them early in life. It is less clear if this is equally beneficial for the mentally retarded child. Most educators agree that mildly retarded children should be mainstreamed for non-academic subjects, as they will live in society and must adapt to it. It seems much less clear that there is benefit to more severely mentally retarded children who will always live a life apart and may suffer at the hands of their schoolmates in a regular classroom setting.

My advice to you about mainstreaming is that your major concern should be that your child is in a program he or she enjoys and in which effective learning occurs. Children who are placed in classes in which the level is too high often feel continually frustrated, while those placed in programs that are not stimulating enough may be bored. Either way, the child may act out with behavior problems. The ideal program should stretch your child's abilities and enable him or her to achieve as much as possible. Finding the appropriate program is often difficult, and requires yearly reassessment.

Recreation

Besides education, you must address the social and recreational needs of your child. He or she needs friends just as much as any other child, and needs the opportunity to play with other children outside of school. Encourage friendships with children who are functioning at your child's mental age, not chronological age. That might mean that your child will play primarily with younger children or with other mentally retarded children.

Generally speaking, children with mental retardation do better in individual or small-group activities than in team sports. Activities that utilize gross-motor skills rather than fine-motor coordination are best. Examples include track and field, swimming, and hiking. The Special Olympics provides many children with a framework for such activities.

Behavioral Problems

We are going to discuss behavioral and emotional problems separately. The basic difference between these two is that behavioral problems are learned, while emotional disorders are part of the child's psyche. Behavioral problems include temper tantrums, food refusal, and refusal to go to bed. As these behaviors are learned, they can also be unlearned! The role of the behavioral psychologist and educator in treatment is critical (see chapter 15). By contrast, depression is an example of an emotional disorder. Emotional disorders are generally dealt with by a psychiatrist, clinical psychologist, or social worker. In differentiating behavioral from emotional disorders, what complicates matters is that children with emotional disorders may also have behavioral problems. For example, a depressed child may show his unhappiness by having temper tantrums. Therefore, it is important to determine if your child has a behavioral problem, an emotional disorder, both or neither.

Behavioral problems can be especially hard to sort out in mentally retarded children. You must keep your child's mental age in mind when assessing the appropriateness of behavior. For example, an aver-

age four-year-old who gets into everything may be considered hyperactive; but a four-year-old with an IQ of 50 may be acting his mental age of two years, in which case excessive exploratory behavior may not be abnormal.

While not all retarded children have behavior problems, they occur more commonly than in nonhandicapped children. Sometimes parents may inadvertently add to these problems. The burden of care, guilt, and frustration can tax parents' child-rearing skills and lead to secondary handicaps. For example, letting a young child get away with things can backfire when the child grows up to be a strong young adult who is undisciplined. Children who are waited on because of disabilities have decreased potential for independence as adults. Parents often fail to understand that even the most severely disabled child can control the family. However, your child is capable of responding to both limits and discipline. Either he will learn to live in your house or you will have to live in his disordered house. Early attention to discipline and emotions often prevents major problems in the future.

There are also medical measures that can sometimes solve behavioral problems. The identification and correction of a hearing or vision problem may decrease frustration from this sensory impairment (see chapters 10 and 13). Treatment of previously undetected seizures or esophageal ulcers due to gastroesophageal reflux will provide relief and decrease irritability (see chapters 8 and 16). Sometimes the short-term use of sleeping pills for sleep disturbances, or treatment of constipation, can help (see chapter 19).

Behavioral problems can also result from an inadequate educational program (for instance, if your child is frustrated or bored), so this should be evaluated first and modified if necessary. Changing the school environment is not often the sole answer. Therefore, behavior-modification techniques and/or medications are frequently needed. Behavior modification involves encouraging appropriate behavior and discouraging inappropriate behavior. This therapy is especially useful for managing children who are noncompliant, aggressive, or show self-stimulatory/self-injurious behavior (see chapter 15).

Although behavior modification is often effective, medication is sometimes needed to control behavior. Stimulant medications such as Ritalin and Dexedrine are beneficial in controlling hyperactive and inattentive behaviors in both children with normal intelligence and those who are mildly mentally retarded. Stronger drugs such as Propranolol, Lithium, Mellaril, Thorazine, and Haldol have also been used (see chapter 19). While these other drugs may be helpful in decreasing hyperactivity, anxiety, and aggressiveness in some mentally retarded children, they also carry greater risks than the stimulant medications. Side effects include sleepiness, decreased attention span, excessive weight gain, depression, worsening of seizure activity, and the development of unusual motor movements after years of use. Therefore, these drugs should be used cautiously, starting with an initial short trial period, during which time parents and teachers should keep a record of attention, behavior, and activity level. The medication should be continued only if it is shown to be effective. Then, each year, the child should be taken off the medication for a short time to evaluate the need for continued treatment.

Emotional Disorders

The prevalence of emotional disorders in the United States is high. In fact, 50 percent of all hospital beds are filled by persons with psychiatric disorders. Considering their physical and cognitive limitations along with their decreased ability to cope with problems, one would expect a high incidence of emotional problems in the mentally retarded population. This is in fact the case.

It is important to differentiate normal from abnormal emotional responses and to identify situational anxiety in the retarded. It is not abnormal for anyone to have occasional outbursts in response to certain situations. Take a child who is in a residential program. He may be scheduled for activities every waking moment of the day. If Saturday morning from nine to ten is laundry time and he wants to sleep in, he may be belligerent in resisting participation in this activity. This may be reported as an emotional disturbance, but could very well just be adolescent rebellion. Some flexibility is needed for these "normal" emotional outbursts.

Situational anxiety is very common and may be misinterpreted as a significant emotional problem. For instance, going to the doctor may be stressful, especially if your child has had previous bad experiences or is fearful of what may happen. This can be avoided by explaining in advance what will occur and how it will affect his normal routine. It is helpful to expose your child to many experiences so he can learn to cope with new situations. If your child is very anxious, the use of a mild tranquilizer such as Atarax or chloral hydrate, under the supervision of your doctor, may be of benefit in preparation for a particularly stressful situation.

There are many individuals competent to diagnose and treat psychiatric illnesses in mentally retarded individuals. Counseling may take the form of teaching parenting skills and understanding the emotional problem. Music therapy has recently been shown to be effective in treating some emotional problems. Relaxation and bio-feedback techniques have also proved valuable for some people. Concrete and simple supportive therapy, nonverbal methods such as play therapy, and group therapy involving the child either with or without the family have all proven helpful.

Evaluating Associated Deficits

The final aspect of treatment involves determining whether your child has other undetected impairments, such as hearing or vision loss or seizure activity. Since these associated deficits may affect school performance, early identification and treatment is essential. Yearly reassessments are important to ensure that your child has a correct school placement, and that there are no new medical problems.

Treating All in the Family

Although we have focused on your child, treatment must also take into account the rest of your family. How are you doing? Do you have enough time for yourself and your other children? What are your feelings about your disabled child? How are your other children faring? The answers to some of these questions may be distressing, and may indicate the need for professional counseling for family members. Your child will be happiest if you are able to spend "quality time" with him or her and if you can avoid resentment. Take care of yourself by using summer camps, respite care, and baby-sitters, so you will not feel overwhelmed by your child's care.

SOME QUESTIONS ANSWERED

Will my child catch up?

"If my child is four years old and is functioning at a two-year-old level, does that mean he will always be two years behind?" The implication is "Will the difference from normal lessen in my child as he grows older?" Will he act like a twelve-year-old when he is fourteen?

Unfortunately, the gap will widen rather than narrow as your child grows older. Consider two four-year-old children, one with an IQ of 100 and the other with an IQ of 50. Each year the child with an IQ of 50 will gain only half the skills and abilities mastered by the normal child. By fourteen years of age, the child with an IQ of 100 will have a mental age of fourteen years, while the retarded child will have the mental age of about seven years. Additionally, there are age limits to brain development: the forty-year-old retarded man or woman will not develop a mental age of twenty; he or she may have reached a plateau at a mental age of eight. As a result, the retarded child's disability will become more apparent over time, not less.

Are errors likely to be made in IQ testing?

Serious errors are uncommon, but possible. They are most likely to occur when testing an infant who may be ill, or a child with an unrecognized vision or hearing problem. Children with hearing or vision impairments may score much lower than their ability unless they are given special IQ tests that take into account their sensory impairment. A severe motor impairment such as cerebral palsy or muscular dystrophy may also interfere with the timed tests in standard IQ batteries and this must be taken into account.

On the other hand, if your child is simply tired or unhappy, her IQ score should not be significantly affected. Psychologists know how to get the best performance from your child. However, it is generally better to test a young child in the morning rather than the afternoon. If there are concerns about the accuracy of the tests, you can return for a second visit so the results can be checked. If your child is found to be significantly developmentally delayed, the psychologist will probably want to retest him or her six to twelve months later. If the second test shows a similar delay, the diagnosis of mental retardation is very likely to be correct.

Can I predict how much my child will learn?

It is difficult to predict your child's eventual intellectual abilities when he or she is very young and being evaluated for the first time. Prediction becomes more exact following reevaluations. For example, if a physician has followed a child with an IQ of 50 for two to three years, and each year the child gains six months instead of 12 months of new skills, the physician can predict the child's eventual abilities with some confidence. It is also more straightforward to give a prognosis for a severely retarded child than for a mildly retarded child.

As a general indicator of your child's eventual mental age, assume that intellectual growth is complete by about sixteen years of age, and then multiply the IQ as a percent of normal times sixteen years. Thus, a child with an IQ of 60 might be expected to have the intellectual abilities of a ten-year-old (60 percent × 16) when an adult. In this case, you could expect your child to attain the abilities to do functional reading and arithmetic and to live independently. However, keep in mind that outcome is not solely a function of intellectual gifts. It is significantly influenced by the home and school environment and by your child's own efforts.

My child had the mental retardation screening test during the newborn period and it was normal! How can he be mentally retarded?

Newborn screening is performed for a number of rare inborn errors of metabolism. The specific diseases tested for vary from state to state but generally include phenylketonuria, hypothyroidism, homocystinuria, galactosemia, and maple syrup urine disease. Such genetically inherited disorders have an incidence of between 1 : 6,000 to 1 : 300,000 births. Thus, they account for very few of the total number of children with mental retardation. The importance of these tests is that they can identify certain diseases that, if left untreated, invariably lead to mental retardation. Early treatment of these diseases can prevent the occurrence of mental retardation. However, a normal result on this screening test only means your child does not suffer from one of the above illnesses; it does not ensure that your child is normal.

If he is retarded, why were his brain wave test and his CT scan normal?

Electroencephalograms (EEGs) measure the brain wave pattern through electrodes pasted to your child's scalp. This test is primarily used to evaluate the possibility of a seizure disorder. Many children with normal intelligence have abnormal EEG patterns, and many children who are mentally retarded have normal EEGs. An electroencephalogram is not a test for mental retardation.

The computed tomography (CT) of the brain, or alternatively the magnetic resonance imaging (MRI) scan looks for major structural brain abnormalities. Most causes of mental retardation involve microscopic changes in the brain architecture and cannot be seen on these scans. Thus the scans may be helpful in detecting a specific abnormality, but they may also be normal even in the presence of severe mental retardation.

Will his physical growth be normal?

The adult height of a child is usually determined by the average height of his parents — tall parents tend to have tall children and short parents have short children. Mildly retarded people generally reach the genetic growth potential of their parents. However, more severely retarded children are usually short and we don't know why. Additionally, certain forms of mental retardation, like Down syndrome, are specifically associated with short stature. Moderate to severely mentally retarded children also tend to mature physically later than normal. Their secondary teeth erupt later, their growth spurt begins later, and menstruation may be delayed in onset.

DOWN SYNDROME (TRISOMY 21) AND OTHER CHROMOSOMAL ABNORMALITIES

Approximately four thousand children are born each year in the United States with Down syndrome, making it the most common genetic cause of mental retardation. As we discuss below, most of these children are moderately retarded, with IQs in the range of 40–54. In the United States, 10 percent of all people who are moderately to severely retarded have Down syndrome.

The overall incidence of Down syndrome is one affected child in every 700 births. However, that risk figure depends to a great extent on the parents' ages (Figure 7.1). In women under twenty-five, the frequency is about 1 : 2,000 births. This risk increases to 1 : 1,300 at thirty years and to 1 : 400 at thirty-five years. The significance of the mother's age becomes very important after the age of thirty-five: at age forty the incidence climbs to 1 : 90 and at age forty-five it is 1 : 32. On this basis it has been suggested that all women over the age of thirty-five be offered prenatal diagnosis in order to detect Down syndrome or other chromosomal abnormalities. Fathers over age fifty also appear to carry an increased risk of having a child with Down syndrome, although the father's age is much less important than the mother's.

LENNY

Laurie and George had two young healthy daughters. When Laurie was twenty-eight years old, she enjoyed an easy third pregnancy. Labor began within two days of the expected date, delivery was uncomplicated, and a son, Lenny, was born.

At the time of birth, the doctors noted that Lenny was floppy and had an unusual, "oriental-like" appearance. His head was small and flattened at the back. Lenny's eyes were slanted upward and there was a fold of skin over their inner corners. This combination of physical traits suggested Down syndrome. The doctors told Laurie and George their diagnosis and later confirmed it by performing a chromosome analysis and finding an extra number 21 chromosome in each of Lenny's white blood cells. Laurie and George were shocked and perplexed. They were young, there had been no sign of trouble, and they had no family history of Down syndrome. They wondered what had gone wrong and what the future held.

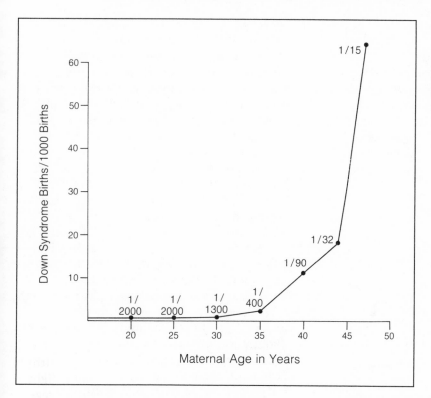

Figure 7.1. *Incidence of Down syndrome in mothers of various ages. The risk markedly increases after thirty-five years of age.*

This chapter will provide some of the answers to Laurie's and George's questions. We will discuss a number of disorders involving chromosomal abnormalities including Down syndrome, trisomy 13, trisomy 18, cat cry (cri du chat) syndrome, Fragile X syndrome, Turner syndrome, and Klinefelter syndrome. We will discuss the cause of each disorder, the risk of having another affected child, and the medical and developmental problems associated with these disorders. We will also advise you how to help your child reach his or her potential.

AN HISTORICAL PERSPECTIVE

Down syndrome is an ancient disorder. Archaeological excavations have revealed a skull dating from the seventh century that displays the physical features of a Down syndrome individual. Portrait paintings from the sixteenth century depict children with a Down's-like facial appearance. However, it was not until 1866 that the first complete description of these children was published by Dr. John Langdon Down, after whom this disorder is named. He indicated the physical characteristics and noticed the "family" resemblance of affected individuals. Unfortunately, he also gave these children the label "mongolian idiocy," a derogatory term that was to persist for almost a hundred years.

THE CAUSES OF DOWN SYNDROME

Since the early part of this century, it has been known that older women have an increased chance of giving birth to a child with Down syndrome. However, it wasn't until 1959 that the cause of Down syndrome was found to be an extra number 21 chromosome in each of an affected child's cells.

The extra chromosome associated with Down syndrome results from a phenomenon called nondisjunction, in which the cells divide unequally (Figure 7.2). This abnormality can occur during the maturation of either the egg or the sperm. As discussed in chapter 4, when a developing

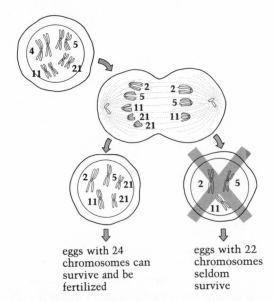

eggs with 24 chromosomes can survive and be fertilized

eggs with 22 chromosomes seldom survive

Figure 7.2. *Nondisjunction: During the meiotic division of the sperm or egg (see Figure 4.1), a mistake can occur in which there is unequal division. As a result, one of the new cells ends up having an extra chromosome and the other cell has one chromosome less than normal. In this figure we have simplified the process by showing only four pairs of chromosomes. As a result of nondisjunction, one daughter cell has five chromosomes and the other three. The cell with one less chromosome does not survive. However, the egg or sperm with the extra chromosome can survive and be fertilized, leading to the birth of a child with forty-seven rather than forty-six chromosomes. The most common chromosome affected by nondisjunction is the twenty-first, leading to the development of Down syndrome.*

sperm or egg cell divides, each of the resulting cells should have one copy of each of the twenty-three chromosomes. But in nondisjunction, one cell may get two copies of one chromosome while the other cell gets none. The cells that lack a chromosome usually die, but those with an extra copy may go on to become fertilized. As a result, the fertilized egg has three copies of one chromosome rather than the normal two. This condition is called trisomy. The most likely chromosome to have an extra copy is number 21, resulting in a child with Down syndrome (Figure 7.3). This is the reason Down syndrome is also called trisomy 21. However, other chromosomes, most notably numbers 13 and 18, can also be affected by nondisjunction. These abnormalities produce children with trisomy 13 and trisomy 18 (see below). Although nondisjunction can occur in either the sperm or the egg, it is more common in the egg. Nondisjunction in the egg is responsible for 95 percent of trisomies, while only 5 percent result from nondisjunction in the sperm.

It is unclear how the extra chromosome actually causes the multiple abnormalities of Down syndrome. The chromosomes contain the blueprint for development and it is suspected that the additional information contained in the third number 21 chromosome scrambles or distorts this blueprint.

THE EFFECT OF PARENTAL AGE

Both the mother's and the father's age affect the likelihood of having a child with Down syndrome because cells of older people are more likely to divide unequally. The mother's age plays an especially significant role. At birth a woman's ovaries contain all the eggs (approximately five thousand) that she will ever have. During

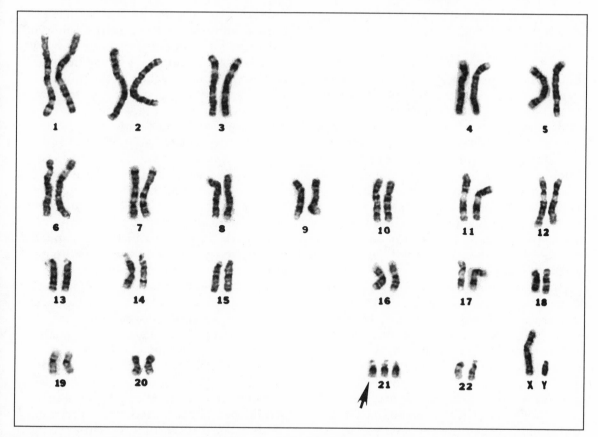

Figure 7.3. *Karotype or chromosomal pattern of a male child with Down syndrome. Note that there are forty-seven rather than forty-six chromosomes, with three copies of the number 21. There is also one X and one Y chromosome, indicating that this is a boy.*

childhood the eggs are immature and have forty-six chromosomes, but between adolescence and middle age about five hundred eggs will ripen sequentially and be released at monthly periods. It is during this ripening process that the cell splits to become an egg cell with twenty-three chromosomes. You can see that in an older woman, the egg cells will have been present for a longer period of time. As a result, the mechanism of cell division is more likely to be defective, leading to an increased possibility of nondisjunction. In men, new sperm cells are produced con-stantly and are therefore less likely to undergo nondisjunction. The risk of nondisjunction does increase, especially in men over fifty, although the precise reason is unknown.

Due to the complex nature of cell division, you might expect mistakes to occur frequently. In fact, nondisjunction does occur frequently, but the resulting abnormality in chromosome number places the developing fetus at an increased risk for miscarriage. Over 80 percent of all Down syndrome embryos are miscarried during the first trimester of pregnancy.

OTHER MECHANISMS THAT CAUSE DOWN SYNDROME

Although 95 percent of all Down syndrome children have trisomy 21 caused by nondisjunction, this is not the only chromosomal abnormality that can produce a Down child. Mosaicism and translocation are two less common mechanisms that are responsible for the remaining 5 percent of Down children.

In mosaicism, abnormal cell division occurs not in the maturing egg or sperm, but at some later point during development of the embryo. As a result, some, but not all of the embryo's cells will be affected; the child will be a "mosaic" of normal and abnormal cells. As many as 75 to 80 percent of the cells may be normal. Children with mosaic Down syndrome are generally less severely affected than those with trisomy 21. The oriental appearance may be less pronounced and there is less likelihood of other malformations such as heart defects. In addition they may be more intelligent. There seems to be some correlation between the percentage of cells affected and intellectual function; the smaller the percentage of cells affected, the higher the IQ score. Some mosaic children have IQ scores in the 55–70 range. In other words, they are only mildly retarded.

Translocation involves a completely different mechanism in which one of the parents is a carrier of an unusual chromosomal rearrangement. This parent has only forty-five chromosomes although he or she appears normal because part of the missing chromosome (number 21) is attached to the arm of another chromosome, usually number 13. In effect, this person has the information of all forty-six chromosomes carried on only forty-five chromosomes. A problem arises when this person passes on a sperm or egg containing the translocated number 13/21 chromosome as well as the normal number 21. The resulting embryo will have forty-six chromosomes, but will actually have a third copy of the number 21 chromosome attached to the number 13. This child has the same physical features and intellectual function as does any other Down syndrome child.

It is important to know whether a Down child has trisomy 21 or translocation because the risk of recurrence in future children is not the same. In the case of a young couple with a Down syndrome child, the recurrence risk for trisomy or mosaic 21 is about one in 100 as compared to about one in 2,000 in the general population. However, when translocation is the cause, the risk is about one in 50 for male carriers and one in 10 for female carriers. Therefore, all children with Down syndrome should have a chromosome analysis performed on their blood cells in order to identify which chromosomal abnormality has caused their disorder. If the child has a translocation, the parents' chromosomes should also be studied to determine who is the translocation carrier. A recurrence figure can be given at this time to help in planning future pregnancies. In addition, other family relations who may be at risk for carrying a translocation can be alerted.

PRENATAL DIAGNOSIS OF DOWN SYNDROME

Down syndrome can be diagnosed prior to birth, by performing either amniocentesis or chorionic villus sampling in the pregnant mother (see chapter 4). The fetal cells obtained by these procedures are analyzed for the presence of an extra number 21 chromosome. These tests are most commonly performed in women over the age of thirty-five and in women who have previously had a child with Down syndrome.

Recently a blood test has been developed to screen pregnant women for the presence of Down syndrome as well as for another malformation syndrome called spina bifida (see chapter 14). The blood test measures the chemical alpha fetoprotein (AFP), a substance that is normally produced by the fetus and is found in the bloodstream of pregnant women. A high level of AFP in the blood of women during their second trimester has been associated with an increased risk of spina bifida in the fetus. A low level has been associated with mothers who are carrying a fetus affected by Down syndrome. High or low levels of AFP do not confirm either diagnosis. It may also be abnormal if a woman is carrying twins or if she is at risk for premature delivery or for a low birth weight baby. If the test result is abnormal, amniocentesis is needed to determine the specific diagnosis.

It is important to realize that the AFP screening test is not sufficiently reliable to confirm a diagnosis. There are many reasons why AFP levels may appear abnormal even if the fetus is normal. In addition, 80 percent of women carrying Down syndrome fetuses will have normal AFP levels. The advantage of AFP testing is that it can identify a group of pregnant women who have not previously had affected children but who could benefit from further testing. The disadvantage is that it may cause needless worry in some women with healthy pregnancies. It is likely that this test will become more widely available and more accurate in the next few years.

PHYSICAL FEATURES OF A DOWN CHILD

Children with Down syndrome resemble one another (Figure 7.4). Infants have small heads that are rather flattened and shorter than they are wide. The soft spot on the top of their heads may be larger than normal, the bridge of their nose is flat, and their neck is shortened and broad. A flattened face and eyes that slant upward give the child an oriental appearance. Often

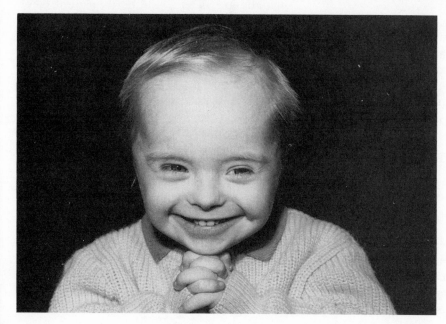

Figure 7.4. *Photograph showing a child with typical features of Down syndrome.*

there is a fold of skin at the inside corner of the eye, called an epicanthal fold, and the iris of the eyes may contain flecks of light colors. Floppy limbs caused by decreased muscle tone are especially apparent in infancy.

As these children become older, they are often nearsighted and the frequency of crossed eyes increases. Both the ears and mouth of Down children are small, their tongue is large, and their teeth may be small, poorly aligned, and erupt late. Down individuals have broad spade-shaped feet and hands. A single line called a simian crease usually runs across their palm and sole, and the small finger and toe are often misshapen. Their skin is mottled and their hair is sparse and fine. Overall, their body appears small and stocky. Growth potential is decreased; the average adult male with Down syndrome is five feet tall and the female is four and a half feet. There are separate growth charts that are used to follow the physical development of a Down syndrome child (see Cronk et al. in references).

There is no correlation between the degree of physical abnormalities and the severity of mental retardation. Some children with subtle physical signs of Down syndrome are severely retarded, while others with many prominent physical abnormalities are only moderately retarded.

MEDICAL COMPLICATIONS OF DOWN SYNDROME

There are a number of medical complications associated with Down syndrome. Approximately 40 percent of Down syndrome children are born with a congenital heart defect. The most common malformation is an opening between the right and left sides of the heart, called an endocardial cushion defect (Figure 7.5). If untreated, this mal-

formation can lead to heart failure and death in early childhood. Fortunately, over 90 percent of the infants who undergo open-heart surgery to correct the defect survive and do well.

There are additional medical complications that occur frequently in Down syndrome children. About 4 percent of Down syndrome children are born with a blockage of the small intestines. This abnormality, called duodenal atresia, must be corrected surgically in the first week of life to permit the normal passage of food. About 1 percent of Down syndrome infants contract a rare form of leukemia, which is often fatal. However, recent developments in chemotherapy have improved the prognosis. In addition, Down syndrome children often suffer from immune system problems that place them at increased risk for infections, especially in the middle ear and sinuses. Down syndrome children are also more likely to lose areas of scalp hair during childhood for no apparent reason. This condition is called alopecia. The hair usually grows back and no treatment is effective or necessary.

Hypothyroidism, which means decreased function of the thyroid gland, occurs in at least 10 percent of the children who have Down syndrome. The incidence increases with age. If untreated, this disorder worsens over time. Symptoms include constipation, increased floppiness, and decreased reflexes. Pediatricians may monitor thyroid function by doing a blood test to determine if there is a need for thyroid supplements.

Recently it has been discovered that some Down children are also at increased risk to sublux, or partially dislocate, their atlanto-occipital neck joint during active sports. In plain English, this means that the spinal column in the upper neck may be unstable, and a sudden jolt could lead to spinal cord damage. To determine if the

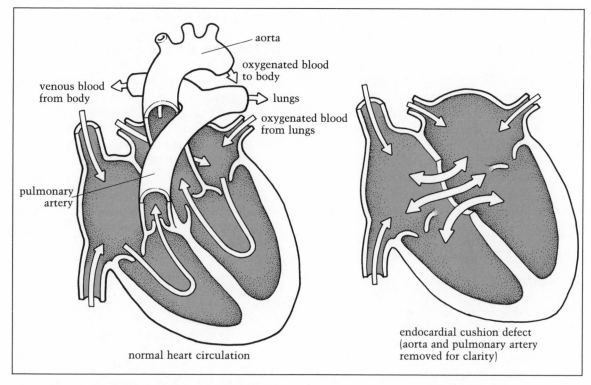

- aorta
- oxygenated blood to body
- venous blood from body
- lungs
- oxygenated blood from lungs
- pulmonary artery

normal heart circulation

endocardial cushion defect (aorta and pulmonary artery removed for clarity)

Figure 7.5. *Endocardial cushion defect: This is the most common heart abnormality found in children with Down syndrome. The wall that normally separates the right from the left side of the heart is not completely formed.*

atlanto-occipital joint is stable, Down syndrome children should have an X-ray study of their neck before participating in gymnastics or contact sports. If the joint is not stable, contact sports should be avoided and an orthopedic consultation obtained to determine if corrective surgery is needed. Because of their low muscle tone, Down syndrome children are also at risk for other orthopedic problems, such as joint dislocations.

Sexual development may be late or incomplete. Males are generally sterile and the fertility rate in women with Down syndrome is low. Approximately 70 percent of children born to a Down syndrome woman have Down syndrome.

INTELLECTUAL FUNCTIONING

All children with Down syndrome are mentally retarded. Although there is a wide scattering of IQ scores, most fall in the range of moderate mental retardation. Infants with Down syndrome often appear to be only mildly retarded because they are very attentive, happy, and responsive; for example, smiling and cooing occur at the expected ages. However, sitting and walking are usually delayed, because of low muscle tone, and by two to three years of age, significant intellectual deficits will be quite noticeable, with lags in language development and in reasoning abilities. Socially, they will continue to function at a higher level than they will academically, and the early gross-motor problems become less apparent over time. However, they will continue to have difficulty with fine-motor skills such as handwriting.

One disconcerting aspect of intellectual function is the possible loss of some abilities in adulthood. A small fraction of Down adults over age forty develop symptoms of Alzheimer's dementia, which include a gradual loss of memory and decreased speech and cognitive abilities.

PERSONALITY CHARACTERISTICS

Down syndrome children are often perceived as being happy and lovable, a generalization that seems to have merit. One study showed that young adults with Down syndrome were more responsible, cooperative, cheerful, and better adjusted than other individuals who were matched for intelligence and other social variables. However, a number of Down children do have significant behavioral or emotional problems, and even the usually happy Down child will have his bad days. As with any group of children, there is great individual variation in behavioral characteristics.

MEDICAL THERAPY

We have previously discussed a number of the medical complications of Down syndrome. Some of these problems, including hypothyroidism and congenital heart disease, require medical or surgical treatment. However, medical therapy cannot improve the IQ score. People have tried treating Down syndrome with vitamins (especially vitamin B_6), trace mineral supplements

(zinc and cadmium), injections of fetal tissue ("cell therapy"), and amino acids (tryptophan), but when these approaches were studied using scientifically valid methods, no differences were found in the IQ scores or motor skills of treated versus untreated patients. Similarly, the use of special breathing or fine-motor training exercises and other physical methods have not been effective in improving intellectual abilities. Treatment with thyroid medications has been beneficial in improving muscle tone in those individuals who are hypothyroid, but it does not improve the mental retardation.

PLASTIC SURGERY

There are plastic surgical techniques that can change the appearance of your Down syndrome child. These procedures include facial reconstruction for correcting the epicanthal folds of the eyes, the depressed nasal bridge, flat cheeks, receding chin, enlarged tongue, and hanging lower lip. The surgery is not particularly dangerous and the complication rate is low. But because this is a new procedure, the potential long-term complications are unknown. Moreover, it is unclear whether such surgery really gives your child a more "normal" appearance. In one study, people rated photographs of Down syndrome children taken before and after surgery. Parents of Down children rated the postoperative photos as more attractive than preoperative photos. But uninvolved lay persons rated the same photos as unchanged or slightly less attractive after surgery. In addition, claims that surgery improves speech articulation have not been substantiated. Thus, at present it is arguable that facial reconstruction is of benefit to Down syndrome children.

EDUCATION

There are many things that can be done to help your Down child reach his or her potential. The approaches to therapy are dictated more by your child's intellectual abilities than by the specific cause of the disability. Thus, your Down syndrome child should be treated as would any other mentally retarded person. Intervention should start in infancy, with an infant stimulation program administered by a private agency or by the public school system. As part of this program, a therapist will work with your child once a week and offer suggestions for exercises that will encourage sitting, walking, and increased vocalizing. The therapist may also help in the selection of play toys and will teach play skills and appropriate social interactions.

When your child is approximately two years old, the program will usually last half a day, three times a week, and may include consultation with a physical therapist, who may suggest exercises to improve muscle tone, and a speech therapist, who can offer help with language skills. It should be noted that Down children will improve their low muscle tone naturally with age.

At school age, your child should enter a special-education program with other children of similar intellectual abilities. Most Down syndrome children are placed in classes for the mildly or moderately mentally retarded, which include children with Down syndrome and other causes of mental retardation. Sports and other extracurricular activities should be encouraged. The Special Olympics program has been particularly valuable, and there are special education Boy Scout and Girl Scout troops and many other programs.

LONG-TERM PROGNOSIS FOR DOWN CHILDREN

In the past, many children with Down syndrome died in infancy of heart or gastrointestinal complications. Today, well over 90 percent of these children survive childhood. Life expectancy is only modestly lower than average. Medical complications later in life include arthritis, complications of hypothyroidism, and long-term heart disease. Deaths most commonly result from complications of malignancies, severe infections, or Alzheimer's disease.

Although institutionalization was the rule for Down syndrome children as recently as fifteen to twenty years ago, this is rarely considered at present. Studies have clearly shown that Down children develop many more social abilities if they remain at home rather than being placed in an institution. It is less clear whether home care has any effect on IQ.

By the end of schooling at age twenty-one, Down individuals may have some "survival" reading and math skills that will enable them to be self-sufficient in many areas. However, they will need supervision, either living with their parents or in a group home and attending sheltered workshops or activity centers. Depending on their level of intelligence, they may be expected to be completely independent in the home as well as being capable of doing errands for the family. They should be able to take care of themselves, make meals, do housework, and take a bus to the store to purchase food items. They can frequently earn money working in sheltered workshops. Higher-functioning adults with Down syndrome can hold jobs. Many Down individuals lead very fulfilling lives, as illustrated by the following story.

KENNY

Kenny is a twenty-one-year-old who, among other accomplishments, has spoken to many first-year medical students about his life. This excerpt was taken from one of his talks:

"Hello, my name is Kenny, I'm twenty-one years old, and I have Down syndrome. I look a little different from you. I have a slant to my eyes. I'm shorter than most people my age, and I have kind of stubby fingers. When I was a baby I had a hole in my heart that was fixed. I am also slow in learning things and I went to a special school.

"But, in most ways, I am like you. I have fun going out with my friends. I like to eat out and I have a girlfriend, named Linda. I want to work as a teacher's aide with special children. I am training to do this. Now I'm a happy person, but I had a pretty hard time when I was a kid. Children can be sort of mean and I looked and acted different. Other kids made fun of me and sometimes hit me. No one ever chose me to play games. Sometimes they just treated me like I wasn't there. My brother helped sometimes, but then they would start calling him names, too.

"My parents are great. They tell me I'm a good kid and they love me. They spend lots of time with me and are my friends. I like being with regular people, but I am really happy with other kids like me. In school I had most of my classes with my friends, but I had gym and art with the other kids. I was in a Cub Scout troop and the Special Olympics — I won a lot of medals! Now I'm older and I understand people more. I live with four kids in a group home. We have a counselor who helps us cook, takes care of our money, and breaks up fights. I finish school this year and then start working full-time. I feel good about myself now."

Kenny's experiences reflect his strengths and those of his family. Many children with Down syndrome will not attain Kenny's level of sophistication and understanding. He has an IQ of 55, which is higher than usual for a person with Down syndrome. But equally important, his parents gave him their love, acceptance, and guidance. Kenny's perception of himself as a good and useful member of society is within the reach of children with Down syndrome and other developmental disabilities.

OTHER CHROMOSOMAL DISORDERS

Trisomy 13 and 18

At the age of thirty-six, Alice gave birth to Sarah. The pregnancy was full-term and uncomplicated, but in retrospect Alice thought the baby did not move around very much. At birth, the obstetrician observed that Sarah was very small, weighing only four pounds. She had a number of malformations including an unusually small and misshapen head, a cleft lip and palate, and deformed overlapping fingers. Sarah was very floppy and had difficulty breathing. Physical examination detected a heart murmur. Because of her small size and her multiple malformations, it was suspected that Sarah had a chromosomal abnormality. Subsequent blood studies showed the presence of an extra number 13 chromosome.

Sarah's health during infancy was complicated by heart failure and respiratory distress. As a result, she spent her first four months in the hospital, during which time Alice visited daily. There were many times when it seemed that Sarah would not survive; but eventually, Alice was able to take her home. Sarah continued to require medications to control heart failure and oxygen to help her breathe. She also was susceptible to infections and needed antibiotic treatment on a number of occasions. Because her sucking reflex was so weak, she had to be fed through a tube placed down her nose and into her stomach.

As exemplified by Sarah, children with trisomy 13 are much more severely affected than are Down syndrome children. This disorder occurs less frequently than Down syndrome, in about one in 3,000 newborns. At birth they are small, often weighing less than five pounds, and their heads are small and misshapen. A protruding back of the skull, low-set ears, weak chin, and small mouth contribute to an unusual appearance. There is often a cleft lip and palate as well. Their hands are clenched, and their index and third fingers overlap. These children grow poorly and have feeding problems. They also tend to have complex heart abnormalities and other malformations. They may have respiratory problems and seizures. Fatalities usually result from complications of the heart defect or severe infections.

At twelve months, Sarah's development has not progressed beyond the newborn level. If she survives her childhood, she will be profoundly retarded and have cerebral palsy. Fortunately, Alice gets both emotional and financial support from her parents. She also has a public health nurse who comes into the home each day to help give Sarah her medications and treatments. Alice hopes to avoid institutionalization for Sarah, preferring instead to care for her at home.

Children with trisomy 18 look very much like those with trisomy 13. They have similar health problems and will also be severely mentally retarded.

As in Down syndrome, the principal cause of these disorders is nondisjunction, and parental age plays a significant role. Translocation and mosaicism can also produce those trisomic syndromes. Additionally, there have been cases of partial duplication of the extra chromosome. In these situations, the fertilized egg contains the extra chromosome, but it is only partially duplicated when the cell divides. As a result, the developing fetus has three copies of only a part of the chromosome. Children with partial duplications may be less severely affected than those with typical trisomy. As in Down syndrome, prenatal diagnosis for any of the trisomic disorders is performed by examining chromosomes obtained in amniocentesis or chorionic villus sampling. The recurrence risk in a family who already has had one affected child is the same as for Down syndrome and depends on whether the cause is nondisjunction or translocation.

Cat Cry (Cri du Chat) Syndrome

Timmy had an unusual appearance when he was born. His head was small and his forehead sloped. He was a floppy infant and had a heart murmur. Perhaps his most unusual feature was a high-pitched and "mewing" cry. Because of Timmy's appearance, chromosome analysis was performed. It showed that in all of his cells there was a loss of the upper portion of one of the number 5 chromosomes. The diagnosis was cat cry, or cri du chat, syndrome.

During the first year of life, Timmy developed very slowly. He did not smile until six months (normally two months) and did not coo or roll over until twelve months (three months). At twelve months of age, he was seen by a pediatric developmental specialist who found him functioning at the three-month level (IQ 25). By school age Timmy had the skills of a twelve-month-old. He had a few words, followed simple commands, and was taking a few steps. He was placed in a class for the multiply handicapped in his local school system, where he received physical and occupational therapy as well as speech stimulation. He has continued to make slow progress. As an adult he will probably function at or below a three- to four-year-old level.

Since Timmy's birth, his parents have had two other children. Both times, Timmy's mother underwent chorionic villus sampling, which diagnosed the fetuses as unaffected. At birth, both infants were confirmed to be normal.

Cat cry syndrome involves a different underlying cause than do the trisomy syndromes. Whereas trisomy involves the presence of extra chromosomal material, cat cry syndrome is caused by the deletion of a portion of one normal chromosome, the number 5 chromosome. This results in the loss of a large number of genes which are normally located on this region of the number 5 chromosome. The child looks unusual, has low birth weight, a very small head, epicanthal folds, low-set ears, and an asymmetrical face. During infancy affected children have a mewing catlike cry; hence the name "cat cry syndrome." This unusual cry results from a malformation of the voice box and will become less evident as the child grows older. These children also commonly have congenital heart defects, which often require surgical repair. Children with cat cry syndrome are severely retarded (IQ 20–30) and resemble each other because of the distinctive physical malformations. The overall incidence is about one in 20,000 births. Individuals usually survive through childhood, although life expectancy is somewhat decreased compared to normal.

In 90 percent of these cases, the cause is a chromosomal deletion and the risk of recurrence in subsequent pregnancies is extremely low. However, in about 10 percent of these children, cat cry syndrome is caused by a translocation, which has a greater frequency of recurrence. As in Down syndrome, translocations are inherited from a carrier parent and the risk of recurrence ranges from 2 to 10 percent. Prenatal diagnosis can be used to detect this disorder in future pregnancies.

SEX CHROMOSOME DISORDERS

Fragile X Syndrome

As an infant, David was floppy but otherwise not unusual in appearance. As a child he was clumsy and "double-jointed," and developed slowly, especially in the area of language skills. By age six he was still having difficulty making his parents understand his needs, and it was hard for him to follow directions. David was also hyperactive and had behavior problems, including some autistic characteristics such as twirling around, playing with string, and acting as if he were deaf. Formal psychological testing at entrance to school revealed an IQ of 45 (moderate retardation).

Physically, David had a normal appearance except for a rather long face, prominent jaw, and large ears. However, when David was nine years old, his pediatrician observed that his testicles were almost double the normal size for his age. A family medical history revealed two instances of retarded boys on the mother's side of the family. This family history prompted the pediatrician to request a chromosome analysis, which showed the presence of fragmented X chromosomes in about half of David's cells. A diagnosis of Fragile X syndrome was made.

Fragile X syndrome is caused by an abnormality of the X chromosome. In these individuals, the X chromosome fragments easily when studied in the laboratory under certain conditions. As discussed in chapter 4, since females have two X chromosomes, one fragile X chromosome can be compensated for by the other normal one. Males, however, lack the second compensating X chromosome. For this reason, Fragile X syndrome mainly affects males, but is carried by females. In affected males, 15 to 50 percent of all cells in the child's body contain the fragile X chromosome. Carrier females have the fragile X chromosome in 5 to 20 percent of their cells.

Recent evidence suggests that as many as 10 percent of males with moderate to severe mental retardation of undiagnosed origin may have Fragile X syndrome. The overall incidence is about one in 1,000 male births. The physical characteristics of boys with Fragile X syndrome are distinctive but rather subtle: their faces are elongated, their ears protrude, and their jaws are prominent. They show decreased muscle tone and are often double-jointed. By adolescence, boys have enlarged testicles caused by an accumulation of fibrous tissue, but their sexual maturation does not differ from normal boys'. About 75 percent of the affected boys have IQ scores in the range of 30–50 (moderate to severe retardation); 15 percent have IQ scores above 50, and 10 percent have scores below 30. A very few have been found to have normal intelligence. In addition to being mentally retarded and having language deficits, many show significant hyperactivity and have autistic-like behaviors.

Although girls are usually only carriers of this disorder, some have intellectual deficits. Approximately 10 percent of female carriers are mildly mentally retarded (IQ 55–69), and as many as 30 percent of the carriers have learning disabilities.

It is important to make the diagnosis of Fragile X syndrome because the disorder is inherited in a sex-linked fashion (see chapter 4). Mothers of affected boys are at risk for passing on this disorder to half of their sons and for passing on the carrier state to half their daughters.

In the mid-1970s, it was observed that the vitamin folic acid could prevent the fragmentation of fragile X chromosomes in tissue cultures. This discovery has led more recently to the idea that children with Fragile X syndrome might benefit from supplements of folic acid. Studies to determine if this treatment has benefits are now being performed, but initial results do not look promising.

Turner Syndrome

Leslie had always been much shorter than her two sisters and than other children her age. She had problems learning to read and her eye-hand coordination was poor, although, with tutoring, she never failed a grade. By the age of fourteen, Leslie still had not begun to mature sexually; she did not have body hair or breast development. Her concerned parents took her to see an endocrinologist, who made a diagnosis of Turner syndrome on the basis of her physical appearance. Chromosomal analysis confirmed the diagnosis.

A girl with Turner syndrome has only a single X chromosome, rather than the normal two X chromosomes, in each of her cells. This situation arises when a sperm or egg with twenty-two chromosomes (lacking an X) joins with a normal cell having twenty-three chromosomes. This is the only situation in which the loss of a complete chromosome does not result in habitual miscarriage. As in the case of Down syndrome, Turner syndrome is usually caused by nondisjunction. There are rare cases of its being caused by mosaicism or translocation. Individuals with these forms of the disorder have less severe abnormalities.

The incidence of Turner syndrome is about one in 5,000 female births. Affected girls are very short, achieving an adult height of only about four and a half feet. Physical features include a lowered hairline and a shield-shaped chest with widely spaced nipples. Their ovaries do not function, resulting in sexual immaturity and sterility. Beginning in adolescence, estrogen replacement therapy is required to bring about the appearance of sexual maturation. Recently it has been found that long-term injections of growth hormone can add three or more inches to final height. Congenital heart disease (usually coarctation, or narrowing, of the aortic blood vessel leading from the heart) is common and may require surgical correction. Plastic surgery can be used to alter the hairline and webbed neck. Intellectual function is usually in the low-normal range, and there is an increased incidence of visual-perceptual problems and learning disabilities. Life span is normal.

Leslie was given hormones to stimulate sexual development, but her parents were advised that she would remain very short and be unable to have children. The disorder was explained to Leslie and she was offered counseling to aid her in adjustment. Eventually she graduated from high school, became an office clerk, and married. Leslie and her husband adopted two children and are doing well.

If a family has one child with Turner syndrome, there doesn't appear to be an increased risk of recurrence. Maternal and paternal age have no effect on the incidence of this disorder, although the missing X chromosome is more likely to be in the father's sperm. As in the other chromosomal disorders, Turner syndrome can be diagnosed using prenatal diagnostic procedures.

Klinefelter Syndrome

Sam was always one of the tallest boys in his class, but his sexual maturation was delayed. At age sixteen he had a rather girlish physique and enlarged breasts; he also had a small penis and testicles. Behavior and academic problems had been frequent during his childhood. Sam had not done well in school and was held back in the second and fourth grades. Formal IQ testing placed him in the range of borderline normal intelligence, with an IQ of 75.

It was the delay of puberty that eventually brought Sam to the attention of a pediatric endocrinologist who thought Klinefelter syndrome was a likely diagnosis. Subsequent chromosome analysis revealed forty-seven chromosomes with the presence of an extra X chromosome. Sam had two X chromosomes and one Y (sometimes noted as XXY) instead of the normal male pattern of one X and one Y chromosome. This disorder occurs as a result of nondisjunction, in much the same way as do other trisomy disorders.

Klinefelter syndrome occurs in about one out of 500 males. Boys with Klinefelter syndrome tend to be tall and thin, with a delayed appearance of secondary sexual characteristics. As adults they have enlarged breasts, a small penis, and small testicles. Little body hair appears after adolescence. The use of the male hormone testosterone has been helpful in producing a more masculine appearance. Most boys will be sterile because their sperm do not develop normally. Intelligence falls in the borderline–mildly mentally retarded range (IQ 55–85). Language development is particularly delayed and behavioral problems are common.

There is only a small risk of recurrence in affected families. Rare cases of mosaicism have been described.

When it was explained to Sam that he would need to take hormones in order to develop sexually and that he would not be able to father children, he became very angry. At first, he refused to take the hormones, but eventually he came to some understanding of the benefits of the medication. Sam continues to require counseling for his feelings of anger and despair. He has graduated from high school and is now entering vocational training to become an auto mechanic.

SOME QUESTIONS ANSWERED

Under what circumstances should my newborn have chromosomal studies performed?

Most infants with chromosomal disorders are unusual in appearance from birth. They tend to weigh five pounds or less at full-term and have very small heads. They usually have other malformations such as a cleft palate, abnormally formed fingers and toes, and heart defects. Children who have combinations of these characteristics should have chromosomal studies performed in order to make a diagnosis

and to help predict the risk of recurrence in future pregnancies. The doctors may be able to give you a prognosis for the future based on their experiences with similarly affected children. Even in the case of Down syndrome, when the diagnosis can be made from physical findings, chromosome studies should still be performed to confirm that the Down syndrome is caused by a trisomy and not a translocation. This is important, because translocations have a relatively high risk of recurrence.

Can chromosomal disorders be cured?

Chromosomal disorders cannot be corrected. The child is born with problems that developed at or shortly after fertilization. The defect involves all cells in the body, so it seems highly unlikely that medication would correct the problem. However, certain plastic surgical or orthopedic procedures have been used to improve the facial appearance and physical deformities of affected children, and surgery can correct heart and gastrointestinal abnormalities. In addition, there are treatment options, just as there are for other developmentally disabled children. Special education programs, physical and occupational therapy, and language therapy are all helpful in allowing your child to achieve his or her potential.

8

SEIZURE DISORDERS

Seizures occur as a result of brief periods of uncontrolled and abnormal electrical activity in the brain. Most people with seizure disorders are not otherwise handicapped and lead normal lives; however, seizure disorders occur more frequently in disabled children than in the general population. About one in 10 disabled children develop seizure disorders, compared with only one in 200 for the normal population. Fortunately, seizure disorders can usually be controlled with the proper medication. However, if left untreated, they can interfere with the full expression of your child's abilities.

Seizure disorders have afflicted people throughout history. In fact, seizures affected some of the world's great historic figures, including Julius Caesar and Napoleon. You may have heard the terms *"fit,"* *convulsion*, or *epilepsy* used to describe your child's seizure experience. A convulsion, or "fit," is a seizure. When a person has experienced multiple convulsions, he is said to have a seizure disorder. The one exception is febrile convulsions, which may occur multiple times in children under four years of age but do not predispose them to a future seizure disorder. Epilepsy

is an equivalent, older term for seizure disorder that has fallen out of favor in recent years. There are other terms used to describe seizures, for instance grand mal, petit mal, and psychomotor. These refer to the different types of seizures, which we will discuss later in the chapter.

EDDY

Eddy had endured a number of complications resulting from a birth injury. By age two he had been diagnosed as having cerebral palsy and moderate mental retardation, and he had undergone operations for an orthopedic problem and a crossed eye. For two years following his diagnosis, he did well in an early-intervention program that provided occupational, physical, and speech therapies. His parents, Steve and Sally, felt they had reconciled themselves to his problems and were adjusting their lives successfully.

But at age four, Eddy suffered another complication — he had his first seizure. All of his limbs shook and he lost consciousness for about two minutes. He was then sleepy for about an hour afterwards. Steve and Sally had been told earlier that children with multiple handicaps were at greater risk than usual for developing seizures, but because he had done so well for so long, they had hoped this complication would not develop.

Eddy had the flu, and when he was first seen in the emergency room, the doctor thought that his seizure might have been brought on by the fever. However, an EEG taken a week later showed a seizure focus in his brain. Two weeks later, Eddy had a second seizure, this time unaccompanied by a fever. His doctor prescribed the anticonvulsant medication carbamazepine (Tegretol), on which Eddy has done well with no side effects. He had one more seizure, but has remained seizure free for the past year. If he continues to do well, an elimination of the medication will probably be tried in a year or two.

Although this new problem was rapidly resolved, for Steve and Sally it still represented another unexpected crisis that led them to ask, "What will happen next? Does this mean he is getting worse?" For a few months afterward they could not recapture their feelings of safety and stability. A year later they are doing much better but are still living "one day at a time." Eddy has not been bothered much by this ordeal. He has no recollection of the seizures or of his parents' distress. He enjoys school and doesn't mind taking his pills.

BRAIN STRUCTURE AND FUNCTION

In order to understand how a seizure happens, we will first review certain aspects of brain structure and function. When fully formed, the brain weighs about one pound and has the appearance of a walnut with many ridges and valleys. The right and left sides, or cerebral hemispheres, of the brain are connected by a central strip of nerve tracts called the corpus callosum (Figure 8.1).

Different regions of the brain have different functions. The cerebrum initiates thoughts and movements. It can be subdivided into four sections, or lobes: frontal, temporal, parietal, and occipital, which control thoughts, movements, sensations, and sight. Seizures usually start in the cortex, or gray matter, of the cerebrum. How the seizure manifests itself depends in part on where the seizure starts. The other major regions of the brain — the basal ganglia, cerebellum, and brain stem — are not sites of seizure origin, although they may be affected by anticonvulsant medications or as a secondary effect of a seizure. The basal ganglia modulate posture, walking, and automatic movements, while the cerebellum controls balance. Unsteady walking is one of the most common side effects of anticonvulsant overmedication, especially with the drug Dilantin. The brain stem controls certain basic bodily functions such as breathing and swallowing. Below the brain is the spinal cord, which connects the brain to the nerves throughout the body.

The basic unit of the brain is the nerve cell (Figure 8.2). A nerve cell consists of a cell body, a long trunk called an axon, and short branches called dendrites. The brain contains millions of nerve cells layered in the cortex, each interconnected with many others through the axons and dendrites (see Figure 5.2). When the nerve cell is activated, an electrical impulse travels down the axon toward the dendrites of the next nerve cell in line. The impulse then jumps to and activates the next cell in line, and so on. One cell affects the next by releasing a chemical substance, called a neurotransmitter, that crosses the space between the cells and permits the electrical impulse to activate or inhibit the next cell in line.

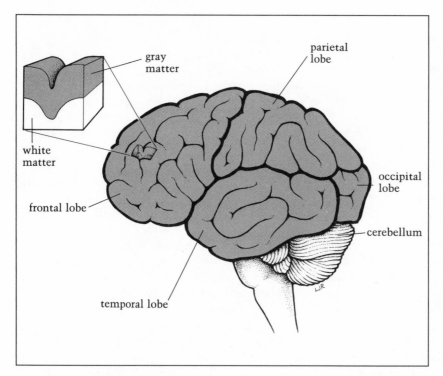

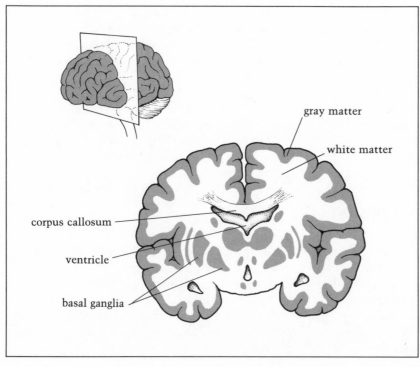

Figure 8.1. (a) A side view of the brain shows that the cerebrum is subdivided into four lobes: frontal, temporal, parietal, and occipital. Gray matter and white matter are differentiated. The cerebellum and brain stem are also shown. (b) A cross section of the brain shows the deeper regions including the basal ganglia, ventricals, and the band of white matter, called the corpus collosum, which connects the two sides of the brain.

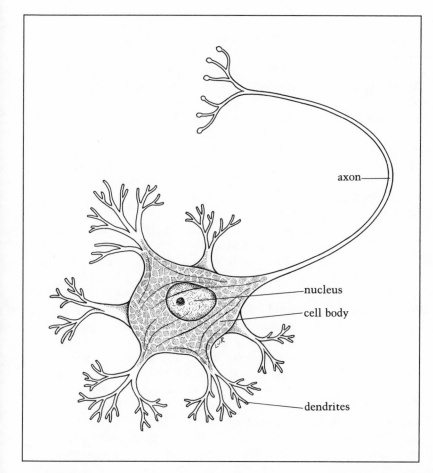

Figure 8.2. *The basic unit of the brain is the nerve cell, which consists of a cell body, a trunk or axon, and branches called dendrites.*

axon

nucleus

cell body

dendrites

SEIZURES

Normally, nerve impulses pass in a controlled, orderly progression. A seizure happens when this order is disrupted and nerve cells start to fire off indiscriminately. In a generalized seizure, all parts of the cerebral cortex discharge their electrical signals excessively at the same time. In a partial seizure, only a small group of abnormal nerve cells in the cerebral cortex begins this excessive electrical firing. This group of abnormal nerve cells is called the seizure focus and can occur in any area of the brain. When the cells misfire, they recruit surrounding nerve cells to fire, re-

sulting in massive and uncontrolled movements or sensations, which we call a seizure. The process has been likened to a short circuit in an electrical appliance, in which there is a massive discharge of electrical activity followed by a lack of activity; the appliance "shorts out." In many seizures, the person will be lethargic or fall asleep afterward. Anticonvulsant medications work to prevent seizures by stopping the initial firing of the nerves at the seizure focus or by interfering with the spread of the unwanted neurochemical transmission.

The physical manifestations of a seizure differ depending on which part of the brain is affected. For example, the temporal lobe of the brain contains the nerves that control memories and emotions. A person having a seizure in the temporal lobe may hallucinate, smell unusual smells, hear sounds, or be frightened as part of the seizure. The frontal lobe controls motor activity; a seizure there may cause uncontrolled jerking movements of the limbs.

Seizures may last for less than a second or for fifteen minutes or more. Some involve unconsciousness and loss of bowel and bladder control, while others simply involve inattentiveness, with fluttering of the eyelids.

CAUSES OF SEIZURES

Among nonhandicapped people, seizure disorders may be caused by a head injury or occasionally a brain tumor, but usually the cause is unknown. For disabled children, the cause of seizures is most often the same as the cause of the disabling condition. For example, if a child suffered severe brain injury during birth or as a result of meningitis, he may suffer from mental retardation, cerebral palsy, *and* seizures.

Most seizure disorders are not inherited, although there are rare inheritable conditions in which seizures play a prominent role. One of these is tuberous sclerosis. In this disorder, children develop seizures during infancy and childhood associated with certain skin abnormalities and mental retardation. This disorder is inherited as an autosomal dominant trait. (See chapter 4 for an explanation of inheritance patterns.) If your child does have a hereditary disorder, a genetic counselor can help you understand the recurrence risk in future children.

In some susceptible children, certain circumstances make seizures more likely to occur. Seizures may cluster just as the

child goes to sleep or awakens. Physical illness, especially if involving fever, may also trigger seizures. Menstrual periods sometimes are related to increased seizure activity. However, emotional stress or fatigue do not appear to bring on seizures unless they have physical consequences, such as extreme sleep deprivation. In most cases, a seizure will occur with no immediate provocation. The best protection is adequate anticonvulsant medication.

Seizures are more likely to occur at certain times in a child's life. The first week of life is a high-risk period. Brain damage that occurred during birth, lack of oxygen, bleeding, severe infection, or chemical imbalances can all lead to seizures. A newborn's seizures look different from those of later life because the brain lacks the multiple interconnections that develop during the first year of life. Thus, generalized seizures in infants are rare; usually they will experience partial seizures with shaking of one or two limbs, sudden jerking, unusual body positions, or eye movements.

The first week of life is followed by a low-risk period for seizures, which lasts until about six to nine months of age. From that time until about four years of age, febrile convulsions are common, occurring in 3 to 5 percent of both disabled and normal children. These generalized seizures occur during periods of high fever (above 39° C, or 102° F). They usually last less than fifteen minutes and do not require treatment. Some types of seizures increase during adolescence, probably due to hormonal changes.

GENERALIZED SEIZURES

Generalized seizures are those in which seizure activity occurs throughout the whole cortex. They include: (1) tonic-clonic, or grand mal, seizures, (2) absence, or petit mal, seizures, and (3) myoclonic seizures.

Grand mal seizures are a very common type. Often, they are preceded by vague symptoms that can occur hours before the attack. These prodromal symptoms include headache, insomnia, irritability, and changes in appetite. When the grand mal (tonic-clonic) seizure starts, the child's eyes roll back, his mouth is held open, and he cries out. He will lose consciousness and may fall to the floor; hence the old name, the "falling sickness." The child's muscles usually become rigid (tonic). He may then stop breathing momentarily, with his lips turning blue. After about ten to thirty seconds, breathing returns as he begins rhythmic jerking or shaking (clonic) movements. The entire seizure usually lasts between thirty seconds and five minutes and is generally followed by a period of relaxation in which bowel and bladder control may be lost. The child usually is disoriented, lethargic, or asleep, and he will not recall the seizure upon awakening. Untreated, these seizures can occur multiple times a day.

Petit mal, or absence, seizures are less common, occurring during later childhood and adolescence. They are called "petit," or small, because there are no forceful tonic-clonic movements as in grand mal seizures. Instead, ongoing normal mental activity and behavior stop suddenly and the child looks vacantly into space, sometimes blinking and losing awareness momentarily. The child will not fall or injure herself and there is no fatigue afterward. However, these seizures may occur over one hundred times per day and can interfere with alertness and learning.

The third type of generalized seizure is the myoclonic seizure. Here, the child has sudden startle-like episodes, in which her body flexes or extends for a brief second.

The most common example of childhood myoclonic seizures is called infantile spasms, which occur in clusters of eight to ten, multiple times during the day. These seizures often begin at around three to six months of age and are difficult to control. They often carry a poor prognosis. Later in the child's life they may evolve into a complex and difficult-to-control seizure pattern called Lennox-Gastaut, which combines features of myoclonic and tonic-clonic seizures.

PARTIAL SEIZURES

The second grouping of seizures is called partial because they are limited to a part, or "focus" in, one side of the brain. The individual appearance of these seizures varies depending on which area of the brain is misfiring. For example, seizures arising from the occipital lobe can lead to visual disturbances, while those from the frontal lobe will result in limb twitching. In "simple" partial seizures, there is no loss of consciousness. Complex partial seizures are associated with a loss of consciousness.

The most common partial seizure arises in the temporal lobe, and was called "psychomotor" in the past because it included mental, or "psychic," as well as physical, or "motor," manifestations. Psychomotor seizures may begin with mental or experiential distortions or hallucinations, which may involve experiencing unusual tastes, smells, or sounds. Or, they may be accompanied by feelings of fear, anger, or déjà vu. The physical expression of the seizure may appear as repetitive fine-motor actions such as buttoning and unbuttoning, lip smacking, walking in circles, or mumbling. Rarely, the child will show rage, usually directed at objects rather than people. Psychomotor seizures generally last a few minutes, but on occasion may turn into tonic-clonic, grand mal seizures. In those circumstances the partial seizure serves as a warning, or "aura," of the impending tonic-clonic seizure.

Some children will have a mixed-type seizure disorder; that is, they will have more than one type of seizure. Children with mixed seizures tend to be more difficult to control using anticonvulsant medication, because the multiple types of seizures may require more than one type of medication.

SEIZURES AND BRAIN DAMAGE

There has been much concern that seizures themselves cause brain damage. This does not appear to be the case except in rare circumstances. However, a child *is* at risk for developing brain damage if seizures persist for many hours or days, a condition called status epilepticus. Poorly controlled seizures, while not causing brain damage, can interfere with normal learning and motor

skills. However, once the seizures are brought under control, skills are regained and there is no evidence of permanent loss of abilities.

THE FIRST SEIZURE

You walk into your child's bedroom because you hear grunting noises and find your daughter thrashing about. Although you have never seen her seize before, it appears that she is having a grand mal seizure. Your initial panic should be held in check by the knowledge that your child is not dying, even though it may seem otherwise. Remove any surrounding objects that have sharp edges and turn your child on her side so that if she throws up, she will not inhale the vomit into her lungs. Loosen her clothing around the neck and check her breathing by noting if her lips are blue and if breath sounds can be heard (Figure 8.3). If she seems to be having trouble breathing, try to explore her mouth to

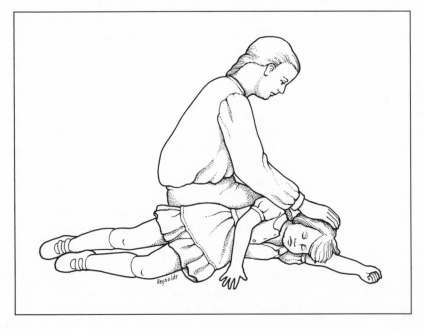

Figure 8.3. *In the event of a seizure, you should remove surrounding objects, loosen your child's clothing, turn her on her side, and check for breathing pattern.*

make sure nothing is blocking the airway. In the unlikely event that she stops breathing for more than thirty seconds, start artificial respiration. You should learn how to perform cardiopulmonary resuscitation (CPR). Short courses approved by the American Red Cross and American Heart Association are given at frequent intervals in local hospitals, public schools and colleges, and YMCAs.

There are certain things you need not worry about during the seizure. "Swallowing the tongue" is a misnomer and a physical impossibility. Placing a spoon between the teeth is difficult because your child's jaw will most likely be clenched. It is also unnecessary and will probably result either in your getting bitten or your child chipping a tooth.

The first time your child has a grand mal seizure, you will likely end up in a hospital emergency room, after either calling your doctor or telephoning "911" for emergency assistance. Your child will probably stop seizing by the time you arrive at the hospital. However, if she is still seizing upon arrival, the doctors may give an intravenous (by vein) medication to stop the seizure. Commonly used drugs in this circumstance include lorazepam (Ativan), diazepam (Valium), phenytoin (Dilantin), and phenobarbital. These drugs generally stop seizure activity within minutes. Medication may also be prescribed for long-term consumption by mouth, including valproate (Depakene), carbamazepine (Tegretol), phenobarbital, or phenytoin (Dilantin) (see chapter 19). It is unlikely that your child will require prolonged hospitalization, but many children are kept overnight for tests and observation.

If your child's first seizure is an infantile spasm or petit mal seizure, she may not require being seen as an emergency patient. Your doctor will probably see you within a day or two and may refer you directly to a pediatric neurologist for further evaluation and treatment.

MEDICAL TESTS FOR SEIZURE DISORDERS

In order to prescribe the correct treatment for your child's seizures, she must be appropriately evaluated. Your pediatrician or family practitioner will ultimately manage your child's seizures. But she may initially seek consultation with a pediatric neurologist who will perform a history and physical, conduct tests, and suggest a specific anticonvulsant medication.

It should be noted that there are many acceptable ways of evaluating and treating seizures, so your doctor may follow a procedure somewhat different from that described here. If the seizure occurred during the newborn period, your doctor is likely to perform tests to detect a treatable disorder, such as an infection or metabolic problem. The evaluation may include various blood tests and a spinal tap. A spinal tap can be used to diagnose a brain infection or hemorrhage. These problems are common reasons for seizures among newborns, though less common among older children. Thus, a spinal tap may not be automatically performed on an older child unless a brain infection is specifically suspected.

The spinal tap seems like a scary procedure, but in fact is safe and causes little pain. During a spinal tap, a small amount of the fluid that bathes the spinal cord is removed for analysis. This fluid, called cerebrospinal fluid (CSF), also surrounds the brain. Thus, infections in or bleeding from the brain can be diagnosed by looking at the CSF. During a spinal tap, also called a lumbar puncture or LP, the doctor numbs a small area on the back and then inserts a hollow needle into a space between two of the vertebrae (the bony segments of the spine) in the lower back. Through this needle, she removes about two teaspoonful of fluid. The procedure carries with it very little risk of infection or bleeding at the site and no risk of paralyzing your child. In adults, spinal taps may be associated with headache or vomiting; however, this is less likely to occur in children.

The most common test used to evaluate a seizure disorder is the electroencephalogram (EEG), or brain wave test. It is usually done several days after a seizure, because the seizure itself or the high-dose medication used to treat it will disrupt the usual pattern of brain wave activity. The test is not painful and you can sit near your child during the procedure. In this test, electrodes are pasted to your child's scalp. The paste is messy and your child will need a shampoo afterward. The electrodes are small buttons with attached wires that can detect electrical activity in the brain transmitted through the scalp. They are attached to a recording device that displays the electrical activity as wave patterns. An electroencephalographic technician will perform the test and a neurologist will interpret the wave patterns, looking for areas of seizure activity. A child may have momentary irregularities of brain electrical activity that indicate the nature of the seizure tendency, even if no actual seizure occurs during the test.

Prior to the EEG, your child may be given a mild sedative so that brain activity can be measured both during sleep and while awake, since seizures can arise in either or both states. In addition, the technician may ask your child to hyperventilate or look at a flashing light. The former helps detect petit mal seizures and the latter, psychomotor seizures.

Figure 8.4 illustrates an EEG from a healthy child and one with grand mal sei-

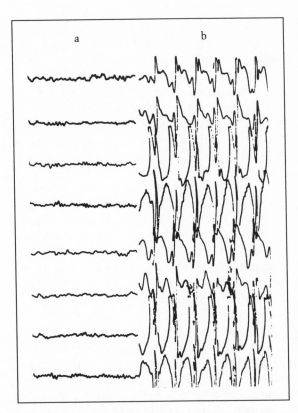

Figure 8.4. *Example of an EEG from an (a) unaffected child and (b) one with grand mal seizures. Notice the regular low voltage pattern in the unaffected child as compared to the sharp spike and wave pattern in the child with a grand mal seizure disorder.*

zures. You can see how the erratic "spike-slow waves" in the latter differ markedly from the regular undulating patterns in the unaffected child. EEGs are useful in diagnosing a seizure disorder and sometimes in evaluating the effectiveness of anticonvulsant medications. Your child, if diagnosed with a seizure disorder, will likely have a number of EEGs performed over time. Complete evaluations of the EEG usually are available after one or two days.

Other tests performed frequently when a seizure disorder is suspected are MRI (magnetic resonance imaging) and CT (computed tomography) scans. Both of these tests create images of the brain but they use different methods of obtaining those images. The scans allow the doctor to search for structural abnormalities in the brain, such as scar tissue, swelling, bleeding, brain damage, or tumors, that might account for seizure activity. However, MRI and CT scans do not show the seizure focus itself, which is an electrical, rather than structural, abnormality.

The MRI scan takes advantage of the magnetic properties of different atoms in the body. By using a strong magnetic field and pulses of radio-frequency energy, the scanner measures the magnetic properties of various tissues and then converts those measurements into pictures. The pictures are extremely detailed and clear. Both the strong magnetic field and the radio-frequency energy are harmless. The CT scan uses X-rays to create its images. The amount of radiation received during a CT scan is very small and safe.

For an MRI scan, your child is likely to be sedated to prevent him from moving. This may involve using oral chloral hydrate given about thirty minutes before the scan, or an injection of a sedative. Once quiet, your child will be placed inside a large cylindrical tunnel containing a magnet. The scanning procedure takes about an hour. A CT scan takes less time. Thus, although the MRI scan may produce better images and avoid exposing your child to X-rays, it takes longer and costs more. For both types of scans, results are usually available within one or two days.

In summary, the workup for a seizure disorder includes a careful history and physical examination, and may include blood tests, a spinal tap, an EEG, and a brain imaging study. After these tests are completed, treatment decisions can be made.

TREATMENT WITH ANTICONVULSANT MEDICATIONS

The goal of treatment is to suppress the electrical output of the abnormal brain cells without sedating the entire brain and thus interfering with learning or physical activity. There are many anticonvulsant drugs available that can accomplish this. They work by different mechanisms, and thus may vary in effectiveness depending on the type of seizure disorder. The most commonly used drugs are phenobarbital (Luminal), phenytoin (Dilantin), carbamazepine (Tegretol), valproate (Depakene), and clonazepam (Klonopin).

With all anticonvulsant drugs, the incidence of side effects usually increases with dose. Overall, the most common side effect is sedation, and the drug with the highest incidence of side effects is phenobarbital, followed in order by phenytoin, valproate, clonazepam, and carbamazepine. A more extensive discussion of anticonvulsant medications and their side effects may be found in chapter 19.

If your child has had a major seizure and has been treated at a hospital, the doctor may begin treatment by giving her a "loading" dose of an anticonvulsant. This is a one-time large dose intended to raise the drug level in the blood rapidly to a therapeutic concentration. Such a dose may protect your child within a matter of hours. The most common side effects to loading doses of anticonvulsants are stomach upset and sleepiness. On rare occasions certain drugs can depress respirations. Whether a loading dose is used or not is determined by the severity of the seizure. The more long lasting and severe the seizure, the more likely it is that a loading dose will be used.

If the seizure is not too severe, the doctor may wait to see if seizures recur before starting medication, or she may begin with a low dose of medication and then gradually increase it, until seizures improve or side effects develop. If side effects occur before seizure activity is controlled, she may substitute a different drug. Blood levels of the anticonvulsant are evaluated periodically to check the adequacy of the prescribed dosage. As your child grows, her dosage will probably need to be adjusted.

In giving your child medications, be sure to follow a few simple rules: First, follow your doctor's prescribing schedule, usually giving the drug two or three times per day. If you miss one dose, you can give a double dose the next time; but if you miss an entire day's dose, don't give a double dose the next day. This could result in side effects. If your child goes without medication for more than two days, he may be unprotected against seizures. The second rule is to double-check your medications. Make sure the dosage is correct and the name of the drug is correct. Drugs have both trade (brand) names and generic names; for instance, Dilantin is the trade name of the generic drug phenytoin. Third, do not use outdated drugs. Fourth, if you are giving your child other medications, check with your doctor or pharmacist to make sure there are no interactions between the drugs that could increase toxicity or decrease effectiveness.

WHEN MEDICATIONS CAN BE STOPPED

In the past, it was believed that seizure disorders required lifelong treatment with anticonvulsant medication. Now this con-cept has been deemed outmoded. For example, in individuals with normal intelligence who have grand mal seizures, a seizure-free period of two years is sufficient to warrant a trial period off medications, especially if the EEG pattern has also shown improvement. Unfortunately, the prognosis is less positive with disabled children who have seizures. They seem less likely to remain seizure free when taken off medication, especially if they have more than one type of seizure. However, if your child has been seizure free for two years, an EEG can be obtained to see if there has been improvement. If so, your doctor may suggest a trial period off medications. At worst, the seizures will return, but they will not cause further brain damage and the medications can always be restarted.

Discontinuing medication should not be done abruptly. Usually, the dose is reduced over a month or more so the brain can adapt smoothly. In addition, some drugs lead to physical dependence and a gradual tapering off can reduce withdrawal symptoms.

KETOGENIC DIET AND NEUROSURGERY

One of the earliest forms of treatment for seizure disorders was the ketogenic diet, rich in fats and low in carbohydrates and protein. On such a diet, the body produces chemicals called ketone bodies, which suppress seizure activity. The ketogenic diet is restrictive and unpleasant, including large amounts of butter, whipped cream, and mayonnaise. However, if maintained accurately, it often works, especially in certain cases of grand mal and myoclonic seizures that are unresponsive to medications. A recent advance has been the use of medium chain triglyceride (MCT) oil as a source of fats. This is a concentrated form of fat that is tasteless and can be mixed with juices. It is more palatable than the classic ketogenic diet. It does not increase the cholesterol level in the child's blood.

The ketogenic diet is not commonly used; but it is worth considering if your child has not responded to multiple-drug therapy. It has virtually no side effects. However, the ketosis interferes with appetite so weight should be carefully monitored. During ketogenic diet treatment, anticonvulsant medications may be decreased or stopped. If successful in controlling seizures, the diet is usually continued for one year, after which seizure control is reevaluated.

Another approach to seizure management is the use of neurosurgery. Surgery is considered only when multiple medications have been unsuccessful in controlling the seizures, and when the seizures are severe enough to greatly impair functioning. The most common neurosurgical procedure is the removal of part of the temporal lobe for treating severe, uncontrolled psychomotor seizures. When the abnormality involves a whole hemisphere and the patient has little useful hand function, a functional hemispherectomy, in which one side of the cerebrum is removed, has been used successfully. For uncontrollable generalized seizures, surgeons have cut the corpus callosum, the network of nerves that connects the right and left hemispheres of the brain, in order to prevent the spread of seizure activity. These operations can have some adverse effects on memory and other cognitive functions. Therefore they are considered last resorts. However, the survival rate is very high and many children have been substantially helped by them.

PSYCHOLOGICAL PROBLEMS ASSOCIATED WITH SEIZURE DISORDERS

An otherwise normal child will often be embarrassed when a seizure identifies him as being different from his peers, especially if the seizure is grand mal and associated with loss of control of bowel or bladder function. With children who have other developmental disabilities, this may be less of an issue. Friends or other children in the class probably have seizures too, so there is less stigma attached to the problem. In addition, your child may not be intellectually sophisticated enough to perceive the seizure as embarrassing. If your child does have emotional concerns as a result of having seizures, explain to her that they are not her fault, but the result of her brain misfiring. Tell her that the medications should help make the seizures less likely to occur. There are many books written for children of different ages explaining seizures; you may want to read one with your child. Make as little fuss as possible about the seizures, but plan ahead by keeping a spare change of clothing at school if seizures are frequent and associated with soiling. Remember that the seizure is not painful and your child will not remember it.

AVOID OVERPROTECTIVENESS

As the parent of a child with a seizure disorder, you may feel so frightened by seizures that you want to protect your child at all costs from having subsequent attacks. This can take the form of restricting her participation in sports, visiting friends, going on trips, and so forth. Try to avoid these restrictions. Seizure medication usually maintains good control and permits your child to participate in most activities.

She should be closely observed without being overprotected, a fine line to follow indeed. For example, swimming and diving are generally permitted, but can clearly be dangerous if your child has a seizure during these activities. Make sure a knowledgeable lifeguard or adult is present at all times. Someone should also be present when your child bathes in a tub. Other circumstances in which accidents may result from seizures including bicycling, boating, and climbing.

Despite medications, some children will still have occasional seizures. If your child tends to fall and injure her head, eyes, nose, or teeth during these episodes, have her wear a lightweight plastic hockey helmet but still allow her to participate in normal activities. As a basic rule, allow as much freedom as possible. Over time, your worries about the seizures will lessen and you will be more comfortable with giving her increased freedom. Try to move through this process as quickly as possible.

PROGNOSIS

Seizures are unlikely to affect the life span of your child. Rarely does a person die as a result of a seizure, especially now that improved anticonvulsant medications can prevent or reduce the severity of seizures. Many studies have suggested that the life span of individuals with seizures is not shorter than normal. If your child has other severe disabilities, his life span is more likely to be reduced by the underlying developmental disorder than by seizures.

SOME QUESTIONS ANSWERED

Does my child's having a seizure mean his condition is worsening?

If your child has been doing well and suddenly starts to have seizures, the obvious concern is that your child's condition is worsening. In the vast majority of children this is not the case. A child may have had an abnormal seizure focus for a number of years before it shows itself. There may have been some precipitating circumstance such as an illness or head trauma. If this is a first seizure, some testing may be done to confirm that there are no new problems that need to be addressed. Usually, treatment with anticonvulsants will return your child to "normal." You will see that he has not lost any skills. However, it may take a month or more to reach the correct dosage that controls seizures but does not cause significant side effects. Until this has occurred, your child will probably not be back to normal.

Can a person with a seizure disorder drive a car?

In most states the only requirement is that the individual be seizure free for three months before he or she drives a car.

9 CEREBRAL PALSY

Cerebral palsy (often abbreviated CP) is the term used to describe a number of disorders of movement and posture that result from brain damage that occurred prior to birth or during childhood. It is rather rare, with an incidence of about 2 per 1,000 births. Despite improvements in newborn medical care during the past two decades, the incidence of CP has remained at this level for two major reasons. First, as we describe below, the brain damage that causes CP commonly occurs during the early months of pregnancy and, for the most part, is not preventable. Second, medical technology has improved the survivability of many very small premature babies weighing one and a half to two and a half pounds. These babies are at a high risk, about 10 percent, of having CP.

A diagnosis of cerebral palsy indicates nonprogressive damage to the brain. However, although the brain damage itself will not worsen as the child grows older, the physical disabilities often change. They may improve as the child grows, as in the case of Marshall, below, or they may worsen over time, as with Sammy. The muscle tone itself may also change, with the floppy infant becoming a spastic child.

As a result of these changes, children with cerebral palsy need to participate in an interdisciplinary program so that appropriate therapies can be altered as needed.

SAMMY AND MARSHALL

Sammy showed signs of trouble from the time of his birth. Though he arrived on schedule, he weighed only four and a half pounds, did not breathe spontaneously, and his limbs flopped, as if he was a rag doll. Within his first twelve hours he began to have convulsions. His first month of life was complicated by a series of problems. He periodically stopped breathing (a condition known as apnea) and continued to experience seizures. His muscle tone was markedly reduced and he had trouble eating, which necessitated the placement of a feeding tube. A brain imaging study revealed abnormal brain development. Sammy's parents were told that he was at high risk for having cerebral palsy and other developmental problems.

Sammy went home at six weeks of age but continued to do poorly. By four months he still could not follow a moving object with his eyes, a skill acquired by most one-month-old infants. He didn't smile and could not hold his head upright. Sucking and swallowing continued to be difficult for him. At this point, a developmental pediatrician indicated to his parents that Sammy appeared to have cerebral palsy and was developmentally delayed.

Now five years old, Sammy's muscle tone has increased and he has been diagnosed as having spastic quadriplegia, a form of cerebral palsy. (We discuss the meaning of this diagnosis later in this chapter.) He is just learning to sit and has had orthopedic surgery to correct a dislocated hip. Eye surgery has corrected his crossed eyes. He remains on anticonvulsant medications for control of grand mal seizures that occur about three or four times a year. He cannot talk but uses a few signs to communicate his needs. Sammy is severely mentally retarded, with a mental age level at present of fifteen months. Despite these problems, he attends a special class for multiply handicapped children and appears happy.

Sammy's neighbor in the newborn intensive care unit (NICU), Marshall, was born two months prematurely and weighed three pounds. Marshall required mechanical breathing assistance for three weeks because his lungs were immature, a condition known as respiratory distress syndrome or RDS (see chapter 3). He also bled into his brain (intracranial hemorrhage). Despite these initial complications, Marshall made rapid improvement and was discharged by six weeks of age, active and feeding well.

Taking into account his prematurity, Marshall's language and social milestones were achieved at fairly normal times. However, he lagged behind in motor skills, especially those involving his legs. By nine months he still was not sitting, even with support. His legs seemed stiff, and diaper-

ing was difficult. A neurologic evaluation at ten months confirmed that Marshall had spasticity of the lower limbs, and his parents were told that this indicated spastic diplegia, a form of cerebral palsy common in premature infants. They were encouraged to learn that over half the children "grow out" of this spasticity by school age.

Marshall was placed in an early-intervention program, where he received physical and occupational therapy. Over time, his muscle tone improved — he sat alone at twelve months and walked at twenty-four months. By five years of age he remained clumsy, but the neurologic signs suggesting cerebral palsy had all but disappeared. Now aged eight years, Marshall has average intelligence with a learning disability. His spastic diplegia is no longer evident, although he is considered awkward.

These two cases illustrate two ends of the spectrum of maladies that come under the heading of cerebral palsy. If your child has been diagnosed with cerebral palsy, you may feel confused and apprehensive about what the future holds. In this chapter, we will discuss the many aspects of this disorder, so you will understand your child's illness and be better able to cope with it.

CAUSES OF CEREBRAL PALSY

Until recently, it was generally accepted that most cases of cerebral palsy resulted from birth trauma. However, it is now clear that this is true of only a small fraction of cases. Most cases result from problems that occurred during the early months of pregnancy. Although children with cerebral palsy are more likely to have had difficult deliveries and to appear neurologically impaired after birth, this seems to be the result of preexisting brain damage rather than the cause of the condition. For example, a brain-injured fetus is less active and is therefore more likely to get stuck in one position. This often leads to a breech (backside first) presentation at birth, a position that results in a more difficult delivery.

Knowing that cerebral palsy usually results from fetal damage does not tell us, however, what did cause the damage. In only a minority of children with prenatal damage do we learn the specific cause. In chapter 3 we discussed the many possible prenatal causes of handicapping conditions, such as illnesses or infection in the mother or exposure to various drugs. Overall, prenatal causes account for about two-thirds of all children who suffer from cerebral palsy. The remainder are divided between birth trauma, prematurity, brain infections, and head injury.

In general, the risk of your having a second affected child is low. The one instance in which there will be a significant risk is if your child has a genetically inherited cause of cerebral palsy. You may want to seek genetic counseling to determine if it is likely that your child has such a disorder (see chapter 4).

TYPES OF CEREBRAL PALSY

Although CP is caused by damage to the brain, the primary effect is on the muscles. The reason for this apparent contradiction is that the brain controls muscle tone. The specific area in the brain that is damaged determines how the disorder will appear. When the damage occurs in the part of the brain that initiates voluntary movement — the pyramidal tract — the disorder is called spastic cerebral palsy. When damage occurs in the part of the brain that modifies or regulates those movements — the extrapyramidal tract — it is called extrapyramidal

cerebral palsy. Damage may occur in both areas, in which case the disorder is called mixed-type cerebral palsy. In these cases, brain damage may be extensive, with significant other problems.

Spastic Cerebral Palsy

Figure 9.1 illustrates how the pyramidal tract controls gross-motor function. When you decide to take a step, the message passes from the cortex of the brain, through the pyramidal tract, down the spinal cord, and into the nerves controlling the muscles that will contract or relax to permit movement. Thus, a single step is a very complex maneuver requiring the coordination of multiple nerves and muscles that must act in concert. If the pyramidal tract is damaged, this coordinated movement will not occur. Instead, the limbs may be tensely extended and then give way suddenly — a condition known as spasticity.

The pyramidal tract has many individual fibers that are programmed to connect with specific limbs (Figure 9.2). For example, the fibers leading to the legs are closest to the blood vessels surrounding the ventricles, or central cavities, of the brain. In premature infants, brain hemorrhages are most likely to occur in this area, damaging that portion of the pyramidal tract. This is why the most common form of cerebral palsy in premature infants involves spasticity of the lower limbs, termed spastic diplegia. When damage is done to large areas of the pyramidal tract, all four limbs will be affected. This condition is termed spastic quadriplegia.

A final type of spastic or pyramidal cerebral palsy is called hemiplegia (or half paralysis). This implies that one side of the body is more affected than the other. We most commonly associate hemiplegia with stroke victims who suffer a hemorrhage

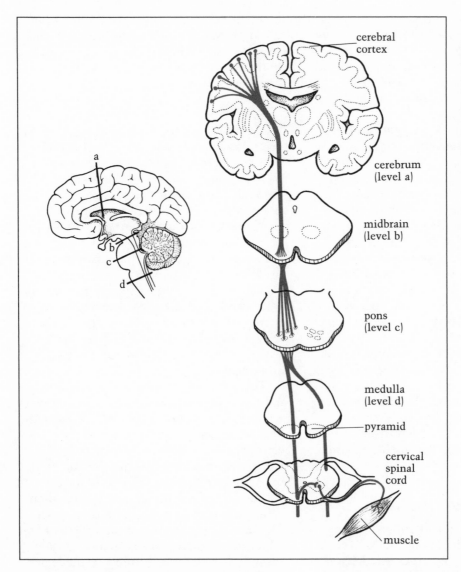

Figure 9.1. *The pyramidal tract. This illustration demonstrates how a movement develops from a thought. The electrical impulse travels from the cortex down the pyramidal tract, through the spinal cord, and connects with the muscle through the peripheral nerve.*

into one side of the brain. Strokes may also occur before birth, but hemiplegia in children is most likely to occur in children who have suffered a traumatic injury to one side of the brain, such as those injured in a motor vehicle accident or a severe fall. As the right side of the brain controls left-sided body movements and vice versa, injury to one side of the brain leads to spasticity on the other side of the body.

Extrapyramidal cerebral palsy

The extrapyramidal tracts are located deep in the center of the brain (Figure 9.3). Damage done to this area will cause a form of cerebral palsy in which fine-motor movements are affected. One example is choreoathetoid cerebral palsy, in which the child will have unusual involuntary writhing movements especially when trying to

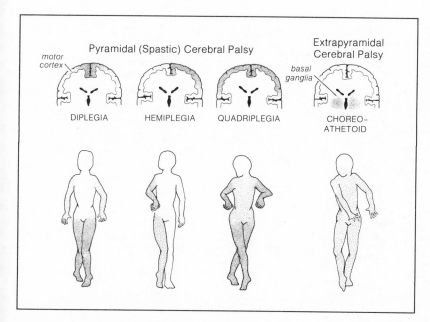

Pyramidal (Spastic) Cerebral Palsy

motor cortex

Extrapyramidal Cerebral Palsy

basal ganglia

DIPLEGIA   HEMIPLEGIA   QUADRIPLEGIA   CHOREO-ATHETOID

Figure 9.2. *Different regions of the brain are affected in various forms of cerebral palsy. The darker the shading, the more severe is the involvement.*

reach for objects. These movements are rarely seen in children under one year of age. Prior to this time, affected children tend to be floppy or rigid.

DIAGNOSING CEREBRAL PALSY

There is no specific medical test that can diagnose cerebral palsy. The diagnosis is based on the presence of a number of abnormal physical signs and neurologic findings. Almost 50 percent of all children with cerebral palsy can be diagnosed by six months of age and over 70 percent by one year of age. As is true of most conditions, the more severe the disorder, the sooner it is detectable.

Certain signs that you see in your child may suggest the possibility of cerebral palsy. In infancy, a normal baby will move all his limbs symmetrically, suck vigorously, and have a lusty cry. A child who is significantly brain damaged is likely to have abnormalities in all these areas. His muscle tone is most often decreased, re-

sulting in his being floppy, like a rag doll. Alternatively, the tone may be increased; he may be "as stiff as a board." If one side of his body is weakened or paralyzed, he may markedly favor that side. Normally an infant will be ambidextrous, developing a hand preference between twelve and eighteen months of age. However, an infant with CP may develop handedness before six months of age.

Often accompanying the abnormal muscle tone is difficulty in feeding. The infant may have a weak suck and require formula feedings from special wide-holed nipples. Breast feeding is often impossible. The problem may be severe enough to require tube feedings, in which a plastic tube is passed through the nose, down the esophagus, and into the stomach. The child may also have a weak cry and show little interest in his surroundings, being unresponsive to noises and not following faces.

Collectively, these findings suggest cerebral palsy. But doctors are often reluctant to use this term during the first six

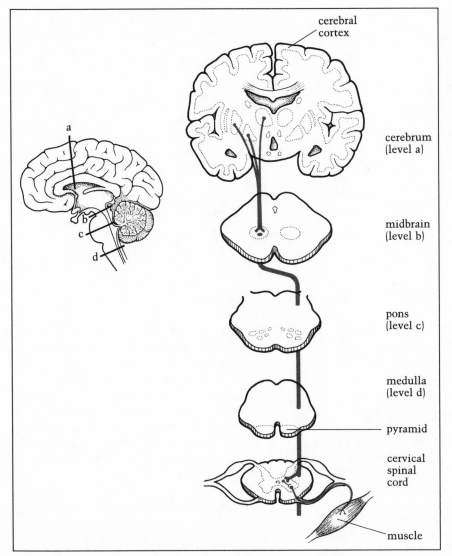

Figure 9.3. *The extrapyramidal tract. The adjustment of fine-motor movements involves a different tract that starts in the basal ganglia rather than the cortex, but also connects through the spinal cord to muscles.*

months of life. They may say your child is "developmentally delayed" or "at risk for cerebral palsy." It is not really necessary at this point to have a firm diagnosis, as long as the appropriate therapies are being given. However, it is rare that the diagnosis cannot be made by two years of age. Although some doctors will avoid using the term *cerebral palsy* because of its negative connotations, the diagnosis can open up resources and financial support for your child.

THE NEUROLOGIC EXAMINATION

As part of the evaluation, your child's doctor will perform a neurologic examination. The doctor will look for specific signs that are consistent with the diagnosis of cerebral palsy. He will check for increased or decreased muscle tone and for asymmetries, such as the legs being more affected than arms, or one side more affected than the other.

Next, he will evaluate reflexes. He will check tendon reflexes by tapping on the knees, ankles, and elbows with a rubber reflex hammer. Over- or underactive reflexes can indicate brain damage. He will also hit the heel of the foot. A foot that continues to shake after the heel is hit — a condition called clonus — indicates spasticity.

Your doctor will also look for the persistence of primitive reflexes, a strong indicator of cerebral palsy. These are reflexive actions that are normal during infancy but should disappear by three to six months of life. Some of these reflex actions are adaptive, such as sucking and rooting toward the breast. Others seem to have little purpose, such as the tonic neck and tonic labyrinthine reflexes. In the tonic neck reflex, if the head of the infant is turned in one direction, his arm and leg on that side of his body extend, and the arm and leg on the other side flex. In the tonic labyrinth reflex, if the neck is extended backward, the shoulders pull back and the legs shoot out.

In addition to being markers for cerebral palsy, the persistence of these reflexes can interfere with voluntary movements. You can imagine the difficulty a child would have rolling over if his arm and leg shoot out in the direction of his turn. Similarly, it is difficult to maintain a sitting position if your arms automatically flex and your legs extend every time you tilt your neck up. One of the major methods of physical therapy, the neurodevelopmental (NDT or Bobath) method, involves teaching children with cerebral palsy to overcome these primitive reflexes so they can sit and walk (see chapter 17).

MEDICAL TESTS FOR CEREBRAL PALSY

There is no specific medical test that will detect cerebral palsy. However, some tests may be performed to determine the underlying cause of brain damage. A brain imaging test (either a CT scan or MRI scan) will be done if a specific region of the brain is suspected to be damaged (see chapter 8). There may be chromosome studies or enzyme levels may be measured in blood specimens if genetic abnormalities are suspected. Other blood tests for viral infections may also be taken. None of these studies is dangerous or painful to your child, but it is only rarely that these tests are helpful in making a diagnosis.

ASSOCIATED DEFICITS

In addition to trying to find a cause for your child's condition, your doctor may perform other tests to determine if there are associated deficits, such as communication problems, hearing loss, vision problems, seizures, or mental retardation. Most children with cerebral palsy have at least one other disability, which may be as much of a problem as the cerebral palsy itself. Usually, the cerebral palsy and associated problems will have the same cause. In general, the likelihood of having associated deficits rises with the severity of the cerebral palsy.

Vision problems include difficulty focusing, crossed eyes, involuntary eye movements, and a decreased field of vision. Your child is likely to require glasses to correct nearsightedness or astigmatism. Crossed eyes occur in about half the children and may require surgery to adjust the muscles that control eye movement. There is no specific treatment for involuntary eye movements. Vision disorders are discussed more fully in chapter 11.

Communication disorders can take many forms. Hearing loss occurs in about 10 percent of children with CP and may require hearing aids (see chapter 10). More commonly, the overall muscle incoordination associated with CP affects a child's ability to form words. Speech may be delayed and/or slurred, especially in choreoathetoid cerebral palsy. The problem may be severe enough to prevent intelligible speech. In this case alternate methods of communication can be used, such as sign language, communication boards, or voice synthesizers. These are discussed in chapter 11. Signing may be difficult because it requires fine-motor coordination that is usually impaired by cerebral palsy. However, the use of computerized communication systems has permitted children with severe cerebral palsy to communicate in a way not previously possible.

Seizure disorders are present in about 20 percent of children with cerebral palsy. The most common type is grand mal seizures occurring in children with hemiplegia or spastic quadriplegia. Children with mixed-type cerebral palsy may have myoclonic seizures. The seizures can occur during the newborn period and then disappear, only to recur later in childhood. They generally respond to appropriate anticonvulsant medication. However, if the medication is stopped, these children are less likely to remain seizure free than children who have seizure disorders not associated with cerebral palsy or mental retardation (see chapter 8).

Approximately 60 percent of all children with cerebral palsy are mentally retarded. The degree of retardation varies from mild to profound, and occurs more frequently with certain types of CP. Children with spastic diplegia and hemiplegia tend to have the highest IQ levels, while children with spastic quadriplegia or mixed-type CP have the lowest. Extrapyramidal disorders are in the middle. However, IQ testing is often difficult with these children because of their motor and speech impairments. This may lead to either underestimation or overestimation of abilities.

Over time, and with repeated testing, the rate of development becomes clearer. If your child gains six months of intellectual skills in six months, this is an excellent sign. However, if he has gained only two to three months of skills in the same six-month period, some degree of retardation is likely.

APPROACHES TO TREATMENT

Because children with cerebral palsy often suffer from a number of problems, a multidisciplinary approach to treatment is necessary. At the center of his care is your pediatrician, but you will likely require services from physical and occupational therapists, speech and language pathologists, nutritionists, and various medical subspecialists. A physical therapist (see chapter 17) will work with your child on posture and movement, while an occupational therapist (see chapter 18) will work on functional skills necessary for basic daily living, such as eating and dressing. A speech and language pathologist (see chapter 11) will help your child learn to communicate. The nutritionist will evaluate your child's dietary needs and help develop an appropriate diet that takes into account his specific disability (see chapter 16).

Below we discuss other specific problems that arise frequently for children with cerebral palsy. In infancy, two major problems are irritability and feeding disorders. In older childhood, drooling, constipation, contractures, dislocations, and decubital ulcers become a concern.

Irritability

Children with cerebral palsy are likely to be irritable for the first twelve to eighteen months of life. This is thought to be a "brain irritability," not under the voluntary control of the child. If affected, your child will tend to cry inconsolably and sleep in short spurts, keeping you awake long after normal infants have begun to sleep through the night. Smiling develops later than usual, and your child may not enjoy being cuddled. Therefore, you may be deprived of many of the small pleasures you anticipated before the baby arrived.

In some instances medications may help. However, these should only be used once it is clear that there is no physical reason for the crying. Chloral hydrate and diazepam (Valium) have been used most commonly. Chloral hydrate is a mild sedative that can be given about thirty minutes before sleep time and should permit undisturbed sleep for about five to six hours. Valium is a muscle relaxant as well as an anti-anxiety agent. Under a doctor's supervision, given in small doses two or three times a day, it may decrease daytime irritability. Over time, the medication may be tapered off. These drugs and others discussed in this section are described in more detail in chapter 19.

Feeding Disorders

Feeding disorders are an important and difficult problem for some children. The child with cerebral palsy may have a poor appetite, be unable to suck, chew, or swallow, and may have defective muscular valves, resulting in reflux of food from the stomach into the esophagus or feeding tube. Additionally, these problems may prevent your child from obtaining adequate nutrition and may lead to episodes of aspiration pneumonia.

The mechanisms of sucking, chewing, and swallowing are complex and involve the coordinated actions of many muscle groups. Therefore, it is not surprising that a child with cerebral palsy should have difficulty with this process. Occupational therapists and speech pathologists are particularly skilled at improving feeding skills, and their help should be obtained.

Drooling

Control of salivation is a particularly vexing problem in extrapyramidal cerebral palsy. Drooling may be excessive, leading to chapping of the lips and face. A more significant concern to some parents is the embarrassing and unhygienic image it projects, making drooling as much a social concern as a medical one. Unfortunately, treatment has proven difficult. Behavior-modification techniques (see chapter 15), often combined with biofeedback (described below), can be successful. Certain medications that decrease salivation have also been tested, but the results usually have not been worth the side effects, which include pupil enlargement in the eyes, dry mouth, and sleepiness. Recently, ENT (ear, nose, and throat) surgeons have repositioned the salivary glands so that they drain directly down the throat; this has been fairly successful.

Constipation

Constipation is a nettlesome and chronic problem. Uncoordinated muscle movements, lack of physical exercise, and decreased bulk food intake all conspire to make constipation inevitable. There are a number of ways of treating constipation. This is important, for constipation can be painful and lead to a further decrease in food intake. Treatment includes exercise, modifying the diet, and the use of stool softeners and laxatives. Prevention and treatment approaches are further discussed in chapter 16.

Decubital Ulcers

When a bone presses against the skin for a prolonged period of time, it can lead to breakdown or ulceration of tissue (Figure 9.4). Children with spastic cerebral palsy are particularly at risk for this complica- tion because they tend to rest in the same position much of the time. In addition, they are often very thin, so there is little fat or muscle to cushion the bone. Once present, decubital ulcers are notoriously difficult to treat. Thus, the primary approach should be prevention. Prevention and treatment strategies are discussed in chapter 19.

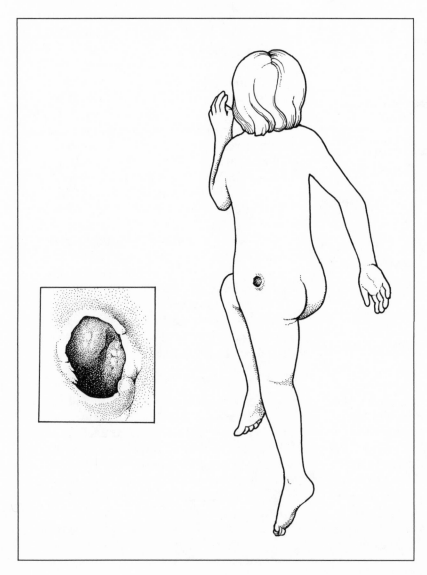

Figure 9.4. *Decubital ulcer: When bone presses against skin for a long time, an ulceration may result. This most commonly occurs in the buttocks area of children who are nonambulatory, as shown in this illustration.*

Spasticity

Spasticity can lead to many muscle and bone deformities; it should be treated as early as possible. Unfortunately, the antispasticity medications available have not proven to be very effective. The drugs that have been used are diazepam (Valium) and its derivatives lorazepam (Ativan) and clonazepam (Klonipin); baclofen (Lioresal); and dantrolene (Dantrium). Valium has been most commonly used.

Biofeedback has also been used to decrease tone. Here your child is hooked up to an apparatus called an electromyogram (EMG) that measures muscle contractions and shows them in graphic form on a TV screen or chart recorder. Your child can actually see the results of her relaxation attempts, which can help her learn to control the muscle contractions. However, this procedure takes a long time to learn, and can be used to control only one or two muscle groups at a time. When multiple muscle groups are involved, as in cerebral palsy, this approach is of limited value.

Other approaches toward controlling spasticity have been more radical, involving neurosurgical operations. Cerebellar or dorsal column implants and dorsal rhizotomies are examples of neurological procedures suggested to control spasticity. These techniques are still undergoing evaluation and are considered experimental. Cerebellar implantation involves the surgical placement of electrodes in the region of the brain that adjusts fine-motor movements. Intermittent electrical impulses to these electrodes by a stimulator implanted under the skin has been shown in animals to decrease both spasticity and choreoathetoid movements. Dorsal column stimulation involves a similar approach but with the placement of electrodes along the upper portion of the spinal cord. Neither of

these approaches has produced convincing results in children. Dorsal rhizotomy involves cutting certain nerve roots of the lower back as they come out of the spinal cord and connect with the spastic limb. Initial results have been encouraging, but adverse effects may include impairment of bowel and bladder function and persisting muscle weakness.

Contractures and Dislocations

Increased muscle tone may become progressively problematic for children with the pyramidal types of cerebral palsy. Spasticity can be uncomfortable or even painful and can inhibit voluntary movements. Over time, this can lead to tendon contractures and joint dislocations that may need to be corrected surgically. If spasticity involves paralysis of only one side, there may also develop, over time, a discrepancy between the lengths of the limbs. The paralyzed limb will not be used, and its growth will be impaired. Leg length differences of two to three inches may result by adolescence. Scoliosis, or spinal curvature, may also develop. As a result of these progressive problems, children who have been ambulatory may lose the ability to walk during adolescence. Motivation plays an important role in maintaining ambulatory skills, as the required therapy is uncomfortable and monotonous, often leading to rebellion in teenagers.

As noted above, sustained spasticity and increased muscle tone can lead to a number of muscle and bone deformities, including contractures and dislocations. The term *contracture* refers to a permanent shortening of the muscle or tendon that occurs when muscles are maintained in a tight contracted position for a long time. Increased muscle tone and spasticity can also pull a bone out of its joint, resulting in a dislocation. These problems may ultimately require orthopedic surgery to correct the deformity, preserve function, or relieve pain. But prior to surgery, braces may be used to delay or even prevent the need for an operation. Some of the more commonly performed operations are described below. These include heel cord lengthening, femoral varus osteotomy, and scoliosis surgery.

Prior to the performance of orthopedic operations, your child, if able to walk, may be sent to a gait analysis laboratory. Here, a number of electrodes will be taped to your child's legs and arms and he will be asked to walk while being videotaped. Your child will also be asked to walk across a force plate, which records foot pressure. A computer will analyze the muscle pattern during walking and suggest proper corrective approaches to decrease spasticity and improve motion. This study may be repeated following surgery to determine if the operation has improved your child's walking.

It should be emphasized that the operations discussed below are performed only following the failure of more conservative measures. For example, children with spastic diplegia will demonstrate toe walking as a result of prolonged spasticity of the Achilles ankle tendon. The initial approach is to use MAFOs (molded ankle foot orthoses), plastic inserts that keep the foot flat on the floor, or short leg braces (Figure 9.5). If these are ineffective in eliminating toe walking, then a surgical procedure is performed to lengthen the ankle tendon. Following surgery the child is placed in a cast until healing occurs, in six to eight weeks. During and following this time intensive physical therapy is important.

The hip presents the next major problem. Because of the unequal pull of spastic muscles, there is a significant risk of the upper leg bone (femur) being pulled or dis-

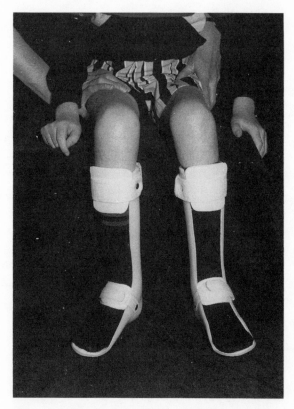

Figure 9.5. *MAFOs are plastic shoe inserts that help correct walking difficulties, including toe walking.*

located from its hip socket. Dislocations prevent a child from walking, but even if your child is wheelchair bound, fixing the hip may make sense because over time painful arthritis is likely to develop in a dislocated hip.

When the hips are only partially dislocated, they are called subluxed. At this point an operation can be performed in which certain muscles and tendons are cut to weaken the spasticity and make the pull on the joint more symmetrical. These operations are called flexor and adductor tenotomies, and may be sufficient to permit the hip joint to function normally. However, over time the problem may recur. If total dislocation occurs, an operation called a varus osteotomy may be performed. Here, the head of the femur is cut and repositioned so that it rests back in the hip socket. Temporarily, a metal plate and screws are attached to hold it in this position.

Scoliosis

A complication of both spastic and extrapyramidal cerebral palsy is a curvature of the spine called scoliosis. If left untreated, scoliosis can cause some children to freeze in "pretzel-like" positions that prevent movement and interfere with self-help skills. The deformity may also affect breathing and prevent the child from sitting.

When your child is examined, your doctor will probably look for a spinal curvature. A small curve must be watched to make sure it doesn't worsen as your child grows. For a more significant curvature, your child may be placed in a molded plastic jacket or a chair insert to try to prevent further curvature or maintain flexibility of the curve. If this does not halt the progression, surgery may be necessary to straighten the spine as much as possible. In this surgery, metal hooks, rods, and wires hold the spine in an improved position while bone graft material fuses the spine in position.

WHEELCHAIRS AND OTHER ADAPTIVE EQUIPMENT

If your child is not ambulatory or has difficulty walking long distances, he will need a wheelchair. There are many types, ranging from manually operated to battery-powered ones. Your child will need to change wheelchairs as he grows. You will also need a transport chair that can be folded up and used on trips. The various

types of chairs and the method for choosing the correct one are described in chapter 17.

If your child has severe communication problems, a voice synthesis system may be used. This involves a computer that can be programmed to produce speech. This equipment is described in chapter 11.

MODIFYING YOUR HOME

Besides treating your child directly, your therapists may also suggest modifications in your home that will help your child achieve a greater degree of independence. For example, a ramp can make it easy to roll a wheelchair into the house. Placing bars in the bathroom may permit your child to stand up and transfer himself. Doors between rooms may need to be widened and table legs shortened. You may also choose to install a computer that will permit your child to control various aspects of his environment; for instance, turning on the radio, television, or lights, or sending an emergency message by telephone. The potential adaptations to aid your child's daily life are limited only by your imagination and finances.

COUNSELING

All of these problems weigh heavily on you, your child, and the rest of your family. You may have held yourself distant from your child for fear of getting too attached and then losing him. Or he may be a child who is difficult to love because of his lack of interaction, irritability, and multiple medical problems. These are not abnormal feelings, but they will engender guilt unless you can discuss and come to grips with them. Social workers, psychologists, and psychiatrists all have the skills to help you, and you should consider using their services.

THE CHILD WITH CEREBRAL PALSY GROWN UP

Having done all these things for your child, you no doubt will wonder what his life will be like when he is an adult. The range of possibilities varies from complete independence to complete dependence. The determining factors are the severity of the disorder and the intelligence and motivation of your child and family. The premature infant with spastic diplegia may well grow out of the cerebral palsy and be unaffected as an adult. At the other end of the spectrum, the child with spastic quadriplegia or mixed-type cerebral palsy combined with severe mental retardation will remain dependent. In between may be the child with choreoathetoid cerebral palsy and normal intelligence who, with the aid of a computer, may work from home as an adult.

Times are getting better for disabled people as legislation has removed many barriers to employment and movement. Despite this, disabled adults have been slow to take advantage of this new freedom. Thus, your pushing to have your child be in as normal an atmosphere as possible is important.

SOME QUESTIONS ANSWERED

Is there value in nonconventional therapies such as patterning?

Because you will find few answers to your questions about cause and little hope for a "cure," you may be tempted to try nontraditional therapies that hold out hope for a miracle. Unfortunately, none has been shown to be of significant benefit and

some carry risks. Patterning is one example. It has been advocated as a way of restructuring brain circuitry. It involves repeating a set pattern of movements with your child many times a day, attempting to train his brain to function more normally. This takes an enormous amount of time and may place an additional strain on the family. Further, it does not appear to have any more benefit than the usual physical therapy approaches. This therapy further recommends periods of carbon dioxide rebreathing and occasional fluid restriction, neither of which has clear benefits.

Megavitamin supplements have also been advocated as a means of therapy, but here too there is no evidence of benefit and, in addition, they may lead to a harmful overdose of vitamins. Special diets have also been advocated. Some use organically grown foods and others are restricted in protein or calories. Again, there is no evidence that these diets help, and some restricted diets may interfere with your child's growth.

Should my child be mainstreamed in school?

This really depends on your child's individual needs and abilities. If your child has normal intelligence and the school has physical and occupational therapists and speech pathologists who can work with him, mainstreaming is the way to go. Such a child should be independent as an adult and needs to have as normal and integrated a childhood as possible. However, if your child is severely mentally retarded and has spastic quadriplegia, he will continue to need care throughout his life. Therefore mainstreaming really has little benefit.

How often should my child's condition be reevaluated medically?

During infancy, change occurs very rapidly.

Your child should probably be seen every three or four months. By two years of age, this can be extended to twice a year. By school age, yearly visits may be sufficient. Obviously, this depends on your child's needs and the extent of his disability. If possible, the evaluation should be done by a multidisciplinary team of specialists. Most major children's medical centers have such a clinic.

10 HEARING IMPAIRMENT

Dan F. Konkle, Ph.D.

The ability to communicate ideas through speech is often mentioned as the most important factor that separates man from lower forms of animal life. One of the most amazing aspects of development during the first three years of life is the growing child's capacity to take what he hears and, from that, develop a complex speech system. When a child has a hearing loss, however, communication development is significantly disrupted, resulting in long-term effects on the child's ability to communicate. The effects can be especially severe if the hearing loss is undetected and uncorrected. For example, if a child hears none or only part of a speech message, he will have trouble understanding the meaning of and imitating speech sounds. However, if a hearing loss is detected early, appropriate management can allow the growing child to develop more normal speech and language skills.

Unfortunately, hearing loss is often hard to detect. It cannot be seen and, with the possible exception of middle ear infections, seldom causes physical pain or discomfort. In addition, infants and young children cannot tell us that they are unable to hear. Babies who are born with a hearing impairment will startle to loud sounds in a manner similar to that of normal hearing babies. Thus, several months or years may pass before a hearing loss is detected.

Each year in the United States about twenty-two thousand infants are born with or acquire a permanent hearing loss, which can be an isolated disability or part of a multihandicapping condition. For example, about 10 percent of children with hearing loss are mentally retarded. When hearing loss is combined with other disabilities, it further impairs the child's ability to function. Even a mild hearing loss may have a disproportionate effect on a mentally retarded child because he has less ability to compensate with other senses.

This chapter provides information about how the ear works, the causes and types of hearing loss, how hearing loss is assessed, diagnosed, and treated, and options that are available for educating the hearing-impaired child.

DAVID, JENNIFER, AND SUSAN

David was born with a cleft lip and palate, mildly deformed ears, and incompletely formed ear canals. A hearing test at three months of age indicated that although he had a moderate hearing loss, both his inner ear and auditory nerve function were normal. During surgical correction of his ear canals, David's middle ears were found to be normal. Following surgery, David had another hearing test that showed that his hearing had been corrected to normal.

Jennifer has Down syndrome. As a baby she had frequent ear infections associated with colds. During one of these infections a hearing test showed that Jennifer had a mild hearing loss in each ear. On examination, both eardrums were "stiff," but the inner ears and auditory nerves appeared to be functioning normally. The doctor recommended antibiotics, and five weeks later another physical examination showed that both middle ears appeared to be normal. A repeat hearing test revealed that Jennifer's hearing had returned to normal.

Susan was born eight weeks prematurely and had numerous medical complications. She had respiratory distress syndrome and required artificial ventilation. She also had a blood infection and received two weeks of treatment with an antibiotic, gentamicin, which can be toxic to the inner ear. She was discharged from the hospital at six weeks of age and developed normally over the next six months, although her mother was concerned about her hearing. By the time Susan was fifteen months old, her mother was certain that "something" about Susan's speech did not seem right. A subsequent hearing test indicated that Susan had a severe hearing loss in both ears. She is now wearing hearing aids and her ability to hear and communicate has greatly improved.

HOW THE EAR WORKS

The normal ear can respond to a wide range of sounds that vary both in intensity (loudness) and frequency (pitch). Hearing tests determine the intensity and frequency of sound that a person can hear. The intensity of a sound is measured in a unit called the decibel, which is abbreviated "dB." As the dB value of a sound increases, it becomes louder. 0 dB is defined as the softest sound a person with normal hearing can distinguish. A normal-hearing person can detect sounds ranging from 0 dB to 140 dB. Normal speech ranges between 40 and 60 dB. Over 90 dB, sound becomes uncomfortably loud, and by the time it reaches 120 dB, it is painful. Many rock music concerts are at a level of 100 to 110 dB and can actually lead to a temporary hearing loss.

The pitch of a sound — that is, whether it is a high squeal or a low tone — is determined by the frequency of the sound wave. Frequency is measured in cycles per second, or units called hertz (Hz). Low frequencies are heard as low pitches, whereas higher frequency sounds are perceived as higher pitches (Figure 10.1). As a point of reference, middle "C" on a piano has a frequency of approximately 256 Hz. Although we can hear sounds with frequencies between 20 to 20,000 Hz, the most important sounds that occur in day-to-day listening have frequencies between 250 and 6000 Hz.

Almost all of the sounds encountered during everyday listening, however, do not occur at a single frequency and intensity. The vowel sounds of speech, for example, contain low-frequency energy between approximately 250 and 1000 Hz, whereas the consonant sounds contain high-frequency information (e.g., between 1500 and 6000 Hz). Vowel sounds also are more intense than consonant sounds. Yet, the consonant sounds convey over 90 percent of the meaning in conversational speech. Speech is an example of a complex sound; it is

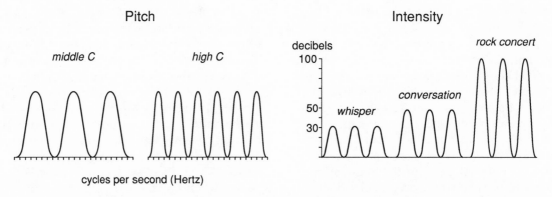

Figure 10.1. *Pitch and intensity of sound waves. The pitch of a sound, its frequency, is expressed as cycles per second, or hertz (Hz). A higher Hz measurement indicates a higher pitch. Intensity of sound is expressed in decibels (dB) and varies from a whisper at 30 dB, to normal conversation at 60 dB, to a rock concert at 100 dB or more.*

continuously changing in frequency and intensity. A hearing loss that affects only high-frequency sounds can seriously impair hearing of all conversation. The person will hear only parts of words or phrases and will have difficulty understanding their meaning. Table 10.1 lists several common sounds and provides the average range of intensities and frequencies associated with each sound.

TABLE 10.1   Common Sounds and Their Average Intensities and Frequencies as Referenced to Normal Average Hearing of 0 dB

Sound	Intensities	Frequencies
Tree leaves in a gentle breeze	0–10 dB	1500–2500 Hz
Soft whisper (speech)	10–25 dB	2000–6000 Hz
Conversational speech	25–55 dB	250–6000 Hz
Vowel sounds	35–55 db	250–800 Hz
Voiced consonant sounds	30–50 db	500–1500 Hz
Unvoiced consonant sounds	25–40 dB	1500–6000 Hz
Window air conditioner	60–70 dB	125–250 Hz
Crying baby	55–65 dB	800–1200 Hz
Barking dog	75–85 dB	300–800 Hz
Telephone ring (loud)	80–90 dB	3300–3700 Hz
Power table saw	95–105 dB	3500–6000 Hz
Helicopter	100–110 dB	3000–6000 Hz
Rock music band	105–120 dB	300–7000 Hz
Jet airplane (80–100 feet from tail)	125–140 dB	3000–7000 Hz

THE PATHWAY OF HEARING

The ear is divided into two general parts. The outside portion is called the peripheral hearing mechanism, while the inside portion is called the central auditory system (Figure 10.2). The outside portion of the ear is divided into the outer, middle, and inner ears. The outer ear includes the auricle on the side of the head, the ear canal, and the eardrum. The eardrum, or tympanic membrane, forms the boundary between the outer and middle ear. The middle ear contains three small bones that serve as a bridge between the eardrum and the inner ear. The inner ear includes a number of delicate and complex structures, most importantly the sensory organ for hearing and the auditory nerve that carries impulses to the brain.

In dogs and cats, the outer ears, or auricles, help to locate the source of sound; whereas in birds and frogs, which have equally good hearing, the auricles are absent. In humans, the auricles are the least important structures for hearing and play only a small role in gathering sound. From a practical standpoint, auricles serve a handy purpose because they hold our eyeglasses in place, and they are convenient structures from which ornaments can be hung.

The ear canal is a small tunnel about one inch long, with the eardrum located at the end. There are two functions attributed to the ear canal. First, it protects the delicate structures of the middle and inner ears. The walls of the ear canal contain glands that produce a sticky wax, which helps keep dirt and other debris from reaching the eardrum. Also, since the eardrum is placed at the end of the canal, deep inside the head, it is protected fairly well from accidental damage and is kept at

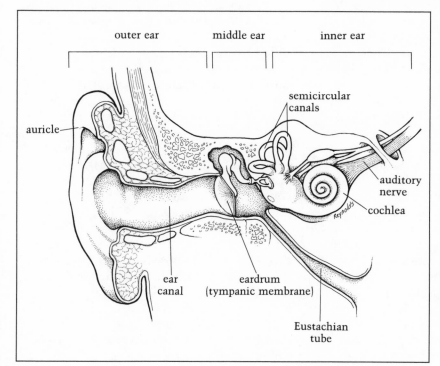

outer ear   middle ear   inner ear

semicircular canals

auricle

auditory nerve

cochlea

ear canal

eardrum (tympanic membrane)

Eustachian tube

Figure 10.2. *The ear. The outer ear includes the auricle, the ear canal, and the eardrum. The middle ear contains three small bones that serve as a bridge between the eardrum and the inner ear, and the Eustachian tube, which connects the middle ear to the back of the throat. The inner ear includes the cochlea, the sensory organ for hearing, the auditory nerve that carries hearing impulses to the brain, and the semicircular canals, which control balance.*

a constant temperature and humidity. Second, the ear canal conducts sound to the eardrum and serves as a "tube resonator" that increases the intensity of sound at the eardrum.

The eardrum transfers the sound conducted by the ear canal to the small bones contained in the middle ear. The eardrum itself is a very thin membrane that is disclike in shape and vibrates with the airborne sound waves. Since the eardrum is connected directly to the bones of the middle ear, these vibrations are transferred easily to the middle ear structures.

The middle ear is a small, air-filled space connected to the back of the throat by a channel called the eustachian tube, which opens and closes during swallowing and yawning (Figure 10.2). The opening and closing of the eustachian tube allows the air pressure in the middle ear to equalize with the pressure of the outside air. There are three small bones in the middle ear that form a bridge between the eardrum and the inner ear. These bones are commonly referred to as the hammer, anvil, and stirrup because of their shapes.

The inner ear is extremely complicated, containing thousands of moving parts, and yet is the size of a small pea. It is responsible for converting the vibrations conducted by the outer and middle ears into nerve impulses that are sent to the brain for interpretation by the central auditory system. Among the many important structures in the inner ear is the sensory organ of hearing, called the organ of Corti. Along the surface of the organ of Corti are over twenty thousand tiny hair cells that are connected to nerve fibers within the auditory nerve. These hair cells are thought to pick up vibrations from the middle ear bones and transfer them to the nerve cells, which transmit impulses to the brain. The large number of these hair cells and their exquisite sensitivity allows the organ of Corti to encode the entire range of frequency and intensity information required for normal hearing.

The auditory nerves that come from each inner ear enter the central auditory system at a structure known as the brain stem (see Figure 10.2) and then pass the sound message to an area of the brain where the information is decoded and shared with input from other sensory systems (vision, taste, smell, and so forth).

TYPES OF HEARING LOSS

A defect anywhere along the hearing pathway will result in hearing loss. The types of hearing impairment are classified as conductive, sensorineural, and mixed. Conductive hearing loss occurs when there is a disorder of the outer or middle ear; sensorineural hearing loss occurs when the inner ear or auditory nerve is damaged. When there is both a conductive and sensorineural component to the hearing loss, it is called a mixed-type hearing loss.

In a conductive hearing loss, the inner ear and auditory nerve are normal, but sound fails to reach the inner ear at the normal intensity because of an abnormality or obstruction in the ear canal, eardrum, or middle ear. Conductive hearing loss accounts for about 95 percent of all acquired hearing losses in infants and young children and is usually caused by middle ear infections (see below).

Most conductive impairments are mild, temporary, and do not cause a substantial threat to overall language development so long as the problem is identified early and medical attention is obtained promptly. Most conditions that cause conductive hearing loss can be corrected either by medication or through surgery. Even if the conductive impairment cannot be completely corrected, hearing aids and special instruction often will allow children to function normally.

The term *sensorineural hearing loss* is used to indicate that the inner ear (sensory) and/or the auditory nerve (neural) is affected. Unlike the case with conductive hearing loss, less than 5 percent of people with sensorineural hearing impairments improve through the use of medication or surgery. This does not mean, however, that there is no treatment. Most children with sensorineural impairments benefit greatly from the use of hearing aids and special-education placement (see below).

CAUSES OF HEARING LOSS

Hearing loss either may be present at birth, in which case it is called a congenital impairment, or it may be acquired after birth. The most common causes of congenital hearing loss are heredity, intrauterine infections, medications taken by the mother during pregnancy, and complications that occur during the birth process.

Until the early 1970s, one of the most feared causes of hearing loss in childhood was congenital rubella syndrome (see chapter 3). Extremely rare now, it has been replaced in importance by another intrauterine viral infection, cytomegalovirus, or CMV. Though CMV is far more common than rubella ever was and has more varied effects on the fetus, it often goes undetected in the mother. Affected children may initially have only a mild hearing loss, but as they grow older, it becomes progressively worse. The principal manifestation of CMV is sensorineural hearing loss. Other intrauterine infections have also been implicated in hearing loss, including syphilis and toxoplasmosis. Specific blood tests can be done in infancy to detect these infections.

There are many other causes of hearing loss besides intrauterine infections. Childhood infections, especially middle ear infections, can cause conductive hearing loss. Other infections, such as measles, mumps, meningitis, and encephalitis, can lead to significant sensorineural hearing loss. Certain antibiotics used to treat infants, especially those born prematurely, can also damage the inner ear or auditory nerve. Between 2 percent and 5 percent of babies who graduate from a newborn intensive care unit will have a significant hearing loss either due to medications, lack of oxygen, or birth trauma. This was the case with Susan. Hearing loss can also be acquired later in life. For instance, if the ear or temporal bone of the skull is damaged in an accident, the middle or inner ear also may be affected, causing hearing loss.

Finally, hearing loss can be of genetic origin. A number of chromosomally inherited disorders are associated with abnormalities in the formation of the ear or its contents. These include Down syndrome, trisomy 13, and trisomy 18 (see chapter 7). Further, children with cleft palate invariably have recurrent middle ear infections and associated hearing loss. Isolated sensorineural hearing loss may also be inherited either as an autosomal recessive or dominant trait (see chapter 4). Despite our knowledge of the many causes of hearing loss, we only have about a 50-50 chance of diagnosing the specific cause in any particular child.

OTITIS MEDIA: MIDDLE EAR INFECTIONS

Virtually all children will have at least one middle ear infection during the first two years of life. These infections may not be associated with any noticeable symptoms, or your child may cry, pull at his ear, and/or have a low-grade fever. When an ear infection is suspected, the pediatrician will examine your child's ears with an otoscope to see if the eardrum is inflamed or if fluid has collected behind it. Fluid behind the eardrum interferes with the normal conduction of sound and can cause a mild or moderate conductive-type hearing loss. If an infection is found, the pediatrician will prescribe antibiotics and/or a decongestant, which should alleviate symptoms within a few days. The doctor will probably want to recheck your child's ears one to two weeks later, by which time the eardrum should appear normal. If hearing is tested during the infection, there may be a mild or moderate conductive hearing loss, but this should also disappear following treatment.

Problems occur when there are recurrent ear infections, when the infection goes undetected, or when fluid remains behind the eardrum despite treatment. In these instances, the child can develop a persistent mild or moderate hearing loss. If the fluid lasts for several weeks, or if your child has recurrent bouts of middle ear infections, he or she should be seen by an audiologist for a hearing test. If these problems do not resolve in a reasonable period of time (i.e., six to ten weeks), your child may be placed on long-term antibiotic therapy or have ear tubes placed surgically (described below). Children with certain developmental disabilities, such as Down syndrome or cleft palate, and children who are born prematurely are at increased risk for having repeated middle ear infections.

EARLY IDENTIFICATION OF A HEARING LOSS

If you suspect that your child has a hearing loss, get his or her hearing tested as soon as possible. It is far better to find out that your child has normal hearing, and perhaps to suffer some embarrassment for being an overly worried parent, than to wait several months or years to discover that your child has been hearing-impaired or hears distorted sounds. Even a mild hearing loss is worthy of being diagnosed and corrected. We recommend that hearing testing be done prior to the age of six or seven months for all children who are premature or who have developmental disabilities, chromosomal abnormalities, recurrent ear infections, or intrauterine infections, because of the high risk of hearing loss associated with these conditions.

As your child grows, you can watch for signs that suggest a hearing loss. Between birth and four months of age, a hearing child will awaken momentarily if you talk loudly while he is asleep, whereas a hearing-impaired child may not. However, even children with significant hearing loss may startle momentarily to a loud noise.

The talking behavior of a baby or young child may also reveal clues about hearing ability. Between four and six months of age, both normal hearing and hearing-impaired children will babble. However, a deaf child (i.e., one with profound hearing loss) will stop babbling by around nine months of age and may be silent thereafter. By five to seven months of age a normal hearing child should turn consistently toward a voice and will begin imitating sounds made by adults and other children. The hearing-impaired child will do neither. Mentally retarded children with normal hearing will also be delayed in the achievement of these language milestones; however, all their skills will be similarly delayed, while the hearing-impaired child will have much slower development in language than in other skills.

HEARING ASSESSMENT

No child is too young for a hearing test; even the hearing ability of newborn infants can be tested. However, unlike older children and adults, who usually can be tested in a single session, it sometimes takes several test sessions to assess the hearing of an infant or young child. Whenever possible, children under five years of age should be tested by an audiologist at a clinic that specializes in pediatric assessment.

A hearing assessment should address three questions: Is hearing normal? If abnormal, what is the severity of the hearing loss? Finally, what is the type of hearing loss — conductive, sensorineural, or mixed? The results of the assessment can also be used to compare the hearing of one ear to the other ear, and can determine the "shape" of the hearing loss; that is, whether hearing is better at some frequencies than at others.

Infant hearing tests can determine if hearing is impaired but cannot accurately predict the degree and type of hearing loss. In children over six months of age, more precise information can be gathered about each ear and about the shape of the hearing loss.

Hearing Assessment of Infants Less Than Six Months Old — Brain Stem Response Audiometry

As might be expected, the methods used to test a child's hearing vary with the age of the child. The best procedure to assess the hearing of young infants is most commonly called Brain Stem Response Audiometry (BSRA) or Brain Stem Evoked Auditory Response (BEAR). This test is ideal for evaluating the hearing of infants because it requires no active participation.

In fact, the best test results are obtained when the baby is asleep.

The procedure used in BSRA testing consists of taping small electrodes to your infant's forehead and on or behind each ear. The electrodes record the electrical activity from the brain stem auditory nerves while a series of very brief sounds are presented first to one ear and then to the other. The brain waves are then analyzed by a computer and compared to the brain waves of other infants who are known to have normal hearing. Based on this comparison, normal or abnormal hearing can be diagnosed. Figure 10.3 shows the brain stem responses obtained from an infant with normal hearing compared to the responses from a hearing-impaired infant. Note that the responses from the normal hearing baby have three distinct waves that are labeled as waves I, III, and V. The response from the hearing-impaired baby does not have this characteristic wave form.

Although BSRA has become a valuable tool to test hearing in young infants, there are two limitations with this procedure. First, BSRA is not a true test of hearing; it provides information about the workings of the ear, but does not tell us what the baby actually hears. Second, the sound stimulus used in BSRA is made up of frequencies that are most intense between 2000 and 6000 Hz. If hearing is impaired for frequencies below 1000 Hz, but normal between 2000 and 6000 Hz, BSRA would indicate normal hearing even though a low-frequency hearing loss actually existed. Fortunately from a test standpoint, low-frequency hearing losses are rare. Conversely, if hearing is normal for the lower frequencies (i.e., below 1000 Hz) but impaired at the higher frequencies, BSRA results would indicate the high-frequency

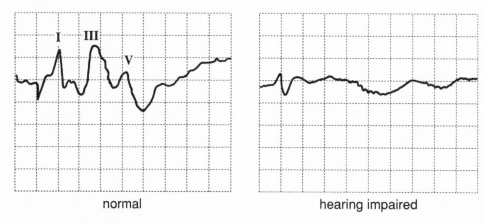

normal   hearing impaired

Figure 10.3. *Test results from Brain Stem Response Audiometry in an infant with normal hearing and in one with severe hearing loss. Note that the responses from the normal hearing baby have three distinct waves that are labeled as waves I, III, and V. The response from the hearing-impaired baby does not have this characteristic wave form.*

hearing loss but not the normal low-frequency hearing ability. Thus, BSRA results provide limited information about the shape of a hearing loss.

Hearing Assessment from Six Months to Two Years of Age — Visual Response Audiometry

By the time a child reaches a mental age level of about six or seven months, he has become very curious about what is going on around him and actively interacts with his environment. Most infants at this age will attempt to locate the source of an interesting sound. Hearing tests take advantage of this behavior by presenting a sound at one side of the baby's head and then watching to see if the baby turns toward the sound. If the same sound is presented several times in a row, infants usually lose interest and stop responding. However, if a visual reward is provided for each correct head turn in response to a sound, the infant will continue to perform the task indefinitely.

This type of testing, in which the natural head turn response to sound is coupled with a visual reward, is called Visual Reinforcement Audiometry (VRA). The visual reward, or reinforcer, which can be a motion toy such as a bear playing a drum or a dog with a wagging tail, is placed in a dark glass box. When the infant makes a correct head turn, lights inside the glass box go on and the toy is activated for several seconds. The audiologist repeats this procedure multiple times with decreasing sound intensities to determine the softest intensity of sound that continues to elicit a head turn. This sound is called the threshold of hearing. The Visual Response Audiometry procedure can be used to test several different frequencies of sound. Thus, this procedure is more precise than BSRA responses in determining both the degree and type of hearing loss.

Hearing Assessment in Children Two Years of Age and Older — Play Audiometry

The hearing of children between the ages of two and four years can be tested successfully using a procedure called "play audiometry." Actually, play audiometry does not differ much from the procedures used with adults except that the procedure is designed to be more play oriented and appealing to children. For example, an adult being tested might be instructed to push a button or to raise his hand whenever he hears the sound. In play audiometry, the child is asked to perform a simple play task, such as placing a ring on a peg, whenever he hears the sound.

Whenever possible, the hearing test is performed using earphones so that the ears can be tested separately. Not all young children, however, are willing to wear earphones. When this happens, the pure tone sounds are presented by a loudspeaker and the responses obtained are called "sound field responses." This indicates that the sounds were presented to both ears at the same time rather than to each ear separately. Thus, sound field thresholds represent a combination of the hearing in the better ear and in the more impaired ear.

Like the other hearing tests, the goal of play audiometry is to find the threshold, or the softest intensity at which a sound can be heard. It also permits the determination of threshold levels for low-frequency and high-frequency sounds. Although many young children can be taught to respond as an adult would (i.e., push a button or raise their hand), it has been found that play audiometry increases the attention span of most children, thereby allowing more information to be collected during a test session.

Types of Audiometry

When thresholds are obtained using either earphones or a loudspeaker, the procedure is referred to as air-conduction testing. In air-conduction testing, pure tone sounds travel down the ear canal to the eardrum, across the three bones of the middle ear to the inner ear, and so on to the brain. The results of air-conduction testing, therefore, represent the response of the total hearing mechanism.

Air-conduction audiometry can determine whether hearing is normal or abnormal. It can also tell the minimum intensity and the range of frequencies that your child can hear. Air-conduction testing by itself, however, cannot determine whether a hearing loss is conductive, sensorineural, or mixed. To do this, a different type of measurement, called bone conduction, is necessary. In bone-conduction testing, a small vibrator is placed just behind the ear and pure tones are presented to the inner ear in the form of vibrations on the skull. Thus, the "sound" bypasses the outer and middle ear systems. Bone-conduction tests measure the hearing threshold of the inner ear, auditory nerve, and central auditory pathways.

When air-conduction measurements are used in combination with bone-conduction thresholds, it is possible to differentiate between outer or middle ear disorders (conductive hearing loss) and problems of the inner ear and neural pathways (sensorineural impairment). If your child has a hearing loss by air conduction yet shows normal hearing by bone conduction, the impairment is probably due to an obstruction or blockage of the outer or middle ear. However, if the thresholds by both air and bone conduction show the same extent of hearing loss, the impairment is sensorineural.

The results of a hearing test generally are displayed graphically on a chart called an audiogram. Figure 10.4 provides examples of audiograms illustrating various degrees of hearing loss.

Assessing Middle Ear Function — Tympanometry

Regardless of your child's age, the hearing assessment should include, besides

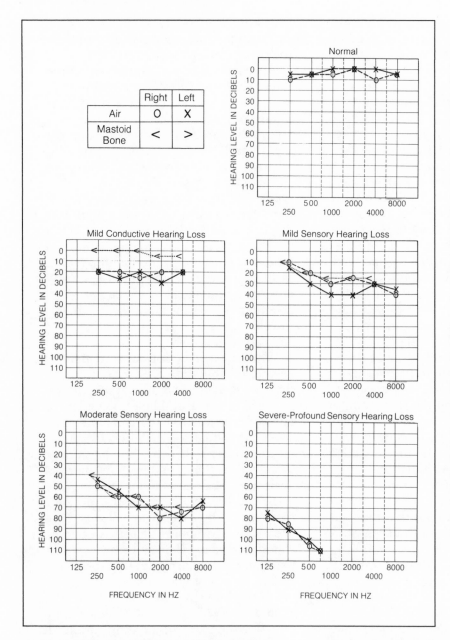

Figure 10.4. *Audiograms are used to plot the findings of pure tone air and bone conduction threshold testing. Various degrees of hearing loss are indicated. The individual frequencies, in Hz, that are tested during the assessment are displayed along the bottom of the audiogram and hearing intensity levels, in dB, are listed along the sides of the audiogram. The 0 dB reference line represents average normal hearing. Values greater than 0 dB indicate how much louder an individual frequency must be made in order to be heard. The frequencies of 125, 250, 500, 1000, 2000, 4000, and 8000 Hz represent single frequencies, commonly called pure tones. When testing young children, thresholds are usually obtained for only the most important frequencies of 250 through 4000 Hz.*

audiometry, a special test called tympanometry. Tympanometry is not an actual hearing test, but is designed to assess middle ear function by measuring how well the eardrum transmits sound to the middle ear. This is a simple test that does not require a response from your child, although he must sit still. The test is conducted by placing a small earphone in the outer part of the ear canal. During the test your child hears a low-frequency tone, usually around 220 Hz, and feels a slight pressure in the ear, much like the pressure sensation felt when riding up a fast elevator. The entire test takes only about five seconds for each ear. This test most commonly detects middle ear infections that alter the ability of the eardrum to transmit sound.

Extent of Hearing Loss

There are varying degrees of hearing impairment, ranging from slight to profound, that will be identified by audiometry. The degree of hearing impairment is assessed by measuring the softest sound that can be perceived at three different frequencies and then averaging the three measurements. If, for example, the average threshold for the three pure tone frequencies was 35 dB, the hearing loss would be described as mild, suggesting that your child will have difficulty understanding speech of normal loudness.

Table 10.2 lists the varying degrees of impairment associated with different amounts of hearing loss as well as their probable effects on a child's ability to understand speech. A slight loss (threshold of 15–25 dB) is most often associated with a middle ear infection and usually will have no significant effect on function. If a slight hearing loss persists for longer than six

months in your child when she is less than three years old, we recommend speech/language evaluations every three months. If speech and language skills are developing normally, special attention is not necessary. However, if a delay in speech/language development becomes evident, it may be necessary to fit your child with a hearing aid and begin a program of language stimulation. As she becomes older and enters preschool or kindergarten, she should sit in the front of the room where she will be able to hear better.

A mild impairment is defined as a 25–40 dB hearing loss. As compared to the child with a slight hearing loss, children with mild impairments are at a greater risk for delayed speech or language. Again, we recommend that the speech and language skills of these children be monitored carefully — every three months if they are less than three years of age, and every six months if they are three years of age or older. If a speech or language delay is discovered, your child should be fitted with an amplification device and be provided with language therapy. If these guidelines are followed, children with mild impairments should develop normal speech and

TABLE 10.2   The Extent of Hearing Loss for Varying Degrees of Impairment and the Associated Handicap for Hearing and Understanding Speech

Lowest dB heard	Extent of loss	Handicap
0–15 dB	Normal limits	No significant difficulty with faint speech
15–25 dB	Slight hearing loss	Difficulty only with faint speech
25–40 dB	Mild hearing loss	Frequent difficulty with normal speech
40–60 dB	Moderate hearing loss	Frequent difficulty loud normal speech
60–90 dB	Severe hearing loss	Can understand only shouted or amplified speech
Over 90 dB	Profound hearing loss	Usually can hear but cannot understand even amplified speech

language and will not need special educational placements.

The moderately hearing-impaired child (40–60 dB loss) has difficulty understanding loud normal speech. There is some speech/language delay, and articulation defects are usually present. These children will benefit from the use of hearing aids and language-stimulation programs. While many of these children attend normal schools, they often will require extra help for classes that depend upon language skills, such as English, social studies, or history.

The child with a severe loss (60–90 dB) will hear only very loud speech. Although he may be aware that he is hearing speech, he will not be able to understand what is being said unless he wears a hearing aid. Most of these children will have a limited vocabulary and immature language; their voice quality also may be abnormal. The ability of these children to function in a normal school setting will depend on how well they develop speech and language skills. Even if they attend a normal school, however, they will require special assistance in the form of tutors and instructions.

The child with a profound hearing loss (greater than 90 dB) may not be able to hear speech even with the use of amplification. These children will have severe speech and language delays and most will have to rely on signing. Typically, children with profound hearing loss attend special schools for the deaf and have a difficult time interacting with the hearing community.

TREATMENT OF HEARING IMPAIRMENT

Treatment for a hearing-impaired child should be multifaceted. It may include surgical procedures, the use of hearing aids, speech therapy, special education, and psychosocial counseling.

Surgical Procedures

The most common surgical operation on the ear involves the placement of tubes through the eardrum. If your child has a persistent ear infection, or has had multiple ear infections in any one year, your ear doctor (otolaryngologist) may suggest placing tubes in the affected ear(s). This is an outpatient surgical procedure in which a slit is made in the eardrum and a small plastic tube is inserted into the middle ear. This equalizes the pressure, reduces pain, and allows ventilation of the middle ear space. Once placed, these tubes remain for a few months and generally fall out spontaneously. The eardrum will heal after the tube comes out.

If recurrent ear infections are associated with large infected adenoids, the ear specialist may also suggest removing the adenoids. In years past, tonsillectomies were often performed in combination with adenoidectomies as a way of preventing ear infections. However, today we know that tonsils have nothing to do with ear infections and, furthermore, that they provide immunity for the child against other infections.

Rarer surgical procedures involve repairing or reconstructing the small bones in the middle ear, repairing a torn eardrum, and placing cochlear implants. The last of these procedures was developed to replace part of a damaged inner ear. The cochlea is the portion of the inner ear that contains the nerve cells and fibers that conduct sounds to the brain. Sensorineural hearing loss commonly involves abnormalities of the cochlea. Cochlear implants are devices that stimulate the nerve cells directly in an attempt to provide partial restoration of hearing. In children, the device is limited in use to those over two years of age with profound sensorineural impairment who cannot benefit from any other form of amplification.

Hearing Aids

Less than one of every thousand hearing-impaired children is completely deaf. Thus, most children with hearing loss can benefit from hearing aids. When hearing loss is congenital or acquired prior to the third year of life, it is especially critical that your child receive amplification as soon as the hearing loss is identified. Hearing aids provide a vital link between your child and all the sounds that are important for language development. If several months elapse before he is fitted with hearing aids, it can substantially affect speech development and language comprehension. When medical or surgical procedures cannot help, the hearing aid is the single most important rehabilitative tool available for the hearing-impaired child.

Some professionals feel that children with mild hearing losses are not candidates for hearing aids. This viewpoint probably results from the observation that many adults with slight or mild impairments do not gain significant benefit from using them. It is not appropriate, however, to generalize this notion to young children who have not fully developed their language skills. Rather, it is important to explore the potential of using hearing aids with any hearing-impaired child before deciding that it is unwarranted. All children with hearing loss can potentially benefit from amplification.

Both body-level and ear-level aids are available for children. Both consist of a microphone, an amplifier, a power supply, and a miniature loudspeaker called a receiver. The electronics of the body-level aid are contained in a small box that is clipped to a piece of clothing. A cord runs from the box to the receiver, which is placed in the ear. The ear-level aid has all the parts in one piece that fits in or behind the ear. At one time it was felt that body-type hearing aids should be used with all young children, especially those with severe or profound hearing loss. We now know, however, that ear-level hearing aids provide superior quality and more natural amplification than body-type instruments. For younger children, behind-the-ear hearing aids should be used rather than all-in-the-ear instruments. While in-the-ear aids are less noticeable, they require more frequent changes as your child's external ear grows bigger. In-the-ear aids are also more difficult to keep in place and tend to fall out of the ears of infants and very young children. Unless the hearing in one ear is significantly poorer than that of the other ear, binaural (both ear) amplification is preferred. Each ear should be tested separately for a specific aid.

The hearing aid selection process begins with making ear molds from an impression taken from each of your child's ears. Once the ear molds are ready, the audiologist will begin the process of selecting the most appropriate type of amplification. This can take several weeks or even months as the hearing aids are "fine-tuned" based on information obtained during formal testing sessions and by observations of your child's behavior. During this process, your child should be wearing the hearing aids so he will receive the benefit of amplification even if it is not yet optimal. It is important to have realistic expectations about the benefits to be derived from amplification. Unlike eyeglasses, which can completely correct most visual problems, hearing aids cannot restore a hearing impairment to normal. The purpose of a hearing aid is to make sound more intense so that it can be heard better. Unfortunately, this does not always imply that the sound received through a hearing aid is heard normally. In most cases, extensive training is required in order for the child to make effective use of the amplified sound. As a result, progress using newly fitted hearing aids often appears to be frustratingly slow. Bear with it — in the end your child will hear better.

Most children will eventually adapt to wearing hearing aids. At first, they may not like the sensation of having something stuck in or behind their ears, especially if they are too young to appreciate its purpose. After a few trials, however, most children will tolerate the devices. In fact, young children often become upset if they are not allowed to wear their hearing aids all the time.

Occasionally, a child will refuse to wear a hearing aid despite all efforts to convince him otherwise. If this happens with your child, you may need to employ behavior modification techniques (see chapter 15). Initially, try having your child wear the aid for a few minutes at a time, several times throughout the day. After your child has worn the aid for a few minutes, let him know that it is all right to remove the aid. Be sure to provide a reward of praise and a favorite treat. If your child attempts to remove the aid before the designated time has elapsed, let him know that he must leave the hearing aid in place. If he takes the hearing aid out, replace it but do not provide any reward until the aid is worn for the complete time.

As your child is becoming accustomed to wearing the aid, be sure the volume control is adjusted to the level recommended by your audiologist. After your child is able to wear the aid for one-hour periods, begin using the aid during games

and other activities in which he will see its advantages in dealing with other children. Expose him to new sounds such as a TV, vacuum cleaner, or telephone. Take him outside and explain the environmental sounds he can now hear. Continue to increase the amount of time the aid is worn until it can be kept in for the entire day. From this point on, routine is important. Your child should learn to put in the aid as he dresses and take it off at bedtime.

For ear-level hearing aids, you can teach your child how to insert the ear mold by using a doll. The more independent your child is, the better. If he throws the aid against the wall or flushes it down the toilet, he may just be acting up. However, he may also be trying to tell you that the ear mold does not fit correctly. Poor fit may cause his ear canal to become sore or the aid may emit an unpleasant "squeal" when the volume is adjusted. To ascertain the cause of your child's refusal to wear the aid, first inspect your child's ear for inflammation that suggests a poor fitting ear mold. Then, have the aid and ear mold tested to make sure both the fit and amplification are correct. If no problems are found, try using behavioral techniques to get him to accept the aid. You should use positive reinforcement rather than punishment.

Your audiologist should check your child's hearing aids at routine intervals, usually every three months for the first year and then yearly thereafter. Your child should also have repeat hearing tests during these checkups. Hearing levels may change; the ear mold may become too small as the ear canal grows; or the aid may not be functioning optimally. These potential problems can be discovered during routine checks and steps can be taken to assure that your child continues to receive optimal amplification.

Practicing Speech at Home

In order for your child to get the greatest benefit from hearing aids, you may need to make adjustments at home that will encourage auditory learning. For example, you cannot expect your hearing-impaired child to understand what you are saying from across a large room while a television set is playing in one corner, other children are engaged in a noisy game, and you are running the vacuum cleaner. This does not mean that your home must be deathly quiet all the time. However, you may need to make some compromises in order to find several times during the day when on-going background noise is at a minimum. During these times, talk to your child about your activities, using words that are within her vocabulary. If you are unpacking groceries, for instance, explain that you are taking a can out of a bag, you are putting the can on a shelf, you are putting the milk in the refrigerator, you are closing the refrigerator door, and so on. Try not to engage in one activity while talking about a different activity.

EDUCATING THE CHILD WITH A HEARING IMPAIRMENT (see also chapter 20)

Your hearing-impaired child should begin a therapy program as early as possible. Federal law (PL 99-457) mandates that children with developmental disabilities, including hearing loss, begin receiving services in infancy. These free services will be provided either by the health department or by the local school district and may include having a specialist, such as a speech/language pathologist or an educator of the hearing impaired, come into your home. Alternatively, your child may be enrolled in a preschool program for the hearing impaired. The law also mandates services for

testing your child's hearing, for fitting her with hearing aids, and for follow-up care. You should take advantage of these services as soon as a hearing loss has been identified.

The type of educational program your child needs will depend more on her language and speech skills than on the extent of hearing loss. Another important consideration is whether there are other developmental disabilities associated with the hearing impairment. In general, however, it has been found that the majority of children with slight, mild, or moderate hearing losses are able to attend regular schools, although they often require the help of special-resource teachers or classes. Children with severe or profound hearing losses usually attend special schools for the deaf. There is one college specifically for deaf people, Gallaudet College in Washington, D.C. Special classes in the public schools and programs for the hard of hearing usually teach the oral method of communication, which encourages children to rely as much as possible on speaking and understanding speech. In contrast, schools for the deaf may emphasize the manual method (signing). However, both types of schools are now moving toward a total communication philosophy, which includes both approaches (see chapter 11).

As noted previously, many children need to wear hearing aids in order to function at an acceptable level in the classroom. The use of hearing aids alone, however, may not be sufficient to permit hearing and understanding of classroom conversations. The ambient noise in most classrooms is so high that it may interfere with explanations or instructions given by the teacher, or obscure the comments offered by other classmates. In order to overcome this problem, special classroom amplification systems have been developed that are used in combination with your child's personal hearing aids. These systems operate much like a radio station, transmitting the teacher's voice directly to your child's hearing aid using either a special FM radio signal or an infrared light beam. Classroom amplification systems can significantly improve your child's ability to hear and communicate in noisy conditions because they reduce the disturbing effects of ambient noise. However, they are in limited use in classrooms, at present, because of their expense.

For the profoundly hearing-impaired (i.e., deaf) child, hearing aids often have only limited value. These children are most likely to be placed in self-contained classes for the deaf. An added complication is that they often have learning disabilities in addition to the hearing defects. Therefore, the teacher must take into account the child's intellectual and educational abilities as well as the hearing loss. As with all special-education programs, there should be a yearly Individual Educational Program developed for your child.

You may wonder whether to send your child to a neighborhood school or to a special school for the deaf. All things being equal, your child will function more normally if he stays in a community school with his friends and neighbors. However, if his problems are complex and the local school is unable to provide for your child's needs, a special school is an option worth exploring. Tuition will be paid by the local school if they agree that it is necessary. If you disagree with their decision, you may appeal their judgment (see chapter 20).

The number and availability of programs specifically designed for hearing-impaired children depends upon where you live. Your audiologist can provide a list of programs that are available in your area and can explain how each program may be able to help your child. Before you decide to place your child in a particular program, however, you should plan to visit various programs in order to find out firsthand which one best meets your child's needs. You should ask your audiologist to give you the names of other parents with hearing-impaired children who live in your community. Call these parents and discuss the pros and cons of those programs that interest you. Finally, you can contact any of the agencies listed in the Selected Readings and References for this chapter for additional information about programs for the hearing impaired located in your area.

PSYCHOSOCIAL ISSUES

Being hard of hearing is very frustrating, especially for a young child. His difficulty expressing his needs and desires may translate into acting out to get attention or flying into rages when he is not understood. When angry, he may turn off his hearing aid so he does not hear you. These episodes need to be dealt with quickly before they become regular parts of your child's behavior. First, you need to be sure that the hearing aid is working well and that your child is in an appropriate school setting. You also need to be sure there is not some emotional crisis brewing. Then you can use behavior-modification techniques (see chapter 15). Basically, you must reinforce appropriate means of getting attention and ignore or punish inappropriate outbursts. Try not to let your feelings of sympathy impair your ability to discipline your child when necessary. A hearing-impaired child needs to conform to the same standards and rules of behavior as does a normal-hearing child and needs to learn to express himself in appropriate ways.

OUTCOME

Your child's eventual abilities will depend on many factors, including intelligence, the degree of hearing loss, the age of diagnosis, and the family environment. The higher your child's intelligence, the more adaptive she will be and the faster she will learn. However, the more severe the hearing loss, the harder you and your child will have to work to be successful. In one study of deaf children with normal intelligence, the average reading level at the end of high school was only eighth grade. The age of diagnosis is important because the earlier the identification, the more effective the therapy will be, especially in your child's development of speech and language. Finally, the family environment can either help or hinder. Concerned, helpful parents and siblings can make a major difference in the outcome of a hearing-impaired child. You can make your child feel normal and wanted and can help in the therapy programs.

SOME QUESTIONS ANSWERED

How do I choose the right audiologist or speech/language pathologist?

You will need to choose both an audiologist and a speech/language pathologist. You want professionals who are competent, have experience in working with children, and are sensitive to your and your child's needs. You may find such an individual in your school system, a children's hospital, or in private practice. The American Speech, Language, Hearing Association (ASHA) has a listing of audiologists and speech/language pathologists with specific interest and abilities in pediatrics working in your area.

Does a hearing aid amplify sounds equally and from all directions?

Hearing aids are directional. They tend to focus sounds that are presented in front of your child's face and weaken sounds to the side and back. Depending on the shape of your child's hearing loss (that is, low frequency or high frequency), different sounds will be amplified to a different extent. The goal is to provide your child with as much of the acoustic information contained in conversational speech as possible.

Can a hearing aid overamplify and cause further damage?

Many studies suggest that hearing aids are unlikely to cause further damage to your child's hearing by being turned up too high. The best way to determine that the hearing aid is not causing problems is to have your child's hearing tested every three months during the first year after he gets a hearing aid, and annually thereafter.

What do I need to know about my child's hearing aids?

You cannot simply put a hearing aid on your child and then forget about it. When you first get the hearing aids, your audiologist will explain how they work, how to replace the batteries, how to insert the ear molds, and how to tell if the aids are working correctly. It is better for your child not to wear hearing aids at all than to wear ones that function poorly. You should visually inspect and listen to them daily. It is important to check your child's ear to be sure that the ear mold is not causing soreness because of a poor fit. If the ear mold does not fit, see your audiologist to have the problem corrected or a new ear mold made. Be sure that you take the same precautions in storing the hearing aid's extra batteries as you would with medicine. Hearing aid batteries are small, and if swallowed can cause a toxic reaction. This problem can be avoided if you are careful to keep extra batteries in a safe place where they are out of the reach of young children.

Will my child, who has a severe hearing loss, be able to talk?

Almost all children with an isolated hearing loss, regardless of severity, learn to talk. Children with slight, mild, and moderate impairments usually will develop normal or nearly normal speech. Children with severe impairments will have more difficulty learning to talk and their voice quality may be abnormally high pitched, but their speech usually is understandable. Children with a profound hearing loss have the most difficulty learning speech because, even with amplification, their ability to monitor and receive feedback about their own speech is severely limited. With extensive training, however, even these children can learn to communicate orally. However, if your child has other developmental disabilities, such as mental retardation or cerebral palsy, the hearing loss will add to the disability and may make the difference between your child's eventually talking or having to use alternate means of communication.

11 COMMUNICATION DISORDERS

Ken M. Bleile, Ph.D.

Communication may seem simple, but in fact it is probably the most difficult activity a human can perform. Just the physical act of speaking involves the coordinated activity of the brain, chest, stomach, mouth, and lips. Then there is the truly complicated part of communication — having something to say. This requires a host of abilities, from understanding what someone else just said, to organizing what you want to say, to putting words together to make a sentence.

Communication disorders range from relatively mild speech problems in the normal population, such as pronouncing the word *rabbit* as "wabbit," to severe problems with understanding language or expressing oneself in a child with a developmental disability. Many times the neurological damage leading to a physical disability also leads to a communication disorder. For example, children with cerebral palsy, autism, and mental retardation often have communication problems. Other children may have communication problems and be perfectly fine in other areas. In this chapter, we will discuss the various forms of communication disorders that affect disabled children.

JIMMY, LISA, JANE, AND BILLY

Jimmy is three years old and has cerebral palsy. Although he appears to understand everything that is said to him, his speech is slurred. Even Jimmy's mother can't always understand what he is saying.

Lisa is a nine-year-old with learning disabilities, and although her words are clear, her sentences are all jumbled up, making her difficult to understand. Lisa complains that she can't always think of the precise word she wants to use.

Jane is six years old and is mildly mentally retarded. She is functioning at a four-year-old level in all areas except for language. Her speech is difficult to understand because she has trouble with many speech sounds, such as *k*, *s*, and *l*. Jane also seems to have trouble understanding what people are saying to her. Her mother says that Jane uses the same types of sentences her older sister used at age two.

Billy is ten years old and has a severe hearing impairment. Billy's speech is difficult to understand, and he seems to have trouble putting his words together into sentences.

139

These four children illustrate a wide range of communication disorders in children with disabilities. Jimmy, who has cerebral palsy, has difficulty with the physical act of speaking and is therefore said to have a speech disorder. Lisa, who is learning disabled, has no difficulty with speech itself, but has trouble understanding and using language to express herself. In other words, she has a language disorder. Jane, who is mentally retarded, has both speech and language problems that are more severe than her other cognitive deficits. Finally, Billy's hearing impairment has resulted in speech and language difficulties.

Children may have speech disorders or language problems without other associated disabling conditions. However, children with developmental disabilities, especially those with cerebral palsy, mental retardation, and hearing deficits, are at increased risk for having associated communication disorders.

NORMAL DEVELOPMENT OF COMMUNICATION SKILLS

The development of communication normally occurs in the following sequence: babbling at six months, saying a single word at twelve months, developing a five-word vocabulary by eighteen months, speaking in two-word phrases by twenty-four months, and forming complete sentences by three years. By five years of age, the normal child can distinguish verb tenses and relate experiences.

In order for communication skills to develop normally, your child must hear accurately what is said to him, and possess the physical ability to speak and the brain connections to understand what is being said. A deficiency in any of these areas can iso-

late him from normal social and intellectual interactions.

If you suspect a communication disorder in your child, you should have a speech and language pathologist identify if there is a specific deficit and, if present, plan appropriate therapy that will allow your child to develop skills that compensate for his deficiencies.

SPEECH DISORDERS

Speech problems are the most common type of communication disorder in both the normal population and in children with disabilities. There are two factors that combine to make speech deficits likely. First, speech occurs very rapidly. For example, the word *big* contains three speech sounds: b-i-g. Each must be shaped in sequence by the mouth and throat. Even in casual speech, this must be done at a rate of fourteen sounds a second. Second, much more than the mouth and throat is involved in speech production. The parts of the body required for speech are collectively called the speech mechanism and include certain pathways and structures in the brain, various nerves leading from the brain, the voice box, throat, nose, mouth, and tongue (Figure 11.1). A defect anywhere along this pathway will limit effective communication.

Speech disorders that arise from problems of the mouth, nose, throat, and voice box include voice disorders of phonation and resonance, and certain types of articulation disorders.

An extreme example of a voice disorder is the premature infant who has required prolonged placement of a tube down the windpipe to permit ventilation of his immature lungs. Because the tube bypasses the voice box, no speech can occur. Speech

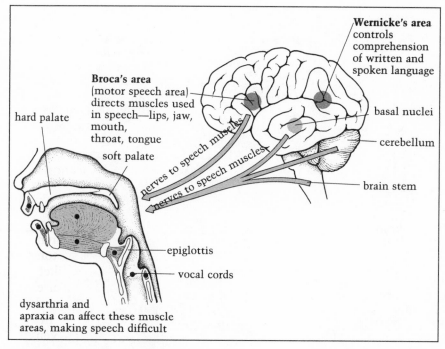

Broca's area
(motor speech area)
directs muscles used
in speech—lips, jaw,
mouth,
throat, tongue

soft palate

hard palate

nerves to speech muscles

nerves to speech muscles

Wernicke's area
controls
comprehension
of written and
spoken language

basal nuclei

cerebellum

brain stem

epiglottis

vocal cords

dysarthria and
apraxia can affect these muscle
areas, making speech difficult

Figure 11.1. *The
mechanism of lan-
guage: The tongue,
hard and soft palates,
and vocal cords are
all essential to pro-
duce speech sounds.
The brain is equally
important to control
the muscles used in
speech (Broca's area)
and to insure that
there is a relationship
between what is
heard and what is
spoken (Wernicke's
area).*

therapy with such children focuses on developing alternative means of communication. Sign language and computers are sometimes used to give these children a means to communicate until the tube can be removed (sometimes at three to four years of age). These children also can be taught to produce some speech by swallowing and then expelling air. The result is a voice that, while sounding somewhat deeper than normal, can with practice be clear and easily understood.

Resonance disorders occur in children who have abnormalities of the oral or nasal tracts, the most common example being cleft palate. Speech therapy for these disorders involves teaching the child to speak without allowing excessive amounts of air to escape through the nose. Figure 11.2 shows how air normally flows during speech. When a child has a cleft palate or other malformation of the structures in the nose and mouth, he may be unable to make certain sounds, such as *b, d,* and *g.* In severe cases, the child may have difficulty making any sounds except *m, n,* and *ng.* In cleft palate, there will be marked improvement in speech following surgical correction. However, speech therapy may still be needed to overcome remaining physical deficits in the oral and nasal tracts, and to extinguish bad speech habits the child might have acquired prior to surgery.

It should be emphasized that your child's speech articulation problem is unlikely to result from a physical abnormality of the mouth or tongue. In fact, one of the surprises about speech is how different even "normal" mouths are from each other. Extreme damage to the mouth or tongue must occur before speech is affected. Unless your child has an obvious physical problem with his mouth, it is

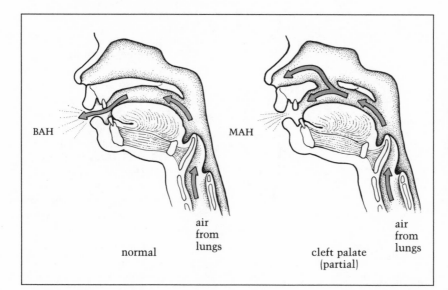

Figure 11.2. *The effect of cleft palate on speech: This illustration shows (a) how air normally flows during speech, and (b) how it flows when a child has a cleft palate. The leakage of air through the open palate makes the child unable to pronounce certain sounds, such as "b," "d," and "g."*

likely that his speech disorder results from problems elsewhere in the speech mechanism.

SPEECH MOTOR DISORDERS

When the mouth, tongue, nose, throat, and voice box are normal, but the brain is unable to control them effectively, a child is said to have a speech motor problem. The most common of these are fluency disorders (stuttering), dysarthria, and apraxia.

Stuttering

The exact cause of stuttering is unknown, but it is thought to result from the brain having difficulty in controlling the timing of speech movements. Stuttering appears to be more prevalent in mentally retarded and learning-disabled children than in the general population. It should be noted that many of the grimaces, contortions, and tics often found in stutterers are the result of attempts to "force out the words" and do not represent neurological impairments.

The best advice I can give you about your child's stuttering is to pay attention to what your child is saying and not to how he says it. You should avoid finishing your child's sentences for him, even during the longest stuttering block. You should also not ask your child to repeat words that he stutters on.

Many times stuttering disappears of its own accord, especially in children during the preschool years. It can also be improved through speech-language therapy. However, there is no known complete cure for stuttering, and you should consider carefully before engaging the services of a person offering a cure.

Dysarthria

Dysarthria, a problem of poor muscle control, arises from damage to the parts of the brain that direct the action of the speech muscles. If your child has dysarthria, he probably has difficulty with speech and other activities that involve coordinated movements of the mouth or throat. For example, your child may have difficulty moving his tongue both when speaking and when eating. The speech of children with dysarthria varies according to where the damage to the neurological system occurs. Some types of dysarthria make speech appear slurred, almost as if the child were drunk. Other forms make speech sound monotone, hoarse, or strangled. This disorder is most commonly found in children with extrapyramidal cerebral palsy (see chapter 9).

Speech therapy for dysarthria consists of helping your child work around his problem, or developing alternative ways to communicate. For example, if your child has a weak diaphragm (as in muscular dystrophy), he may be taught how to sit better to produce a louder voice. If speech therapy is ineffective, alternative means of communication can be considered, including special computers called augmentative communication devices, which can be programmed to help your child communicate (see below).

Speech Apraxia

Apraxia is a disorder affecting voluntary activities such as moving the mouth and throat during speech. Brain damage to an area just behind the forehead, called Broca's area, causes apraxia. Broca's area is thought to be responsible for control of voluntary mouth and tongue movements. A child with apraxic speech may be unable to touch his tongue to his lip if asked to do so; however, he may reflexively use his tongue to wipe a crumb off his lip while eating dinner. This does not reflect stubbornness. Rather, the brain damage limits his ability to perform voluntary but not reflexive activities.

Speech apraxia is often found in children who have suffered severe brain injury such as that resulting from a motor vehicle accident or removal of a brain tumor. Treatment for speech apraxia often involves helping your child learn to gain voluntary control over the muscles that control articulation. In its severest forms, apraxia may leave your child unable to speak intelligibly. In this situation, he may be taught to communicate through the use of computers or other speech aids.

LANGUAGE DISORDERS

Speech is merely the act of producing sounds for the purposes of communication. Language involves having something to say. While language is not the only way we communicate, it is the most important way we understand others and express ourselves. Language is largely acquired during the first three years of life, and is almost completely mastered by ten years of age. Yet, many children with developmental disabilities need a much longer time to acquire language, or language learning may stop short of being completed.

Language disorders are classified by the skills affected. Receptive (comprehension) language disorders are those that involve difficulty understanding or processing what is said. Expressive language disorders are those that involve difficulty expressing oneself.

A comprehension disorder means that your child has trouble understanding what he hears; it does not mean he cannot hear. Similarly, an expressive communication problem does not mean your child cannot make speech sounds; it means that he cannot use language to express himself. Language problems have been divided into disorders of semantics, syntax, pragmatics, and discourse.

Semantic Disorders

A child with a semantic disorder has trouble understanding the "meaning" of language. This problem can involve comprehension (receptive language), expression, or both. For example, if a child has a semantic comprehension disorder he might have trouble learning colors, names of common objects, and adjective pairs such as big/little and up/down. If it is an expressive semantic problem, he has "word-finding" problems. Although everyone has experienced not being able to find the right word, for the child with an expressive semantic problem, this happens so frequently or severely that it interferes with his ability to make his meaning understood.

Children without semantic disorders mostly learn meanings of words during conversation. However, children with semantic disorders may require direct teaching of meaning. For example, your child might be taught the meaning of "house" and "baseball," or the difference between the meanings of "up" and "down." If your child has word-finding problems, he might be taught techniques that can help him find the right word.

Syntactic Disorders

To communicate, we must also understand grammar or syntax. Knowledge of grammar tells us, for example, that the sentence, "Mary was kissed by John" means that "John" is the kisser and "Mary" is the person being kissed. Similarly, we know that the phrase "the boys" refers to more than one boy.

An example of a syntactic comprehension disorder would be a four-year-old child who understands sentences at a two-year-old level. Such a child might not understand that "The cat scratched the dog" occurred in the past, because he does not yet understand that "-ed" means past tense. Your child would be said to have an expressive syntactic problem if he has trouble using sentences to communicate.

Therapy for syntactic disorders focuses on teaching grammar. For example, your child might be taught that "-ed" at the end of "scratch" means that scratching occurred in the past, or that "-s" after "boy" means more than one boy.

Pragmatic Disorders

Communication requires more than understanding word meaning and grammar. We must also know how to use language to interact with others, an aspect of language called pragmatics. This involves not only knowing such terms as *please* and *thank you*, but also knowing how to take turns during a conversation and how to adjust our language depending on the person we are talking to. For example, we use a different manner of speaking at a football game than in a bank.

All children have difficulty using language in social settings now and then. However, a child with a pragmatic disorder has consistent troubles in this area. Such a child has difficulty understanding the rules that govern the use of language in social situations. For example, she might not allow others to speak in a conversation even though she understands that she is not supposed to speak as much as she does. Therapy for pragmatic disorders focuses on teaching the social rules of language. For example, an adolescent retarded child might be taught how to interact with clerks in a grocery store or waiters in a restaurant.

Discourse Disorders

Because people speak more than one sentence at a time, to communicate we must know how to organize sentences into a discourse or conversation. For example, we must know how to organize sentences into stories, recipes, jokes, lectures, and so on. As adults, we take the knowledge of discourse organization for granted, and we forget that learning such organizations can pose significant problems to children, especially those with language handicaps.

As with the other language disabilities, discourse problems can affect both comprehension and expression. An example of a discourse comprehension disorder is a seven-year-old child who has difficulty identifying the basic plot in a simple story. An example of an expressive discourse disorder might be a nine-year-old child who, though he can understand simple stories, is not able to tell such a story himself. Children with learning disabilities often have discourse problems. Therapy would focus on helping your child organize sentences into a whole. For example, she might be helped to figure out the main point of a story, or taught to relate an experience accurately.

EVALUATION OF SPEECH AND LANGUAGE DISORDERS

If your child has a communication problem, a speech and language evaluation is the first step to developing a therapy plan. The person performing the evaluation should be a licensed speech-language pathologist, have a master's degree or a Ph.D., and be certified by the American Speech, Language, Hearing Association (ASHA).

A speech-language evaluation typically begins with a parent interview during which the therapist will ask basic questions about your child's development, medical problems that might affect his speech and language, and the extent of his problem. If you have reports from previous speech-language evaluations, the evaluator may ask to see them. After the interview, the evaluator may ask you to leave the room so she can see how well your child

performs in a therapy or school-like setting. In other cases, especially if your child is very young, you may be asked to stay for the evaluation, which lasts anywhere from one to two hours. If your child is sick, young, or distractible, the evaluation might be given in shorter periods over a number of days.

A complete speech and language evaluation covers all aspects of speech and language development and should also include a hearing screening to determine if a hearing loss is contributing to the communication difficulties. The evaluation involves giving your child a number of tests. Many consist of the evaluator asking your child to point to pictures or move objects. The speech portion of the evaluation typically requires your child to name the objects in pictures aloud and perhaps to tell stories. The evaluator will also want to look in your child's mouth. This may involve using a tongue depressor in order better to see the teeth and the roof or back of the mouth. The evaluation should not be unpleasant for your child.

The speech-language pathologist will determine how your child compares to other children her age and at what age level she is functioning. A percentile score allows the evaluator to compare your child to children her own age. For example, suppose your child is six years old and is given a vocabulary test on which she scores in the twelfth percentile. This means that out of one hundred six-year-old children tested, eleven know fewer and eighty-seven know more vocabulary words.

The age-equivalent score compares your child's development to the expected developmental level of a child her age. For example, in chapter 5 we presented a table showing selected developmental milestones. One milestone indicated that children between two and one-half and three years old typically speak in three- and four-word sentences. If your child is six years old and typically speaks in three- and four-word sentences, then she would receive an age-equivalent score of two and one-half to three years old.

Not all differences between children can be measured quantitatively. For this reason, a number of qualitative tests are also used. Qualitative tests rely on the educated opinion of the evaluator, rather than on numerical scores. Qualitative tests are commonly used to evaluate oral-motor abilities and spontaneous language, especially in the areas of pragmatics and discourse. For example, an evaluator might observe your child during play and say, "Your child has difficulty following the content of a conversation." Such a description does not quantify your child's performance in that it doesn't give you either an age-equivalent score or a percentile ranking. However, qualitative descriptions can provide important insights into your child's communication problems.

After the evaluation, the evaluator should sit down with you to explain what she found and to answer your questions. Many times, the evaluator will also be your child's therapist. However, it is not uncommon to have different people do the evaluation and therapy. This is often the case when you have an evaluation performed by a specialist in a large regional hospital or in an academic setting. Whether or not the evaluator will also be doing the therapy, the report will contain a list of suggested therapy goals.

THERAPY FOR SPEECH AND LANGUAGE DISORDERS

If your child has a communication disorder, he will need speech-language therapy. Not all therapy programs are alike. For this reason, it is important to shop around to find the program that you feel best meets your child's needs. Primarily, you want to be certain that the program is designed for disabled children. Assuming the program meets this requirement, there are a number of factors you should consider. These include: Where will the therapy take place? What type of therapy will my child have? How much therapy will my child receive? What treatment methods are being used? What are the objectives of therapy?

Approaches to Therapy

There are essentially three different approaches to therapy: direct therapy, stimulation, and parent training.

Direct therapy consists of a therapist working with your child, alone or in a group, on some aspect of communication. Until approximately fifteen years ago, drill was the primary technique used in direct therapy. Drill involves the repetition of specific sounds, words, or phrases. However, it was found that many children found drill too boring. Today, drill is only one tool in a battery of therapy techniques. Other therapy techniques can be almost as structured as drill, but are more interesting. For example, a structured therapy technique might be a "game" that requires your child to name objects in pictures. Still others may look more like play than work. These techniques are often used with children too young to do well in more structured activities. For example, the therapist might coax your two-year-old to name objects while playing with a toy garage.

Stimulation is the second approach to therapy. There are two basic types of stimulation programs: speech-language stimulation (also called developmental stimulation) and oral-motor stimulation. Speech-language-stimulation programs typically use play as a tool for encouraging your child to use language appropriately and to learn better communication skills. An example of a developmental program would be a therapist playing peekaboo with a nine-month-old child who has cerebral palsy. Peekaboo teaches the child that communication is enjoyable, that people take turns in conversation, and that speaking is a means of interacting with others. Speech-language stimulation is usually employed with children who are too immature developmentally to engage in more structured therapy activities. It is commonly used in early-intervention programs.

The second form of stimulation is called oral-motor stimulation, which is commonly used with children who have problems with the physical act of speaking. It involves physical stimulation of the mouth, face, and throat as a means of improving your child's oral-motor abilities for later speech. For example, a twenty-two-month-old child with cerebral palsy might receive oral-motor stimulation that consists of feeding and rubbing his cheek with a soft object.

Parent training is the least direct form of therapy. The goal is usually to educate you about your child's disabilities and to teach you specific techniques to assist in your child's development. You should receive both written information and verbal instructions as part of your parent training. For example, a therapist might instruct you in how to teach your baby to make babbling noises, and give you a pamphlet on the importance of babbling to the development of speech. Parent training should be included in all other forms of therapy. At certain times, especially when the child is young or newly diagnosed, parent training may be the most important aspect of therapy.

Therapy Settings

Therapy services are typically offered in one of three locations: a treatment room, a classroom, or at home. There are advantages and disadvantages to each setting.

The treatment room is the most common setting. It is likely to be located in a hospital, a school, or a clinic. The room should be quiet and uncluttered, so your child will not become distracted. While the treatment room may be the ideal location for teaching new skills, it is less ideal when teaching your child to apply previously learned skills to daily activities. When application of the skills becomes important, your child will benefit from therapy in a more natural environment, such as an uncluttered and relatively quiet classroom.

Home therapy is typically provided on a short-term basis as a transition between release from the hospital and enrollment in a community program, or because the child lives too far from any therapy center. The advantage of home therapy is that it provides therapy to children who might not otherwise receive it. As with therapy in other settings, home therapy should be conducted in a relatively quiet and uncluttered location. While parents and siblings may provide the therapist with useful information about the child's performance, they typically are not asked to be present during therapy because they can excite or distract the child. The exception to this rule occurs when the speech-language pathologist is specifically training members of the family in various therapy techniques that have been found to be effective.

Types of Therapy

Therapy can be individual or group. Many children do — and should — receive both types of therapy at the same time. In individual therapy the therapist works one-to-one with your child. This approach is especially useful when she is acquiring a new skill, such as learning to make a difficult speech sound. Individual therapy is less successful in encouraging your child to apply those skills in real-life situations. For example, individual therapy doesn't provide the opportunity to practice a new speech sound when speaking with other children.

Individual therapy typically occurs in a treatment room. Classrooms, if they are quiet enough, can be almost an ideal setting, because your child may later find it easier to apply her skills in conversations with other children. However, if the classroom contains too many distractions, it is likely that she will not receive the benefits of individual attention.

The second type of therapy occurs in groups. Therapy groups typically consist of two to five children. Group therapy can be very useful in helping children learn to apply new skills. Further, in good therapy groups the more advanced students tend to help "pull up" the less advanced students.

Groups work best when they are small and when the children are at similar developmental levels. For children one to three years old, their developmental levels should be within six months of each other; for three- to six-year-olds, within one year of each other; and for six- to eighteen-year-olds, within two years of each other.

Amount of Therapy

The frequency of speech therapy varies from once a week to five times a week. Once a week is appropriate for children with relatively minor communication problems, or for children who are on a plateau. As we discussed in chapter 5, your child's development will proceed with plateaus and peaks. During a plateau the therapist might work with your child once a

week, chiefly to monitor progress and to work to maintain skills. Parents sometimes ask, "Why not increase the amount of therapy in order to help move my child off the plateau?" Therapists typically will increase therapy on a trial basis to see if greater changes can be produced. However, this needs to be done with caution. Especially in children with severe communication problems, progress in speech and language therapy is often set by neurological development. Plateaus generally represent periods when your child is not neurologically ready to advance. Sometimes pushing him beyond what he can do results in frustration and a dislike of therapy. Then, when your child is ready to change, he may be uncooperative because of his history of failures.

Therapy two to three times weekly is appropriate for most children with communication disorders, even those whose problems are severe. Therapy at this level is often sufficient to produce major developmental changes, but is not so frequent that your child becomes bored and uncooperative.

If your child is seen four or five times weekly, he is receiving intensive therapy. Autistic children, for example, may need this level of therapy. Intensive therapy sometimes can produce quick changes in development. However, children typically become weary of this level of treatment over a long period of time.

Occasionally, a therapist will see a child either less than once a week or more than four or five times a week. If your child is seen less than once a week, the therapist is probably not trying to improve your child's communication abilities, but is monitoring your child's development, maintaining skills, and serving as a resource for you. At the other extreme, a therapist may see a child up to twice a day, for four or five times a week. For example, a child might receive that amount of therapy during recovery from neurological surgery or a car accident in order to facilitate return of communication skills.

ALTERNATE MEANS OF COMMUNICATION

There are some instances when speech will not be sufficient to permit adequate communication. This may occur in a child with cerebral palsy, whose speech is unintelligible, a child who has suffered brain damage in a car accident, a deaf child, or a child with a severe developmental communication disorder such as autism. In these instances, oral communication will need to be supplemented with or replaced by other methods of communication. These alternate methods include sign language and augmentative communication.

Sign Language

Sign language is most commonly used by children and adults who are deaf. In most parts of the United States, the language of the deaf is American Sign Language (ASL). ASL is a language, just like English. Children can be taught ASL at a young age. In fact, it has been found that hard-of-hearing children born to deaf parents learn ASL a little quicker than hearing children of hearing parents learn English.

The difficulty with ASL is that it limits the child's ability to communicate with the outside world. Further, unless the child's parents are very proficient in ASL, parent-child communication can be impaired. For this reason, not all hard-of-hearing people or parents of hearing-impaired children favor the use of ASL. Many parents opt instead for a combination of speech and sign language, a program called total communication.

Sign language is also used by children who are not hard of hearing but have relatively long-term or permanent communication difficulties. For these children signing has been found to reduce the frustration of being unable to communicate. For reasons that are not entirely clear, sign language is a particularly effective tool for severely mentally retarded children who have not developed language but who have the physical and intellectual abilities (mental age of eighteen months or higher) needed to attempt signing.

If your child's therapist is advocating the use of sign language, you should ask whether the goal is to use sign as your child's only language or whether it is to use sign language to augment speech. If the goal is to use sign as his language, the therapist should be proficient in ASL. Unfortunately, very few people outside the deaf community are proficient. Instead, many therapists use signs that do not belong to a real language. If your child is not being taught ASL, this means he is not being exposed to a real language. On the other hand, if the goal is to use sign language in conjunction with speech, any number of different sign systems, not just ASL, can be used. If your child is learning sign language, you should learn it as well. Not only does it facilitate better communication, but it also sends your child the message that you accept his problem and that you *want* to communicate with him.

Augmentative Communication

Most children go on to become speakers, but a small number of children have such severe mental or physical disabilities that normal speech proves impossible for them. The majority of such children are mentally retarded or have cerebral palsy. These children may be helped by augmentative communication (AC) — special tools that can substitute for language as a form of communication. For example, a four-year-old child with cerebral palsy may only have 10 percent of her speech intelligible to others. She might find that AC helps her to express herself.

Candidates for AC should have a mental age of at least eighteen months. Children developmentally younger than this age are occasionally taught prerequisite skills to AC, such as how to point to pictures or how to press buttons to operate mechanical toys. However, there is no evidence that these activities help the child go on to become proficient in AC. A therapy program attempting to promote AC for a child developmentally under eighteen months should be considered with caution.

An augmentative communication evaluation generally consists of two parts. First, the evaluator determines your child's mental or language age. Assuming his mental age is eighteen months or above, the evaluation is likely to focus on his physical abilities. In order to assess physical abilities, the evaluator will have your child manipulate switches and buttons similar to those he will need to use on the apparatus. If your child has good arm movement, but poor finger control, the evaluator will attempt to design an AC system that maximizes his ability to use his arms, but does not depend on precise finger movements. In many cases, the speech-language pathologist will seek the help of an occupational therapist to evaluate your child's fine-motor skills.

There are many types of AC devices. The simplest are flat boards upon which are placed squares containing pictures or words. The child points to the square containing the word or picture he wants to indicate. Until recently, such boards were the most commonly used augmentative device. With the advent of the computer,

they are typically used only in temporary situations, such as in a hospital when the child is unable to speak, or when a child's electronic communication board is being repaired.

Electronic, computerized communication boards have many advantages over the older boards. For example, electronic boards can be equipped with a voice synthesizer. The voice will say aloud whatever appears on the screen. Electronic boards also permit much more rapid communication. For example, a board can be programmed so your child need touch only one square to say a long sentence such as "I want to go play at the park." Finally, electronic boards offer greater flexibility. They can be reprogrammed to include new words and sentences as your child's vocabulary, needs, and interests change. This greater flexibility also includes alternate means of controlling the board. Perhaps the most innovative way the board can be accessed is through light. For example, if your child has severe physical limitations, he can use a beam of light attached to his forehead to activate the board.

Electronic communication boards have greatly improved the quality of life of persons with severe communication disorders. However, there are still important limitations to these devices. Although faster than the older boards, they are still a fairly slow way to communicate. The speed of the board will be influenced by the extent of your child's physical limitations, his intellectual abilities, and the number of squares he must touch to make a message. Speed of communication can be a particular hindrance for children of lower intelligence and/or impaired physical skills who have boards that contain a large number of squares. If the communication becomes too slow, options to consider include changing how your child accesses the board or reducing the number of squares on the board. For example, access to the board might be changed from pointing to a light beam, and the number of squares might be reduced from thirty-two to sixteen.

A second problem with electronic AC devices is that they can be expensive. Prices range from several hundred to many thousands of dollars. Fortunately, medical insurance and charitable organizations often can help defray the expenses for augmentative communication. Typically, the speech-language pathologist who evaluates your child will assist you in acquiring the necessary augmentative equipment and information about funding sources.

SOME QUESTIONS ANSWERED

Why does my child's ability to learn new skills seem so variable; good one day and bad the next?

Frequently, parents come to believe their child is lazy because he is variable in his communication ability. For example, it is common to hear frustrated parents complain, "Sometimes he can make the *s* sound just fine. Other times he can't. He's just not trying." However, variability in performance is the hallmark of learning any new skill. Additionally, you may unintentionally be confusing your child by not asking him to perform the same task each time. For example, the first time you ask your child to say "*s*," you may be pointing to a picture of the sun, the second time to a picture of a star, and the third time to a picture of a bus. While these words may seem to be of nearly equivalent difficulty, in reality *s* in the beginning of words ("sun") is typically learned a full year before *s* in consonant clusters ("star") or *s* at the end of words ("bus"). In such a situa-

tion, your child's failure to say "*s*" consistently is due to the varying difficulty in the tasks he is being asked to perform. Subtle but important differences in task complexity are very common in most aspects of speech and language, so be careful.

Will using baby talk with my child slow his communication development?

Actually, baby talk often helps children learn to speak, so long as the baby talk is not so simple that your child finds it boring or silly. Baby talk is good to use because it brings you down to your child's level. In general, you should talk to your child in a way that helps you have enjoyable interactions. This often means using baby talk.

My child is developmentally delayed and does not speak yet. What is the latest age at which he might learn to speak?

The vast majority of children with developmental disabilities go on to speak. The general rule of thumb is that if a child is to speak, he will start to speak words by five years old. However, every professional can cite exceptions to this rule. Further, speech is not all or none. Many more disabled children use speech in conjunction with other means of communication — such as sign language and augmentative systems — than do not speak at all.

Are all children with language disorders mentally retarded?

Most children with language disorders are not mentally retarded. Mental retardation means that both verbal and nonverbal reasoning skills are significantly subnormal. A language disorder is a problem with language but not necessarily with nonverbal reasoning abilities.

12 | AUTISM

Autism is a syndrome, that is to say a group of clinical symptoms that leads to a diagnosis. It has been diagnosed in children suffering from many different conditions ranging from Fragile X syndrome to phenylketonuria. The diagnosis is, in many cases, an educated guess. This will likely remain the case until we can find a "marker" or specific test for autism. The major symptoms of autism are delayed and abnormal language, an inability to relate to people, and stereotyped, repetitive behaviors.

Unfortunately, we do not understand autism much better than did Dr. Leo Kanner when he first described the disorder in 1943. But we do know better what it is not. It is not due to ineffective parenting or other psychosocial issues, as was commonly believed in the 1950s. Nor is it a subcategory of childhood schizophrenia. Rather, autism appears to result from abnormal brain development in which the limbic areas (responsible for mood) and cerebellum may be affected. It is a fairly rare condition, occurring in about one or two out of every 1,000 children, with boys outnumbering girls 4 : 1. Heredity may play a role in the illness. In studies of identical twins, when one twin is autistic, the second twin is also likely to be affected.

JOEL

For the first few months of life Joel appeared normal, but by twelve months of age, his parents noticed that his language skills lagged behind those of other one-year-olds. He could walk and manipulate toys, but he did not utter a word. At two years of age he was still not talking, although he was running around the house and loved to build block towers. He showed little interest in interacting with his parents and shied away from other children. Joel was particularly attached to an empty detergent bottle. He carried it around all day and would scream if it was taken from him. When not engaged in an activity, he often rocked back and forth repeatedly.

As Joel grew older, these features persisted and he seemed more and more abnormal. He required a regimented schedule from dawn to dusk. He had unusual behaviors, like moving the furniture around so that each piece was in a certain position, and spending hours lining up toy cars and

152

pushing them down the stairs. He neither spoke nor used signing to communicate, although he seemed to understand much of what was said to him. At three years of age his parents brought him to a developmental center where he underwent formal psychological testing. These tests revealed an IQ of 65, and a severe language impairment. His language skills were at a twelve-month-old level, while other reasoning skills were at about a two- to two-and-a-half-year-old level. Putting together his history, the behavioral features, and the testing results, the doctors diagnosed Joel as having autism.

DIFFERENTIATING AUTISM FROM MENTAL RETARDATION

It is sometimes very difficult to differentiate autism from mental retardation. The reason is that many children who are severely mentally retarded will also exhibit some autistic behavior. For example, they may have stereotyped behavior and poor language, although they usually interact well with people. What leads to further confusion is that the majority of children with autism also have some degree of mental retardation. However, there are clearly differences between these two disorders, as described below.

CHARACTERISTICS OF THE AUTISTIC CHILD

Although children with mental retardation may have autistic features, infantile autism is quite distinct. The autistic child has problems with social interactions. He will often treat parents and other people like pieces of furniture, making little eye contact, showing no interest in being comforted, and stiffening when held. He will not actively participate in games, but pre-

fers to play alone. He shows little empathy for others.

Autism also involves problems with both verbal and nonverbal communication, which are more severe than deficits in other cognitive areas. Speech generally develops late or, for approximately half of autistic children, not at all. It is rare for an autistic child to speak before two years of age. Autistic children who are not speaking words by five years are unlikely to develop useful speech later in life. If present, speech is often abnormal in volume, pitch, rhythm, or intonation, making it sound singsong or monotonous. The content of speech is also abnormal, often being echolalic (echoing what has just been said) or stereotypic (reciting set phrases). For example, some autistic children repeat commercials over and over while others recite lists, such as train schedules. The autistic child has difficulty starting or sustaining a conversation. His speech may sound flat and he may gesture or use body language infrequently. The autistic child tends not to use language to communicate socially but merely to get things he needs. He rarely engages in imaginative play or shows an interest in storytelling. Not all autistic children have all of these features, but multiple behavioral features should be present before a child is diagnosed as autistic (see Table 12.1).

The behaviors and interests of an autistic child are usually quite limited, stereotypic, and self-stimulatory. For example, he may arrange and rearrange a line of cars or toys for hours on end or form a strong attachment to a specific object, as Joel did with his detergent bottle. The autistic child may carry this object at all times, often sniffing or tasting it. He requires "sameness" and may go into a tantrum if a chair is moved from its accustomed place or his daily routine altered. This translates

TABLE 12.1   Diagnostic Criteria for Autism (from DSM-IIIR, American Psychiatric
Association, 1987)

At least eight of the following sixteen items should be present, these to include at least two items from A, one from B, and one from C.

A. **Qualitative impairment in social interaction as manifested by the following:**

(The examples within parentheses are arranged so that those first mentioned are more likely to apply to younger or more handicapped, and the later ones to older or less handicapped persons with this disorder.)
(1) marked lack of awareness of the existence or feelings of others
(2) no or abnormal seeking of comfort at times of distress (e.g., does not come for comfort even when ill, hurt, or tired; seeks comfort in a stereotyped way, e.g., says "Cheese, cheese, cheese" whenever hurt)
(3) no or impaired imitation (e.g., does not wave bye-bye; does not copy mother's domestic activities; mechanical imitation of others' actions out of context)
(4) no or abnormal social play (e.g., does not actively participate in simple games; prefers solitary play activities; involves other children in play only as "mechanical aids")
(5) gross impairment in ability to make peer friendships (e.g., no interest in making peer friendships; despite interest in making friends, demonstrates lack of understanding of conventions of social interaction, for example, reads phonebook to uninterested peer)

B. **Qualitative impairment in verbal and nonverbal communication, and in imaginative activity, as manifested by the following:**
(1) no mode of communication, such as communicative babbling, facial expression, gesture, mime, or spoken language
(2) markedly abnormal nonverbal communication, as in the use of eye-to-eye gaze, facial expression, body posture, or gestures to initiate or modulate social interaction (e.g., does not anticipate being held, stiffens when held, does not look at the person or smile when making a social approach, does not greet parents or visitors, has a fixed stare in social situations)
(3) absence of imaginative activity, such as play-acting of adult roles, fantasy characters, or animals; lack of interest in stories about imaginary events
(4) marked abnormalities in the production of speech, including volume, pitch, stress, rate, rhythm, and intonation (e.g., monotonous tone, question-like melody, or high pitch)
(5) marked abnormalities in the form or content of speech, including stereotyped and repetitive use of speech (e.g., immediate echolalia or mechanical repetition of television commercial); use of "you" when "I" is meant (e.g., using "You want cookie" to mean "I want a cookie"); idiosyncratic use of words or phrases (e.g., "Go on green riding" to mean "I want to go on the swing"); or frequent irrelevant remarks (e.g., starts talking about train schedules during a conversation about sports)
(6) marked impairment in the ability to initiate or sustain a conversation with others, despite adequate speech (e.g., indulging in lengthy monologues on one subject regardless of interjections from others)

C. **Markedly restricted repertoire of activities and interests, as manifested by the following:**
(1) stereotyped body movements, e.g., hand-flicking or hand-twisting, spinning, head-banging, complex whole-body movements
(2) persistent preoccupation with parts of objects (e.g., sniffing or smelling objects, repetitive feeling of texture of materials, spinning wheels of toy cars) or attachment to unusual objects (e.g., insists on carrying around a piece of string)
(3) marked distress over changes in trivial aspects of environment, e.g., when a vase is moved from usual position
(4) unreasonable insistence on following routines in precise detail, e.g., insisting that exactly the same route always be followed when shopping
(5) markedly restricted range of interests and a preoccupation with one narrow interest, e.g., interested only in lining up objects, in amassing facts about meteorology, or in pretending to be a fantasy character

into an unwillingness to try new things or see new people or places. These children are inflexible and often have temper tantrums when change is forced.

Stereotypic behaviors may include unusual body movements such as hand clapping or hand washing, spinning, swaying, staring at lights, or head banging. The child may also be preoccupied with smells or sounds, which leads him to spend much time going around sniffing objects or making strange noises.

THE DEVELOPMENT OF THE AUTISTIC CHILD

As noted above, the most obvious abnormality in development involves language. Although cooing may develop normally at three months and babbling at six months, speech often does not progress beyond this point. In fact, the child may stop babbling before twelve months of age and remain silent thereafter. A child with autism will also be less likely to use signing or other gestures to indicate his needs. If language does develop, it is usually deviant. Words are taken literally so that jokes and metaphors are not understood, even when the child is older. He may also reverse pronouns, saying, for example, "You want this" when he means "I want this."

An autistic child may have exceptional "splinter skills" that make him seem brighter than he is. Such a child has been referred to as an idiot savant. For example, a child may have a prodigious memory, which allows him to memorize pages of the phone directory, or be able to add numbers as fast as a calculator. He may also be able to remember complicated travel directions or put together complex puzzles. Unfortunately these rote skills have little practical application and simply add to the bizarre behavior pattern.

Formal IQ testing of autistic children (described below) reveals a spectrum of capacities. About 70 percent of autistic children have IQ scores that fall in the mentally retarded range (35 percent mildly retarded, 15 percent moderately retarded, 20 percent severely-profoundly retarded). Twenty-five percent have IQ scores in the 70–100 range. Only about 5 percent have IQ scores above 100. While speech and reasoning abilities are delayed, motor skills are less affected, although the child may be somewhat awkward.

ASSOCIATED NEUROLOGIC DEFICITS

Autistic children are more likely than normal children to have certain neurologic problems, including hyperactivity, abnormalities in muscle tone, and seizures. Although they tend to be overactive, inattentive, and distractible, autistic children are not likely to respond to stimulant medications, such as Ritalin. In fact, stimulants are generally avoided as they may increase the stereotypic behavior. Muscle tone may be either increased or decreased. These changes in tone are far less severe than those found in cerebral palsy and rarely interfere with walking.

Autistic children may also suffer from seizures. Brain wave tests (EEGs) are abnormal in about 80 percent of autistic children, and about 25 percent have seizures beginning by adolescence. The seizures are usually grand mal or psychomotor in type and generally respond to anticonvulsant medications (see chapter 8). Among anticonvulsants, phenobarbital should be avoided if possible as it may worsen hyperactivity or lead to mood alterations.

HOW TO KNOW IF YOUR CHILD IS AUTISTIC

Children who are severely mentally retarded may act deaf, spin, rock, or bang their heads. Such a child might appropriately be said to have "autistic features." However, the autistic child will have a prominent language delay, while the mentally retarded child tends to be delayed similarly in both verbal and nonverbal intellectual areas. Also, mentally retarded children enjoy interactions with their parents and show affection and the need for social contact; autistic children lack interest in social contact.

Certain psychiatric conditions can also imitate autism. For example, schizophrenia is marked by delusions (such as believing oneself immortal), hallucinations (hearing voices or seeing things that do not exist), and thought disorders that may mimic the bizarre behaviors of autism. However, the autistic child does not have delusions or hallucinations. Also, schizophrenia develops in later childhood in a child with normal intelligence, whereas autism becomes evident before three years of age in a child who shows developmental delays.

CONDITIONS ASSOCIATED WITH AUTISM

The most common condition associated with autism is Fragile X syndrome (see chapter 7). Boys affected with this disorder are mentally retarded and many of them are autistic. Prior to the development of effective treatment for phenylketonuria in the 1960s (see chapter 16), these children often exhibited the syndrome of autism. There also seems to be a predisposition for autism in children who have suffered birth injury and in those who have a family history of autism. However, in most children with infantile autism, the cause remains unknown.

MEDICAL TESTING FOR AUTISM

There is no specific medical test for autism. Therefore, the specific diagnosis is based on parent and professional observation of a series of abnormal behavioral patterns, social interactions, and language deficits that have been defined in the *Diagnostic and Statistical Manual of Mental Disorders* (DSM-IIIR) (see Table 12.1). Eight features need to be present to make this diagnosis.

Blood tests and brain wave tests may be abnormal but are nonspecific. In experimental studies, brain imaging tests have detected certain abnormalities in the cerebellar region of the autistic child's brain, but it is not clear whether these changes are significant, and they have no therapeutic implications at present. Your doctor may order a number of tests in order to detect certain specific causes of autism. For example, he may obtain chromosome studies to determine if your child has Fragile X syndrome, or metabolic studies to diagnose an inborn error of metabolism. He may obtain an EEG, especially if your child appears to be having seizures, or a brain imaging study to look for specific areas of brain damage. He will also arrange for vision and hearing testing, as sensory deficits may lead to some autistic behaviors.

PSYCHOLOGICAL TESTING

IQ tests also do not give definitive diagnostic information. The commonly used psychological tests — the Bayley, Wechsler Scale of Intelligence for Children–Revised (WISC-R), and Stanford-Binet (see chapter 6) — can be administered to autistic children. These tests help to identify an autistic child's strengths and weaknesses and to design an appropriate educational program. However, they do not reveal whether a child is, in fact, autistic. If language is severely impaired, your child may be given only the nonverbal parts of these tests, or he may be given cognitive tests that are designed for deaf children and do not depend on language, such as the Leiter scale. Modifying psychological testing in this manner permits a fairly good assessment of your child's intellectual function.

TREATMENT

There is no specific medical treatment for autism. As a result, you may be tempted to try nonconventional therapies such as special diets, vitamin supplements, or allergy treatments, to name a few current fads. There is no evidence that these approaches are helpful. They may simply distract you from getting appropriate educational and behavioral help. At worst they may be medically harmful to your child.

The most appropriate approach to treatment is multifaceted, involving education, speech and language therapy, behavior-modification techniques, and possibly medication. Where should you go for this therapy? You would think this is an easy question to answer, but it is complicated by the fact that autism was first thought of as a psychiatric illness and only recently has entered the domain of neurology and child development. Therefore, you may find a child psychiatrist, child neurologist, or developmental pediatrician who has the appropriate expertise to treat your child medically. Whichever specialist you choose, find one who has a specific interest in and experience with autistic children. As this is a rare disorder, there may not be more than one or two physicians in any given city who can claim expertise. There

are a number of multidisciplinary autism clinics in university settings.

Educational Programs

The educational program should be directed at your child's intellectual level and delivered in a structured environment. If your child has normal or near-normal intelligence, he should be taught at his chronological age level, although he will probably need special help in social and language areas. If he is mentally retarded, he should be placed in a class with similarly functioning children. The class size should be kept small, around four to eight students.

Autistic children need educational environments in which activities are kept interesting and varied, and in which tasks are broken down into simple subunits, with each task taking less than thirty minutes to accomplish. This programmatic planning should hold your child's interest and decrease stereotypic behavior. One-to-one interactions with teachers and fellow students should be encouraged. In addition, you should develop a close working relationship with your child's teachers, so that what is learned in school can be practiced at home. As with other developmental disabilities, your child's educational experience should start in a pre-school early-intervention program that stresses communication skills and social interactions.

Social Skills Training

No matter what your child's level of intelligence, he will need social skills training. This involves learning how to act in social situations, how to interact with people, and how to develop relationships. This generally begins with teaching your child to maintain eye contact, something seldom done by autistic children. It is followed by play-acting situations involving social contact. Here your child is placed in a particular social situation and taught appropriate verbal and nonverbal interactions.

Speech and Language Therapy

Because language is significantly impaired, speech and language therapy is extremely important. Communication is kept short and simple. Conversations are interactive and meaningful, and echolalia is discouraged. Alternative means of communication may be taught if speech is not present or is severely restricted. Communication can often best be taught in a self-contained communications-disorder class (see chapter 11).

Behavior Modification

Behavior modification techniques have been used successfully with autistic children to decrease stereotypic behaviors. They will also be helpful in decreasing temper tantrums. This will make your child more socially acceptable and may move him away from compulsive behaviors that interfere with his ability to learn new skills. These techniques are discussed in detail in chapter 15. Although behavior modification is helpful, psychotherapy is of little value for these children, who have limited communication skills.

Medication

Many medications have been used with varying success to control hyperactive and bizarre behaviors in children with autism (see chapter 19). Antipsychotic medications such as haloperidol (Haldol) and thioridazine (Mellaril) were commonly used in years past, but have fallen out of favor because of ineffectiveness combined with potentially severe side effects, including liver toxicity and the development of abnormal movements. More recently, antidepressants have been tried with some success. These medications include imipramine (Tofranil), lithium, desipramine (Norpramin), and fluoxetine (Prozac). Antianxiety drugs such as buspirone (Buspar) and propranolol (Inderal) have also been used, especially for children who exhibit a lot of anxious behavior. The anticonvulsants carbamazepine (Tegretol) and phenytoin (Dilantin) have been used to treat episodic behavioral outbursts, especially those that might be stereotypic and consistent with a seizure disorder. Finally, fenfluramine (Pondimin), originally used as a weight-control drug, has been put forward as an aid for autistic children. Unfortunately, the trials of fenfluramine have not proven very successful and it has significant side effects, including irritability, lethargy, and decreased appetite. In sum, medications are likely to yield at most only modest benefits. If your child tries a medication, it will generally be stopped if it proves ineffective during the first months of treatment.

THE ROLE OF THE FAMILY

What is learned in school must be practiced at home in order to be retained. Therefore you must act as co-therapists to your autistic child. You will need to use the same teaching and behavior-modification techniques at home as in school. An example would be mealtime interactions. Your child should be taught to sit at the table with the family, wait his turn for the food, and, if possible, carry on a conversation. During the summer, he should be enrolled in a camp that specializes in special-needs children. He can then learn to interact with children in sports and other extracurricular activities.

COPING WITH AN AUTISTIC CHILD

Your autistic child will place many emotional demands on your family. The first problem is accepting the diagnosis. An autistic child looks normal; he does not have the abnormal facial appearance of Down syndrome or the physical abnormalities of cerebral palsy. Further, he develops quite normally in early infancy. For these reasons, and because of the lack of a specific diagnostic test, it may be difficult for you to accept that your child has infantile autism.

Second, this child may give you less pleasure than your other children because of the lack of social interactions. He may not show you a great deal of affection or attachment. He, in fact, may not treat you differently from other adults. This is very difficult to take emotionally. However, you must believe that although your child has difficulty acknowledging or demonstrating affection, he does love and need you.

Third, you may find his bizarre behaviors embarrassing in social or community settings. His behaviors in the playground or school may also create problems for his siblings. Hopefully, the use of behavior-modification techniques will improve this.

Fourth, his diminished communication abilities may make it difficult for you to understand his needs, leading to frustration on both his and your part. This may be accentuated by physical hyperactivity and inattentiveness.

How will your family cope with all these problems? Most of the general mechanisms for families coping with a developmentally disabled child apply to your autistic child (see chapter 1). You will need to find a team of professionals that you trust to provide care for your child. Behavior-modification techniques may al-

ter some of his unusual behaviors, and speech and language therapy will result in improved communication skills. Social as well as academic skills will be worked on in the school placement. Joining a parent group may be particularly helpful so you can share your troubles and successes with others who have faced similar problems.

You should also take advantage of respite care opportunities to go out with your spouse or take vacations with other family members. You will need a rest from this very demanding and difficult child. In terms of the day-to-day care of your child, try to involve your whole family. Your other children could share some responsibility appropriate to their ages and abilities.

FUNCTIONING OF THE AUTISTIC CHILD AS HE/SHE GROWS UP

Autistic features generally improve as your child grows up and the stereotypic behavior decreases. In adolescence, your child's level of functioning will principally depend on his intelligence and speech skills. The autistic child with moderate to severe mental retardation (IQ less than 54) will function in a manner similar to other significantly retarded children, although with poorer language skills, possibly better problem-solving abilities, and a lack of interest in people.

The autistic child whose intelligence falls in the mildly retarded range (IQ 55–69) will interact with his peers, but in a "programmed" fashion. Typically, these children will answer questions asked them but have little spontaneous conversation. Or, the child may have a ritualistic series of questions and comments he uses when he first meets someone. For example, he may say, "How old are you? Are you married? It's a nice day today." Following this monologue, and not waiting for answers, he may turn around and leave, his social duties completed. Close relationships with people are unlikely to develop.

Children with borderline normal intelligence (IQ 70–100) are more likely to be mainstreamed in school, a situation with both positive and negative consequences. In a regular school, your child will have more opportunities to participate in normal interactions with nonautistic children, and thus may develop better social skills. However, his behaviors will stick out more prominently in a regular class, which may lead to him being ridiculed by his schoolmates. He may become a fanatic collector of anything from stamps to baseball cards to toy cars, and become incredibly knowledgeable about facts concerning his collections.

The autistic child with average to above-average intelligence will function still more effectively. He will participate more fully in conversations, although his answers to questions may tend to be concrete rather than abstract. If he is lucky, his encyclopedic knowledge of certain subjects will gain him some special status. However, he will remain a loner, undisturbed by his isolation.

In sum, as with many other handicaps, your autistic child's future is best predicted by his intelligence and communication skills. The brighter child with better language skills will appear more "normal," although his underlying problems with communication and social interactions will continue to identify him as being different. This difference will remain throughout life. As a result, autistic individuals, even those with average intelligence, are unlikely to marry. They also tend to choose jobs that are well ordered and repetitive. The majority of autistic individuals live at home or in group home situations.

SOME QUESTIONS ANSWERED

If my child is autistic, what are my chances of having a second affected child?

This is difficult to predict because there appear to be many disorders that lead to the syndrome of autism. Overall, if you have had one autistic child, you have a 2 to 3 percent risk of having a second affected child. However, if your child's autism is genetically based, the risk may be higher. For example, if your son has Fragile X syndrome, there is a 50 percent risk for subsequent boys to be affected. Prenatal diagnosis is available for this disorder, so you should seek genetic counseling.

What does the term pervasive developmental disorder mean?

The term *pervasive developmental disorder* (PDD) is sometimes used interchangeably with autism. However, PPD is actually a broader term that refers to autism and other autistic-like behaviors including hyperlexia and Asperger's syndrome.

13 VISION AND ITS DISORDERS

Mark L. Batshaw, M.D., and David B. Schaffer, M.D.

Vision is the baby's window on life outside the womb. Even before she can physically move about, understand language, or recognize her parents, she experiences the world through sight. While still in the delivery room, a newborn baby already has color vision and can see her mother's face, although her eyesight is still immature and she does not yet see things clearly. She "bonds" to her mother through both physical touch and vision during the first days after birth. The shape of the human face most attracts her, and bright colors catch her fancy. By one month of age she can fix her gaze on her mother and follow her with her eyes. By two months, she will follow a mobile as it rotates near her head and smile at the facial antics of her parents. At three months, she will turn from one face to another, differentiating mother from father and her parents from strangers. By four months of age, a normal child should be able to perceive depth and discriminate between near and far.

Hence, although vision is present at birth, it is not mature. Visual acuity is only about 20/400. At six months, vision has improved to 20/40 and sometime between twelve and twenty-four months vi-

sion should reach the adult level of 20/20. Binocular vision begins around four months and is well developed by six months, permitting the child to have depth perception and three-dimensional vision. The baby will also accommodate better to changes in lighting.

Not only does vision permit the child to focus on the world about her, but it is integral to the development of her other abilities. For example, learning to move normally depends on seeing how others move. Blind children learn to walk later than normal. Likewise, the development of speech involves imitation of mouth movements, meaning that in the blind child language may also be delayed. Thus, vision disorders, even if not associated with other disabilities, can interfere with normal development.

In addition, a substantial proportion of children with handicaps will have visual difficulties as part of their disability. In general, the more severe the disability, the more likely are vision problems to be present. Thus, vision should be tested early in all disabled children and efforts at correction made at a young age. A few case histories are discussed below to illustrate

161

the spectrum of visual deficits that may occur in children with developmental disabilities.

CARL, ROBIN, AND JONATHAN

Carl has spastic cerebral palsy. At six months of age his parents noted that his eyes crossed. When the left eye looked at an object, the right eye tended to drift inward. Carl's pediatrician referred them to an ophthalmologist who diagnosed him as having esotropia, which means an inward crossing of the eye. He advised Carl's parents that the eye muscles should be surgically repaired before two years of age in order to maximize Carl's likelihood of developing binocular vision.

Robin was born three months prematurely. Because of the risk of vision impairment as a complication of prematurity, an ophthalmologist examined Robin's eyes before she was released from the nursery. He found that new blood vessels were growing abnormally into the jelly-like interior part of the eye, an early sign of retinopathy of prematurity, eye damage that is commonly associated with prematurity. Using cryosurgery, the doctor was able to halt the damage and spare Robin's vision. However, she is very nearsighted and has needed to wear glasses since she was two years old.

Jonathan, aged four years, was born severely mentally retarded. He has cortical blindness, in which the damage is to the brain rather than to the eyes themselves. Although Jonathan's eyes appear to be normal, his brain does not process the images sent to it. During infancy his eyes moved about randomly, without focusing on objects. He seemed to be completely blind. However, as he grew older, his parents noted that Jonathan was turning toward lights. By three years he could reach toward objects held in front of him. His vision may continue to improve, although the ultimate level of recovery remains unclear.

Carl, Robin, and Jonathan illustrate the range of vision problems that can occur in young children. Some are associated with other developmental disabilities, as in the case of cerebral palsy in Carl and mental retardation in Jonathan. At other times, as with the premature infant Robin, the visual impairment may be the child's only significant problem. And in some instances, as with Jonathan, the condition may improve over time. In this chapter we will describe the normal function of the visual system, the various problems that can cause visual impairment, and the related difficulties that arise in visually impaired children. We also discuss methods of treating and living with vision deficits.

EYES AND THEIR FUNCTION

Your eye works much like a camera. The lens of the eye brings an image into focus on the retina, the "photographic film" at the rear of the eye. The retina captures the image, which is then transported in the form of electrical signals to the brain. The brain integrates this visual information with sounds and memories, leading to perception. A defect anywhere along this pathway will interfere with vision.

The eyeball itself is a globe (Figure 13.1). On the front of the eyeball, we can see a central opening, called the pupil, which appears black. Surrounding the pupil is the colored part of the eye (usually brown or blue), called the iris. Like the shutter on a camera, the iris opens and closes in response to light, opening wide (dilating) so that the pupil looks large in dim light and closing to a pinpoint in

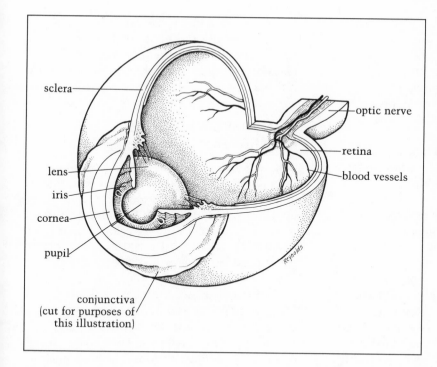

Figure 13.1. *The eye: The front of the eye consists of a central aperture (the pupil), a surrounding colored area (the iris), and a clear covering window (the cornea). At the back of the globe lies the film-like retina, blood vessels supplying the eye, and the optic nerve carrying visual impulses to the brain.*

bright sunshine. In front of the iris is a protective, clear window called the cornea. Behind the iris is the lens. Light rays hit the cornea first and are refracted, or bent, by the cornea and lens on their way to a focal point on the retina. Between the lens and the retina, the eyeball is filled with a jelly-like substance called the vitreous humor. Different cells on the retina, called rods and cones, interpret light, dark, color, and shape; and send the information via the optic nerve to the brain.

CONDITIONS REQUIRING GLASSES

Because the cornea and lens are responsible for bringing the image into focus on the retina, a defect in either — or an eyeball that is too short or too long — can cause difficulties with focusing. These focusing problems are called refractive errors. The most common refractive errors in children are farsightedness, nearsightedness, and astigmatism.

The reasons for farsightedness and nearsightedness are as follows: If the cornea or the lens (see below) bends light rays too much, or if the eye is too long, the point at which the light rays converge, the focal point, will occur in front of the retina. This is known as nearsightedness, and will cause blurred vision. Conversely, if the cornea or lens is too flat and does not bend the light sufficiently, or if the globe is too short, the focal point will occur behind the retina, and the person will be farsighted. Farsightedness can lead to crossed eyes.

Astigmatism results when the cornea is improperly shaped. For example, if the cornea is more cylindrical, like a football, rather than spherical, like a basketball, the angle of refraction will be different at various points along the cornea. As a result, a point of light comes to focus as a streak of light, resulting in a blurred image (Figure 13.2).

All these conditions are readily corrected by glasses or contact lenses. In the case of nearsightedness, a concave (inwardly curved) lens is used to counteract the excessive bending of light waves. In farsightedness, a convex (outwardly curved) lens is used to increase the bending of light waves. For astigmatism, a cylindrical lens is used with different angles of bending, compensating for the irregular cornea (Figure 13.2). It is generally a good idea to have a spare set of glasses, as they tend to get lost or broken with distressing regularity by young children.

Contact lenses generally work as well as glasses, although preteenagers often are unable to wear and care for them. Soft lenses are the most commonly used type of contact lens except in the case of astigmatism, which is treated with gas-permeable "hard" lenses. The lenses should not be worn overnight and good hygiene is essential. In an otherwise healthy eye, either glasses or contacts should correct vision to normal.

DISORDERS OF THE LENS: CATARACTS

The lens is a globular body placed about one-quarter of the way between the cornea and retina. It is stretched or relaxed by the attached ciliary muscles, becoming thinner or thicker, to accommodate looking at near or far objects. In older people, it becomes more rigid and less adjustable, often leading to the need for bifocals.

The major disorder associated with the lens is the formation of cataracts. Although a disease primarily of older adults, it can on rare occasions occur before birth or in early childhood, most often as part of

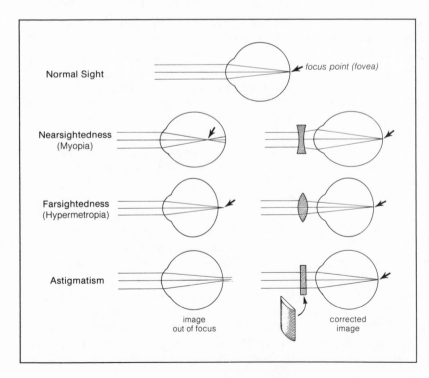

Figure 13.2. *The lenses in glasses are curved to correct for the refractive error. Here are shown lenses for nearsightedness, farsightedness, and astigmatism.*

a disabling condition. Cataract refers to any defect in the clarity of the lens. The cataract can be any shape and usually appears white in direct light. If large enough, it can be detected by the naked eye; smaller cataracts are detected during the ophthalmologic exam. Small cataracts often remain stable and do not need to be removed. However, if a cataract is large, it will significantly obscure vision. The lens itself will then need to be removed. A large cataract left alone can cause irreversible loss of vision through disuse of the affected eye. Cataract removal is done using an operating microscope and a suction tube through which the contents of the lens are aspirated. This is a fairly straightforward operation. The principal consequence of removing the lens is the need to wear thick glasses or contacts to compensate for the loss of the lens's refractive power.

DISORDERS OF THE RETINA: RETINOPATHY OF PREMATURITY

Behind the lens, the gelatin-like vitreous humor maintains the shape of the eyeball and conducts the light waves to the retina.

Blindness most commonly results from damage to the retina. In a premature infant, damage to the retina can occur as a side effect of treatment with a mechanical ventilator and oxygen used to save the baby's life (Figure 13.3). In this disorder, called retinopathy of prematurity, or ROP, blood vessels in the retina may begin to proliferate and invade the vitreous. Eventually they stop growing, leaving a fibrous scar that contracts and, in the most severe cases, pulls the retina away from the back of the eye. If enough retina is pulled away, the child will suffer blindness in that eye. As this process is likely to involve both eyes, affected premature infants may become permanently blind.

To try to avoid blindness from retinopathy of prematurity, ophthalmologists routinely check the retinas of premature infants while they are still in the nursery. The abnormal blood vessel growth can then be detected early and corrected with cryosurgery, which freezes and destroys the damaged part of the retina and the overgrowing new vessels. This is done before

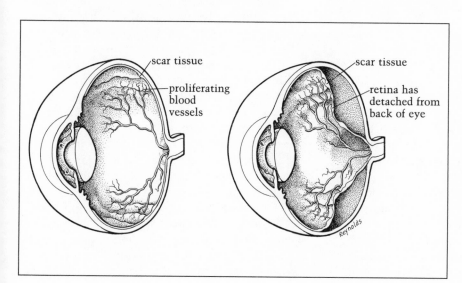

Figure 13.3. *In retinopathy of prematurity, blood vessels in the retina proliferate. Eventually they stop growing, leaving a fibrous scar that contracts and, in the most severe cases, pulls the retina away from the back of the eye.*

the vessels contract and cause the retina to detach. Although not always effective, this approach has resulted in a marked reduction in blindness in premature infants.

CONES AND RODS: COLOR BLINDNESS AND NIGHT VISION

The retina itself is a rather complex structure. It has two types of light-sensitive nerve cells, the rods and cones. Rods are plentiful on the edges of the retina and are involved in night vision. Cones are prominent in the central, or focal, point of the retina and are used for reading, seeing distant objects, and for color vision. There are three subtypes of cones for the colors blue, green, and red. By combining the signals of these different cones, the eye can see all the colors of the rainbow. The most common defect of the cones involves color-blindness, a sex-linked trait that primarily affects boys. Simple color-blindness does not cause a decrease in vision and is not associated with educational handicaps. However, it will prevent the person from discriminating certain colors, red from green being the most common defect. Damage to the rods, associated with vitamin A deficiency and other causes, results in poor vision after dusk.

EYE MUSCLE PROBLEMS: STRABISMUS

The brain not only receives visual information from the eyes but also sends back signals that control the movement of the eyes. This permits us to look toward an object, focus on it, and then follow it as it moves. Six small muscles that surround each eye coordinate these movements. However, if the brain cannot accurately control these muscles, the eyes will not move in synchrony and strabismus will result. Strabismus refers both to "crossed

eyes," in which the eyes turn inward, and "wall eyes," in which they turn outward. These are common problems for children with cerebral palsy and are not uncommon for otherwise normal children.

When the two eyes are not working in concert, the brain receives confusing images, which results in "double vision." If this persists, the brain corrects for the double vision by simply ignoring the weaker visual image transmitted by the nonpreferred eye. This eventually results in a permanent impairment of vision in the nonused eye. An eye which has lost vision from this type of disuse is referred to as a "lazy," or amblyopic, eye. Therefore, treatment needs to be instituted as soon as strabismus appears.

Treatment of strabismus may involve patching, glasses, or surgery, depending on the cause and severity of the disorder. Although eye exercises have been proposed by some eye-care specialists, there is little evidence that they are helpful in most types of strabismus.

Patching is used to prevent loss of vision due to disuse of the nonpreferred eye. An adhesive-backed gauze pad is placed over the good eye for part or all of each day, forcing your child to use and strengthen the weaker eye. Patching is not easily accomplished in young children, as they do not like having their good eye covered. However, it is most effective if done before a loss of vision occurs. Behavior-modification techniques may be needed to get your child to comply. Elbow cuffs (plastic splints preventing movement around the elbow) can also be used to prevent him from tearing the patch off.

Glasses are used to improve visual acuity and to straighten some types of crossed eyes. Surgery is needed when patching and glasses do not work and should be performed early, preferably before two years of age, if the strabismus continues to be present.

PINK EYE OR CONJUNCTIVITIS

In addition to these chronic conditions, your child may have certain acute problems affecting the eye. The most common of these are conjunctivitis and traumatic injury. Conjunctivitis, or "pink eye," may result from chemical irritation, allergy, or infection. It involves inflammation of the small blood vessels that run through the surface membrane (conjunctiva) that covers the white of the eye. If this is caused by irritation or allergy, eye drops or antihistamines may be helpful. If it is due to an infection, an ointment containing an antibiotic should be applied to the lower eyelid. This infectious type of conjunctivitis commonly accompanies a bout of middle ear infection and is quite contagious, spreading easily from one eye to the other. With proper treatment, the infection should clear up in a few days.

Conjunctivitis can also result from chemical injury. If your child's eyes are irritated by chemicals or fumes, immediately flush the eye with water. You may need two people to do this; one to hold your child on his back with his eyelids stretched open and the second to flood the eye with water. About a cup of water in each eye is usually sufficient.

Rarely, the conjunctivitis may be a sign of increased pressure inside the eye, a condition called glaucoma. Like cataracts, glaucoma is usually a disease of senior citizens. But it can occur in children, especially following eye trauma, and is detected by measuring the pressure inside the eye by using a special instrument. If a pink eye persists, have your child examined by an eye doctor as the increased pres-

sure can damage the blood vessels in the retina, leading to blindness.

EYE TRAUMA

Trauma to the eye is quite common in children. It most often involves something getting stuck under the eyelid or having an object scratch the surface of the cornea. Small objects can usually be removed from the eye through the combined action of tears and by sliding the upper lid of the eye over the lower lid repeatedly, as if you were pulling down blinds. A Q-tip can also be used to carefully remove small objects.

If your child complains that he has been hit in the eye and has pain that persists for a few hours, he should be seen in an emergency room. Here the doctors can determine if there has been a corneal abrasion, a hemorrhage, or more serious damage. The doctor will apply a drop of dye onto the cornea that will allow him to see any scratches that are present. If one is found, eye drops containing a muscle relaxant are applied to dilate the pupil, and an antibiotic solution is applied. Frequently a patch is also needed. This treatment takes away the discomfort and rests the eye. The injury is usually not serious and the cornea, a derivative of skin, can repair itself readily.

Pain and fuzzy vision can, on rare occasions, be caused by bleeding from the blood vessels in the iris leading to a collection of blood in the chamber of the eye just behind the cornea. Your doctor can see the bleeding through a microscope. This type of injury usually requires patching and probably hospitalization or bed rest with daily checkups. As with other types of bruises, the blood is reabsorbed and there should be no long-term consequences unless glaucoma has occurred.

Eye injuries rarely cause a retinal detachment severe enough to result in blindness in the affected eye. However, retinal swelling and hemorrhaging are not infrequent. They too improve spontaneously if the eye is rested over a few days.

VISION TESTS

The average child receives his first vision test during a well-child checkup or in school at around five to six years of age. The most commonly used test is the Snellen eye chart, with its rows of progressively smaller letters (Figure 13.4). With one eye covered, the child is asked to read the letters until they become too small to distinguish. Normal vision is also called 20/20 vision, which means that a child can read, from twenty feet away, the letters that a population of normally sighted individuals can also see at twenty feet. On the eye chart, this is the bottom row and the

smallest letters. Vision of 20/200 indicates that the smallest letter the child can read from twenty feet away is the size that a person with normal vision can read from as far away as two hundred feet. On the eye chart, this is represented by the large E at the top.

For this test to be accurate, the child needs to know his alphabet and to be able to pay attention. Thus, it is difficult to use this eye chart for a child with a mental age below five years. Another chart, called the tumbling E chart, can be used for children three to five years old (Figure 13.4). On this chart, as on the Snellen chart, each row of figures gets progressively smaller. However, instead of different letters, all the figures are Es, placed in different orientations — upside down, backward, pointing up, and pointing down. The child is asked to point with his hand in the direction the E is facing.

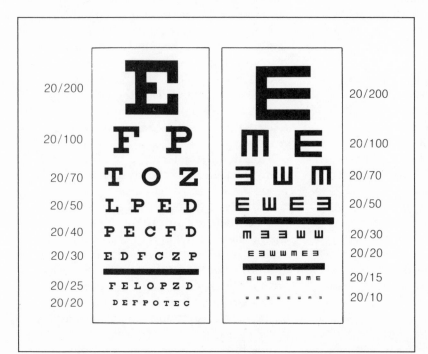

Figure 13.4. *Eye charts: The Snellen eye chart is shown to the left and the tumbling "E" chart for young children on the right. On the Snellen chart, the largest letter can be seen by a person with at least 20/200 vision, the smallest by a person with 20/20 vision.*

Another approach is used to test vision in children aged six months to three years. The "preferential looking test" is based on the observation that infants prefer to look at patterned rather than plain objects. To conduct this test, the examiner hides behind a partition and positions progressively smaller grated or solid gray cards to the right or left of the child (Figure 13.5). By watching the child's eye and head movement, the examiner can see whether he looks to the right or left. He will consistently look to the patterned card up until the point at which he can no longer distinguish the pattern from the solid gray. His visual acuity is determined by the smallest pattern that he can distinguish.

Like the other tests, preferential looking requires the cooperation of the child. For infants or severely retarded children, cooperation is a major problem. For these children, visual evoked responses (VER) may be used to test vision. In this test, EEG (brain wave) electrodes are attached by adhesive to the back of the child's head and a light is flashed in front of the child. If he is able to see, his eyes will focus on the light, and an electrical wave will

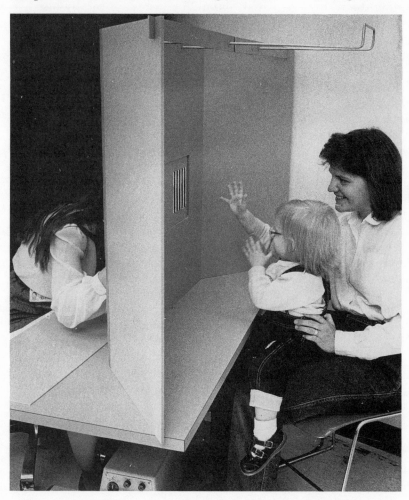

Figure 13.5. *The preferential looking test. The examiner hides behind a partition and positions progressively smaller grated or solid gray cards to the right or left of the child. By watching the child's eye and head movement, the examiner can see whether she looks to the right or left. This is used in testing very young children.*

register on the EEG machine. This shows that the light has passed successfully through the eye and has reached the brain. It does not measure visual acuity as do the other tests, but only that the child can see.

While the VER measures the effect of light on the brain, another electrical test, the electroretinogram (ERG), measures the effect of light on the retina. An electrode attached to a contact lens is placed over the cornea. The retina is then stimulated with light. The electrode registers the retina's response to light, which is a measure of retinal functioning. Combining the results of the VER and ERG tests, the doctor can differentiate between blindness resulting from retinal damage versus cortical blindness (see below).

New imaging techniques have also been helpful in detecting eye problems. The three techniques used are ultrasound, computed tomography (CT scan), and magnetic resonance imaging (MRI). Which specific test is used to visualize the inside of the eye depends on the specific problem. Ultrasound is the simplest procedure and will detect many problems including hemorrhages, tumors, and retinal detachment in the eye. CT or MRI will show tumors or objects trapped in the eye. These techniques are described in more detail in chapter 8.

VISION IMPAIRMENT AND BLINDNESS

Vision impairment comes in various degrees, the most severe of which is blindness. The legal definition of blindness is that vision in the best eye, after correction by glasses, is poorer than 20/200, or that the field of vision is so narrow that it encompasses only 20 degrees rather than the normal 105 degrees or so. Restricted field of vision means that the person has tunnel vision.

Within blindness there are also degrees of severity. Individuals with corrected vision of 20/70 to 20/200 are called partially sighted and can read large newsprint. Those with 20/200 vision can count fingers placed twelve inches in front of their eyes, but cannot see well enough to read. Many people who are legally blind, that is, with less than 20/200 vision, can still distinguish shades of light. Totally blind people will not even have light and dark perception. Of those people who are vision impaired, about 25 percent are totally blind, 20 percent have light perception, 25 percent can count fingers, and 30 percent can read large print. In addition to visual acuity, there is also the issue of visual efficiency. This means that the child who has vision loss and is also nearsighted will have worse functional vision than a child with visual loss alone.

Overall, the incidence of partially sighted children is about one in 500 births. The incidence of total blindness is four per 10,000 births. Blindness is most commonly caused by abnormalities or damage to the optic nerve or retina. Blindness occurring when the eyes themselves are healthy is called cortical blindness. This involves damage either to the nerve tracts that send visual information to the brain or damage to the part of the brain where these electrical signals are interpreted. Head trauma, brain infections, stroke, and lack of oxygen can all cause cortical blindness. Unlike retinal blindness, which is irreversible, cortical blindness can improve over time, although the mechanism for improvement is unclear. It is suspected that another area of the brain takes over the function of the damaged area. It is difficult to predict the ultimate visual ability of a young child with cortical blindness.

Overall, prenatal injury, infection, or congenital malformation of the eye accounts for about 50 percent of total blindness in children. An additional 40 percent of blind children lose their vision in the first year of life, most commonly because of retinopathy of prematurity, tumors which required removal of the eye, or traumatic injury to the eye.

DIAGNOSING VISION IMPAIRMENT

Blindness can be missed in the newborn period. But by about two months of age, the inability to fixate visually, combined with a lack of visual responsiveness, should indicate a problem. Most totally blind children will have roving eye movements — their eyes constantly search for a point on which to fix their gaze. In partially sighted children, sudden, jerky, sideways eye movements, called nystagmus, occur intermittently as the child tries to seek and focus on objects. Neither of these types of movement are under the child's voluntary control. In severely retarded infants, it may be unclear whether there is a vision problem or if the child is just not interested in his environment.

There are several ways you can test for blindness in addition to the vision tests noted above. First, you can see if your child focuses on your face or on a brightly colored object. Red works best. You can rapidly place your hands before her eyes and see if she blinks. You can shine a flashlight into her eyes and observe whether the pupils constrict. Last, look to see if your child holds an object very close to her eyes; this may be a sign of vision impairment. Once a visual deficit has been identified, it may take months before you will know how much vision has been preserved. This is especially the case when there is cortical blindness rather than a primary disorder of the eye.

THE DEVELOPMENT OF A BLIND CHILD

Although most partially sighted children have normal intelligence, about half of totally blind children have developmental disabilities. These include most prominently cerebral palsy, mental retardation, and hearing impairments.

Even blind children with normal intelligence have delays in the development of reasoning, language, social, and motor skills. The sighted child learns many of these skills by following the comings and goings of her parents and by seeing how her parents and others react to her. The blind child can't see people leave and then come back and so she has difficulty understanding the concept of object permanence — that is, that even when her parents leave the room, they still exist. As a result of the delay in the development of object permanence, blind children tend to be fearful of being left alone. Similarly, it is difficult for a blind child to understand that what she does has an effect on another person's actions (cause-and-effect relationships).

Visual imitation is very important in the development of language and social skills. The social smiling of an infant imitates the parents' facial expressions, and the forming of words is also done by mimicry. Our facial expressions and body language are both consequences of visual interactions. All these are lost on the blind child. Though a blind infant may have a dull facial expression, this does not necessarily mean that she is sad or uninterested. You will learn to watch for subtle head and body movements that give hints of mood. Her lack of normal social interactions may also lead to difficulties relating to peers. Maintenance of immature gestures is quite common in teenaged blind children. For example, they may continue the child-like activity of jumping up and down and clapping their hands when happy or excited.

Language may also be somewhat delayed. Your child may be echolalic, repeating words said to her without necessarily understanding their meaning. She may also tend to imitate noises around her, such as a car, a dog barking, or a phone ringing. She may refer to herself as "Sally" rather than "I," having difficulty differentiating "self" from "others." Although delayed in onset, speech is usually normal by school age for blind children with average intelligence. However, reasoning abilities remain different from sighted children. Blind children tend to do poorly in abstract reasoning tasks though better in arithmetic skills.

Formal IQ testing can be performed on blind children. However, the results are most accurate when the child is old enough to be tested on language and verbal reasoning abilities rather than on the visual perceptual skills that are prominent in tests used for younger children. The verbal section of the Wechsler or Stanford-Binet scales of intelligence are most often used (see chapter 6). There are no specific intelligence tests for blind children.

Motor skills are also affected in early childhood. Blind infants tend to be floppy and, as a result, sitting and walking are delayed (Figure 13.6). They do not generally sit until eight months, and may not crawl at all. Their average age for walking is eighteen to twenty-four months rather than the normal thirteen to fifteen months. When they do walk, they tend to have a wide-based gait, with their feet turned outward to help maintain balance in the absence of visual cues. Reaching out and grabbing for objects occurs around nine months rather than four months of age. Instead of turning toward sounds at around seven months, the blind child will reach toward the sound at this time. Feeding skills may also be delayed, with the chewing of food starting around nine months

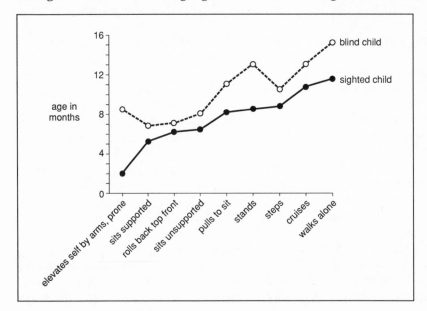

Figure 13.6. *The development of blind children with normal intelligence is contrasted to sighted children. The development of motor skills is delayed in blind children.*

rather than six months. In mentally retarded blind children it may be difficult to distinguish what proportion of the developmental delay is due to vision loss and what to underlying cognitive deficits.

It has been said that vision impairment is compensated for by the heightening of other senses. This does not occur automatically; it must be learned. For example, blind infants tend not to use their hands much, as they mostly end up grabbing at air. Thus, you need to interest your child in different textures and shapes that can be explored manually, or toys that make sounds when squeezed or turned. Crib gyms are also good for practicing motor skills. On the other hand, furry or fuzzy toys often frighten blind children, as may real animals. Feet are used a lot since they permit mobility. Therefore, extra stimulation of the feet is not usually necessary.

Blind children can also become more sensitive to sounds. They can develop their hearing for use in locating objects that they cannot see. For example, many blind people can navigate around rooms without bumping into things by memorizing the location of objects and by listening for the echoes from their steps bouncing off solid objects. This is their use of sonar. There is no magic to it, only hard work. This training is frequently offered by physical or occupational therapists.

BEHAVIORAL ABNORMALITIES IN BLIND CHILDREN

Blind children tend to show "autistic-like" mannerisms. Your child may, for example, exhibit repetitive, self-stimulatory behaviors such as playing with her hands in front of her face, twirling, rocking, or banging her head. She may intermittently blink forcefully, gaze at lights, press her fingers into her eyes, roll her head, or sway her body. These behaviors become less evident after four years of age in blind children with normal intelligence, but may persist throughout life in blind, mentally retarded children.

The reasons for the self-stimulatory behaviors are not completely known. They may be attempts by the child to compensate for the sensory stimulation that she is not able to achieve visually. A child with some dark/light vision may enjoy the changes of shading that she can produce by playing with her hands in front of her eyes. Another explanation is that a totally blind child may "see" light when her head is banged or eyes pressed. This is not the case for cortically blind children, who do not eye press. Rocking is another form of tactile stimulation. If these behaviors become a significant problem, behavior-modification techniques can be used to decrease their frequency (see chapter 15).

Sleep problems may also occur. It is not unusual for a blind child to reverse day and night. Also, blind children appear to need less sleep, although this is not usually true for their parents! Try to avoid daytime naps so your child is adequately sleepy at night.

TEACHING THE BLIND INFANT AND CHILD (see also chapter 20)

Different approaches to stimulating residual vision or other senses are required at different ages. For the infant, a mirror attached to the crib, brightly colored mobiles, or Christmas lights will all stimulate the use of residual vision. Keep toys in the same part of the crib so your child knows where to find them. Toys can be attached by strings to a high chair so they can be thrown and then retrieved. Note that dolls carry little interest as the young blind child has no idea of the shape of the human body or face.

To encourage fine-motor skills, give finger foods that are unlikely to be crushed easily: celery, cookies, crackers, bacon, french fries, M&Ms. Avoid soft messy foods such as fruit slices; blind children generally do not like their hands being sticky. Use a deep dish with straight sides to train spoon feeding, and a Tommy Tippy cup to teach cup drinking. A plastic sheet placed strategically under the high chair will make your life easier. Stacking blocks, nesting cubes, and colored rings may improve eye-hand coordination. Other fine-motor tasks can include using a toy workbench with toy hammer and "nails," unscrewing bottle caps to obtain desired objects within, and stringing large beads. In teaching dressing skills, when possible use Velcro straps for shoes, pants, and shirts rather than relying on buttons that can be missed.

Given the fact that vision-impaired children will learn by using touch and hearing, these senses should be stimulated and utilized. You must remember that a child who has been born blind will have no concept of the structure of the world about him. On the other hand, a child who has had vision and then loses it will not have this problem, especially if blindness occurred after two years of age.

What do colors mean to a totally blind child? What is distance? What are trees? The way a blind child learns is by touching an object while you explain what it is, its function, and its physical composition. Your child will explore by smelling, touching, tasting, turning over, and examining each object. This exploration and discrimination of shapes, orientation, and distance in space should be encouraged by placing your infant on his belly rather than his back and by giving him toys that have in-

teresting surfaces to explore and that make noises.

There are special early-intervention programs for vision-impaired infants beginning at six months of age. Besides language and exploration, the teachers will work on motor skills. They will try to help your child develop protective reactions, such as extending her arms when balance is lost. She will need these quick reactions in sitting and walking so she will have more confidence in exploring her environment. There may be little motivation and a lot of fear involved in learning to walk. Try using a desired object or destination (like the refrigerator) to motivate your child. Use your voice to guide her in the right direction. You will have to learn not to be overprotective. Safety considerations will demand close observation on your part, but you must allow your child as much freedom as possible. She may also need to touch and smell objects or people in a way that may not be socially acceptable. Some compromises in propriety may be necessary in order for her to learn, but she must eventually follow appropriate social mores.

Regarding language, when approaching a blind child, start talking while you are distant from her so she will not be startled by your sudden presence. Explain everything you plan to do with or for her. You should talk to your child as much as possible in a responsive way. She needs to react to your questions and take part in conversations, not just listen passively. Placing your child in front of a television set so she will learn words can lead to simple repetition of words or phrases she hears rather than real interactive language. A multisensory approach will be most helpful to her. For example, as she eats her Cheerios, have her smell and touch the cereal, feel how it floats in the bowl, melts in the mouth, and tastes different from other foods. Outside, have her play in the grass, jump in the leaves, dig in the dirt while you explain what these things represent. In your interactions with your child, use touch and physical affection. Remember, she cannot pick up on "body language." A summary of age-related toys and activities is listed in Table 13.1.

The dull facial expression and sense of isolation tend to make contact with peers difficult. Your child needs to be taught appropriate social interactions, including control of self-stimulatory behavior, conversational skills, and appropriate participation in activities. In general, blind children can be mainstreamed in school if they do not have other developmental disabilities. However, if they are multihandicapped, they may best be placed in classes for the vision impaired or in a school for the blind.

AIDS FOR THE VISION IMPAIRED

As your child grows older and is ready for schooling, the question of reading arises. A child with better than 20/200 vision who can read quarter-inch letters can and should be encouraged to read large-print books. Children with less vision will need

TABLE 13.1   Toys and Playthings for the Vision-Impaired Child*

Infants		
Mobiles	Little bells	Busy box
Rattles	Squeaky toys	Cradle gym
Strings of beads	Spring mattresses	Mirror
Buttons on elastic	Water beds	
One to Three Years		
Flashlights	Toddler trike	Beach balls
Slinky	Foil pie plates	Spring horse
Party noisemakers	Clothespins and box	Plastic pool
Leather belt	Pull toys	Bath toys
Old vacuum hose	Rubber tubing	Squeeze toys
Riding toys	Cartons of all sizes	Empty boxes
Three to Five Years		
Nesting cans	Beads	Slide
Bean bags	Construction toys	Sand box
Screw jars and tops	Toy phones	Swing
Bottle and tops	Nuts and bolts	Big cartons
Jack-in-a-box	Dolls	Tricycle
Talking toys	Inner tubes	Doll carriages
Low swing with soft seat	Rope ladder	Books
Small radio	Firm ladder	Light displays
Record player		
Five to Six Years		
Toy hammer and nails	Walking beam	Stoves
Scissors	Stunt bar	Tree house
Poster paints	Play Doh	Play house
Fingerpaints	Pop or siren guns	Trampoline
Roller skates	Toy dishes, brooms	
Tape recorder	Books	

* From Scott, E. P., J. E. Jan, and R. D. Greeman, *Can't Your Child See?* 2nd ed. Austin TX: PRO-ED, 1985.

to read Braille, a symbolic language formed as a series of raised dots on a page. Braille libraries are extensive and there is a federally funded free lending library that will provide books by mail. This library also has an enormous collection of books on tape, especially for children. They will provide both the tape recorder and recordings free of charge. A monthly magazine is sent to describe new titles in stock (National Library Service for the Blind and Physically Handicapped, Library of Congress, 1291 Taylor St., NW, Washington, DC 20542). Books on tape are also becoming common in public libraries and bookstores.

The availability of personal computers has opened up an entire range of new possibilities for the vision impaired. There are talking calculators and voice-activated computers. Via modems, computers can connect the blind person to libraries or jobs. Computers can also control various functions in the house, such as turning off lights, dialing phones, and locking doors, thereby permitting greater independence for blind people as well as those with other physical disabilities. As a result, many previously unemployable disabled people are now able to hold jobs that allow them to work at home.

The need for walking aids is controversial. Generally speaking, a child who can see fingers held twelve inches away will be able to travel around independently. For those with less vision, canes, dogs, or human helpers can assist. However, dogs can be prohibitively expensive and are often frowned upon because they reinforce the idea that blind people are not self-sufficient. As a result, white walking canes have become the primary aid for the vision impaired. They are now so sophisticated that they function more like a bat's sonar system than as an old-fashioned tapping stick.

PROGNOSIS

The blind child's future depends primarily on the amount of residual vision and the intelligence of the child. The less the visual impairment and the higher the IQ, the better the prognosis. At one end of the spectrum are people like the famous singer and pianist Stevie Wonder, and Harold Krents, who was born prematurely and developed retinopathy of prematurity, but ultimately graduated from Harvard Law School and wrote an amusing and poignant autobiography (see the references at the end of the book). At the other end of the spectrum is the child who is severely mentally retarded, has cerebral palsy, and is blind. Here, the blindness probably has had little effect on the outcome, the other disabilities being so restrictive. In between these two extremes are most blind children, whose limits may be evident only once they reach adulthood. In one study of eighty-two children who were blind (eighteen were also mentally retarded), thirty-three did well in a mainstreamed school setting, forty-one had a mixed result, and eight did poorly. At twenty-five years of age, seventeen were married while forty-three still lived at home. Sixty-six traveled independently with a white cane and twenty-seven were gainfully employed.

SOME QUESTIONS ANSWERED

How old must my child be to wear glasses?

Glasses can be worn by an infant as young as six months. In the case of a severe visual deficit, correction with glasses should be attempted immediately. However, a less severe refractive error of between 20/40 and 20/60 does not need to be corrected in a preschooler. Once primary school has started, correction to 20/20 should be attempted. Headbands may be needed to hold the glasses in place on your child's face, and plastic lenses will prevent breakage when he drops or throws the glasses.

Why do some children with developmental disabilities and blindness have unusual-appearing eyes?

Some children with severe disabilities have an unusual-looking face; abnormalities of the eyes are a common feature of this. The eyes may be small, malformed, or they may be more widely spaced than normal. In thinking of how this may relate to an underlying developmental disability, it is important to remember that as an embryo, a child's eyes are positioned at the side of the head. As the fetus grows, the eyes move toward the center of the face. Thus, alterations in the size or placement of the eyes suggest some abnormality that occurred early in the growth of the fetus. When this happens, it is usually also associated with altered brain development. Therefore, eye abnormalities may mirror underlying brain damage.

Do blind children dream?

Blind people do dream, but the dreams are not illustrated. Images are present only if the blindness occurred sometime after age seven.

14

NEUROMUSCULAR DISORDERS
Spina Bifida and Muscular Dystrophy

Edward B. Charney, M.D., and
Mark L. Batshaw, M.D.

Neuromuscular disorders affect a child's ability to move and are a result of abnormalities in the nerves or muscles. This is in contrast to cerebral palsy (see chapter 9), which arises from problems in the brain's control of movement. The most common neuromuscular disorders of childhood are spina bifida and muscular dystrophy. Although they both affect movement, these two disorders have more differences than similarities. Muscular dystrophy primarily involves an abnormality of muscles, while spina bifida indicates a spinal nerve problem. Muscular dystrophy is inherited, while spina bifida is sporadic in occurrence. Children with spina bifida are identifiable at birth, while muscular dystrophy is a progressive disorder that is not clinically evident until early childhood. As these two disorders differ so much, we will discuss them separately

Spina Bifida

JONATHAN

Jonathan was born after an uncomplicated pregnancy and normal labor. At birth, he weighed seven pounds and moved vigorously, but had a large fluid-filled sac covering the lower third of his back. His parents were told that he had a birth defect called spina bifida, or myelomeningocele. He was transferred the next day to a children's hospital, where a team of specialists evaluated him. These doctors told Jonathan's parents that he had a high lumbar spinal cord lesion with paralysis of both legs. Although his head was of normal size, the doctors said that enlargement of the head was a common complication for children with spina bifida and that Jonathan would probably need a shunting procedure. A neurosurgeon closed the opening on Jonathan's back on the third day of life. On day nine, a shunt was inserted to drain excess fluid away from his head.

Jonathan required shunt revisions at three and twelve months of age. Shortly after his first birthday, he was fitted for long leg braces and began to receive weekly physical therapy for walking. He was also enrolled in an early-intervention program once a week. By three years of age, Jonathan was walking independently with his braces and crutches. He achieved bowel continence shortly after four years of age, and became continent of urine at five using a procedure called clean intermittent bladder catheterization. Now seven years old, Jonathan is enrolled in a regular first grade class and is doing quite well. He is able to catheterize himself and continues to be an excellent walker. He enjoys singing in the school choir and playing with his friends and with his five-year-old brother.

WHAT IS SPINA BIFIDA?

As noted above, spina bifida, also called myelomeningocele, is a birth defect in which the spinal cord fails to develop properly. At birth, the spinal cord is seen to be open and exposed rather than internally contained in the back. The term myelomeningocele refers to the fluid-filled sac that protrudes from the defective spine (the spina bifida) and contains the malformed spinal cord (Figure 14.1). Nerves below the defect fail to develop, leading to paralysis and sensory loss. As noted in chapter 5, the spinal cord is responsible for carrying messages from the brain to all parts of the body via nerves coming out of

the cord at various levels. For example, in order for us to walk, there must be a message transmitted from our brain, through the spinal cord, to the nerves that direct leg muscle movement. The spinal cord also transmits sensory messages in the opposite direction, from our body to the brain. For example, in order to feel a pinprick, nerves in the skin pick up the message and transmit it through the spinal cord to the brain, where it is perceived. If there is an abnormality in the spinal cord that disrupts this pathway, there is loss of sensation. Likewise, the message that runs from the brain to the finger, telling it to respond to the pinprick, will also be disrupted. Thus, spina bifida involves a loss of both sensation and movement. This often results in paralysis of the legs, loss of control of bowel and bladder function, and insensitivity to pain.

CAUSE, INCIDENCE, AND INHERITANCE

The defect causing spina bifida occurs very early in pregnancy. At around the twenty-eighth day of embryonic development there is a failure of a portion of the cord to

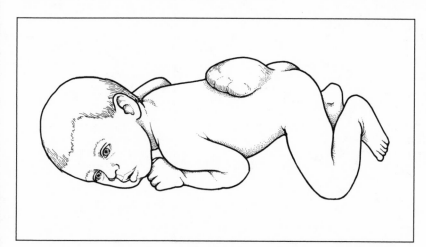

Figure 14.1. *A newborn with spina bifida. The meningomyelocele sac covers the malformed spine.*

form a neural tube (Figure 14.2). This leads to incomplete closure of the spinal cord. Why this happens is not known, although many theories have been proposed. Ongoing studies are being conducted to determine whether maternal dietary deficiencies around the time of conception, particularly in folic acid and/or other vitamins, may be a factor in causing this abnormality. *Keep in mind, though, that your baby's birth defect is not a result of something you did wrong. No one knows the cause of spina bifida.*

Spina bifida occurs in approximately one out of every 1,000 births in the United States. Although this disorder is not inher-

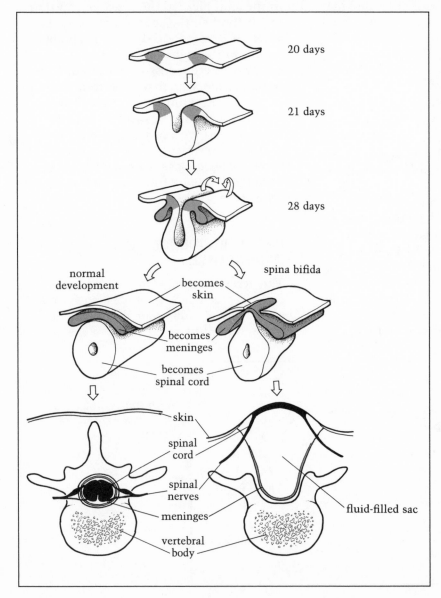

Figure 14.2. *The formation of the neural tube (spine) during development of the fetus and what goes wrong in spina bifida. The tube does not close completely, for as yet unknown reasons.*

ited as a genetic trait, as is muscular dystrophy, there is a familial predisposition. Couples who have had one child with myelomeningocele have an increased risk (approximately one in 20) that a future pregnancy will result in an affected child.

As noted in chapter 4, prenatal diagnosis of spina bifida may be established through amniocentesis at the sixteenth to eighteenth week of pregnancy. Fetuses with an open spinal tube will usually have an increased amniotic fluid level of alpha fetoprotein (AFP). Unfortunately, the newer approach to prenatal diagnosis, chorionic villus sampling, cannot be used to detect spina bifida since amniotic fluid is not obtained in this procedure. Obstetricians may screen pregnant women for the presence of spina bifida in their fetus using a blood AFP test which is often, *but not always,* elevated at sixteen to eighteen weeks in mothers carrying an affected fetus. The blood AFP test is a screen only. If levels are high, the test must be followed up with amniocentesis and/or diagnostic ultrasound.

MANAGEMENT OF SPINA BIFIDA IN THE NEWBORN PERIOD

The diagnosis of spina bifida can be made in the delivery room if not prior to birth. A neurosurgeon will usually close the myelomeningocele defect within the first few days of life. The surgery provides skin closure over the cord and minimizes the likelihood of an infection developing in the cord or brain. However, the surgery cannot repair the malformed portion of the spinal cord and therefore does not improve the child's neurologic function.

Besides problems in the spinal cord, children with spina bifida can also have hydrocephalus. Hydrocephalus occurs when cerebrospinal fluid circulation is

blocked and the fluid builds up in the head. Either before or shortly after the surgery, your baby will probably have a brain imaging study: a CT (computerized tomogram), MRI (magnetic resonance imaging), or ultrasound to evaluate this potential problem (see chapter 8). These studies provide information about the size of your baby's ventricles (the chambers in the center of the brain containing cerebrospinal fluid) and permit the diagnosis of hydrocephalus (Figure 14.3). If the ventricles are enlarged, a shunt will be placed to prevent fluid buildup. This procedure will be performed within a few days of the closure of the back (see below).

Another potential problem is a kidney abnormality. Therefore, an intravenous pyelogram (IVP) or renal ultrasound test is likely to be performed. The ultrasound is usually done first. It is noninvasive and almost totally risk free. The IVP, which uses an X-ray-sensitive dye to image the kidneys, is performed only if a problem is suspected. If a problem is found, clean intermittent catheterization (see below) or a surgical procedure may help the bladder drain better.

If there are no complications, your baby will probably be discharged home within a week after the shunting procedure. During this time, you will be taught to care for the back wound, to position your baby so he will be comfortable, and to do range of motion exercises for his legs. Some newborns with congenital clubfeet, a frequent accompaniment of spina bifida caused by inactivity in utero, will require casting prior to discharge. This would be managed by your orthopedist.

HYDROCEPHALUS

Almost all children with spina bifida have a defect of the brain called the Arnold-

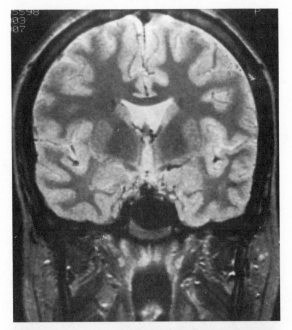

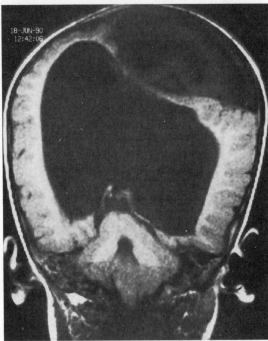

Figure 14.3. *The MRI scan on the top reveals a normal ventricle (the small white area at the center of the image). The MRI scan on the bottom reveals the enlarged ventricle (the large dark area) of hydrocephalus in a child with spina bifida.*

Chiari malformation. Here, the brain stem and part of the cerebellum are displaced downward toward the neck, rather than remaining within the skull. This malformation interferes with the normal flow of cerebrospinal fluid and results in the development of hydrocephalus. Hydrocephalus is found at birth in 60 to 90 percent of all children with spina bifida. Additional complications associated with the Arnold-Chiari malformation may include swallowing difficulty, hoarseness, and crossed eyes (strabismus).

If hydrocephalus is present, a neurosurgeon will perform a shunting operation (Figure 14.4). He inserts a small plastic catheter through a burr hole in the skull

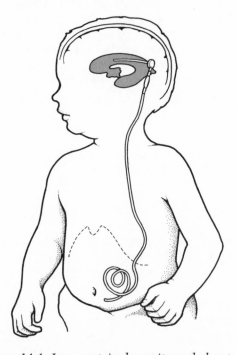

Figure 14.4. *In a ventriculo-peritoneal shunt, the neurosurgeon places a catheter into a hydrocephalic ventricle. This connects through a pump to tubing that runs under the skin and to the abdomen.*

into one of the enlarged ventricles. This catheter is then connected to another catheter that is placed under the skin behind the baby's ear. This catheter runs under the skin of the neck and chest and into the abdominal or peritoneal cavity. Called a ventriculo-peritoneal or V-P shunt, this permanently placed device diverts the excess fluid from the brain ventricles into a cavity in the body from which it can be absorbed into the bloodstream. Less frequently, if there is a problem in absorption from the abdominal cavity, the neurosurgeon may attach a catheter from the ventricle directly to the bloodstream via the jugular vein of the neck; this is called a ventriculo-jugular shunt. Either shunt usually has two plastic bulbs or "bubbles" that are attached behind the child's ear. These can be pumped by your doctor if there is a concern that the shunt is blocked or not working.

Shunt Malfunctions

Once a shunt has been placed in your child, you are likely to be worried about whether it is working properly. Although extra tubing is left in the abdomen so that as your child grows it can uncoil without getting clogged, blockages sometimes occur. There are a number of signs that you and your doctor can watch for to ensure that the shunt is working. You should first understand that it is unusual for the shunt suddenly to stop working and require emergency care. More often, the young infant with a malfunctioning or blocked shunt will show an excessive increase in the growth of his head over a several-week period. During each well-baby visit, your doctor will measure your baby's head circumference and plot it on a graph. If there is an unexpected acceleration in head growth, and/or the soft spot on the top of the head feels full or tense, your doctor

will suspect that the shunt may not be working.

Usually, your baby will not look sick since the buildup of fluid in the brain is gradual and is accommodated by a spreading of the skull bones. However, you will need to consult your neurosurgeon, who will consider revising the shunt. A less common sign of a malfunctioning shunt is a croupy cough. This results from the increased pressure affecting the nerves that control the vocal cords. If your baby makes a loud noise when breathing, that sounds like the croup, it may be necessary to consult your neurosurgeon.

Although shunt malfunction is more common during the first year of life, it can occur at any age. Once the infant's skull bones have fused, some time after one year of age, the symptoms of shunt blockage become more acute and must be dealt with rapidly. This is because pressure builds up as the brain tries to expand into a closed space. The child will generally develop headache, vomiting, irritability, and sleepiness. However, since these symptoms are also seen in children with a viral illness, it may be difficult to discriminate between a blocked shunt and the flu. When in doubt, be conservative and consult your physician.

If a blocked shunt is suspected, a CT or MRI brain scan may be performed to determine if the ventricles have enlarged. A pressure reading may also be taken through the shunt tubing to see if the spinal fluid is under increased pressure, another sign of blockage. It is not always easy to tell whether a shunt is blocked, and your doctor may want to wait to see if there are worsening symptoms before operating. If there is evidence of a block, the neurosurgeon will remove the blocked part of the shunt and replace it with a new catheter. Prior to surgery your child may be placed on a medication to decrease the production of cerebrospinal fluid. These medications include acetazolamide (Diamox), dexamethasone (Decadron) and furosemide (Lasix). A shunt revision usually requires several days of hospitalization.

A rarer complication is a shunt infection. A shunt infection may have the same signs as a shunt blockage, but with an associated fever. Shunt infections most commonly occur within the first three months after a shunt operation. If your neurosurgeon suspects a shunt infection, she will withdraw a sample of cerebrospinal fluid through the tubing, culture the fluid for bacteria, and, if necessary, treat your child with intravenous antibiotics. The shunt may need to be removed and replaced as well. This treatment course usually requires hospitalization for two to three weeks.

The signs and symptoms of a shunt malfunction or infection are not to be memorized so that you can be constantly fearful. Rather, familiarity with them should be reassuring, so you can recognize if your child's shunt may not be working. You can then feel comfortable in making the appropriate telephone calls and arranging for the necessary evaluations.

EARLY DEVELOPMENT OF CHILDREN WITH SPINA BIFIDA

Many infants with spina bifida have delays in motor development. This is more common when the lesion is high on the spinal cord, resulting in floppiness and paralysis of both legs. But motor delay may also occur in infants with low-level paralysis. Most children with myelomeningocele are not mentally retarded. However, many school-aged youngsters display visual-perceptual deficits that predispose them to learning disabilities.

RELATIONSHIP OF THE LEVEL OF DEFECT AND MOTOR ABILITIES

Your child's degree of motor paralysis and sensory loss depends on where the lesion occurs. To understand levels of paralysis, it is helpful to look at the structure of the spine. The twenty-nine vertebrae of the spine are named according to their location: seven neck, twelve thoracic or chest, five lumbar or back, and five sacral or lower-back vertebrae (Figure 14.5). High-level paralysis is defined as a spinal cord malformation beginning in the thoracic or high lumbar (signified as lumbar 1, lumbar 2, or L1, L2) region; midparalysis beginning in lumbar 3 (L3), and low paralysis beginning in lumbar 4, lumbar 5 (L4, L5), or the sacral region.

Remember that spinal nerves will not develop normally below the lesion. Thus, if an infant has a thoracic-level lesion, it means that the spinal cord malformation also extends throughout the lumbar and sacral region. Such an infant would have complete paralysis of both legs, with variable weakness in control of his torso. A child with a high lumbar lesion (L1, L2) can flex his hips, but is unable to voluntarily move his knees or ankles (Figure 14.6). Yet many of these children will walk if provided with proper bracing and therapy during the toddler and preschool years.

An infant with a midlumbar lesion, starting around the lumbar 3 (L3) region, can produce strong movements of the legs, but will be unable to move his feet. The majority of these children should be able to learn to walk with proper bracing and therapy.

An infant with a low lumbar lesion, beginning at the lumbar 4 or lumbar 5 (L4, L5) region, is able to flex her hips, straighten her legs at the knee, and move gion will have nearly normal movement of the legs, feet, and toes. Almost all these children will eventually walk with minimal or no bracing.

LEARNING TO WALK

For the average child, the toddler years are marked by increased mobility as the child learns to walk, run, and explore his environment. To achieve this same level of independence, a child with spina bifida needs assistance in establishing some form of mobility. For most of these children, even those with a high level of paralysis, walking with braces and crutches is a realistic goal. To walk well, children with high or midlevel paralysis will require bracing of the ankles, knees, and hips, as well as crutches. Children with low-level paralysis may require only bracing of the foot and ankle.

The vast majority of children with myelomeningocele need extensive physical therapy as well as bracing in order to learn to walk. Depending on your child's prewalking skills (that is, the ability to sit alone, crawl, and use her arms), most programs will prescribe walking braces between twelve and eighteen months of age. If your child is not ready to walk at this age, a special standing frame may be suggested to encourage her to interact with the environment in an upright position.

Yet, spending even several hours a week in braces with a physical therapist is not enough time to learn to walk. Your child will need to practice walking at home. But be patient. Children with high or midlevel paralysis may not independently walk with their braces and crutches until three years of age or later. Most children with low-level paralysis learn to walk independently sometime between eighteen and thirty months of age.

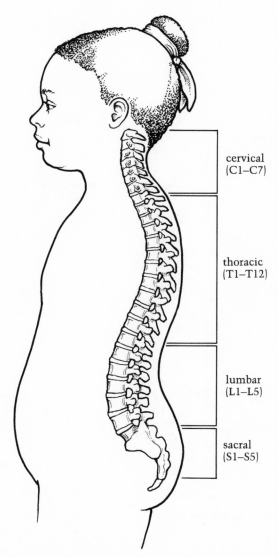

cervical (C1–C7)

thoracic (T1–T12)

lumbar (L1–L5)

sacral (S1–S5)

Figure 14.5. *The vertebral column contains and protects the spinal cord. It is divided into seven neck (cervical), twelve chest (thoracic), five back (lumbar), and five lower-back (sacral) vertebrae. Spina bifida most commonly affects the thoraco-lumbar region.*

her feet at the ankle. Almost all these infants will learn to walk with bracing.

An infant with a malformed spinal cord beginning at the bottom of the sacral re-

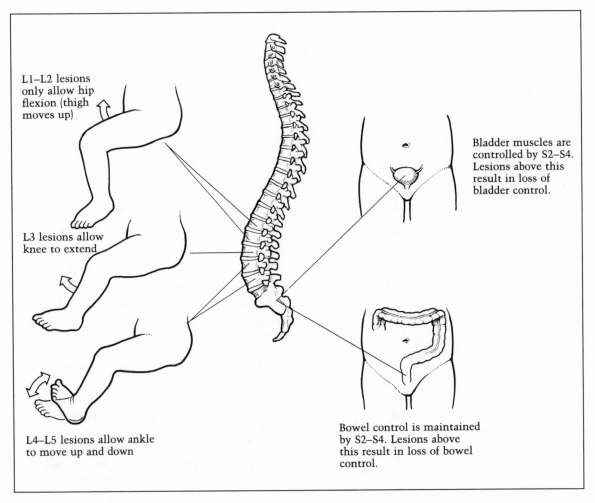

L1–L2 lesions only allow hip flexion (thigh moves up)

L3 lesions allow knee to extend

L4–L5 lesions allow ankle to move up and down

Bladder muscles are controlled by S2–S4. Lesions above this result in loss of bladder control.

Bowel control is maintained by S2–S4. Lesions above this result in loss of bowel control.

Figure 14.6. *An illustration of the effect of various levels of spina bifida on the child's ability to move and control bowel and bladder functions.*

Unfortunately, not all children with spina bifida will be functional walkers. If your child has not learned to walk by six years, she is unlikely to be a functional walker as an adult and will need a wheelchair. However, wheelchairs may be avoided for children younger than five years old, because of the concern that their use may decrease your child's motivation to walk. However, if walking is clearly not an option, a wheelchair may be used even for a young child.

BOWEL AND BLADDER ABNORMALITIES

Most children with myelomeningocele, irrespective of the level of spinal cord lesion, will have problems with bladder and bowel control. This is because the muscular control of the bladder and bowel is located in the lowest portion of the spinal cord, sacral levels 2–4. Not only is muscular control affected, but the sensation of fullness is either totally or partially absent.

The bladder has two major functions. One is to store the urine that has been produced by the kidneys. The second is to empty the urine when the bladder is full. Children with myelomeningocele generally have a bladder that cannot store urine effectively, or one that does not empty it well. The child who has a bladder that cannot store urine may experience intermittent "dribbling." For the child whose bladder does not empty well, urine will remain in the bladder for a prolonged period of time, leading to the excessive growth of bacteria and resultant bladder infections. Many hospital centers that specialize in the care of children with myelomeningocele recommend a small daily dose of an antibiotic such as trimethoprim-sulfamethoxazole (Bactrim or Septra), to minimize the likelihood of a bladder infection. Consult your doctor if this is a concern for your child.

Bowel control presents a similar problem. Normally, sensory messages travel from the bowel wall through the spinal cord to the brain, signaling the presence of stool in the rectum. This message tells us to squeeze the muscle around the anus, which holds in the stool until a toilet can be reached. Children with myelomeningocele often cannot control this muscle. As a result, when they are ready to have a stool, they have difficulty holding back the bowel movement until reaching a toilet. Alternately, some children with spina bifida do not have the ability to contract or relax the muscle inside the rectum voluntarily, leading to diarrhea or constipation respectively.

ACHIEVEMENT OF BOWEL CONTROL

When your child is still an infant, bowel management requires awareness of routine well-baby dietary recommendations. Early introduction of foods that tend to be constipating, such as cereals, should be avoided. If your baby seems to be straining and having hard bowel movements, you may need to add some water or fruit juice to her diet.

The preschool years are normally marked by increasing independence in self-care skills, including toileting, dressing, bathing, and grooming. Although most children will have achieved toilet training by three years, this is uncommon for children with myelomeningocele. Bowel training using the timed-potty training method can usually begin at around three years of age. At this time, you may sit your child on the potty for several minutes after every meal. Often, the large intestines will reflexively contract after a meal. This, accompanied by gentle belly pressure, can lead your child to have a bowel movement. The goal is to have your child empty her rectum of as much stool as possible, so that later in the day, any remaining stool will not accidentally leak out. It is very helpful if your child can assist this effort by straining so that the bowel emptying is more complete. Many children can learn to strain for a bowel movement by attempting to blow up a balloon while sitting on the potty.

Attention must also be given to your child's diet. The goal is for her to have stools that are soft enough to pass without great difficulty but not so soft that there is leakage between timed-potty sittings. In general, it is safer to avoid excessive amounts of foods that soften stools, such as fruit juices or candies, and use more foods that firm up the consistency of a bowel movement, such as high-fiber foods including vegetables and grains. As with any child, success in potty training should be reinforced with praise. Punishment or other negative interactions should be avoided.

If after approximately six months of timed-potty training you are having little success, your child may benefit from the use of a rectal suppository such as bisacodyl (Dulcolax) to assist in stimulating regular and complete bowel emptying. Aim for no more than one bowel accident per week, and none when your child is in school. To achieve this, you may need to give a suppository each night around mealtime, and then have your child sit on the toilet for approximately twenty minutes after dinner. The suppository should stimulate the large intestines to squeeze more effectively. With your child providing some strain, a more complete bowel movement should be accomplished.

Success in this bowel-training program does not happen overnight. It requires the commitment of your family and the cooperation of your child. Here are a few tips for success. First, it is important that your child's large intestines are "cleaned out" with an enema a few days before beginning the trial with rectal suppositories. Second, have your child sit on the toilet each morning before beginning her day's activities. Finally, make sure your child is sitting comfortably on the toilet with both feet touching the ground, so that she can adequately tighten her belly.

After the bowel program has met with success, which may take several weeks or months, your child may still have days of unexplained loose-bowel accidents. Often, this is a sign of constipation, as poorly absorbed intestinal contents sneak around the hardened stool at the end of the intestines. This problem can be managed with a once-a-month enema to enhance bowel emptying.

You may be concerned that regular use of suppositories or enemas will be habit forming or harmful to your child. However, this is unlikely, and it should be noted that chronic constipation itself has several medical complications, and continued bowel accidents in school have significant social repercussions.

ACHIEVEMENT OF BLADDER CONTROL

Attempts at achieving urinary control should begin after your child has already gained bowel control. If family commitment and child cooperation was necessary for a successful bowel program, at least three to four times more effort is required for a successful bladder program. When both child and family are ready, usually when your child is three and a half to four years of age, you will be instructed in the clean, but not sterile, insertion of a plastic tube or catheter through the urethra and into the bladder. The urethra is the channel that runs from above the vagina in girls or through the penis in boys to the bladder. Once the catheter is placed, urine is allowed to flow until the bladder is completely empty. This usually takes one to two minutes and should be accomplished easily and without pain.

For some children, this clean intermittent catheterization (CIC) performed four times a day will be sufficient to maintain dryness. However, for others, oral medication may be needed to help gain urinary control. For example, in some children, the muscles in the bladder contract when they should not, making the bladder unable to store urine sufficiently to keep the child dry between CICs. Drugs such as oxybutynin chloride (Ditropan), taken one to three times a day, may prevent these uninhibited bladder wall contractions and allow your child to remain dry. Another example of a bladder problem that can be treated with medicine is a condition in which there is insufficient tightening of the urethral muscle that acts like a cork to hold back urine. In this situation, you may notice that a cough, laugh, or just regular increased physical activity can make your child wet or damp between CICs. Some oral medicines (e.g., ephedrine and imipramine [Tofranil]) may alleviate this problem. If your doctor thinks medication may be necessary, he will want to know the volume of urine produced with each CIC and may order a special bladder-contraction test, called a urodynamic study.

Achieving bladder control has significant positive social implications for your child, freeing him up to take part in many activities. This may be accomplished as early as the preschool years. With time, he should be able to become increasingly independent by learning to perform CIC himself. Some children can be relied upon to take care of their own catheters, perform bladder catheterization, and maintain their own schedules by the time they are eight or nine years old.

If urinary control has not been achieved after an adequate trial of CIC, surgery may be indicated. Surgical procedures are generally reserved for well-motivated, school-aged youngsters in whom urodynamic studies have confirmed the presence of a bladder that cannot adequately store urine. Bladder storage capacity can be enlarged by surgically cutting out a small piece of the large intestine and then attaching it to the bladder.

Besides bladder control, surveillance of kidney function is important in children with myelomeningocele. This is usually done at two-year intervals using renal ultrasound. If the kidneys are found to be enlarged or otherwise abnormal, this might be another reason to perform the bladder surgery noted above.

OTHER PHYSICAL ABNORMALITIES AND MEDICAL PROBLEMS ASSOCIATED WITH SPINA BIFIDA

Spinal Deformities

Spinal deformities include scoliosis (curvature of the spine) and kyphosis (hump in the spine). Kyphosis, present at birth in about 10 percent of infants with spina bifida, is a result of deformed vertebrae. Scoliosis is either the result of deformed vertebrae (in less than 10 percent of infants), or of weakness of the muscles supporting the spine (in at least 50 percent of children with high-level paralysis). Kyphosis may become worse in childhood and require surgery. Scoliosis usually does not become a major orthopedic concern until preadolescence, a period of rapid growth, when it may interfere with sitting and/or walking. Spine X-rays may be required and, at some point, the orthopedist may recommend that your child wear a plastic scoliosis jacket for most of the day. This jacket can slow down the progression of the spinal curvature. If the curve progresses beyond a certain point, the orthopedist may recommend spinal fusion.

Obesity

Besides the above physical abnormalities, there are a number of secondary medical problems that are more common in children with spina bifida than in the general population. These include obesity, skin sores, impotence, and seizures.

It is very easy for children with spina bifida to become overweight, especially in the preadolescent years. This is particularly true for children dependent on wheelchairs for mobility. Even though your child may not overeat, his reduced activity level results in a lower than normal caloric requirement. Too many calories taken in with too little activity to burn them results in too much fat. Thus, dietary surveillance must continue throughout the school years (see chapter 16).

Recreational activities can also help your child maintain a normal weight. At the same time they can give him a feeling of accomplishment and of being out there with the rest of the "gang." Team or individual sports should be encouraged and efforts should be made to identify appropriate and accessible recreational facilities in your community. These might include horseback riding, bowling, wheelchair sports, or swimming.

Skin Sores

As your child is expanding his ability to explore the environment, minor scrapes got while crawling or from tight-fitting shoes or braces can develop into skin sores. Regular skin checks for these sores are necessary since your child will not feel the discomfort and, therefore, will not complain about the sores. Efforts should be made to keep your child from crawling about with exposed legs over hot surfaces (e.g., a midday sun-lighted porch), rough surfaces (e.g., cement borders of a swimming pool), or near hot objects (e.g., radiator, clothing iron, hot tub water).

In adolescence, particularly for children with higher-level paralysis, pressure sores become a problem. Your child may become dependent on a wheelchair for both social and school activities and, as a result of the hours spent in the chair, develop pressure sores, especially over the buttocks. Prevention of undue pressure is the best treatment. Your adolescent should be reminded to change positions frequently while sitting in the wheelchair. Another aid for preventing these sores is a special cushion on the chair that will evenly distribute your child's weight and minimize excessive pressure on any one site. Treatment of skin sores is discussed in chapter 19.

Impotence

Adolescence is normally marked by maturation of the body, establishment of opposite-sex relationships, enhanced independence, development of one's identity, and planning for the future. Adolescents with myelomeningocele generally do not have any problems with physical maturation. In fact, many affected girls develop breasts, pubic hair, and menstruation earlier than usual. They should have no significant problem in getting pregnant as adults. Boys with spina bifida also have normal development of secondary sexual characteristics — lowering of the voice, enlargement of testes and penis, and growth of pubic hair. However, they may have difficulty maintaining an erection and ejaculating because of the spinal cord abnormalities. If this is a problem for your marriageable-age son, there are now devices available to assist in maintaining erections.

Seizures

Approximately 15 percent of individuals with spina bifida have seizures at some time in their life. These most commonly occur during childhood and may be associated with a blocked shunt. Usually these seizures are grand mal and respond well to medication. If your child remains seizure free, the medication can be stopped. Please refer to chapter 8 for a more detailed description of seizure disorders and their treatment.

APPROACHES TO PSYCHOSOCIAL ISSUES

We have focused on physical and medical issues to this point. However, the social, educational, and behavioral aspects of treatment are equally important in encouraging your child to become more independent.

Working toward Independence

Ongoing efforts should be geared to improving your child's walking ability and gaining independence in activities such as dressing and undressing. For some children, particularly those with higher-level paralysis and extensive bracing, dressing and undressing can be difficult. Though your child may need assistance in putting on and removing pants, try to assist him without doing it for him. Your child may also need assistance in bathing, particularly getting in and out of the tub. Efforts should be directed at getting your child to become as independent as possible in these areas of self-care. One mother of a child who achieved significant independence summarized her parenting approach as follows: "If he fell down in his braces, no matter how much my heart said to go over and help him up, I first let him try on his own. If he couldn't do it, I was there to help him."

Social Interactions

Play activities with other children normally begin between two and three years of age and are important for all children, whether disabled or not. Most children with spina bifida are outgoing. Take advantage of this strength and encourage play activities. Your child will benefit from playing both with children who have similar physical disabilities and with "able-bodied" children. Association with other children with disabilities will help your child recognize that there are other children who may need help in walking and running. Early-intervention programs (see chapter 20) can provide the setting for this socialization with other special-needs children beginning in early childhood.

Adolescents with myelomeningocele should be encouraged to maintain social interactions with other teenagers while continuing to work hard in school and make plans for the future. Realistic goals need to be developed based on both physical and intellectual strengths and weaknesses. Career planning should begin by ninth grade, so that educational emphasis may be directed toward both their strengths and interests. It should be emphasized that life expectancy is not significantly reduced.

Educational Program

An educational program may be started at two years of age or younger. Specialized preschool programs developed for children with other developmental disabilities are also helpful for children with myelomeningocele. Not only do they provide an opportunity for your child to receive appropriate therapy, but they also have the potential for expanding your child's socialization skills. Many of the programs also afford you the opportunity to share with other parents similar experiences about raising children with special needs.

Throughout the school years, emphasis

should be directed at establishing or maintaining self-care skills and peer relationships, as well as success in academics. Achievement in these areas is very important for your child's self-respect and confidence. You must therefore identify the proper school.

Although the majority of children with myelomeningocele and shunted hydrocephalus are not mentally retarded, some are learning disabled. They may have difficulty maintaining consistent and focused attention, completing written assignments on time, or remembering things taught them several days earlier. These difficulties may adversely affect their performance in all of their academic subjects and often require some form of specialized educational intervention.

In choosing the appropriate school setting for your child, you should consider his physical, emotional, and learning needs. What may be right for one child may be wrong for another carrying the same diagnosis. For instance, some children do quite well in a regular school setting; others can attend a regular classroom with supplementary help in a resource room; and still others require a full-time special-education setting. Formal psychological testing may be done prior to school entry in order to evaluate your child's intellectual abilities and his learning strengths and weaknesses. The earlier a problem is identified, the earlier appropriate intervention can be implemented and the more likely there will be a successful outcome.

The school setting must also be appropriate for your child's physical needs. For example, a child who walks well should be in a school with a limited number of physical barriers, such as steps. A child who requires a wheelchair should be in a school that is wheelchair accessible, with ramps, elevators, and other appropriate building modifications. The physical setting should encourage your child to be independent: The child who walks should be encouraged to maintain this ability, while the child who requires a wheelchair should establish competence in wheelchair skills, including transfers in and out of the chair. Physical and occupational therapy (see chapters 17 and 18) are helpful for achievement and maintenance of skills both in school and in the community.

Muscular Dystrophy

The second neuromuscular disease we will discuss is muscular dystrophy. The most common and unfortunately the most severe form of muscular dystrophy is called Duchenne type and is described below. Other less frequent and less severe forms of muscular dystrophy are the Becker type, facioscapulohumeral form and the various limb-girdle dystrophies. The Becker type, like Duchenne, begins in childhood and primarily involves the pelvic girdle. But it has a slow progression, and is associated with normal intelligence and school function. The facioscapulohumeral form begins in later childhood, involves the face and shoulder girdle only, and is inherited as an autosomal-dominant condition, unlike Duchenne and Becker, which are sex-linked disorders. Limb girdle dystrophy occurs in adulthood and involves the shoulder or pelvic girdle only and is inherited as an autosomal-recessive disorder. A child with Duchenne muscular dystrophy (DMD) generally develops normally during the first year of life, but then experiences progressive weakness associated with muscle degeneration. At present there is no cure or effective treatment for DMD.

THOMAS

Tommy seemed normal during the first year of his life, rolling over, sitting, and pulling to stand at the usual times. He began walking at around sixteen months, a bit later than usual. During his second year of life, concerns mounted when his gait remained awkward and waddling. He often fell and couldn't run, jump, or walk up steps. When lying on the ground, he could not directly get up but first had to get to a sitting position. Despite this weakness, he had enlarged calf muscles. Tommy's pediatrician was concerned about his symptoms and ordered a blood test, which strongly suggested Duchenne type muscular dystrophy. Other tests confirmed the diagnosis, and Tommy started attending the muscular dystrophy clinic at a local children's hospital.

Things remained stable until Tommy was eight years old, when his walking deteriorated so much that he needed long leg braces. In first grade he did not do well academically. An educational evaluation revealed learning problems, and he was placed in a self-contained learning-disability classroom.

Tommy received physical therapy daily. But despite these measures, his muscle weakness worsened and his walking continued to deteriorate. By ten years of age he needed to use a wheelchair most of the time. As his activity level decreased, he started to gain excessive weight. The loss of skills and independence was hard for him to accept, and Tom became depressed. Supportive therapy with a social worker helped both him and his family.

Now fifteen, Tom is quite disabled and needs help with most eating and dressing activities. He can no longer walk but gets around well in his electric wheelchair. He attends a special class for the physi-cally disabled and has formed friendships with his classmates as well as with other boys he meets at the muscular dystrophy clinic. He knows the future is not bright, but he faces it with dignity and a sense of humor.

INCIDENCE, INHERITANCE, AND CAUSE

DMD is a rare disorder, occurring in about one per 3,300 males. It is inherited in an X-linked fashion, as described in chapter 4. Thus, boys are affected and mothers carry the abnormal gene. A carrier mother is usually not affected but has a 50 percent chance of passing DMD to her sons. In over half of the cases, however, the disorder arises from a new mutation. This means the defective gene first occurred in the child and was not passed on by the mother. If this is the case, the mother is not a carrier and is, therefore, not at risk of passing DMD to other children. Genetic testing and counseling (chapter 4) and prenatal diagnosis can now provide families with information about risks and about whether a fetus is affected.

Although DMD remains untreatable at this time, scientists have recently made tremendous strides in their understanding of the disease. In 1987, the gene for DMD was isolated and shortly thereafter the gene product was identified. Children with DMD do not make dystrophin, a protein that surrounds and protects muscle fibers. In its absence the muscle degenerates and is replaced by fibrous tissue (Figure 14.7).

CLINICAL COURSE OF THE DISEASE

During the period of one to two years of age, symptoms of muscle weakness become evident, although the signs may be subtle. Parents often discount the waddling

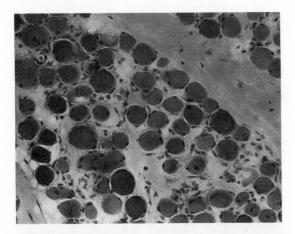

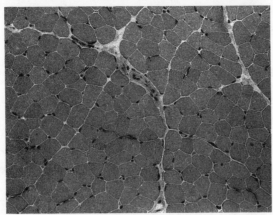

Figure 14.7. *Example of a muscle biopsy from a child with Duchenne's muscular dystrophy and from an unaffected child. Note that the muscle biopsy from the child on the top, with MD, has decreased numbers of muscle fibers and increased fat and fibrous tissue compared to the normal biopsy on the bottom.*

gait and frequent falls as merely signs of clumsiness.

In the third year of life, the abnormalities become prominent, and most children are diagnosed between three and four years of age. There is frequently a "honeymoon" period between three and six years of age when no deterioration occurs and there may even be some improvement. Parents may be lulled into the feeling that the di-

agnosis is in error. Unfortunately, loss of skills becomes a considerable problem between six and eight years, as walking becomes more difficult. Affected boys may walk with stomachs sticking out and backs arched in order to maintain balance. They usually walk on their toes and fall frequently. By twelve years of age, most boys with muscular dystrophy are wheelchair bound and will not walk again. However, it should be emphasized that there is variability in the rate of progression.

DIAGNOSING MUSCULAR DYSTROPHY

If your neurologist suspects DMD, she may perform three tests: creatine phospho kinase (CPK), an electromyogram (EMG), and a muscle biopsy. The first is a blood test for an enzyme, CK, which is released by damaged muscle cells. This test requires only about a teaspoon of blood taken from an arm vein. In a three-year-old with DMD, the levels are usually fifty- to a hundredfold elevated. There are very few other disorders that produce these elevations. This finding is confirmed by performing an EMG, a muscle function test in which electrodes are placed on an affected muscle and the muscle is then electrically stimulated. In DMD there is an abnormal electrical pattern indicating muscle damage. This test carries with it the discomfort of having small needles stuck into a muscle, but it is not particularly painful.

Finally, the specific diagnosis of DMD can be made by taking a biopsy of a diseased muscle. A small piece of muscle tissue is removed, usually through a needle under a local anesthetic. Sometimes a more extensive surgical procedure is performed requiring a general anesthetic. The tissue is prepared by a pathologist, who stains and examines the muscle cells under a microscope, looking for specific abnormalities (Figure 14.7). The combined results of these tests should permit a definitive diagnosis of muscular dystrophy.

ASSOCIATED DEFICITS

Muscle Weakness

Muscle weakness is the central feature of DMD. The muscles that are closest to the torso are most affected, and the legs are more affected than the arms. However, in the end, all major muscle groups become weak, and it is difficult for the child to lift any weight against gravity. This weakness may also be associated with muscle pain or cramping, which often responds to aspirin or acetaminophen (Tylenol).

Contractures

As muscle weakness increases, the child becomes inactive. As with paralysis in cerebral palsy (see chapter 9), lack of joint movement leads to contractures. This is particularly a problem at the hips, knees, and ankles. It may result, for example, in a fixed inturning of the feet. Contractures often can be prevented by active and passive range-of-motion exercises directed by a physical therapist (see chapter 17). If contractures become severe, they may require surgery to release the shortened tendons.

Scoliosis

We noted that scoliosis may be a significant complication for children with spina bifida. It is an even more critical problem for boys with DMD and can prove to be life-threatening. Scoliosis is rapidly progressive during the teenage years when the child is no longer walking. The spinal curvature results in a smaller chest cavity and interferes with expansion of the lungs. Combined with worsening muscle weakness, scoliosis can contribute to the development of respiratory failure.

Until recently, scoliosis was usually treated by fitting the child with a plastic chest jacket that would prevent further worsening of the spinal curve. However, success was limited. Fusion surgery was considered problematic because the commonly used Harrington rod procedure required prolonged immobilization, which in turn led to contractures. A more recent operation, called the Luques procedure, uses external rather than internal fixation to stabilize the spinal column and does not require prolonged casting. As a result, orthopedic surgeons are now more likely to operate early, while the curvature is less than 50 degrees and respiratory status is still fairly good. Better lung function makes the operation itself less hazardous. It should be noted that anesthesia is a somewhat greater risk for children with DMD than for other developmentally disabled children. This is both because of the underlying lung problems and because they are at greater risk than normal to develop high fevers with anesthesia, for reasons that are not entirely clear. As a result, certain anesthetic agents are avoided. You should discuss the options with your child's surgeon prior to any operation.

Respiratory Problems

Respiratory problems have been alluded to already. As muscle weakness increases, the diaphragm, which normally acts as a "bellows" to help expand and contract the lungs, works less efficiently. This is compounded by the scoliosis. Frequent chest infections can also damage the lungs, making them stiff and less able to hold oxygen. These three complications may significantly impair breathing capacity by the teenage years, causing shortness of breath, fatigue, and excessive sleeping. Respiratory function tests performed by a lung specialist, in which the child is asked to breathe into a machine, are used to evaluate his ability to expand his lungs. It is not uncommon for a DMD patient to have lost well over half of his lung capacity by the midteens.

In the late stages of this disease, breathing capacity is so severely limited that minor respiratory infections may become serious medical problems. Therefore, such infections must be treated aggressively with antibiotics, postural drainage, and possibly respiratory support with oxygen, intermittent positive pressure breathing, or, in extreme situations, artificial ventilation.

Postural drainage techniques will be taught to you by a respiratory therapist. You will learn to pound on your child's back to loosen secretions in the lungs and stimulate coughing. The respiratory therapist also will be involved in the control of positive pressure ventilation. This involves forcing air/oxygen under pressure through a mask or breathing tube into your child's lungs to keep them expanded.

Finally, artificial ventilation is used if your child is in respiratory failure. This means he is not taking in sufficient oxygen to survive for a long period of time. Artificial ventilation requires the placement of a breathing tube in the windpipe. This can be done either by intubating your child — placing a plastic tube through the mouth or nose, down the throat and into the windpipe — or by performing a tracheostomy. Here, the tube is placed through an opening cut directly into the windpipe in the neck. In either case, the tube is connected to a ventilator that breathes for your child as long as is necessary. Unfortunately, some children may not be able to come off the ventilator

once placed on it. This will also interfere with speech, and alternate means of communications may need to be learned (see chapter 11).

Heart Function

Cardiograms (EKGs) performed on children with DMD usually show abnormalities in function of the left side of the heart. After the teenage years, there is a significant risk of developing congestive heart failure. There is nothing that can be specifically done to prevent this, as it is the result of worsening lung function. However, it can be treated medically.

Gastrointestinal and Nutritional Problems

There are three potential gastrointestinal problems: obesity, constipation, and acute stomach dilatation. As with spina bifida, the lack of activity for DMD patients leads to decreased metabolism and the risk of excessive weight gain. Thus, your child's weight needs to be watched closely and dietary restrictions may have to be imposed. Inactivity also leads to constipation, which can be treated as in spina bifida.

Unlike spina bifida, there are no problems with bowel or bladder continence. However, there is a problem with stomach emptying. Sometimes the child simply feels bloated or full. But a more dangerous problem is acute stomach dilatation, which involves a sudden swelling of the abdomen associated with severe pain. There may actually be an obstruction. These symptoms should lead to immediate hospitalization as they may prove life-threatening.

Learning Problems

It appears that Duchenne muscular dystrophy not only affects muscle strength but also learning abilities. The average IQ of DMD children is somewhat lower than that of their parents. Most children with DMD do attend regular schools. The associated learning problems are similar to those of other learning-disabled children, so school programs specifically for DMD children are not needed. They can fit into a learning-disability or slow-learning class provided their physical rehabilitative needs are also met.

Emotional Issues

Children with DMD are predisposed to depression, for understandable reasons. Symptoms include weight change, sleep disturbance, decreased energy level, and sadness. These episodes may relate to certain life events: (1) entering school at age six where the other children are able-bodied, (2) no longer being able to walk as an adolescent, or (3) in the late teens realizing that this is an ultimately fatal disease. If your child becomes depressed for a prolonged period of time, he may benefit from seeing a psychotherapist (psychiatrist, psychologist, or social worker). Sometimes antidepressant medications are useful (see chapter 19).

Children with DMD may also suffer from psychological problems that result from overprotection by parents and manipulative behavior by the child. Chronic illness may lead you to treat your child differently, to be more accepting of bad behaviors. Your child in turn may take advantage of this situation to manipulate you for more attention, affection, and favors. Overprotection can lead to a spoiled child who acts hatefully to others, ultimately isolating himself from social contacts. You may create a monster, borne of guilt, who devours himself as well as the rest of the family. You should at least be aware of these issues and be ready to deal with

them. They are discussed further in chapter 15.

TREATMENT APPROACHES

An Interdisciplinary Approach

After a firm diagnosis has been made, your pediatrician will likely refer you to a muscular dystrophy clinic. These multidisciplinary programs are found in most large cities, usually associated with a children's hospital, and are supported by the Muscular Dystrophy Association. A typical treatment team consists of a physician specialist, an orthopedist, a physical therapist, an occupational therapist, an orthotist, and a social worker. Thanks to the work of Jerry Lewis and others, the Muscular Dystrophy Association is able to use its considerable financial resources both to subsidize the care provided by these clinics and to provide financial support for bracing and wheelchairs when needed. Children are generally seen twice a year in such a clinic. Each of the treating disciplines has a specific role to play; these are described below.

Physical and Occupational Therapy

The length of time over which your child will continue to walk is partially dependent on the effectiveness of the therapy he receives (see chapters 17 and 18). Try to have him continue walking for as long as possible, since once he spends some time in a wheelchair, he is likely to remain there. The physical therapist is essential to this process by minimizing contractures and maximizing muscle strength. She will work on preventing contractures in the legs, elbows, and hips, and on maintaining walking ability. This is done by teaching your child to participate in an active exercise program and training you to perform passive range-of-motion exercises to keep limbs supple. Your child should be on his feet about two hours a day if possible. Once he is no longer able to walk for more than an hour a day, bracing will be used. If your son is no longer walking, the therapist may recommend a standing brace for twenty minutes twice a day to maintain weight-bearing ability. This also helps to maintain bone strength and make pathological fractures (resulting from minor injuries that would not cause a fracture in normal people) less likely to occur. Don't worry about overexercising your child. Even if he is exhausted at bedtime, if he is rested after a night's sleep he is not being overly stressed.

The occupational therapist will work on self-help skills such as eating, dressing, and personal hygiene, including the use of assistive devices and adaptive clothing (see chapter 18). When the time comes, she will work together with the orthotist to develop wheelchairs and braces that will optimize your child's well-being and independence. She may also recommend certain sleeping positions or even a special bed that will allow your child to sleep more comfortably and safely. Some sleeping positions — for instance, flat on the stomach or on one side — can compromise your child's breathing capacity.

When your child is no longer able to walk, he will need to be fitted for a wheelchair. A proper fit is essential; if the chair is too big it will not give the necessary support. If it is too small, it will be uncomfortable and may lead to pressure sores. The wheelchair also should recline so your child can use gravity to help him maintain a seated position. Special neck supports may also be needed. Once fitted, your child will need to be re-

assessed at regular intervals to make sure he has not outgrown the bracing or wheelchair.

Orthotist

As noted above, braces are important in the treatment of DMD. The technical specialist who makes braces and splints is called an orthotist. Your first experience with an orthotist may come as early as the preschool years, when your child will need to have short leg braces or molded ankle-foot orthoses (MAFOs) to prevent heel cord contractures.

Orthopedic Surgeon

Once your child is wheelchair bound, contractures often accelerate and orthopedic surgery may be needed. The orthopedic surgeon will work with the therapists and orthotist to determine if, and when, bracing is needed and to decide when to perform surgery. The most common surgical procedure is for scoliosis (see the spina bifida section). Other procedures include release of contracted tendons at the elbows, heels, lower legs, or hips. Orthopedists have found that early intervention is most effective, and therefore recommend the surgery early and more frequently than in the past.

Physician

The physician specialist may be a pediatric neurologist, physical medicine and rehabilitation specialist (also called a physiatrist), or developmental pediatrician. Each is trained to work with developmentally disabled children and to serve as the hub around which the other specialists revolve. This individual should direct the overall care of your child. She will document changes in your child's abilities, adjust medication, and bring in additional specialists as necessary.

Medications

Many medications have been proposed to treat DMD. Unfortunately, few have been successful. Vitamins and trace metals have been suggested as helpful, but in scientific studies have been found to be ineffective. Allopurinol and mazindol are two of the drugs that were recommended at one time and later found to have little worth in improving muscle tone.

The one medication that seems to have benefit is the steroid prednisone. It appears to slow the progression of the disease and improve lung function and walking in some patients. However, it is not without considerable risks, which include cataracts, diabetes, bone fractures, obesity, and high blood pressure. Thus, this approach is used with caution.

WHAT THE FUTURE HOLDS

The unhappy fact is that, at present, children with DMD rarely live beyond young adulthood. They die either from respiratory or heart failure or from infection. What has changed the prognosis somewhat in recent years is the use of ventilators for young adults with DMD. As discussed above, a tracheostomy tube may be placed and the patient attached to an artificial ventilator during the night when breathing is at greatest risk. This can be done at home, although nursing assistance is often required. Ventilators plus the aggressive use of antibiotics for suspected chest infections is increasing the life span of some affected young men to the thirties. However, until we treat the underlying progressive damage to muscles, prolonged survival will remain uncommon. There are ongoing experiments in which immature muscle cells (called myoblasts) containing the gene for the deficient dystrophin are being injected into dystrophic muscles to see if they will protect the muscle from further degeneration. If successful, this research may open up a new era in the treatment of DMD and offer a brighter future.

SOME QUESTIONS ABOUT MUSCULAR DYSTROPHY

Why are some of my son's muscles enlarged if he is so weak?

These muscles have been infiltrated by fat cells and connective tissue. While this makes the muscle big, in actuality, fat and fibrous tissue are replacing the muscle cells that would permit movement. Thus, the muscle seems large, but it has a rubbery consistency and does not work well.

How do I explain to my child that he may die from this disease?

Wait until he asks. Generally this will not be an issue until he is a teenager. Then, try to be truthful. You may want your doctor to address this issue with him. If he is depressed, consider his meeting with a psychotherapist.

IV Approaches to Treatment

15

LOVE AND DISCIPLINE
Managing Behavior

John M. Parrish, Ph.D.

A major part of your job as a parent is balancing love and discipline. Just because your child has a disability does not immunize him or her from having behavior problems or excuse you from managing these problems effectively. Treatment involves identifying a specific behavior as being a problem and then setting up a behavior-management approach to change the behavior. In most cases this approach involves skill-building and positive reinforcement. In a few cases, especially for dangerous behaviors, discipline may need to be used in combination with positive reinforcement. In order optimally to promote your child's development, it may be necessary for you to learn and practice sound behavior-management procedures.

Each of us has personal views about what constitutes a behavior problem. Some of us are upset by our child's slightest whimper, while others can tune out a tag team match! We will define a behavior problem as being an action that occurs too often or too seldom, or one that is inappropriate. As described below, Betty's overeating is an example of an excessive behavior, while George's refusal to take his seizure medications is an inappropriate behavior.

Table 15.1 lists some behavior problems that are common among developmentally disabled children.

When a child's behavior puts him or others in danger of injury, it's definitely time to get help, as in the case of Mary's skin picking (below), which could cause an infection. With a less severe behavior problem you may wait, hoping it will get better. However, in many instances misbehavior only gets worse. When in doubt, it is wise to ask for assistance *before* the behavior becomes unmanageable. One good rule of thumb is that if you are spending more time telling your child what not to do than enjoying what he does, then it is time to seek help with the management of his behavior.

BETTY, MARY, AND GEORGE

Betty is six years old and very overweight. She has been diagnosed as having Prader-Willi syndrome, a congenital disorder marked by a huge appetite and associated obesity, short stature, and mental retardation. She regularly begs for food and, if left unattended, will scavenge until she finds it. Betty is also quick to whine and cry.

TABLE 15.1   Behavior Problems Commonly Presented by Developmentally Disabled Children

Academic underachievement	Impulsivity
Aggression	Inappropriate sexual be-havior
Attentional deficits	Lack of self-help skills
Bedtime problems	Dressing
Breaks curfew	Feeding
Dawdling	Toileting
Disruptive behaviors	Lying
Inappropriate vocalizations	Noncompliance with
Interruptions	Parental requests
Encopresis (soiling)	Teacher instructions
Enuresis (bed wetting)	Medical recommendations
Feeding problems	Phobia
Food selectivity	Pica
Inappropriate textures	Property destruction
Loss of appetite	Rumination/vomiting
Length of meal	Self-injury
Obesity	Self-stimulatory behavior
Habit disorders	Body-rocking
Hair-pulling	Hand-flapping
Nail-biting	Social skills deficits
Thumb-sucking	Tantrums
Motor tics	Verbal abuse
Hyperactivity	

When she doesn't get her way, she usually has temper tantrums.

Mary is a teenager who is moderately mentally retarded. She has developed a number of set routines and prefers things to stay the same. When her father became ill and was hospitalized, Mary began to pick at her skin, creating several cuts on her arms, hands, and legs. Her mother attempted to stop the skin-picking by wrapping Mary's arms and legs with bandages and by putting gloves on her hands, but Mary continued to pick.

George is a mildly mentally retarded boy who has a seizure disorder. When he takes his medication, he remains seizure free, but he resists taking the drugs and consequently has multiple grand mal seizures that interfere with his functioning at school and at home. Cajoling and punishment have not improved his compliance.

SELECTING A BEHAVIOR MANAGER

Friends and relatives are often quick to offer advice about your child's behavior problems. It seems that everyone is an expert when it comes to managing the bad behavior of any child but their own! If common-sense approaches have not worked and you feel concerned about your child's behavior, you may want to seek the help of an expert in child-behavior management, usually a psychologist or an educator. Whatever the individual's title, be sure that she has experience dealing with the behavior problems of developmentally disabled children. Ask the therapist to outline how she would approach certain types of problem behaviors. A qualified therapist will give you practical advice on what to do and what not to do.

To locate a skilled behavior manager, begin by asking your pediatrician. If you live near a child-development center, you may be able to find a qualified behavior-management specialist there. In addition, you can contact the psychology or special-education department of hospitals or universities in your area. Often such departments either offer services themselves or will refer you to a qualified professional.

If you cannot find someone in your area who specializes in treating disabled children, consider finding a nearby therapist who would be willing to consult with a specialist from some distance away. Ask the local therapist to find the expert for you. Alternatively, you may choose to travel some distance in order to arrange an evaluation by a specialist yourself, and then ask this individual to assist you in designing a program that can be conducted with the help of therapists closer to home.

The behavior analyst will expect you to be an active participant in your child's evaluation and therapy. You will be asked to keep appointments, to make a good-faith effort to follow recommendations, and to keep records of your child's performance as a way of quantifying his progress in treatment. Avoid therapists who claim that they can solve any problem you can present, or those who say they will work just with your child, not with you or your child's teachers. Professional organizations that may be able to recommend a highly skilled therapist are listed in the references at the end of this book.

THE BEHAVIOR-MANAGEMENT PROGRAM

At your initial visit, the behavior analyst will work with you to determine the nature of your child's behavioral problems, including the occasions that elicit misbehavior. This assessment may include semi-structured interviews, rating scales or questionnaires, and direct observations of your child during interactions with you. The therapist will ask about your general concerns and for specific examples that illustrate those concerns. For instance, if you say your child is "mean" or "lazy," the behavior analyst will want to know what your child does that warrants those labels. Does he hit other children? Does he fail to complete chores at home?

Once your child's problem behaviors have been defined, the behavior analyst will explore those of greatest concern to you. He will ask you to estimate each problem behavior's frequency, duration, and intensity. You will be asked to de-

scribe the circumstances under which each problem behavior is most likely to occur. For example, if your child has frequent tantrums, the analyst will want to know what triggers them. Do they start when you ask your child to stop some activity that he likes, or when you ask him to complete a task that he doesn't like? Or, does withholding a treat or privilege from your child precipitate a tantrum?

The analyst will also want to know how you react to your child's misbehaviors. Whether your child continues to misbehave depends, in large part, on the consequences he faces. For instance, if you give in to your child's demands when he has a tantrum, the tantrums are likely to continue or even increase. Or, if you allow him to avoid completing a chore when he has a tantrum, he is likely to exhibit the same behavior again the next time he is asked to complete a chore.

In addition to questioning you about the antecedents and consequences of the problem behavior, the behavior analyst is likely to arrange situations during which he can observe your child's problem behaviors firsthand. Toward the conclusion of the assessment, the analyst will ask you what behaviors you most want changed and what strategies, successful or not, you have already tried.

After completing the evaluation, the analyst will advise you as to whether treatment is warranted. If a number of behaviors require attention, the order in which they are addressed will depend upon the relative severity of each problem, the degree of effort required on your part to manage the behavior, and, most important, your preference about where to begin. The therapist will want a commitment from you to participate actively in a short-term treatment program.

Behaviors that can be managed using

positive reinforcement or those that are potentially dangerous are usually targeted first. Intervention for behaviors that are not dangerous but are difficult to alter, such as hand-flapping, body-rocking, or persistent screaming, is often delayed until you have experienced some early success with more malleable behaviors.

POSITIVE REINFORCEMENT

Before tackling the problem behaviors, the therapist may advise you to work on strengthening appropriate behaviors. This is done through positive reinforcement. Reinforcement involves presenting a preferred object or event after a target behavior occurs, in order to increase the frequency of that behavior in the future. Appropriate reinforcers include things as simple as words of praise or more concrete rewards such as special foods or activities. Social activities — for example, playing a game with a parent — can be highly motivating rewards. The list of reinforcers is nearly endless and will vary from child to child, and from time to time.

You may want to ask your child to suggest what she would like as a reinforcer. However, with younger or more intellectually limited children, you may have to take a more indirect approach by simply permitting the child to do what she chooses to do. If your child repeatedly chooses to lie down on the couch, stare at the back of her hand, watch television, listen to music, twirl string, suck her fingers, eat a cookie, or make noises, each of these would be a potential reinforcer for appropriate behavior. You should not assume that what you like, or what you think your child should like, will necessarily be an appropriate reinforcer for her.

Many parents of severely disabled children believe that their children have no reinforcers. This is almost always not the case. Even severely disabled children have likes and dislikes. These may be more difficult to detect, but they exist nonetheless. Using systematic methods, the behavior analyst can help you determine what they are.

Once you have identified your child's preferences, you must determine whether each one would be an appropriate reinforcer. Several characteristics should be considered. First, you should be able to deliver the reinforcer immediately after the behavior has occurred, rather than after some delay. In this way your child can more easily recognize which behaviors result in reinforcement and which do not. Second, the reinforcer should be provided only when appropriate behavior occurs and should not be available at other times. Third, reinforcers should be provided frequently and in small doses: It is better to give verbal approval several times a day than to offer the child a movie ticket at the end of a week of good behavior. As an alternative, you may want to use reinforcers such as points or tokens, which can be redeemed at a later date for a variety of special treats. Fourth, offer a variety of reinforcers in small quantities so that your child does not lose interest too quickly.

Finally, the reinforcers should be compatible with the goals of your child's treatment program. An overweight child should not be given high-caloric snacks as a reinforcer, nor should a withdrawn child be permitted to spend long periods of time alone in her room as a reward. The reinforcers should be inexpensive, readily available to you but not to your child, easily dispensable, interesting, novel, and should not cause side effects. Once reinforcers have been identified, you need to provide them consistently. When interacting with your child, one of your principal aims should be to "catch" him being good so that you can reinforce that behavior.

PLANNED IGNORING: WHEN IT'S BETTER TO LOOK THE OTHER WAY

Children frequently misbehave in order to get attention. You will be more successful in encouraging good behavior if you can avoid giving a lot of attention to your child's misbehavior. For example, if you give your child attention when he whines, you may be increasing the likelihood of whining in the future. Similarly, when you scold your child for interrupting your conversation or making loud noises, you may be reinforcing that behavior. If children continue to receive attention for their misbehavior, it is likely that their poor conduct will continue or even increase.

In such situations, a procedure called planned ignoring can be effective in decreasing the rate of a problem behavior. (Please note that planned ignoring should *not* be used to treat dangerous or destructive behaviors.) Planned ignoring means that you withhold reinforcement (attention) following the occurrence of a problem behavior. Consistent ignoring of your child's nagging, whining, or crying will usually result in a decrease in these bothersome acts. However, planned ignoring typically does not work immediately. At first, you may actually see an increase in the rate, duration, and intensity of inappropriate behavior before a reduction is ultimately achieved.

In order for planned ignoring to be effective, you must use it consistently over an extended period of time and you must be willing to endure flare-ups in your child's behavior. For example, consider when your child was a toddler and routinely pleaded for a cookie before supper. You may have responded to his pleas by asking him to wait, but ultimately you may have given in to the persistent requests and crying in order to quiet him. Using planned ignoring, you would have simply reminded your child once that he could have a cookie only if he finished his supper. You would also say that you would ignore any additional requests. Then, if he continued to beg for a cookie, you would go about your business without further talk about the cookie. The first few times such a procedure was implemented, your child would probably ask for the cookie over and over again. However, with consistent ignoring, over time the begging and crying would gradually decrease and he would learn to wait. If, on the other hand, you occasionally gave in to his crying and produced a cookie, you would have taught him that if he begs and cries long enough, he will get his way. Planned ignoring must be followed to completion to be effective.

Although easy to understand, this procedure is sometimes hard to follow. You may find it difficult to ignore annoying behavior. Instead, you may find yourself issuing a string of "no," "don't," and "stop" commands. Unfortunately, by providing this attention, negative though it is, you would be unintentionally reinforcing your child's problem behaviors. So the next time your child gets on your nerves with some frustrating behavior, try to ignore it!

DIFFERENTIAL REINFORCEMENT: BEING MINDFUL OF WHAT YOU REINFORCE

Your child may exhibit some behaviors that you want to change and others that you want to reinforce. In this case, positive reinforcement and planned ignoring can be combined to form a procedure known as differential reinforcement. For instance, you would be providing differential reinforcement if you ignore your child's tantrums, but praise her cooperative play. In many situations differential reinforcement is preferred over planned ignoring because it teaches a youngster when his behavior is appropriate and when it is not.

SHAPING: HELPING YOUR CHILD LEARN NEW SKILLS

You may want to teach your child a behavior that is not present in his repertoire. Because he is not already exhibiting this behavior, you have no opportunity to reinforce it. In these cases, you may use a procedure called shaping. Shaping involves reinforcing selected behaviors displayed by your child that most closely resemble the behavior you wish your child to learn. Multiple opportunities for your child to learn and to practice new skills should be arranged. Whenever your child behaves in a manner that approximates the desired skill, his efforts should be rewarded.

To illustrate, consider teaching your disabled youngster to shoot a basketball in preparation for the Special Olympics. You first teach prerequisite skills such as how to stop dribbling, how to grip the basketball when shooting, how to position the body for a shot, how to pinpoint the basket, and how to deliver a shot in proper form. Each time your child's performance approximates a component skill, reinforce her efforts. Once such basic mechanics have been taught, have her practice shooting from a very short distance until several baskets in a row are scored. Then direct her to move back a few steps and so on until she can shoot accurately from greater and greater distances.

Shaping is most often employed to help disabled children learn new skills, such as how to dress, use utensils, toilet train, select clothing, cross the street, use public transportation, and so forth. For detailed information about how to teach your child specific daily living skills, please refer to a very useful book entitled *Instructional Programming for the Handicapped Student* by D. R. Anderson, G. D. Hodson, and W. G. Jones (1975).

INSTRUCTION AND IMITATION: SHOWING YOUR CHILD WHAT TO DO

Besides shaping, two other procedures are commonly used to teach new behaviors. One is termed instructional training and the other imitation training. Instructional training is used to teach new behaviors to children who can follow verbal directions. You simply describe what you want your child to do; then you acknowledge and praise your child when she attempts to follow your instructions. If your child lacks adequate language skills, you may train her by imitation. With imitation training, you demonstrate how to do the task or behavior and then have your child copy what you just demonstrated. Again, praise your child for any attempt she makes to imitate what you did.

Instructional and imitation training can be combined. For example, when Judy's parents wanted to teach her to go to the bathroom and brush her teeth, they gave verbal instructions and reinforced them with demonstrations (imitation training). They began by having her look directly at them as they issued the request. This got her attention. Next, they issued a simple and specific request in a matter-of-fact but firm voice: "Judy, go to the bathroom and brush your teeth." Children are not likely to comply with requests that are expressed in either an angry or apologetic manner, or ones that are framed as questions. After giving the instruction, Judy's mother silently counted from 1,001 to 1,010, thereby giving Judy approximately ten seconds to begin her trip to the bathroom. The therapist had told Judy's parents that they should not reason with or cajole her during this time, but should just wait. This was perhaps the most difficult part of the process.

If Judy headed toward the bathroom, the parents were to express their approval. If she whined or threw a tantrum, they were to ignore her. When Judy hadn't moved by the count of 1,010, her mother repeated the request exactly as she had stated it the first time. This time, however, she also pointed in the direction of the bathroom, thereby adding a gestural prompt to her verbal instruction. After ten seconds, if Judy still had not headed toward the bathroom, her mother was instructed to guide her there gently, ignoring any protests. This proved not to be necessary.

Once Judy was in the bathroom, her mother reminded her to brush her teeth. However, Judy did not know how to perform the task, so her mother taught her by breaking down the task of toothbrushing into small steps. These steps included finding the toothbrush and toothpaste, wetting the toothbrush, putting on the toothpaste, holding the toothbrush at a 45-degree angle to the teeth, brushing the top teeth in a circular fashion, and so forth.

To teach a skill such as toothbrushing, you can either begin with the first step or with the last step. The former process is called forward chaining, the latter, backward chaining. In forward chaining, the first step in the task is learned and then the second step is learned and combined with the first. This chaining is continued until all steps have been learned and practiced together. With backward chaining, you would start by helping your child with every step except for the last one. Then you would give her an opportunity to complete this final step by herself before offering any feedback or assistance. If she needed help, you would give it repeatedly until she learned this step. The next time, you would help with every step except the last two. When those two steps were mastered, you would help with all but the last three steps, and so on. An advantage of backward chaining is that with each trial, your child successfully completes the task.

NEGATIVE REINFORCEMENT

So far, we have focused on the use of positive reinforcement and planned ignoring, in combination with instructional and imitation training, to shape your child's appropriate behavior. However, there is another group of procedures that you can employ to increase the frequency of appropriate behaviors. These procedures rely on negative reinforcement and are often confused with punishment. Negative reinforcement of a particular behavior occurs when that behavior results in the removal of an aversive or unpleasant situation, thereby increasing the rate of that behavior in the future. We use negative reinforcement often in our daily lives. We move inside to escape the cold, we stop at a red traffic light to avoid an automobile accident, we wear sunglasses to reduce glare, and we take off a shoe to remove a pebble that is bothersome.

Negative reinforcement may already be in operation in your relationship with your child. Indeed, it is possible that your child's misbehavior is being maintained by negative reinforcement. For example, if your child refuses to eat spinach (an inappropriate behavior), and in response you throw out the spinach, you are negatively reinforcing his inappropriate behavior because you have removed the unpleasant situation (spinach on his plate). In other words, you are encouraging your child to continue to refuse spinach through negative reinforcement.

When your child's problem behavior is maintained by negative reinforcement, the needed intervention is no longer to allow the inappropriate behavior to result in avoidance of the task at hand. For instance, rather than giving in and throwing out the spinach, the effective parent ignores the child's complaining and refusal to eat, and structures the situation so that the child completes the task at hand (eating spinach) before he is permitted to engage in a preferred activity (eating dessert).

Negative reinforcement can also be used to promote appropriate behaviors. Consider the child who is such a fussy eater that she becomes underweight. Her parents and therapists have tried varying the variety, texture, and temperature of her food. They have tried cajoling her to eat; but nothing works. At this point a behavior analyst may become involved and use both negative and positive reinforcement to encourage her to accept food.

During the learning sessions conducted at mealtime, the therapist presents the child with a spoon laden with food and says, "Take a bite." If the child accepts and swallows the food, the therapist immediately gives her words of praise, hugs, and offers her a brief opportunity to play with a toy. In this way positive reinforcement is contingent on food acceptance. If she refuses to accept the food immediately, the therapist waits three seconds before gently manipulating the child's jaw so that she *must* accept the food. The child quickly learns that she can avoid the physical guidance by accepting presented bites. This "avoidance learning" is a direct result of the process of negative reinforcement.

PUNISHMENT

Positive and negative reinforcement both result in an increase of a targeted behavior. In contrast, punishment of a behavior is a process that leads to a decrease in the frequency of that behavior. For example, you might punish your child by yelling at him for running into the street. Punishment can also involve withdrawal of a privilege; for instance, taking away television for being aggressive, not permitting play outside after school for failing to complete a homework assignment, or removing a favorite toy for having a tantrum.

Applied behavior analysts typically avoid the use of punishment whenever possible, because it can result in negative side effects, such as oppositional behavior on the part of the child. In contrast, positive-reinforcement strategies can usually promote the child's adaptive behavior, while being less disruptive to the child's and the family's routine.

Perhaps most worrisome, punishment procedures can be, and sometimes are, misused. A punishment may be so effective in stopping a problem behavior that it leads parents to use this method to control other less severe behaviors. Over time, however, punishment typically becomes less and less effective and the parent may find that he must use increasingly severe punishments to have any effect on his child's behavior.

Yet, in some cases, punishment procedures may be necessary following the failure of positive reinforcement. For example, some disabled children exhibit self-injurious behaviors that place them at high risk for tissue damage, sensory loss, recurrent infection, loss of mobility, and restrictive educational and/or residential placement. Even with the most severe behavior disorders, however, punishment procedures should be employed only after positive-reinforcement strategies have been shown to be ineffective. Furthermore, positive reinforcement of appropriate behavior should continue in conjunction with the use of punishment.

Scolding

The mildest punishment involves issuing a warning or reprimand following your child's misbehavior. As suggested previously, this scolding may suppress the problem behavior, but it may also serve as a reinforcer for gaining attention. The manner in which verbal disapproval is given may determine the degree of its effectiveness. It has been shown that soft, yet firmly stated reprimands are more effective than shouting. Negative verbal statements should be used sparingly and should never be made in a way that demeans your child.

Time Out

Unfortunately, statements of verbal disapproval often make little difference to a young or mentally retarded child. A more effective punishment strategy could entail "time out," in which you remove your child from his reinforcers. Time-out procedures include brief isolation, such as having him sit in a chair placed in a corner of a room, or preventing him from receiving reinforcement by having him wear a time-out ribbon, which reminds peers and teachers not to interact with him following a misbehavior.

Effective use of time out hinges upon several considerations. During time out, all preferred objects and activities must be beyond reach or out of sight. Time out will not work if your child has simply been removed from the scene of the problem be-

havior. For instance, a mistaken use of time out could occur when parents send a child to her room because of misbehavior. If the room is filled with toys or if removal results in the child's avoiding the task that led to the misbehavior, time out may actually reinforce the bad behavior.

Sometimes the use of time out may be ill advised. For instance, some disabled children will engage in self-stimulatory behaviors such as body-rocking or excessive masturbation. If placed in a relatively isolated, nonstimulating environment, the self-stimulatory behavior may increase. Another example of a poor use of time out may occur when an unruly child lacks social skills. For this child, time out may serve only to isolate him further at a time when the development of social behaviors should be the focus of treatment. Time out is also not a sensible alternative when the child is so resistant or combative that he cannot be safely kept in the time-out area.

When used, time out should be administered as consistently as possible and preferably in response to only one or two problem behaviors at a time. The duration of time out should be kept short, usually one to three minutes. Brief time outs are often effective in suppressing misbehavior, whereas longer time outs can be counterproductive. Having your child engage in a desirable, alternative behavior along with the time out often enhances its effectiveness. For example, if your child enjoys joining in adult-to-adult conversations, then time out is more likely to be effective if it is given with the understanding that following the time out he will be allowed to join such a conversation. Although time out is very effective, like other punishments it remains so only if it is employed infrequently.

Removing a Privilege

Sometimes effective punishment consists of taking away a privilege or imposing a penalty when your child misbehaves. The precise fine to be assessed with each type of misbehavior should be determined in advance and applied consistently. In order to implement this strategy, your child must be receiving positive reinforcement that can be withdrawn if he misbehaves. For instance, removal of privileges is frequently used within more comprehensive programs in which points or tokens are dispensed for appropriate behaviors and taken away for infractions. Indeed, removing a privilege often has its largest impact after a child has experienced success in earning rewards. He is then more eager to avoid losses, and small fines can be very effective.

It is important to inform your child in advance that particular behaviors will result in rewards and that certain problem behaviors will lead to fines. As with other punishment strategies, removal of privileges or the imposition of a fine may result in negative side effects, such as avoidance of or aggression toward you. In general, however, this approach to punishment is relatively easy to implement, especially when employed together with positive reinforcement procedures.

Overcorrection

Another punishment procedure that involves a penalty for engaging in undesirable behavior is overcorrection. This involves two steps: restitution and positive practice. First, your child corrects the damages caused by the inappropriate behavior (restitution) and then repeatedly completes an acceptable, alternative behavior (positive practice). An overcorrection procedure is frequently employed with handicapped children who are learning independent toi-

leting skills. When an accident occurs, you would guide your child to provide restitution for the accident (e.g., remove and replace wet clothes, bed linens, etc.) and then have him begin positive practice, which might involve trying to go to the bathroom at hourly intervals. Overcorrection could also be used when your child mischievously throws a glass of milk on the kitchen floor. Here, restitution would involve having him sponge up the milk, and positive practice would entail his using the sponge to scrub a much larger area of the kitchen floor than that covered by the milk. If overcorrection is to be successful, it is important that both the restitution and positive practice components be applied immediately after the problem behavior. Your child should have no access to reinforcement throughout the procedure.

Overcorrection has several advantages. It promotes learning of new skills, a function not inherent in other punishment strategies. However, overcorrection is not without its own difficulties. Your child may be unwilling to complete the required tasks. If substantial physical force is necessary to guide a resistant child, another disciplinary strategy should be considered. Overcorrection also requires more supervision than some alternative punishments.

Using Punishment Responsibly and Effectively

The use of punishment of any variety is controversial. If punishment is used, you should be clear about why you are using it and, when possible, review the reasons with your child. If, under the guidance of a behavior analyst, you decide to use a punishment procedure, it is important to keep in mind the following guidelines:

1. Be sure that your child cannot escape a warranted punishment. The punish-

ment is not likely to be effective if your child can ignore verbal reprimands, play with a favorite toy during time out, or talk his way out of losing a privilege.

2. Punishment should be applied firmly and confidently, and not in graded steps. For example, a firm but matter-of-fact "no" is better than an apologetic request to stop, followed by successively louder and louder reprimands when your child does not obey. Firm punishment does not mean, however, that you should use extended time outs or excessively large fines.

3. From the onset of a behavior-management program, apply punishment every time the targeted inappropriate behavior occurs. Punishment is effective only if delivered consistently.

4. Apply punishment immediately following the misbehavior. In this way, your child is more likely to understand what behavior is being punished.

5. Eliminate any reinforcement that maintains the problem behavior. Parents often reinforce the very behaviors they hope to eliminate. For instance, when your child has been aggressive, you may provide attention by scolding, issuing threats, or lecturing. It would be far better if you withheld your attention and instead simply stated the contingency and then enforced it. For example, you might say: "You hit your sister. Go to time out."

6. Be careful that the delivery of punishment is not associated with the later delivery of reinforcement. For example, you may be overwhelmed with guilt after spanking your child for misbehaving. As a result, you then shower him with affection and reassurances of your love. In so doing, your child has learned that punishment precedes reinforcement and he may, consequently, increase the misbehavior in order to get the affection.

7. Avoid prolonged or extensive use of punishment. If used too often, punishment loses its effectiveness. Further, a coercive relationship between you and your child may develop.

8. Frequently, a problem behavior does not occur in isolation, but as part of an escalating sequence of problem behaviors. In such instances, provide punishment early in your child's performance of an undesirable behavior. For example, a self-injurious behavior such as head-hitting may be preceded by noncompliance with a request, followed by object-throwing, tantrums, or hitting. Punishment for the earlier noncompliance may reduce self-injurious behavior to a greater extent than would punishment that is delivered after the self-injurious behavior has occurred. In essence, it is wiser to punish your child when he reaches for a match than after he has set the fire!

9. Positive-reinforcement strategies should be attempted before punishment. Typically, punishment will only reduce inappropriate behaviors temporarily and, except in the case of overcorrection, it does little to teach your child acceptable behavior.

Helping George

To illustrate how these behavior-management techniques can be combined to help resolve a behavior problem, consider George's refusal to take his seizure medication. The behavior analyst first determined the percentage of doses George accepted. She then made sure that George had the necessary skills to swallow his medication without difficulty. In fact, George did have trouble swallowing pills, so the behavior analyst systematically taught him how to take his medication through instruction and demonstration. Initially, very small capsules were administered. When George showed that he could swallow such capsules consistently, capsules progressively larger in size were presented, until George was able to swallow capsules of the size originally prescribed. While this shaping procedure was under way, any successful swallows were acknowledged and, based on his performance, George was entitled to select and enjoy a special privilege. At the same time, if George resisted accepting presented capsules by turning his head, using his hands to block the capsule, whining, or crying, these annoying yet nondangerous behaviors were ignored. Rather than backing away when these problem behaviors occurred or scolding George for his misbehavior, the behavior analyst calmly continued with the administration of the capsule, thereby not permitting these behaviors to be reinforced negatively. If George attempted to avoid taking the capsule by showing aggressive behavior toward the trainer, he was placed in a brief "time out," followed immediately by continuation of the capsule administration. If he threw the capsules on the floor, he was required to pick them up and throw them away, followed by the loss of a privilege. As George's resistant behaviors subsided, he was increasingly given the opportunity to practice how to take the capsules himself with minimal adult guidance. Throughout this training sequence, the behavior analyst maintained records of George's performance in order to make adjustments in his

behavior-management program and to determine when systematic training was no longer necessary. In addition, the frequency of seizures was monitored to determine if George's increasing compliance was associated with improved seizure control.

PARENT EDUCATION AND TRAINING

Behavior management is most effective if it is designed by a behavior analyst, but carried out by you. Thus, behavior analysts have numerous parent-training approaches to help you manage your child's behavior problems. These range from telephone consultations to intensive, clinic- or home-based parent-training programs. Less structured forms of parent training include "how to" books on behavior management, articles on positive approaches to parenting found in popular magazines, and lectures and workshops.

Parent training begins with the behavior analyst describing the processes that underlie your child's problem behaviors and the treatments needed to change these behaviors. Basic principles are presented using examples drawn from your daily life. Next, the behavior analyst will prescribe specific procedures for you to carry out at home. He will demonstrate the recommended management strategies either by working directly with your child, by role-playing, or by showing a videotape of what to do. Following this, you will be given a chance to rehearse the demonstrated skills. This gives you the opportunity to refine your newly learned skills under simplified circumstances, while the trainer provides you with feedback about your performance.

Once you have mastered these behavior management skills in the clinic, you will need to try them out at home. To assist you, the behavior analyst will often give you a written protocol summarizing "do's" and "don'ts." Part of your homework assignment will be to observe and record the occurrence of targeted appropriate and inappropriate behaviors. When you have implemented the prescribed procedures for one to three weeks, you will be asked to review your child's progress. Based upon your records and a description of your child's behavior, the behavior analyst will help you adjust the management program until it works well.

Once your objectives have been reached, you will no longer need to attend regularly scheduled appointments. Instead, the behavior analyst will remain in contact with you via telephone. Through these telephone contacts, the analyst will be able to continue to "troubleshoot" with you. If your child's behavior takes a turn for the worse, it may become necessary for the clinic visits to resume. Otherwise, you can occasionally call in to your behavior analyst and keep her posted about your child's progress.

SOME QUESTIONS ANSWERED

Can children with mental retardation learn new skills?

All children, however retarded they may be, can learn new skills. In order to learn, however, more than the usual amount of structure and practice is required by the child. And more savvy and patience is required of the parent and teacher.

Do all developmentally disabled children have behavior problems?

Many disabled children do not have behavior problems. However, children with disabilities are at an increased risk to develop behavior problems compared to nonhandicapped children.

As a parent, I should know how to manage my child's behavior. Isn't asking for help admitting that I have failed as a parent?

Baloney! Parenting any child is hard, but special skills are particularly required to parent a disabled child. Just as is true with any other skill, these special skills must be learned. And sometimes they can best be learned with the guidance of a trained professional. Don't let your pride stand in the way. If your child has behavior problems, you may need to do more than to read just one book on your own.

Behavior is multiply determined. Many factors, both biological and environmental, combine to determine how your child behaves. The important message to retain is: You may or may not be a part of the problem (often we don't really know), but for sure, you can be a big part of the solution.

16

NUTRITION AND DENTAL CARE

Adequate nutrition is important for growth and development, to prevent infections, and to keep the bones and muscles strong. A child with a developmental disability may have different nutritional needs from the average child and may require either more or less food. She may not be able to feed herself or may have difficulty chewing and swallowing her food. She may not get hungry or may be unable to tell you when she does want to eat or drink. As a result, providing adequate food and nutrition may be complicated and frustrating. In addition, providing preventative mouth and dental care to a developmentally disabled child can be difficult. She may be unable to brush her teeth herself and unwilling to open her mouth so you can brush them for her. In this chapter we will discuss nutritional and dental needs of the disabled child. We will also discuss inborn errors of metabolism.

ESTHER

Esther has extrapyramidal cerebral palsy. When she was four years old, she was admitted to a children's rehabilitation hospital for a nutritional evaluation. Her parents

had become frustrated because, although they were spending up to an hour, five times a day, trying to feed her, they could not get her to take in enough food to stay well nourished. They were primarily using pureed baby foods and formula, but Esther would push the spoon away with her hands because she didn't like the feel of it on her lips. She also had an involuntary tongue thrust reflex that caused her to push out most of the food that entered her mouth. When she did swallow food, she would often choke on it. In addition, she often vomited about thirty minutes after a meal.

Upon admission to the hospital, Esther was seen by a speech therapist, who began working to desensitize her to the negative feeling of food against her lips. The therapist also positioned Esther's head and neck so the tongue thrust reflex was less of a problem, and she thickened the formula feedings with cereal so there was less choking. She fed Esther in a semisitting position, and then placed her on her belly after meals. Esther was given medication to decrease the vomiting. During a one-month hospitalization, Esther gained three pounds. Her parents participated in her treatment and carried through at home after discharge. Esther now feeds in four half-hour sessions per day and continues to gain weight. As her overall nutrition and growth have improved, her irritability has decreased, she seems happier, and is doing much better in preschool.

NORMAL GROWTH

An infant normally grows at a fairly predictable rate. By four to six months birth weight will have doubled, and by twelve months it will have tripled. From one year of age to the start of the adolescent growth spurt, the average child will gain about five pounds a year. Height usually increases by 50 percent at twelve months and doubles by the fourth birthday. The average four-year-old weighs forty pounds and is forty inches tall. During this period, the child's head also grows. The circumference of the head, measured just above the ears, increases by half to three-quarters of an inch per month and the brain weight doubles by two years of age.

These parameters may not apply to your developmentally disabled child, whose growth and development may be delayed. However, the general pattern of growth should still apply. Every child grows taller and gains weight at his own rate. A problem may be indicated if your child strays from his own pattern.

NUTRITIONAL NEEDS

Children require more calories per pound of body weight than do adults. This is especially true during early childhood, when growth is rapid. For example, an infant requires about forty-five calories per pound per day while an older child requires about thirty calories per pound and an adult less than fifteen calories per pound.

Further, there is variation from child to child; this is especially so for a child with a disability. A child with choreoathetoid cerebral palsy who is constantly in motion may use up a huge amount of energy and may require up to one and a half times the normal caloric intake. Conversely, a child who has a restricted capacity for movement because of weakness or paralysis may only require three-quarters of the normal caloric intake. These individual variations need to be taken into account in planning your child's diet.

The best way to gauge whether your child is being adequately nourished is to monitor his growth. Each time your child goes to the pediatrician, he will be weighed and measured, and these measurements will be plotted on a growth chart. This chart also shows the normal range of heights and weights for each age. If your child's height and weight fall within the normal percentiles, he is probably getting adequate calories and nutrition. This is especially true if his growth parallels a certain percentile over time. If his growth is below normal, he may still be adequately nourished, providing his growth rate is not slowing down. If it does slow down, you will see him "cross" or "fall off" the normal growth curves (Figure 16.1). Many disabled children, such as those with Down syndrome, will end up being short people even when they are fully grown. No matter how much you feed them, their height will be subnormal. They will only get fatter with more calories.

For some disabled children it will be difficult to measure height accurately because of contractures, scoliosis, or other physical deformities. An additional approach to determining the adequacy of nutrition is to measure skin fold thickness. This is done using a tool called a caliper that measures the thickness of skin at the fleshy area

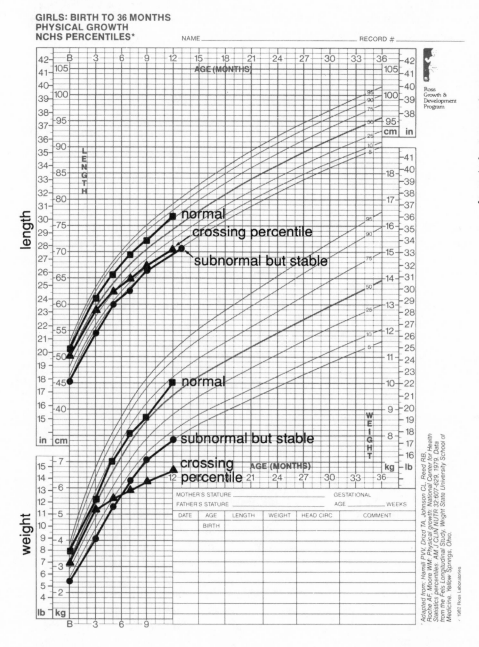

GIRLS: BIRTH TO 36 MONTHS
PHYSICAL GROWTH
NCHS PERCENTILES*

Figure 16.1.
Growth patterns are shown for a child with average growth, a child with subnormal but stable growth, and a child whose growth is "crossing" the percentiles, indicating a growth problem.

above the elbow. Norms have been established for the caliper measurements that will determine if your child has too much or too little body fat.

PREVENTING OBESITY

Certain developmental disabilities predispose children to becoming overweight. These include Prader-Willi syndrome, Down syndrome, muscular dystrophy, and spastic cerebral palsy. Prader-Willi is a syndrome associated with mental retardation and massive obesity that is present from childhood. These same characteristics are also seen in many Down syndrome children. Children who are wheelchair bound as a result of muscular dystrophy or spastic cerebral palsy may become obese as a result of decreased physical activity. Whether you can control your child's weight depends to a large extent on his level of independence. If he can get to the refrigerator and feed himself, he may develop a lifestyle of overeating. If your youngster cannot feed himself, the only way he can get fat is if you overfeed him.

Obesity is better prevented than treated. Having said this, we must admit that it is often not easy to accomplish. One of your child's most enjoyable activities may be eating. And while you will not want to deprive him of this pleasure, you can place certain limits. At mealtime, one helping of food is sufficient and between-meal snacks can be healthful and low caloric, such as fruits and vegetables. Exercise also influences weight gain. Even if your child is nonambulatory, there are active and passive range-of-motion exercises that help prevent obesity. If you need help instituting a weight-control plan, you may want to consult with a nutritionist, who will develop a diet, and with a physical therapist, who will plan an activity program. Inade-

quate weight control is not just unsightly; it can limit your child's mobility and damage his overall health, with effects ranging from elevated blood pressure to an increased risk of fractures.

PREVENTING FAILURE TO THRIVE

The opposite extreme of the obese child is the child who has little appetite or cannot communicate when she is hungry. She eats little and does not gain or even maintain weight. Consequently, her growth starts to fall off the charts. This problem must be approached from a number of angles. If your child has difficulty telling you she is hungry or thirsty, try using a communication board or other means of communication. If this does not work, try feeding her at different times of the day in order to find out at which hour she tends to eat best. Then follow her schedule. You may find that she will eat her largest meal at breakfast or lunch rather than at dinner. You can also try pairing foods she likes with less favored ones. For example, you might insist that she eat one bite of spinach in order to get one bite of chocolate. Try making all meals high in calories and use dietary supplements to enrich her diet further. For example, you might add butter and cream to regular foods and offer food supplements, such as Carnation breakfast bars, Sustacal liquid, or Ensure puddings as between-meal snacks. Finally, you may wish to try a medication, cyproheptadine (Periactin), which has had some success as an appetite stimulant. If these measures are insufficient, tube feeding may need to be considered (see below).

MECHANICS OF EATING

Eating is a complicated task and many things can go wrong. It starts with the

desire to eat and ends with the production of a bowel movement. After your
child decides to eat something, she must
first reach for the food using her fingers,
fork, or spoon; and then accurately
place it inside her mouth. Next, it
must be chewed and swallowed. Finally
the food must make its way into
the stomach and through the intestines.
During this transit, nutrients and
water are absorbed out of the food and
waste material is added to form stool.
Abnormalities can occur anywhere along
this path.

Getting Food to the Mouth

If your child has cerebral palsy or muscular dystrophy, getting food from the
plate to the mouth may require a major
effort. Uncoordinated movements or weakness may make it difficult for your child to
handle a fork or spoon accurately, so that
the food, if it can be picked up at all, lands
everywhere but in her mouth. The effort
needed may be so large that your child
avoids eating altogether. A number of
adaptive devices can help her become independent in feeding (see chapter 18). These
include bowls with high sides, spoons with
curved handles, and cups with rocker bot-
toms.

If your child is unable to feed herself,
you will need to feed her. Here, too, there
may be problems. Like Esther, your child
may reject food either because she doesn't
like the feel of it against her lips or because her involuntary tongue thrust pushes
the food out rather than taking it in. An
occupational therapist or speech pathologist can work with your child to position
her appropriately and gradually introduce
new food textures until she starts to accept
them.

Sucking and Chewing

Once the food reaches the mouth, it
must be sucked or chewed. Suckling is the
most basic feeding skill a baby possesses. It
permits him to gain sustenance from his
mother's breast. However, some children
with disabilities, especially those with cerebral palsy, have an abnormal suck that
interferes with normal feeding. If your
child has this problem, a number of approaches can be taken. Appropriate positioning of your child's head and neck is
critical. If your child normally lies in an
extended, arched position, you must cradle
him in a flexed posture so that the body
parts needed for eating are lined up properly. By manually pursing your child's lips
and holding his jaw stable, you can help
him develop improved tongue and lip control (Figure 16.2). The therapist may try to
teach your child to drink from a straw.
This is especially helpful for the child who
has a tongue thrust. The therapist may
also alter the consistency of the feedings.
In some cases, children will do better with
thickened feedings — for example, by adding cereal to the formula, as was the case
with Esther. Through observation and clinical response, the therapist will help you
adjust feedings to the best advantage.
When your child begins to consume a
greater volume of food and starts to gain
weight, you will know that these efforts
are working.

Chewing is a more advanced form of
eating than suckling. It normally develops
around six to nine months of age and permits the child to start eating solid foods.
However, chewing may be significantly
delayed or abnormal in some disabled children, especially those with cerebral palsy.
Though the development of chewing skills
will depend, in large part, on brain matura-

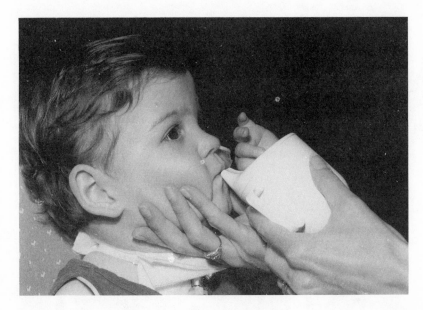

Figure 16.2. *By manually pursing your child's lips and holding the jaw stable, you can help your child develop improved tongue and lip control.*

tion, certain steps can be taken to promote chewing ability. One approach is to place food between the upper and lower back teeth; this forces your child to use tongue and jaw movement to dislodge the food. Thick crackers or teething biscuits are often used for this purpose.

Swallowing

Once the food has been sucked or chewed, it must next be swallowed. Swallowing has three components. Your child must be able to collect the food into a lump, then move the food from the tongue to the back of the throat, and finally, propel the food down the tube (esophagus) to the stomach. Poor coordination of any of these phases will lead to ineffective swallowing. Poor swallowing not only affects your child's ability to eat, it may also result in escape of food into the windpipe, which leads to the lungs. This is called aspiration, and can cause your child to cough in an attempt to expel the aspirated food. In the worst cases, aspiration may lead to

pneumonia. In normal children, aspiration is avoided because a flap of tissue called the epiglottis closes over the windpipe when swallowing begins (Figure 16.3). Thus, the food can travel down only the esophagus, not the windpipe. Children with cerebral palsy may have uncoordinated swallowing with incomplete or poorly timed closure of the epiglottis. They are at particular risk for aspiration. If this becomes a major problem, feeding by mouth may need to be stopped.

Movement through the Esophagus and Stomach — Gastroesophageal Reflux

Once the food enters the esophagus and moves into the stomach, it normally stays there until it is ready to proceed through the small intestine. A muscle surrounding the base of the esophagus acts as a one-way valve, permitting food to enter the stomach but not back up into the esophagus. However, if this muscle is uncoordinated or weak, food and stomach acid can back up into the esophagus. This is called

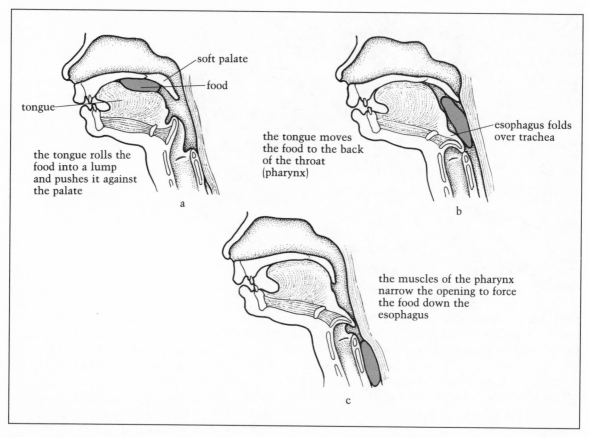

soft palate

food

tongue

the tongue rolls the
food into a lump
and pushes it against
the palate

a

the tongue moves
the food to the back
of the throat
(pharynx)

esophagus folds
over trachea

b

the muscles of the pharynx
narrow the opening to force
the food down the
esophagus

c

Figure 16.3. (a) *After food had been chewed, the tongue rolls it into a lump and pushes it against the palate. (b) It next moves the food to the back of the throat. As swallowing begins, the epiglottis folds over the opening of the trachea to direct food down the esophagus and not into the lungs. Some handicapped children, especially those with cerebral palsy, have defective closure with resultant aspiration into the lungs. (c) The muscles of the pharynx narrow the throat opening, forcing the food down the esophagus.*

gastroesophageal reflux. It presents two problems. First, your child may vomit within thirty to sixty minutes after feedings, losing much of his needed nutrition and being at risk for aspiration. Second, the acid juices from the stomach may cause an irritation of the esophagus. This makes swallowing food painful and will likely lead your child to further avoid eating. Repeated episodes of pneumonia, food avoidance, or back-arching may indicate reflux,

although these symptoms have many other causes as well.

When reflux is suspected, certain medical studies may be performed, including an upper GI (gastrointestinal) study, a milk scan, and a pH probe analysis. For an upper GI study, your child is given liquid barium to drink; X-rays are then taken after specified periods of time to assess how well the barium moves through the stomach into the intestine. This procedure can reveal structural abnormalities in the esophagus, stomach, and intestines, and reflux if it occurs during the study (Figure 16.4). A second study, called a milk scan, gives information on how fast food moves out of the stomach, as well as the presence of reflux into the esophagus or aspiration of food into the lungs. The milk scan involves having your child swallow formula that is laced with a small amount of radio-activity. The esophagus, stomach, and lungs can then be scanned to pick up the radioactivity at certain times to see when the formula has left the stomach, and whether it has refluxed into the esophagus or been aspirated into the lungs.

Reflux may be intermittent and, therefore, may not be seen on either the upper GI study or the milk scan. If these tests are negative but reflux is still suspected, a pH

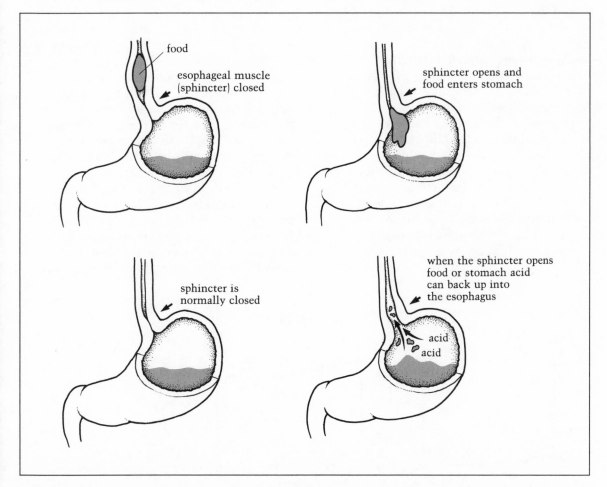

Figure 16.4. *Gastro-esophageal reflux: Food normally passes down the esophagus, through the esophageal sphincter, and into the stomach. Normally the sphincter then closes, acting as a one-way valve. However, if the muscle is weak, there can be reflux of acidic stomach contents back up into the esophagus.*

probe test may be indicated. For this test, the doctor inserts a small thin tube through the nose and advances it to just above the muscle valve at the junction of the esophagus and stomach. A pH probe is attached to the end of the tube. This probe measures the acidity of the surrounding fluid. If the gastroesophageal valve is allowing reflux, the probe will record an increase in acidity, which means a drop in pH. The probe is left in place for twenty-four hours and the results are analyzed by a computer. Normally there is a fairly constant pH. When the pH fluctuates significantly, reflux is indicated (Figure 16.5). This is most likely to occur in the hour after meals or after bedtime when the child is placed on his stomach.

Treatment of reflux may involve changing the volume of your child's meals and positioning him differently while he eats. For example, your child may do better if he sits up for thirty to sixty minutes after meals. This allows the food to slide down easily into the stomach and makes it less likely to back up into the esophagus.

However, these steps may not be enough. In this case, the medications be-

thanechol (Urecholine), metoclopramide (Reglan), cimetidine (Tagamet), and/or ranitidine (Zantac) may be used. Bethanechol and metoclopramide work to tighten the muscle, and cimetidine and ranitidine counteract the stomach acidity, thereby decreasing the irritation of the esophagus. Your child may feel more like eating if he is more comfortable. If these measures seem to be working, a second pH probe may be inserted to prove that the reflux has improved.

If these medical measures do not work, surgery may be considered, especially if aspiration pneumonia occurs repeatedly. The surgical procedure, called a fundal plication, involves strengthening the muscle valve at the stomach-esophagus junction by wrapping the top of the stomach tightly around the esophagus. After the operation your child can still be fed by mouth, but reflux should no longer occur.

Not all vomiting is a consequence of reflux. It can also result from a behavior disorder called rumination. This term refers to a digestive process observed in cows, in which the cow swallows food and then brings it up again from its rumen to

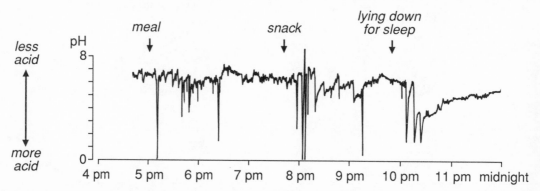

Figure 16.5. *Results of a pH probe. A tube containing a pH electrode has been placed down the esophagus and positioned just above the stomach. Although the pH (acidity) should remain constant, it increases in this child after meals, snacks, and when he is sleeping, giving evidence of gastro-esophageal reflex.*

rechew it. Some severely mentally retarded individuals will practice rumination. They will vomit shortly after swallowing and then chew and swallow again. This is inefficient as well as socially offensive, and can often be handled using behavior-modification techniques.

ALTERNATE METHODS OF FEEDING

Despite the above efforts, some children will still be unable to eat enough to thrive. Parents may spend as much as two hours at each meal trying to feed their child, yet the child still does not gain or even maintain his weight. In these instances, a nasogastric or NG feeding tube is used. This is a plastic tube that is passed through the nose and down into the stomach. A liquid formula or blenderized food is then given directly into the stomach (Figure 16.6). NG feeding can allow your child to gain as much as five pounds in a matter of a month or two. The feedings can be given as boluses (single large volumes) of three

to eight ounces every three to six hours, or they can be administered as a continuous drip throughout the day or overnight.

The advantage of bolus feedings is that they do not interfere with normal daily activities. The feeding itself takes about twenty minutes. However, the large volume may be difficult for your child to tolerate and may lead to vomiting or abdominal discomfort. If this happens, you may want to try continuous-drip feedings, in which a Kangaroo or similar type electric pump delivers the formula at a set rate. Sometimes tube feedings are used to supplement oral feedings. In this case, you will want to encourage your child to take in as much food orally as she can. Therefore, it is best to use the tube feedings at night, so her stomach will not be filled during the daytime.

In placing the tube you must be careful that it is in the stomach and not in the lungs; otherwise you may inject formula into the lungs, causing pneumonia. To avoid this, when the tube is first placed, a

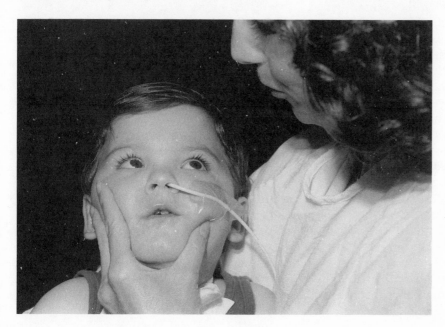

Figure 16.6. *This child receives nasogastric tube feedings because he is not able to take in sufficient food by mouth to maintain his weight. He is now learning tongue and lip control by the therapist's manually pursing the child's lips and holding his jaw stable. It is hoped that the tube will be removed soon.*

syringe is used to push air through the tube while you listen with a stethoscope above the stomach. If you hear a rumbling sound, like a burp, you are in the stomach and formula can be given through the tube. In the unlikely event that the tube is in the lungs, no sound will be heard, and you will need to withdraw and reposition the tube.

The nasogastric tube works well for a few months but can be irritating to the nose as well as the stomach when used for prolonged periods of time. If long-term tube feeding is needed, it is best to place a gastrostomy feeding tube (or G tube). In this procedure an incision is made through the skin and muscle tissue into the stomach. A replaceable rubber tube is then threaded through this hole, and formula or blenderized food can be given. Formulas such as Sustacal, Isocal, and Pediasure are specially formulated for tube feedings and are different from infant formula. They have a higher protein content and more calories. Thus, more nutrition can be given in a smaller volume of formula. Remember that having a tube does not prevent you from feeding your child by mouth unless there is concern about aspiration into the lungs. Combining oral and tube feedings, a young child requires about two to two and a half ounces of fluids per pound of body weight per day, divided into four feedings.

The surgical placement of a gastrostomy tube can be performed under either local or general anesthesia. Once the tube has been placed, you must be sure it is maintained properly to avoid complications. The area surrounding the tube should be washed daily to keep it clean and the tube needs to be changed every few months, a task that you can do at home. If the skin area around the tube has some bleeding, it may need to be cauterized using silver nitrate sticks. If formula leaks around the outside of the tube, the tube can be taken out for a few hours at a time, and the hole will shrink in size so there will be a better fit. Finally, if the area is inflamed, or "weeping," it means that stomach acid is seeping out. The use of Duoderm or another occlusive dressing, such as Vaseline, should help. If oral feeding improves over time and tube feeding is no longer necessary, you can simply remove the gastrostomy tube under your doctor's supervision and the hole will close over without additional surgery.

TRAVEL THROUGH THE INTESTINES: CONSTIPATION

Food is passed through the stomach and into the intestines, where water and nutrients are removed. The result is a bowel movement about once a day. A prolonged period (more than three days) without having a stool or having a very hard stool is called constipation. Constipation is a major problem in children with disabilities. Decreased physical activity, a reduced intake of fluids and foods, and uncoordinated bowel contractions all contribute to the problem.

Treatment methods vary. Dietary intervention may be sufficient to prevent constipation. As much fluid as possible should be added to the oral or tube feedings. Bulky and high-fiber foods, such as whole-grain cereals, bran, fruits, and vegetables should be eaten to increase gastrointestinal activity. If necessary, a fiber supplement, such as Unifiber, can be mixed with the formula and given by tube. Prune and apricot juices act as mild natural laxatives. Increased exercise is certainly a help and should be encouraged when possible.

Stool softeners, such as docusate (Colace), may be used regularly to help encourage movement of the stool through the gut. Note that it takes one to three days for stool softeners to start working. When more powerful laxatives or suppositories are necessary, milk of magnesia, Malt-Supex, Senokot, Kondramul, Dulcolax, or glycerine suppositories are effective. Enemas, such as Fleet's pediatric enema, may also help the problem, but constant use of enemas may interfere with rectal sphincter control and should be avoided. A combination of these approaches may be needed to establish regular bowel movements. Keep in mind, however, that it is not necessary for your child to have one stool each day; once every three days may suffice.

INBORN ERRORS OF METABOLISM

To this point, we have focused on both the normal nutritional needs and the problems of the disabled child. However, some children become disabled as a result of a condition in which their bodies cannot metabolize foods properly, which leads to the accumulation of toxins and results in brain damage. This is called an inborn error of metabolism. An affected child is born with absent or deficient levels of an enzyme necessary to break down a specific component of food. Most commonly it involves problems with protein breakdown. Because the toxins that accumulate are difficult to remove, the major approach to treatment involves restricting the diet to prevent accumulation of toxins in the first place. Unfortunately, a side effect of this dietary therapy may be interference with normal growth. As a result, these children have a whole new group of problems.

Inborn errors of metabolism are inherited, usually as an autosomal-recessive trait (see chapter 4). Thus, a family who has had one affected child is at increased risk for having future affected children. Prenatal diagnosis is available. Perhaps the best-known inborn error of metabolism is phenylketonuria (PKU). When a child has PKU, he lacks the enzyme necessary to break down the amino acid phenylalanine, one of the building blocks of protein. If the PKU is untreated, phenylalanine accumulates and results in severe mental retardation. Early treatment with a special diet can prevent this.

This treatment requires identification in infancy. We can now successfully identify PKU and some other inborn errors of metabolism in the first weeks of life using newborn screening techniques. You may remember that your newborn baby had a drop of blood taken from his heel before he was discharged from the hospital. This blood spot was sent to a state laboratory where a test for PKU and certain other inborn errors was performed. Doctors are notified of abnormal test results in a matter of days, and if the child is confirmed to be affected, treatment is started.

Treatment for PKU and many other inborn errors requires long-term use of a diet that is not very palatable and that can interfere with normal growth if not monitored closely. This problem of maintaining adequate nutrition has led to the search for other approaches to treatment.

One approach that has been tried involves vitamin supplementation. Some enzymes require vitamin cofactors in order to become active. In certain inborn errors of metabolism, large doses of a specific vitamin have been found to enhance residual enzyme activity and improve the child's condition. For example, vitamin B_{12} has been used in treating methylmalonic aciduria, vitamin B_6 to treat homocystinuria, and biotin to treat multiple carboxylase deficiency. If untreated, each of these disorders leads to symptoms ranging from vomiting and fatigue to stroke and coma. Treatment frequently results in marked improvement, and in some cases vitamins can decrease or even eliminate the need for a restricted diet. Unfortunately, the success of "megavitamin" treatment for these rare disorders has led some people mistakenly to promote megavitamin therapy for everything from Down syndrome to schizophrenia.

Another approach to treating inborn errors involves developing biochemical detours around the enzyme block. In urea cycle disorders, also called hyperammonemia, toxic amounts of ammonia accumulate from the breakdown of protein. Such severe protein restriction is needed to lower the ammonia level that malnutrition results. To avoid this, certain medications have been developed (such as Ucephen) that convert the accumulating ammonia to a nontoxic product that can be excreted in the urine. Thus, even though the normal pathway for getting rid of ammonia is blocked, a new pathway is substituted. This permits a less restricted protein intake and improved growth and development of affected children.

Organ transplantation has been tried as a method of curing inborn errors of metabolism. Many enzymes are in high concentration in certain organs of the body. If the organ with the defective enzyme is replaced with a healthy organ, normal enzymes can be produced. For example, in the disorder tyrosinemia, the affected organ is the liver. It has been found that if a child affected with tyrosinemia undergoes liver transplantation, the disease is cured.

Another example of the value of organ transplantation for the treatment of inborn errors has been the use of bone marrow transplantation in the treatment of metachromatic leukodystrophy. This disorder results from a deficiency of the enzyme arylsulfatase A and results in the storage of toxic compounds in the nervous system.

This leads to a progressive loss of physical and intellectual abilities. In bone marrow transplantation, marrow is harvested from a matched donor, usually a relative, and injected into the patient. The injected marrow, which contains many enzymes including arylsulfatase A, replaces the patient's marrow, which has been destroyed as part of the procedure.

While transplantation has proved useful in tyrosinemia, metachromatic leukodystrophy, and certain other inborn errors, it is both expensive and dangerous. The cost is about $100,000 and there is a mortality rate of about 10 percent. These problems limit the use of transplantation.

An obvious and simpler solution to replacing the whole organ is to replace the missing enzyme itself. This has proved more difficult than expected. To this point, the only disorder that has been successfully treated using enzyme replacement is combined immune deficiency (the Bubble Baby syndrome). In this disorder, the child lacks the enzyme adenosine deaminase. This enzyme is essential for the proper functioning of white blood cells, which are necessary for fighting infections. Without the enzyme, any infection can lead to a life-threatening illness. Thus, an affected child must be kept in isolation. However, in 1987 enzyme replacement became available, and now weekly injections of the deficient enzyme can reverse this condition. It is hoped that successes in other disorders will follow.

Yet, even if enzyme replacement were easy, it would still require continued treatment throughout life. The ideal solution would be to replace the gene that codes for the defective enzyme. If this could be accomplished, the person would regain the ability to produce the enzyme himself. This approach is now being tested for use in combined immunodeficiency.

In sum, inborn errors of metabolism present major nutritional problems because treatment frequently requires restrictive diets that interfere with normal growth. Even with treatment, many affected children will have developmental disabilities that compound their nutritional problems. However, there are a number of new approaches to therapy, which hopefully will make reliance on dietary restriction less of an issue in the future.

DENTAL CARE

Nutrition starts with the teeth. Care of the mouth and teeth is important to prevent dental decay, gum problems, and bad breath. For a child with a disability, however, good dental care can become a significant struggle. The areas of difficulty may include the child's physical ability to care for his mouth and teeth, his willingness to cooperate, and/or a number of problem behaviors that can compromise oral health.

Problem Behaviors

There are a number of habits common in children with disabilities that can cause problems in the mouth. These habits include mouth-breathing, tooth-grinding, and finger-sucking. Mouth-breathing can lead to dryness of the mouth and inflammation and enlargement of the gums, especially in the top front area. Sometimes, mouth-breathing is simply a bad habit that can be stopped through behavioral-modification techniques. This might be the case, for example, if your child habitually holds his jaw open. However, mouth-breathing may also result from diminished muscle control that leads to an unusual jaw position at rest, or from a partial obstruction in the nasal passages (for example, enlarged adenoids). If your child is breathing through his mouth because of a partially blocked airway, medical treatment using nasal sprays or even removal of adenoidal tissue may provide relief.

Tooth-grinding (bruxing) occurs in many children with severe mental retardation. It can occur at night, during sleep, or intermittently during the daytime. When done constantly, it can become nerve-racking to parents and other caregivers. In addition, bruxing wears down the teeth and may eventually change the child's bite or interfere with efficient chewing. In some cases, the child will outgrow the grinding. If the habit does not resolve itself, treatment might involve behavior-modification techniques in which the child is rewarded for not grinding. This approach is most successful when he is grinding simply because he is bored or inactive. Another approach to treatment, if tolerated, consists of a protective mouth guard, fabricated by the dentist to fit over the teeth and protect them from the trauma and wear of grinding. For some children with this problem, there is no definitive treatment.

Another oral behavior problem common to all children is thumb- or finger-sucking. This usually is not a serious problem and tends to resolve itself by the age of five, although it does tend to persist longer in children with developmental disabilities. For any child, this habit may contribute to the development of a malocclusion (bad bite), which may in turn predispose the child to tooth injury because the top front teeth are in an extremely prominent and exposed position. If this habit is severe enough and the malocclusion great enough, there may also be problems with normal chewing, swallowing, and/or speech development. The cause of thumb-sucking is often psychological. In light of this, the benefits of simple dental intervention must be weighed against your child's emotional need to engage in this habit.

Dental Decay

Cavities most commonly occur before adolescence. The process of dental decay begins with plaque, a clear sticky mass that clings to the teeth and gums. Plaque is composed of bacteria, saliva, salivary products, and food particles. Bacteria use the sugars from food to make acid as a waste product. The acid, over time, destroys tooth enamel, causing a cavity. Plaque may also harden and form tartar. Plaque and tartar both cause inflammation of the gums. Over a long period of time, this may lead to bone loss, loose teeth, and increased tooth sensitivity.

Gum Disease

Painful overgrowth of the gums is a particular problem with the prolonged use of the anticonvulsant Dilantin. Once Dilantin is stopped, the gums will go back to normal in a matter of months. If the gums become very painful during therapy, the excess tissue can be cut back surgically. The high-calorie, high-fat diets used to treat children with failure to thrive also place them at risk for gum disease. Good dental hygiene is essential to avoid the buildup of high-caloric material between the teeth and gums that will lead to inflammation.

Routine Dental Care

Dental decay and gum disease are preventable through a combination of tooth brushing, flossing, fluoridation, and periodic dental visits. Although it is ideal to brush and floss after every meal, thorough cleaning before bedtime is usually sufficient to prevent cavities or gum disease. A small, soft, polished nylon bristle brush should be used. It should be held at a 45-degree angle to the tooth and gums, while brushing in a circular motion. Brushing should be done systematically in order to ensure that all teeth are cleaned during each session.

If your child is not able to hold a toothbrush, an occupational therapist may be able to adapt the handle so it can be used more easily. We always encourage parents to involve children in their own oral hygiene maintenance. Use of an electric toothbrush, either by parent or child, is an alternative that may be considered in order to improve mechanical cleaning of the teeth.

If you must brush your child's teeth for him, position him either lying down or seated with his head tipped back so that you can see the brush contacting his teeth. This kind of position will also permit you to control your child's head. A very small amount of a fluoride toothpaste may be used on the brush, but if your child has problems with choking, spitting, or excessive swallowing of the paste, the brush may instead be soaked in a fluoride rinse prior to use. It is also acceptable to brush using plain tap water. The most important point is that each tooth should be carefully cleaned. After brushing, dental floss should be used to remove plaque and foreign material from between the teeth, where brush bristles cannot reach. This is often difficult with special children, but the use of a floss holder can be very helpful. Together, brushing and flossing can thoroughly remove plaque from teeth, thereby minimizing the possibility of cavities and gum disease.

Research has shown that fluoridation of community water supplies is the single most effective decay-preventive measure available. If your child does not drink much water, fluoride drops or tablets are advisable. You should consult your pediatrician or pediatric dentist regarding this decision. It has been unequivocally proven that fluoride in low doses has a significant anticavity effect and that it is safe. Additional decay-preventive benefits are also obtained from periodic fluoride applications, which are given in your dentist's office.

Routine dental checkups will help prevent problems and catch difficulties early. Pediatric dentists are specially trained to care for disabled patients, but many general dentists also have had experience caring for special children. Periodic dental visits should start at twelve to eighteen months of age. A regular, periodic schedule of care, for example every six months, can then be set for your child. During these visits, the dentist will evaluate the health of mouth and gums, and examine teeth and bite carefully. The dentist will also clean your child's teeth thoroughly and perform an office fluoride treatment.
X rays will be taken if indicated. The dentist may also suggest use of a pit and fissure sealant, a preventive technique in which a plastic cover is painted on the biting surfaces of the back teeth, in order to minimize further the possibility of developing cavities.

Nursing Caries

Nursing caries are cavities that occur in both bottle-fed and breast-fed babies, especially in those who are sent to bed with a bottle. Prolonged contact over hours with sugars from the liquid in the bottle can cause tooth damage. Any kind of sugar can cause problems, including the natural sugars present in milk and fruit juice.

SOME QUESTIONS ANSWERED

Does my child need vitamin supplements?

This depends on how well he is eating and whether he gets enough sunlight to provide vitamin D. If he has a fairly normal diet or is receiving a formula that has vitamin supplements, then no daily vitamins are needed. If your child is confined to a wheelchair and rarely gets outside, a daily multivitamin (such as Flintstones) may be helpful. Children under two years old may benefit from multivitamin drops or tablets such as Tri-vi-sol or Poly-vi-sol.

What about megavitamin therapy?

The theory that huge doses of certain B-complex vitamins as well as vitamins A and C will help nutrition and mental function is incorporated into megavitamin therapy. Doses of vitamins one thousand times the daily needs are used. As noted in this chapter, the basis for this approach is that there are certain rare inborn errors of metabolism that do respond to high doses of one specific vitamin. This concept has been broadened to suggest treatment with vitamins for everything from cancer to schizophrenia, including mental retardation. A number of studies have now been performed that clearly show that megavitamin therapy has no effect on intellectual function or nutritional balance. Therefore, there is no rational reason to use megavitamins and there may be problems with toxicity from overuse.

Should I be giving my child supplements of trace minerals?

Here again we are dealing with nontraditional concepts similar to those associated with megavitamin therapy. It has been suggested that many problems of developmentally disabled people result from deficiencies in selenium, zinc, and other trace minerals. Daily supplements of the trace elements are suggested. However, there is no evidence to support the use of trace mineral supplements.

How do I strengthen my child's bones so he is less apt to get fractures?

The best way to strengthen bones is to exercise them either passively or actively. A child who is nonambulatory is more likely to have weak bones and to get fractures from such simple activities as sitting up or moving in or out of a wheelchair. This bone weakness may be accentuated if your child receives the anticonvulsants phenobarbital or Dilantin. Some studies have suggested that supplements of activated vitamin D benefit these children by strengthening their bones. Calcium supplements alone have not been shown to be helpful.

How much water should my child drink?

Babies should drink one and a half to two and a half ounces per pound per day. Older children will not need extra fluids, providing they are receiving a normal diet. Disabled children who have a poor oral intake and can't tell you when they are thirsty should follow the rules for infants.

What about the value of "alternate" diets?

Alternate or nontraditional diets include organic foods, vegetarian diets, and macrobiotic diets. Organic simply implies that the food was grown, or animals raised, without the use of pesticides or other chemicals, hormones, antibiotics, or additives. There is nothing at all wrong with eating organically grown food, but it has not yet been shown to be nutritionally superior to food purchased in a supermarket. The only complication is the cost of organically grown food, which may be as much as double the usual food price.

Vegetarian diets can also meet your child's nutritional needs providing there is an adequate mixture of carbohydrates, fats, and protein. The one complication is that the increased volume of fruits and vegetables needed to supply adequate nutrients may be too much food for a disabled child to consume. Also, if a nursing mother follows such a diet, her infant may develop deficiencies in calcium, vitamin D, vitamin B_{12}, and iron. A child or a pregnant woman on a vegetarian diet should therefore receive supplements of these vitamins and minerals.

The one diet clearly to avoid is the macrobiotic diet. The goals of this diet are largely religious rather than nutritional. It involves eating cereals and other grains almost to the exclusion of other foods. Strict adherence may result in malnutrition, scurvy, rickets, anemia, and low calcium levels.

Can I do anything about my child's short stature?

Most growth problems in severely impaired children are related to decreased food and calorie consumption leading to chronic undernutrition. Weight is more affected than height. Treatment involves increasing food intake to keep up normal "fat stores." Then your child's growth will not be limited by his nutrition.

In cases of very short children, there is now the possibility of increasing the height potential through using shots of growth hormone. This has been used to treat girls with Turner syndrome who have an absence of one X chromosome and reach an adult height of only about four and a half feet. Shots of genetically synthesized human growth hormone given three times per week for about two years during the adolescent growth spurt have added four or more inches to their final height.

There are at least two aspects that should be considered before you think of using this therapy for your child. First, it is very expensive, upwards of ten thousand dollars per year, and is not covered by many insurance policies. Second, height may not be an important issue for a significantly impaired child. Small size may make it easier for you to handle him physically, and a youthful appearance can have social benefits. In general, if your child's growth curve is paralleling the normal curve, you probably do not need to worry about his size.

17 PHYSICAL THERAPY

Shirley A. Scull, M.S., P.T.

Physical therapists specialize in disorders of gross-motor development, that is, in movements involving the large muscles of the body. A variety of techniques are used, including exercise, developmental therapy, and assistive devices such as braces, walkers, and wheelchairs to maximize your child's physical capabilities.

The average child goes from being unable to hold his head up in the newborn period, to walking near his first birthday. The child with a developmental disability may follow this same sequence but at a much slower rate; or his progress may be arrested at any point. Children with severe problems may never develop the ability to sit by themselves or even to control their heads, while children with less severe problems may learn to walk, but may need the assistance of braces or crutches. Physical therapists guide children through the normal developmental sequence, trying to maximize the potential for gross-motor development.

In addition to being delayed, a child with a developmental disability may also use movement patterns that are different from those of the average baby. For example, she may stand with her legs crossed or

scissored, which could lead to difficulty in balancing and standing. In addition, she could develop some orthopedic complications, such as a dislocated hip, from standing in this position. To prevent this, the physical therapist works to encourage leg separation, for example, by teaching her to stand with her legs apart. She may also make splints that will keep her feet flat to the ground.

LAURA, JOSEPH, AND MATTHEW

Laura is a two-year-old with cerebral palsy. Born two months prematurely, she suffered brain damage from an intracranial hemorrhage. Her legs are stiff and her motor development delayed. Laura's motor skills are similar to those of a six-month-old child; she can roll over and sit briefly if placed in the position.

Joseph is a two-year-old child with spina bifida. He can bend his hips and straighten his knees, but otherwise his legs are paralyzed. He has been able to sit without support since the age of nine months. His arms are strong, and he can drag himself from place to place on his stomach.

Matthew is an eleven-year-old boy with

Duchenne muscular dystrophy, a progressive neuromuscular disease that leaves him very weak. Matthew had learned to walk when he was two, but he always walked on his toes with a side-to-side waddle. This walking pattern was caused by the muscle weakness in his legs. His weakness has progressed and he now uses a wheelchair for mobility.

All of these children are being helped by physical therapy. Laura, for example, needs exercises to keep her joints and muscles flexible, play on her tummy to help make her back and arm muscles strong, and practice balancing in the sitting position. Joseph needs exercises for building strength and braces to help him stand and walk. Matthew needs stretching exercises to prevent contractures of his joints and a wheelchair for mobility. All of their parents need to learn how to continue their children's physical therapy programs at home. Physical therapists provide these services — exercise and developmental therapy, consultation on assistive devices, and parent training.

THE PHYSICAL THERAPY EVALUATION

Your first visit or two to a physical therapist involves a comprehensive assessment. The therapist will evaluate the flexibility, or range of motion, of all of your child's joints, making measurements using a protractor-like tool called a goniometer. Objective measures like this will allow her to assess your child's progress over time. She will move your child's arms and legs to assess muscle tone (normal, spastic, or floppy), noting the patterns of tone and postures. In some conditions, such as spina bifida and muscular dystrophy (see chapter 14), the therapist will test the strength of various muscles in the arms, legs, and trunk. She will grade their strength based

on the ability to move the limb against gravity, and if possible, against some extra resistance provided by her hands.

Gross-motor development will also be assessed. Your child will be tested for head control and the ability to prop up on his tummy, roll, sit, crawl, stand, and walk. The therapist will observe not only whether your child can perform these skills, but also how they are done. Some therapists will administer a standardized test of motor development. Other therapists will put your child in a variety of positions and make observations. Tests of your child's ability to orient his head in space, called righting reactions, and ability to balance in different positions will also be performed. She may try to elicit certain reflexes in your child that may be interfering with normal motor development. An example is the asymmetrical tonic neck reflex or ATNR. When the head is turned to one side, the arms assume a fencing pattern, with one arm straight and one arm bent. The retention of this reflex would make it impossible for your child to develop symmetrical motor patterns such as bringing his hands to his mouth. It also interferes with learning to roll over.

The therapist will ask questions about your child's typical day, and may want to observe you holding your child or ask you about how you position him in his bed, stroller, or other baby equipment. She will be interested in finding out what has helped you so far, and what problems you are having.

All of these evaluations will be analyzed and documented in a written report. Your therapist will probably send a copy to your doctor, and should share the results of the assessment with you. The conclusions will allow her to identify specific long-term and short-term goals and to determine how much and what type of therapy your child will need in order to accomplish these goals.

It is important that your physician, the physical therapist, and you all agree on these goals. Make sure you understand them, since you will be expected to carry out portions of the program at home. If you feel that the goals are inappropriate or need modifying, speak to your physical therapist about this right away.

Laura's physical therapist established the following short-term goals:

1. Maintain range of motion of all joints of her body.
2. Improve the flexibility of the ankles by 10 degrees so that her feet can be brought to a flat foot position.
3. Decrease the stiffness in her legs, especially when standing.
4. Increase the length of time that Laura will sit.
5. Practice balance reactions in sitting so that when Laura falls to the side, she corrects her head and body back toward the center, and uses her arm to catch herself.
6. Increase the strength in Laura's back muscles so that she can play for longer periods on her stomach and is able to hold herself more erect in the sitting position.

Long-term goals were as follows:

1. Laura will sit with her hands free to play.
2. Laura will assume a hands-and-knees position and start to creep.

Laura's therapy program began with direct treatment three times a week, splints for her feet, and a special seat insert for her stroller and high chair. A home program was taught to her mother to be practiced daily. Regular reexaminations were planned to review Laura's progress and modify the goals if necessary.

TYPES OF PHYSICAL THERAPY

Physical therapists are trained in a variety of ways to provide treatment for your child. They use exercise, developmental therapy, braces or splints, ambulation training (walking or other forms of mobility), adaptive equipment, and training for other daily-living activities. The type of therapy will depend on the goals that have been set for your child and will likely change as your child grows. Gradual progress toward the short-term goals may even be evident while your child is in the therapy session.

Exercise

Exercises are used for three different purposes: to improve flexibility or range of motion, to increase muscle strength, and to improve cardiovascular fitness. Exercise programs vary depending on the goals set for your child.

If your child needs to work on flexibility or range of motion, the therapist will most likely prescribe stretching exercises, called passive range of motion, that require someone other than your child to move his limbs. These exercises need to be done daily, at home as well as in therapy sessions. Therefore, you will be trained to perform them properly. You will need to know the proper positioning of your child, where to place your hands, how far to move the limb and in what direction, and how much force to exert. Stretching usually works best if the limb is moved slowly and then held in position for a minute or so. A child with spasticity may need even longer to relax into a position of maximum stretch. Make sure you understand how far you are trying to move the joint. Practice the exercise with your therapist watching you. Ask for directions in writing, with a drawing to illustrate the exercise. You will feel awkward at first, but your therapist should be able to help you learn to do it correctly.

Stretching exercises can help prevent the development of contractures, in which joints become fixed in one position. Contractures can make it difficult to position your child, to dress him, or to care for him in other ways. The therapist will monitor your child's flexibility from time to time, to see that you are achieving the goals established.

Exercises to build muscle strength must be done by the child himself. For a young child who cannot follow directions, strengthening exercises may need to be incorporated into play. For example, riding a tricycle can be used to strengthen the muscles of the hips and thigh; pulling apart pop-beads can be used to strengthen the arms; playing on the stomach can be used to strengthen the back and arm muscles. The therapist will select activities and toys that are developmentally appropriate for your child and that will help improve his muscle strength.

Other strategies may be needed to encourage muscle strengthening in some children. Preschool-aged children may learn through imitation. For instance, a game of "Simon Says" can improve both flexibility and strength of the arms and neck. Leg strengthening can be accomplished by tying a band of elastic called "Thera-Band" around your child's legs and then having him try to stretch the band by spreading his legs. The resistance applied from the band makes these strengthening exercises more effective than some other types of exercise. If your child has spina bifida or any other disability that results in paralysis of the leg muscles, arm-strengthening exercises are extremely important as he will need to use his arms for crutch-walking.

Exercises designed to improve cardiovascular endurance are called "aerobics" and are needed by children who are inactive as a result of developmental disabilities. Aerobic exercise programs increase the heart rate above its resting level for about twenty minutes and should be done at least three times a week to be effective. Your therapist will design an aerobics program that takes your child's disabilities into account. You may want to help him improve his endurance by providing some motivational reward, such as a chart with stars for each day's progress.

Developmental Therapy

Developmental therapy is another form of therapeutic exercise in which your child is moved into the various developmental postures involved in learning a particular skill. For example, if the goal is to achieve sitting balance, the therapist might first design exercises that encourage him to lift his head and upper body while lying on his belly. The therapist might also move your child from one posture to another in order to practice movement transitions such as rolling over, getting to sitting, pulling to stand, and so forth. The therapist uses her hands to support your child when necessary or to assist in trying a new movement pattern. Some positions may be beneficial and will be encouraged, while other positions may promote abnormal tone and will need to be avoided.

Developmental therapy is particularly valuable for children who have cerebral palsy. For example, a child with spasticity may become stuck in a tonic neck reflex pattern if he is left on his back (see above). This position increases abnormal tone, and interferes with your child's ability to develop more advanced skills such as rolling over. Developmental therapy works to inhibit the influence of the tonic neck reflex and encourages more mature reactions that align the head in space (righting reactions) and allow the body to maintain balance in various positions (equilibrium reactions). The therapy follows the developmental sequence. Balance reactions are practiced by tilting your child slightly to disturb the center of gravity. Sometimes this is done on a flat surface or your lap. Other times a therapy ball or rocking board may be used. A special type of developmental therapy is known as neurodevelopmental treatment, or NDT (see chapter 18).

Gait Training and Bracing

Gait training, or teaching your child to walk, is another form of physical therapy. In order to be ready for gait training, your child must have progressed to the point of being able to sit unsupported and to creep on his hands and knees. Usually a child who has the potential to walk will have developed these prerequisite skills by the age of two. Other signs of readiness include pulling to a standing position and walking sideways while holding on to furniture, or cruising. If your child has spina bifida and his legs are paralyzed, he may show sitting balance and an interest in moving from place to place by dragging himself on his stomach or by scooting in the sitting position. These skills are also sufficient to begin gait training.

Your therapist will start by introducing your child to the standing position. Standing in proper alignment may require the use of supportive orthotics, or braces. Most braces today are made of molded plastic that is custom fit from a plaster cast of your child's limb. If your child can support her weight while standing but has a ten-

dency to stand on her toes, she may only need molded ankle-foot orthoses, or MAFOs, which will help her to stand on a flat foot. MAFOs are plastic shells that cover the calf, the ankle, and the sole of the foot, and usually have a fixed ankle joint (see Figure 9.5). They are made to slip inside a sneaker or other shoe and have Velcro straps that allow them to be removed easily. Children who require greater support in standing may need braces that go up to the groin, the waist, or even as high as the armpits. Most braces are designed with movable joints at the hip and knee so your child can use them to sit as well as stand.

For some children, the therapy program will include a special standing brace called a parapodium. This brace has a large stable base that allows your child to stand without crutches or other assistive devices. It is inexpensive compared to other braces, and does not require custom molding to be fit. Another device for standing is called a prone-stander (Figure 17.1). This is an inclined board on which your child rests on his stomach, with supports for his body, hips, and feet. The angle can be changed between lying flat and standing upright. A prone-stander allows a child with cerebral palsy to stand in good alignment. This helps to maintain the calcium in his bones to avoid pathological fractures and to deepen the sockets of the hip joints. A tray is usually provided so your child can play while standing. Your therapist will guide you in developing a standing schedule. Usually your child can build up to standing an hour at a time, twice a day, which is all that is required to help strengthen the bones.

Walking may require the use of an assistive device such as crutches or a walker. Walkers with wheels are called rollators. Some rollators are designed to be used

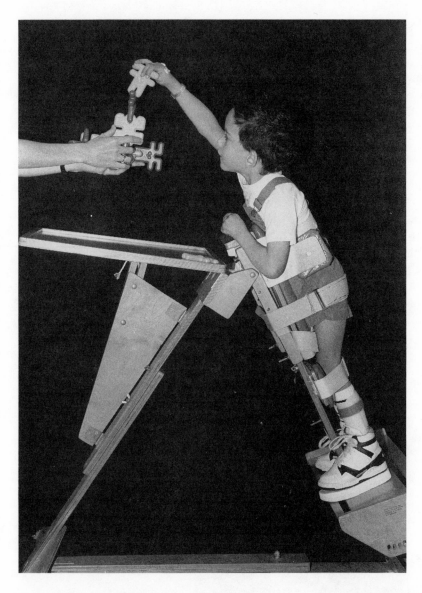

Figure 17.1. *A prone-stander allows this child with cerebral palsy to stand in good alignment.*

backward, and encourage more erect posture. There are also many different types of crutches. Axillary crutches are the standard wooden type that are held under the arms. Proper fitting is necessary to reduce pressure under the armpit. Otherwise, sensitive nerves that run through the armpits and down the arm can be damaged from the pressure of leaning on the top of the crutches. Crutches which stop below the elbow are called forearm or Loftstrand crutches. These are harder to use, but may be better since there is no risk of damaging the nerves.

You will probably need to practice walking with your child every day until he has enough balance to be independent. Use a sturdy leather belt around your child's waist to guard him from falling. Usually it is best to stand slightly to the side and back, while holding the belt with one hand and placing the opposite hand in front of his shoulder (Figure 17.2). Listen carefully to the verbal cues your therapist uses, and give the same commands. If your child does not yet know right from left, you may substitute colors, or touch the leg or arm you want him to move next. Choose an area without carpet or throw rugs to start gait training.

Once your child can walk on level surfaces, it will be time to teach more advanced skills such as walking on uneven ground, climbing ramps, curbs, and stairs, and falling safely to the floor and getting back up. Your therapist may also set a goal of greater walking distance for your child.

Some children continue to use wheelchairs for longer distances, and walk only in limited areas such as in the classroom or around the house. This level of skill is called household ambulation. Children who walk everywhere are called community ambulators, while those who are still learning to walk are called exercise ambulators.

Positioning

If your child has a developmental disability that prevents mobility, the position in which he sits or lies is very important for the prevention of other problems. Positioning your child can be done using various adaptive equipment, depending on his treatment goals. A severely affected child may be limited to lying on his back, stom-

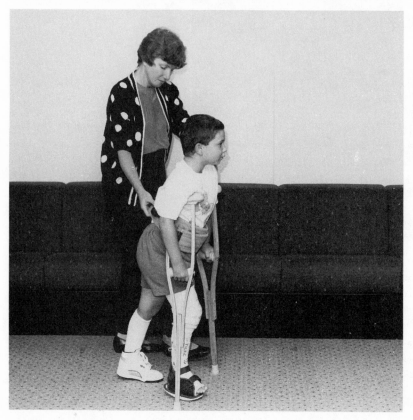

Figure 17.2. *Practicing walking using a belt around the waist for safety.*

ach, and both sides. When on his back, his legs should be bent and his hands positioned toward his mouth. A blanket rolled up and placed under his knees, with smaller towel rolls under his shoulder blades, may help to accomplish this. Additional towel rolls may be needed to keep his head in the middle. Alternately, the child can sometimes be placed in a hammock on his back for short periods of time to achieve a similar posture. This is especially good for the child who tends to arch his back.

Lying on the side can help reduce muscle tone, develop symmetry, and bring the hands together toward the mouth. This position also permits your child to see what is happening in the world around him better than if he is lying on his back. A special piece of equipment called a sidelyer may be used to promote good alignment while on his side (Figure 17.3). It is basically two padded boards which are connected together at right angles, with straps for the body and the legs. Your child lies on the bottom board with his back against the backboard. The sidelyer is designed so

he can be easily shifted from the right side to the left side.

Lying on the stomach is an important developmental step. The ability to hold the head up against gravity and to strengthen the muscles of the back in preparation for sitting is first developed in this position. Many pieces of equipment can be used to help your child support her weight while lying on her stomach. A small towel roll placed under her chest, or a small wedge can be used to support some of her weight (Figure 17.4). For a child who is ready to crawl on her stomach, but still drags her legs, a scooter board on casters can assist in providing mobility.

Adaptive Equipment

Many pieces of adaptive equipment are available to support your child in the sitting position. For young children, an insert and special straps for the infant seat, high chair, or stroller may help. A special car seat may be needed for transportation, or a travel wheelchair may be ordered that converts from a car seat to a wheelchair. For the older child, adaptations may need to be

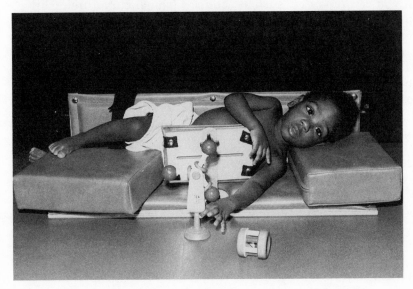

Figure 17.3. *A sidelyer is used to reduce muscle tone and bring the hands toward the midline.*

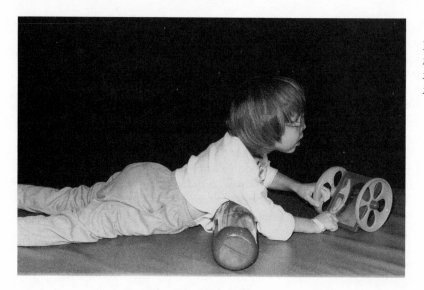

Figure 17.4. *A child uses a roll under the chest to assist in lifting the head while lying on tummy.*

made to the wheelchair, or to the school-room chair. For example, a tray may be added to the sitting equipment in order to provide a convenient work or play surface.

While adaptive equipment is useful, it should not be overused. One problem is that staying in one position for too long can cause deformities. Besides this, you will want to find times when you can remove your child from the equipment to cuddle and hold her as well as provide alternative positions for her joints. When planning for adaptive equipment, consider both the equipment available for normal children as well as equipment made specially for disabled children. If you have a handyman in the family, equipment can be customized, under a therapist's guidance, to meet your child's needs. In addition, the therapist should plan for the equipment to grow as your child grows, so that it can be used for several years.

Wheelchairs

If a wheelchair is necessary, it should be chosen carefully to ensure that it meets your child's needs as well as the limitations of your environment. The fit of the wheelchair is especially important — your child should have one inch of space on either side of his body. In addition, a number of customized features may be needed to help maintain posture. Poor posture can lead to contractures or postural deformities such as scoliosis (spinal curvature). Children with abnormal tone, weakness, or poor posture may need a solid seat or back, or pads called laterals that keep the hips or body centered in the chair. A child with low tone may need to be reclined in the wheelchair to maintain proper alignment. If head control is poor, a special head support may be required. Examples of these wheelchairs are shown in Figure 17.5.

Safety is another factor you should consider when ordering a wheelchair. Every child should have an automobile-style seat belt to secure him safely in his wheelchair. Rear antitipper devices will help prevent the chair from tipping over backward on steep grades or when too much downward pressure is placed on the push handles. A

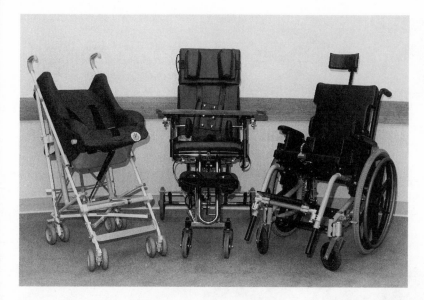

Figure 17.5. *Various types of wheelchairs are individually prescribed to meet a child's seating and mobility needs.*

child with limited hand function but good intellectual function may be able to drive a battery-powered wheelchair if his environment is accessible. Battery-powered chairs may be controlled using a joystick, or by a switch activated by that part of the body over which he has most control. For example, a child with quadriplegia may control the chair with his head.

Make sure that your child receives a thorough evaluation prior to purchasing a wheelchair. Usually a team of professionals including a physical therapist, occupational therapist, wheelchair vendor, and social worker evaluate your child together to prescribe adaptive equipment. You should see your child in a similar chair before ordering one.

Your family's needs must also be considered when choosing a wheelchair. The size of your car trunk and the location of stairs in your home may limit your selection. Lightweight wheelchairs or sport chairs are good looking and may be easier for your child to maneuver than standard chairs. In addition, they will be easier for you to lift into the trunk of your car, since they are

only 18–22 pounds. However, special care must be taken when ordering a lightweight chair or collapsible stroller. If your child is not well supported in good postural alignment, he may be at risk for developing contractures. If your child needs a power wheelchair, a van with a wheelchair lift may be required.

Most parents are sensitive to the way special equipment looks. The first time a wheelchair is ordered may be particularly stressful for you. If you are concerned that your child may become dependent on a wheelchair or might look more handicapped to outsiders, share these concerns with your therapist. Some wheelchairs are now designed to look similar to baby strollers. Other equipment comes in designer colors such as "hot pink," lavender or blue.

Other kinds of equipment may also be helpful in improving mobility for your child. A child who has some sitting balance may be able to ride a tricycle adapted with a trunk support and foot straps (Figure 17.6). Pedaling the tricycle is preferable to bunny-hopping or crawling as a way to

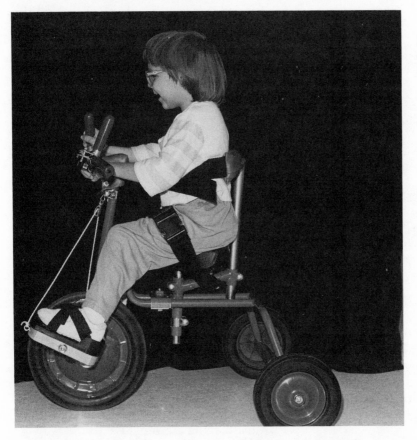

Figure 17.6. *A specially adapted tricycle can be an alternate means of mobility.*

get around. Children with spina bifida may also be able to ride tricycles adapted so they can be controlled by the hands rather than feet.

Activities of Daily Living (ADL)

The physical therapist and the occupational therapist work together to teach those skills required to live independently. For example, feeding, dressing, toileting, and moving about in the environment are all ADLs. The physical therapist will teach wheelchair propulsion, and how to move from the wheelchair to other pieces of furniture or equipment such as the bed, toilet, car, sofa, or school chair. This important skill of moving from one place to another

is called transferring. If your child cannot transfer independently and needs to be lifted, the physical therapists will train you to lift your child without hurting your back.

ARCHITECTURAL BARRIERS

For the child with physical handicaps to be truly independent, barriers in your home or school environment may need to be modified with ramps or other arrangements. In the ideal situation, a child who requires crutches or a wheelchair should live on one floor. If you are selecting your first home, look into a ranch style with plenty of open space inside. You also will need adequate space near the entrance for a ramp. In general, you need twelve feet for every one foot of rise from the ground level to the front door. If you already live in a two-story home, consider installing a stair glide or modifying the dwelling to put a bathroom and bedroom on the first floor. This will save you from carrying your child up and down the stairs.

You may also wish to make special accommodations in specific rooms in the house. Wider doorways can give the wheelchair-bound child access to more areas of the house. In the bathroom, a sink with adequate space underneath for the knees can allow a wheelchair to pull up close. A faucet with lever arms is easier to work than one with knobs. The toilet may need space around it to park a wheelchair for transfer. A higher toilet and grab bars may make transfer easier for the wheelchair-bound child. The preschooler may benefit from a potty chair that is low to the floor with armrests, a seat belt, and other appropriate supports. The bathtub may be modified with grab bars for a child who can walk but has difficulty climbing in and out of the tub. Small children with poor sitting balance may need a special tub seat with straps to make bathing easier. Older children who are too heavy to lift may require a hydraulic lift to move into the tub. A hand-held shower hose may make it easier for you to wash your child or for your child to wash himself.

Many parents have been quite creative in designing bedrooms to meet their child's special needs. For example, the parents of a child with arthritis had a bureau built with drawers on rollers so they were easier to pull out. Clothing was arranged on open shelves and on hangers that were at their child's height.

A child-sized armchair may make it easier for your child to dress himself. Your therapist can advise you about the optimal position for learning dressing skills and about various devices that can help. You can also encourage your child to be more independent by installing environmental-control units set to activate the radio, tape recorder, lights, or other switches that might otherwise be inaccessible. Toys can be modified with special switches that allow your child with special needs to play.

When your child is young, it is tempting to overcome all of these barriers by carrying him and by doing many tasks for him. This approach may work for a while, but by the preschool years you should begin to plan for greater independence, for his sake as well as yours. You will need to do plenty of lifting during your lifetime, and it is important to learn good body mechanics in order to protect your back and make tasks as easy as possible.

HOW PHYSICAL THERAPY SERVICE IS PROVIDED

Pediatric physical therapists work in a variety of settings. Some work at children's hospitals or at pediatric rehabilitation centers while others work in schools. Early-intervention programs serve infants and toddlers from birth to age three and may be either center-based or home-based. In addition, some physical therapists work in a private practice and may treat your child at your home or in their office.

In most states, a physical therapist will see your child following a written referral from your doctor. The physician should specify your child's diagnosis and the goals to be accomplished. The physician should also give instructions regarding any precautions to be taken.

Selecting a physical therapist to meet your child's needs can be difficult. Your physician or another parent can help guide you in selecting a therapist who is knowledgeable and comfortable working with disabled children. You should also look for a therapist who is willing to share her findings with you and provide specific instructions and feedback about what she wants you to practice with your child at home. Don't expect to keep the same therapist forever. Children often change therapists every year without any harm, the same as they change teachers. On the other hand, if you have found a therapist who is successful in working with your child, stick with her as long as possible.

YOUR ROLE IN THERAPY

You will play an important role in providing therapy to your child. The physical therapist may work with your child only one or two hours per week, while the therapy program must be done daily to truly be effective. Your therapist may suggest toys that will reinforce the therapy goals. For example, a child who has left-sided weakness may need to learn to do things using both hands together rather than neglecting the weaker hand. His play toys should be large enough to encourage use of both hands together — for example, a large ball or a truck that can be pushed with two hands. Providing the right kind of toys can be very helpful in reinforcing the goals of therapy, as well as in providing stimulation.

You must also be an advocate for your child. Remember that all children have the right to a free appropriate public education in the least restrictive environment (PL 94-142). This law requires that an individual education plan (IEP) be developed yearly for each child who has special needs. You are a member of the therapeutic team and are given choices in the way your child's treatment needs are provided.

His physical therapy needs will be identified on the IEP, and should be based on a recent assessment by a licensed physical therapist (see chapter 20). Amendments to this law (PL 99-457) extend services to infants, toddlers, and their families.

SOME QUESTIONS ANSWERED

Where can I find a pediatric physical therapist?

Ask your doctor or clinic team to help you locate a pediatric physical therapist. Call the therapy department of a large pediatric hospital, and ask if they can refer you to a therapist in your area. Contact local community agencies that deal with special needs children, such as the United Cerebral Palsy Association or Easter Seals Society. Check the yellow pages of the telephone book under physical therapy. Ask other parents.

What about other treatments such as patterning and chiropractic?

Patterning is not the same as physical therapy. It is a technique in which the child's limbs are passively moved through various crawling patterns. The theory behind patterning is that these passive movements will encourage your child to develop the appropriate neurological connections needed to control movements. There is no evidence that this form of treatment is effective. In addition, it requires a great deal of family time and many volunteers to pattern a child. Because of the amount of time and effort required, and the lack of clear benefit, it is not recommended by most medical experts.

Chiropractic involves manipulation of the spinal column, and will not improve the problems associated with developmental disabilities. Further, a child's bones still have open growth centers, which can be damaged by manipulation. In general, these techniques are not recommended for children with developmental disabilities.

Can physical therapy cure my child?

Most developmental disabilities do not disappear. However, physical therapy can prevent secondary problems, such as contractures or muscle weakness from disuse. It can help your child make the most of the physical potential he has. Your therapist can offer advice and guidelines for your family to manage certain problems. But, physical therapy is not a cure.

18 OCCUPATIONAL THERAPY

Lisa Kurtz, M.Ed., OTR/L

One type of therapy that is often useful for developmentally disabled children is occupational therapy, or OT. Very few parents have heard of occupational therapy, and may wonder at first what type of "occupation" will be taught to their disabled infant or child. Adults tend to think of occupations as "jobs," since work is the primary occupation of most adults. But therapists view "occupation" as having a much broader meaning, relating to how an individual occupies his time performing routine daily-living tasks. Occupational therapy helps children who have disabilities engage in those activities or occupations that are appropriate to their age or developmental level, their interests and motivations, and the requirements of the environment in which they must function.

PETER

Susan and Don are the parents of three beautiful children. Although they tried hard not to compare their children with each other, they became increasingly concerned when nine-month-old Peter seemed slower than his older sisters in learning to sit and to use his hands. Peter's pediatri-

cian recommended a developmental evaluation, which indicated that Peter had cerebral palsy.

Susan and Don were devastated by this diagnosis. However, once the initial shock subsided, they were eager to provide Peter with the best treatment available. They enrolled him in an early-intervention program for infants with developmental disabilities where they met Mary, a pediatric occupational therapist. Mary knew that her most important job was to help Susan and Don gain confidence in their ability to care for and teach their young son. At Susan's request, she conducted therapy sessions in their home, and invited Peter's grandparents and baby-sitter to participate whenever possible.

Mary devised a therapy program that consisted of positioning suggestions, exercises, handling techniques, and play activities selected to help Peter learn control of his body. After familiarizing herself with the family's daily routine, she taught them ways to make everyday activities a therapeutic experience. Diaper changes became the ideal time to perform flexibility exercises for his legs and to help Peter learn to reach for his feet. Although Peter had always struggled and cried during his bath, Mary was able to turn this unpleasant experience into a fun time to splash and play by recommending a supportive seat that made him feel safe. Mary instructed all family members in different ways to hold and carry Peter so that he was encouraged to develop balance and strength in his trunk. Using inexpensive materials, Mary made a special chair and tray for Peter that held his shoulders forward and gave him the support he needed to sit upright. Once in this position, he was better able to control his arms and reach for toys.

OCCUPATIONAL BEHAVIORS

Occupational behaviors of childhood typically fall into one of three categories: self-maintenance behaviors, play behaviors, and work behaviors.

Self-maintenance behaviors include such daily-living tasks as eating, dressing, using a toilet, taking a bath, and performing other self-care needs. Play behaviors include sensory exploration of the environment, symbolic play either through art or make-believe, and recreational games. Work behaviors of childhood include those required to function in school, and those that lead to pre-vocational interests and skills.

Occupational therapists rely on play as their principal teaching strategy. Often this involves playing at purposeful activities that correlate with the desired skill. For example, the therapist might select a game of dressing up in costumes to help the child practice manipulating buttons or other clothing fasteners. Or, for a severely disabled infant, the therapist might strategically place a colorful toy somewhere in the crib, encouraging the child to practice looking, moving, and reaching as he attempts to explore and make contact with the toy.

Before a treatment session can begin, the therapist will most likely prepare your child for the activity. This preparation may include psychological or behavioral approaches, sensory stimulation, physical manipulation, or special positioning techniques. Other therapists who work with your child, such as physical or speech therapists, may use similar preparatory techniques, and you may wonder if your child is receiving an unnecessary duplication of services. Usually, each therapist has different reasons for using these techniques, and different objectives. For example, many therapists begin a treatment session with a spastic child by first focusing on relaxation. A relaxed child can better learn communication skills from the speech therapist, movement skills from the physical therapist, and self-maintenance, play, and work skills from the occupational therapist.

SELECTING AN OCCUPATIONAL THERAPIST

Occupational therapists are health-care professionals whose services are available in a variety of settings including hospitals, rehabilitation centers, early-intervention programs, schools, and home-care agencies. Many therapists also work in private practice. You can ask your pediatrician to recommend a particular therapist or program. This is often the best way to get started, since the doctor will likely know something about the quality of programs in your area. However, if you are unhappy with the program your doctor recommends, do not be afraid to investigate other alternatives. As a consumer and advocate for your child, you have the right to select the therapist and setting you like best, as long as the program meets the overall management needs of your child.

There are several ways to obtain information about the occupational therapists in your area. Try contacting the occupational therapy department of the nearest children's hospital for suggestions. Most therapists are more than willing to offer guidance even if you do not plan to have your child attend their program. You can also contact the American Occupational Therapy Association. They can put you in touch with someone in your geographic area who is knowledgeable about pediatric occupational therapy. Finally, you may consider calling local colleges or universities that train occupational therapists.

You may wish to visit several therapists before making a decision. Some parents like to speak to other families who can comment on their personal experience with a therapist, and this can often be arranged. Ultimately, selection of a therapy program should be based on a combination of factors, including the competence and talent of the therapist, her ability to communicate effectively with your child and with you, her ability to set and achieve realistic goals for your child, and the convenience and affordability of the program.

Of course, you will want to make sure the therapist has the appropriate training. Occupational therapists are trained at either the professional or technical level. Professional occupational therapists have either a bachelor's or master's degree in occupational therapy, have completed a minimum of six months in field training, and have passed a national certification examination. Therapists who have completed this training use the letters OTR after their name. In addition, many states require a license to practice occupational

therapy; this is designated by the letters OTR/L or LOTR. All OTRs have received at least basic training in how to work with children. Many therapists who choose to specialize in pediatrics obtain advanced training, either through graduate education or through special training programs such as those which lead to certification in neurodevelopmental therapy (NDT) or sensory integration therapy (SI). These special approaches to therapy will be described later in this chapter. Check to see that your therapist has had practical experience working with children.

Sometimes, especially in rural areas of the country, it may be difficult to locate a pediatric occupational therapy specialist. If you must select a local therapist who has limited experience working with children, you may wish to find a specialist at a more distant hospital or clinic who can serve as a consultant to your direct-care provider. You would see this individual a few times a year and she would then keep in contact with your regular therapist.

Technical level therapists must have completed a two-year associate's degree program in occupational therapy and must also pass a national certification examination. Therapists who have completed this level of training are called Certified Occupational Therapy Assistants and use the letters COTA after their name, or COTA/L if they practice in a state requiring a license. COTAs are required to practice under the supervision of an OTR who has the ultimate responsibility for the child's therapy program. If your child's primary therapist is a COTA, you should check to see that the therapist is receiving regular supervision from an OTR. You may also want to request periodic meetings with both the COTA and the supervising therapist to discuss your child's progress.

THE OCCUPATIONAL THERAPY PROGRAM

Planning an effective therapy program can be complicated, like putting together the many pieces of a jigsaw puzzle. Good therapy is a team effort, guided by the therapist but requiring cooperation and understanding from your child, you, and all others who are significantly involved in the daily care of your child. Before the therapist can select the appropriate treatment, she needs to gather information about your child's ability to perform daily-living tasks and the factors that limit your child's abilities. This evaluation will probably include a review of previous records, an interview and history-taking with you, and direct observation of your child engaging in informal play activities. Formal tests, such as the Bayley Scale of Infant Development, the Knox Play Scale, or the Developmental Test of Visual Motor Integration, may also be used.

During the evaluation period, you may be encouraged to remain with your child so you can offer comfort and reassurance. This also enables you to observe your child's response to testing and to begin to learn what types of observations may be helpful to the therapist. Sometimes, however, your participation is not possible either because of the size of the examination room, or because the therapist believes your child might be too distracted by your presence. If you are unable to stay with your child during the evaluation, be sure to ask your therapist to describe exactly what occurred and to give specific examples of your child's behavior and responses. It is important for you to comment on whether your child's performance during the evaluation is typical of his usual performance. If you think your child normally performs better or worse than was demonstrated during the evaluation, be sure to let your therapist know.

Once the assessment is completed, you, the therapist, and possibly other professionals involved in the care of your child should review the results and agree on a plan for therapy. You should discuss and agree on specific goals for your child, and on how therapy will be structured to meet those goals. Ask the therapist to explain her rationale for selecting a particular therapy approach, and how long she expects therapy to be needed in order to meet the goals. If the therapist says something you do not understand, ask for a better explanation. A good therapist is never annoyed by parents who ask a lot of questions. Rather, therapists know they can best help your child if they have your full understanding and cooperation. If you disagree with something your therapist says, speak up! You know your child best, and should never be reluctant to express your opinions.

TREATMENT APPROACHES IN OCCUPATIONAL THERAPY

Once therapeutic goals have been established, your therapist must select the methods she believes will most likely meet those goals. There are a variety of acceptable treatment approaches in occupational therapy, and different therapists may approach problems differently. Many therapists combine methods or use different approaches during different stages of your child's development. Treatment approaches commonly used by pediatric occupational therapists fall into one of two general categories: developmental therapy and functional, or rehabilitative, therapy.

DEVELOPMENTAL THERAPY

Developmental therapy techniques are used to help the delayed child reach developmental milestones efficiently. As shown in the information presented in chapter 5, we know that normal human development tends to occur in an orderly and predictable manner. For instance, most children sit before they crawl, crawl before they walk, and walk before they run. Occupational therapists have a thorough knowledge of the process of development; they understand the importance of each developmental step, even those that are very small. The therapist identifies your child's current developmental level and determines what the next small stage of development should be. Then, taking into account how your child's disability might limit his ability to progress, the therapist selects, and if necessary modifies, play activities that will allow your child to accomplish that next step. Your child's success in achieving a small developmental gain tends to motivate him to repeat the skill until it is mastered. Then, he can continue on to subsequent steps.

Two specialized developmental therapy approaches are common in pediatric practice; these are neurodevelopmental therapy and sensory integrative therapy.

Neurodevelopmental Therapy

Neurodevelopmental therapy is a treatment approach developed by Dr. Karel Bobath, a neurologist, and his wife, Berta, a physical therapist, during the 1950s. It was designed for treating children with cerebral palsy or other forms of neuromuscular dysfunction affecting muscle tone, and it is widely used by occupational, physical, and speech therapists who work with children who have developmental disabilities.

Muscle tone is the amount of tension present in a muscle when it is resting or when it is working. Children with neuromuscular dysfunction such as cerebral palsy tend to have either too much muscle tone (spasticity), too little tone (hypotonia or floppiness), or fluctuating tone. Abnormal muscle tone interferes with the child's ability to develop the movements that will allow her to maintain balance, move from one position to another, and feel secure that she is in control of her body. A child with abnormal muscle tone tends to get "stuck" in body positions and movement patterns that, while they may make her feel safe, prevent her from developing more precise movements and restrict her from the sensory feedback in normal movement that helps her to learn.

The therapist using NDT techniques will teach you how to position, carry, and handle your child in a way that encourages more normal muscle tone. He can then teach you ways to help your child use this improved tone to develop more normal movement patterns according to the usual developmental sequence. By handling your child in a more therapeutic way as you play, feed, bathe, and clothe her, you will enhance her opportunity to experience the sensation of normal movement and learn from it.

Occupational therapists are taught basic NDT principles in school, but become competent in the techniques through additional training and practical experiences after they have graduated. Therapists may become certified in basic pediatric NDT procedures by taking an eight-week course sponsored by the Neurodevelopmental Treatment Association (NDTA), which maintains a registry of certified therapists.

Sensory Integration Therapy

Another developmental therapy approach commonly used by occupational therapists is sensory integration therapy, or SI. This approach was introduced during the 1960s by Dr. A. Jean Ayres, whose background was in occupational therapy and educational psychology. It is a method of therapy that was originally developed and is most commonly used with learning-disabled children; however, many occupational therapists use SI procedures with children who have more severe forms of developmental disabilities, including cerebral palsy, mental retardation, and autism. Although sensory integration therapy is a controversial method, research suggests that it may be effective for some children. For example, SI has been shown to increase the rate of language development, improve the organization of behavior, and reduce self-stimulatory behavior in mentally retarded and autistic children. SI therapy may also be effective in improving the rate of development and quality of motor skills in children with developmental disabilities including cerebral palsy, although the evidence of this is less clear.

Sensory integration therapy is based on an understanding of the human sensory system and of the relation of the senses to learning. People talk about five senses — sight, hearing, taste, smell, and touch. Occupational therapists add to this list two other senses when they consider how the brain receives and interprets information from the world. These two other senses are called the vestibular sense and proprioception. The vestibular sense originates with the fluid in the canals of the inner ear, and sends the brain information about the effects of gravity and motion. It is therefore important in developing balance and coordinated movements of the eyes, head, and body.

The sense of proprioception works closely with information from the vestibular system to relay information about our body's position in space. Special receptors in the muscles, joints, and tendons give us an unconscious sense of body position. If you close your eyes and attempt to touch the tip of your nose with your left thumb, the sense of proprioception will enable you to complete the motion with a reasonable degree of accuracy.

Sight, hearing, and smell are called the "distant" senses, because they orient us to situations distant from our body. The other sensory systems — the "near" senses of touch, taste, motion, and body position — orient us to our immediate environment. Most people tend to be much more conscious of the information they receive from the distant senses than from the near senses. However, the less-conscious information relating to our body plays a critical role in human learning and behavior.

The touch or tactile system serves two important functions. First, it helps us locate and identify objects without the use of vision. An example of how you might use touch in this way is when you approach a toll booth on the highway and reach into your pocketbook to find a quarter. Your sense of touch allows you to tell your change purse from your hairbrush, and to discriminate the quarters from the dimes. Even the youngest infant uses touch to locate her mother's nipple during breast feeding. The second function of the tactile system is to alert us to potential danger. An obvious example of this is demonstrated by what happens when you accidentally touch a hot iron.

One of the functions of the nervous system is to organize and interpret sensory information so that it can be reacted to appropriately and used as a tool for learning. This process is called sensory integration. When a therapist says that your child has a problem with sensory integration, she means that your child has difficulty taking in and interpreting sensory information so that it is useful for learning. Children who have problems that affect the sensory organs themselves, that is, blind or deaf children, have a different kind of deficit than a child with a sensory integration problem. Signs of sensory integration problems are varied, but may include over- or undersensitivity to touch or movement, abnormally high or low activity level, poorly organized behavior, difficulty learning novel motor tasks despite adequate neuromuscular development, or delays in language or academics despite adequate intelligence. Most children who have developmental disabilities that affect their central nervous system will have problems with sensory integration.

Sensory integration therapy programs are usually fairly intensive. The exact frequency and duration will vary from child to child, but is typically one or two sessions per week for a period of at least six months. The SI therapist selects play activities that guide your child gradually to respond more appropriately to sensory input. Activities typically provide your child with controlled, often intense sensory input, while simultaneously demanding a purposeful reaction to that input.

For example, suppose your child has difficulty organizing information from vision and from her body-awareness senses in order to control movements of her arms. She might have difficulty with such tasks as learning to copy letters and shapes, or learning to throw an object with good aim. A typical treatment activity might involve having her lie on her stomach in a suspended net, then swing back and forth while attempting to throw beanbags at a target. In order to be successful in the purposeful activity (hitting the target), your child must accurately interpret the location of the target (through vision), the speed and direction of her swing (through vision and vestibular information), and the force and direction of arm movement needed to hit the target (through proprioception).

As your child plays the game, the therapist may adjust the amount and type of sensory input needed to ensure success and yet still challenge her to make gradually more mature responses. For example, visual information might be adjusted by changing the location of the target. Vestibular information might be adjusted by having her swing slower or faster, or by twirling around the circle. The therapist might adjust touch and proprioceptive cues by having your child wear a weighted exercise cuff on her arm, or by stroking the back of her neck and spine to remind her to hold her head up.

In sensory integration therapy, specific skills like dressing are not usually taught. Instead, the activities selected by the therapist are believed to help the child develop the underlying abilities that will make skill-learning easier. Many therapists prefer to use sensory integration procedures as only one part of a more comprehensive program that includes the teaching of specific skills and other methods of compensation.

Because sensory integration therapy is a complex and controversial approach to treatment, it may be wise to obtain an evaluation by a therapist with special training in sensory integration before considering it as an option. An organization called Sensory Integration International maintains a registry of therapists who are certified in assessment procedures.

FUNCTIONAL THERAPY

The rehabilitation, or functional, approaches to occupational therapy involve teaching specific skills needed for the performance of such self-care activities as feeding, bathing, dressing, and recreation. The therapist determines whether your child is developmentally ready to participate in self-care activities and analyzes exactly what aspects of the disability interfere with learning. Then she develops a teaching plan that caters to your child's individual learning style and that encourages the practice of new skills. She may prepare your child for the chosen activity by starting a session with motivating play, therapeutic handling, or the use of special positioning devices, such as splints, to help your child "get ready" to practice a new skill.

Of course, the degree to which your child can become independent in self-care will depend ultimately on the severity of disability. A very severely affected child may always require some degree of assistance in order safely and successfully to bathe, feed, and dress herself. However, you should encourage as much self-reliance as possible. Every small gain in independence will increase your child's self-esteem and sense of control over her life.

Teaching Self-care

Teaching self-care skills to a disabled child requires a great deal of patience and creativity. Families of disabled children spend far more time than average in the daily routines of getting dressed in the morning or getting through a meal. It's easy to feel frustrated and to want to do too much for your child because it seems easier or faster. Remember that even non-disabled children need years of practice before they get all their clothes on straight or get through a meal without spilling. Your therapist can help you establish a routine that provides set times for you and your child to work on self-care skills, while still allowing you the time you need for yourself. For example, working parents may find it more practical to help their child learn to use a spoon at dinnertime rather than at breakfast when they are rushing to get out of the house.

Feeding, the ability to get food to the mouth, is usually the first self-care skill that a child learns. It is a different process from eating, which refers to the manipulation of food within the mouth so that it can be swallowed. Chapter 16 discussed the kinds of oral-motor difficulties that might cause eating problems in a disabled child. If your child has oral motor problems that interfere with her ability to chew or swallow, you should seek advice from your therapist before beginning to teach self-feeding. Know what kind of foods are safe and what foods are not safe for your child to eat, and learn what to do should your child begin to choke. How a child is positioned for feeding can influence both her oral-motor skills and the ease with which she can get food to her mouth. Your therapist can show you the best way to position your child and may recommend that a special seating arrangement be used during mealtime.

Accidental spills are commonplace and should be expected when any child first learns to feed herself. The child with poor motor skills may benefit from the added stability of a dish with a slip-proof bottom or a cup with a special bottom that prevents it from tipping, but try not to become discouraged by the inevitable messiness of mealtime (Figure 18.1). You may want to use nonbreakable dishes, and a plastic cloth under the high chair to make clean up easier. If your child takes longer than usual to finish a meal, you may wish to purchase dishes with a reservoir for hot water so that food will stay warm for a longer time.

Figure 18.1. *Scoop dish and built-up spoon: The raised sides of this dish allow the child to push food onto a spoon without spilling. It has a nonskid material on the bottom to keep the dish from sliding on the table. The large handle on the spoon makes it easier to hold on to when the child's grasp is weak.*

As you begin to teach dressing skills to your child, remember that getting dressed requires a great deal of physical movement and can be very hard for a child with poor coordination, balance difficulties, or for a spastic child who tends to stiffen as she moves from one position to another. Get advice from your therapist on how to relax and position your child prior to dressing so that movement is easier. You will want to select clothing for your child that is attractive, durable, and easy to get on and off. Several companies make clothes specially designed for disabled people, but you will also find that many standard clothing styles have features that are helpful to the disabled child. In general, slightly larger sizes, loosely woven neckbands and cuffs, front rather than back openings, and loosely draped styles such as capes or raglan sleeves will be the easiest to manage. Look for clothes that wash easily, since many individuals with disabilities perspire profusely with the effort involved in dressing and moving around. Look for clothes with reinforced seams or ones that can be easily reinforced, as your child may tend to handle clothing more roughly than usual. Try to select clothes with large or easy-to-manipulate fasteners, or, if you are handy with a sewing machine, you can attach Velcro fasteners behind "false" buttons and snaps.

Some children with disabilities will need to have self-care tasks adapted to their unique abilities. Occupational therapists have devised numerous ways of adapting both the methods and tools needed to accomplish various self-care activities. For example, it may be very difficult for a child with extrapyramidal cerebral palsy to learn to put on his shoes. Since he lacks the ability to balance steadily when sitting and must hold on to something for support, he may have difficulty letting go of his support so he can hold on to his shoe. However, if he sits on the floor with his back against the corner of a wall, he can get the necessary support and stability so his hands can be used freely. A long shoehorn may also provide necessary leverage (Figure 18.2).

Tools can be adapted in many ingenious ways to encourage self-reliance. For example, the child who is too weak to raise his arms over his head might comb his hair by himself if given a lightweight comb with an extra-long handle, which compensates for his inability to reach, or a bath seat can offer needed support (Figure 18.3). An occupational therapist can discuss numerous adaptive aids and devices that make self-care easier for your child. Some can be easily made at home, while others must be purchased or custom made. Devices can be simple, or they can be very elaborate. Remember that as ingenious and helpful as some devices may be, they can also be costly, unsightly, and inconvenient to carry if needed outside the home. The fewer pieces of equipment your child needs in order to function independently, the easier his life will be.

The resource list for this chapter includes the names of companies which sell adapted clothing, self-help devices, and special toys directly to parents. It also suggests several books and manuals that offer further discussion on teaching self-care skills to your child.

Exactly what methods or tools are suggested by the therapist will depend on the unique circumstances of your child and your family's lifestyle. However, certain general principles guide the therapist's approach to solving problems. We will briefly discuss the functional problems that most frequently prevent disabled children from

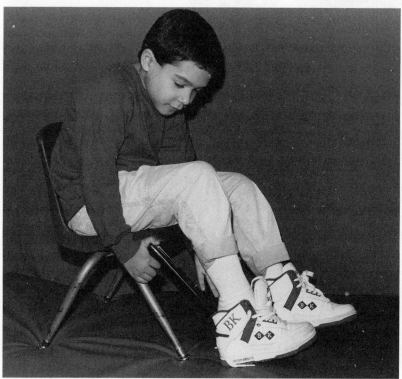

Figure 18.2. *Long shoehorn: This extra-long shoehorn makes it easier to reach shoes without having to bend over.*

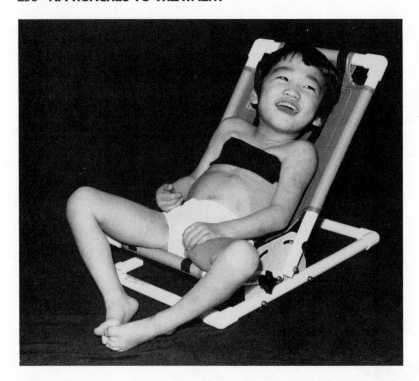

Figure 18.3. *Child's bath seat: This bath seat supports the child safely and securely when sitting balance is a problem.*

developing independence in self-care, and the therapeutic principles used in teaching compensation.

Teaching Skills to a Child with Mental Retardation

Children with limited intellectual function can often achieve a surprising degree of independence in self-care through the use of special teaching methods along with a great deal of patience and practice. Behavioral shaping techniques, discussed in chapter 15, are often successful in encouraging children to repeat desired behaviors and develop new skills.

Dealing with Poor Strength, Endurance, or Limited Motion

If your child's disability causes weakness, the therapist might give your child lightweight tools or change his body mechanics so that less strength is needed to

accomplish tasks. For example, in a child with muscular dystrophy, whose weakness makes feeding difficult, raising the height of the table would allow him to raise his arms a shorter distance in order to reach his mouth. If his arms are extremely weak, he might be fitted with special slings that support his arms against gravity and allow him to move his arms toward and away from his mouth using only slight muscle contractions. If his hands are too weak to hold on to a spoon or fork, he might wear, around his hand, an elastic cuff that has a special pocket to hold a spoon in place.

When the disability causes limited range of motion, the therapist's goal is to find ways of extending your child's reach. Many self-care devices, including sponges, combs, brushes, and spoons can be fitted with extra-long handles that make it possible for your child to reach the necessary body part. Often, though, long handles make a device heavier and more awkward to handle.

Stabilizing Poor Coordination

Problems with coordination require strategies that will provide extra stability. This may involve teaching your child to change her body mechanics or it may require using special tools. For example, a child with cerebral palsy who experiences involuntary movements of the arms may have better control of her hands if she learns to rest her arms against a table top, or to hold her elbows close to her sides when trying to use her hands. Eating may be easier for some children if they use weighted utensils or if they wear weighted cuffs on their wrist.

Coping with Weakness of One Side of the Body

If your child has limited use of one side of the body (hemiplegia), the main therapeutic goal is to teach him to accomplish tasks with only one hand by using substitutes for the other hand. For example, in teaching your child to cut his food, a one-handed rocker knife eliminates the need for using a fork to hold the food still. In dressing, the hemiplegic child should always dress by starting with the affected side, and should undress starting with the unaffected side. With practice, even such complicated skills as fastening buttons or tying shoes can be done using only one hand.

Adaptations for the Blind Child

Children with severe visual impairment need to have an orderly and predictable environment in which to learn self-care skills. This allows them to orient themselves and recognize objects without the use of vision. For example, when learning to feed, the blind child will have difficulty

knowing where the food is located on the plate. You might teach your child to locate food by telling her that meat is always at the "top" of the plate, potatoes or starch at the "bottom," and vegetables on the "side" next to the fork. Your child will need to practice using utensils to feel for food and to gauge the size of a portion by estimating its weight on the utensil.

In dressing, blind children need to learn how to recognize their clothes so they can put together an outfit that looks attractive. You can embroider French knots on clothes to "code" them (e.g., one knot equals red; two knots equals blue), or you can organize closets and dressers so that matching clothes are stored together.

SPLINTS

Splints are a special type of device that can help the child who has limited use of his hands. A splint is a custom-made piece of equipment that supports a weak body part or prevents or corrects deformity or dysfunction. Occupational therapists most often make splints for the hands, while foot splints may be made by an orthotist or a physical therapist. One commonly used splint is the resting hand splint, illustrated in Figure 18.4, which keeps the hand and wrist in a functional position.

Most often, splints are made of a plastic material that is softened by immersion in hot water (140° F to 170° F). Once softened, the plastic is cut to fit your child's hand and is molded directly onto your child while the material is still warm. The process is not painful, but may cause some children to feel a bit alarmed. Once the splint has been fitted, straps are added to hold it in place. The therapist may pad or line the splint to make it more comfortable or to absorb moisture.

It is very important that you understand

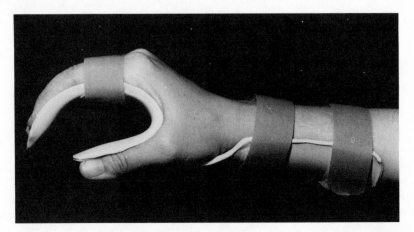

Figure 18.4. *Resting hand splint: This plastic splint helps prevent contractures and holds the hand open so it can be used for assistance.*

how to put the splint on correctly and remember to take it on and off as instructed by the therapist. Ask for written instructions and for a snapshot of the correct application. You should be alert for signs that the splint is causing problems. If your child perspires heavily while wearing the splint, his skin may become irritated or infected. Baby powder, spray antiperspirant, or wearing a stockinette to cover the hand may help prevent this problem. Swelling, redness, or skin irritation that lasts longer than thirty minutes after the splint has been removed could be a sign that the splint has been put on incorrectly or that it no longer fits your child. Discontinue use of the splint until you can contact your therapist for instruction.

To care for a splint, you should wash it daily with cool water and a mild soap. Be careful to keep the splint away from direct sunlight, radiators, or other sources of heat that could cause it to soften and lose shape. Since children are constantly growing and changing in abilities, you should ask your therapist how often she needs to check the splint for fit. If you live far from the therapist or make infrequent visits, you may wish to ask for a supply of replacement straps, as these often become worn, dirty, or lost.

SOME QUESTIONS ANSWERED

My child has just started a therapy program. What can I do at home to help?

Your therapist will probably spend a portion of your child's treatment time teaching you ways of helping your child. You will probably be asked to stay with your child during therapy so that you can observe and try out various techniques. Many parents feel overwhelmed by the expectation that they learn to do therapy at home — after all, it's hard enough just doing a good job of being a parent! If you think your therapist expects too much or too little of you, tell her!

Sometimes, the therapist will ask you to perform a specific exercise or activity at home. But more important, she will help you understand the goals of therapy so you can find ways of incorporating therapy principles into your daily routine. For example, if your child whines or fidgets when you try to teach her to remove her clothes, you might think of a way to motivate her to cooperate, such as by asking her to undress for a splash in the swimming pool. Try to keep sessions short, and stop if either you or your child become frustrated or bored. Remember that the best way to motivate your child is to give encouragement and positive reinforcement for every effort and small success.

How can I select toys that will help my child progress in therapy?

Many toys have educational or therapeutic value, but if your child doesn't think the toy is fun, you can be certain that he won't play with it for very long. Your therapist can suggest toys that offer the appropriate degree of developmental challenge, but freely discuss your own ideas with the therapist. If you think your child would enjoy a drum but your therapist thinks he cannot handle the drumsticks, she might be able to modify the toy or recommend an alternative musical instrument that would be more appropriate.

Some toy companies specialize in toys that are easier for disabled children to play with. For example, puzzle pieces can be fitted with large knobs for grasping, or blocks can be made to stay together more easily using Velcro or magnets.

19 COMMONLY USED MEDICINES

Almost all children require medication at one time or another. However, because of their special medical problems, children with disabilities are more likely to receive several types of medication taken simultaneously or for prolonged periods of time. Medications can be life-saving, as in the use of antibiotics to treat spinal meningitis or pneumonia. They can relieve pain and discomfort from a traumatic injury or improve a chronic medical condition like epilepsy. But they may also have unpleasant or dangerous side effects. In prescribing medication, your doctor will try to balance the likely benefits against the potential risks.

As a general rule, medication should be avoided unless it is clearly needed. Even such common, over-the-counter drugs as aspirin or acetaminophen (Tylenol) can do more harm than good under certain circumstances. Make sure that your child's doctor knows all the drugs your child is taking, both over the counter and prescription.

In this chapter, we discuss the benefits and risks of medications that are commonly used in treating children with developmental disabilities. Some of these are used to treat maladies experienced by all children: fevers, infections, and so on. Other medications are used to treat specific disorders associated with developmental disabilities, for instance, anticonvulsants and antispasticity medications. While this list of drugs is not meant to be all inclusive, it should give you some understanding of the types of medications that may be used in treating your child, and the potential side effects that your child may experience. More specific information is included in the references at the end of the book.

You should keep records of your child's medication history, including notes about any reactions she may have had. This information can be particularly valuable if your child is receiving more than one type of medication, as some drugs cross-react with one another, which alters their effectiveness. By paying close attention to your child's medications, you can help the doctor and pharmacist ensure that your child is properly medicated. Many pharmacists now have computerized systems that will keep track of your prescriptions and flag potential problems or cross-reactions. Try to use the same pharmacy so they can keep track of all the drugs your child is receiving.

When your child must take many different medications, dosage regimens can easily get confused. Plastic pill containers with separate compartments for each day of the week are available in most drugstores and can help reduce the confusion.

GENERIC VERSUS BRAND-NAME MEDICATION

You may be able to save a considerable amount of money by using generic rather than brand-name drugs. In fact, many pharmacists encourage generic substitution and some insurance plans mandate it. Generic drugs contain the same active ingredient that is found in the brand-name agent, although other components of the drug, such as binders and fillers, may differ.

Pharmaceutical companies spend millions of dollars to research and develop a new drug, money that they recover by charging a premium price and gaining exclusive marketing rights for seventeen years. After the patent expires, competitors may copy the drug and sell their copies as generic equivalents. These generic drugs must meet certain federally set standards of equivalency to the brand-name agent. Limited studies are usually required that demonstrate similar dissolution and absorption properties.

For you, this means that rather than buying the brand-name drug Valium, you might buy a generic form of the drug, diazepam, for as little as one-half the price. This principle is true for nonprescription drugs as well. There is no evidence that Bayer aspirin works any better than any other aspirin, nor that Tylenol works better than generic acetaminophen.

Studies have found that in most cases,

generic substitution is safe and effective. However, critics argue that the small variations allowable under the Food and Drug Administration (FDA) guidelines may cause significant problems for certain types of drugs. For example, anticonvulsant levels must be kept within strict limits in order to control seizures with the least likelihood of side effects. However, the FDA allows generic equivalents to vary in absorption by as much as twenty percent. Thus, if you switch from one brand to another, your actual dose may fluctuate significantly.

If you do switch from a brand-name to a generic drug, or from one generic brand to another, keep track of when the change occurred and inform your doctor about the change. Later, if you notice any alterations in symptomatology or side effects, your doctor may be able to trace those changes back to the medication and make appropriate changes.

DIFFERENT SYMPTOMS, DIFFERENT DRUGS

We have grouped the medications below by their uses. First, we discuss those medications commonly used by all children: antibiotics, skin preparations, and fever control, pain, and anticonstipation medications. Then we summarize the medications used for problems more commonly associated with developmental disabilities: behavioral control, sleep, anticonvulsant, antireflux, and antispasticity medications. We also discuss vitamin and mineral supplements, immunizations, and poisonings. The accompanying tables list brand names and generic names, as well as the purpose of the drug and some potential side effects. Please remember that not all possible side effects are listed, and though significant, these side effects occur only rarely.

ANTIBIOTICS

Children with disabilities are somewhat more likely than unaffected children to develop infections that require antibiotics. Common infections include those of the respiratory tract, the middle ear, the urinary tract, and the skin. Thus, your child may require an antibiotic at some point. Antibiotics are medications used to treat bacterial and some fungal infections. They are ineffective against viruses. Antibiotics may be either natural — for example, penicillin, which is derived from a certain mold — or synthetic, like cephalexin. They work by a variety of mechanisms. Some destroy bacterial cell walls, some prevent bacterial multiplication, and some damage the bacterial cells in other ways. Because of their different modes of action, different antibiotics are effective against different microorganisms.

In order to determine which drug will be most effective, your doctor may order culture and sensitivity tests. This involves swabbing the throat, wound, or abscess; or taking a urine specimen or blood test. Bacteria from the infected area are grown in the laboratory, identified by a variety of tests, and then tested against various antibiotics. A pattern of sensitivity to specific antibiotics is then used to help identify appropriate treatment.

For many types of infections, your doctor will make a presumptive diagnosis and then begin treatment even though he has not performed culture and sensitivity tests. For example, most ear infections are known to respond to ampicillin or amoxicillin and most abscesses to cloxacillin (Table 19.1). Tetracycline and erythromycin are commonly used to treat acne. Sulfa drugs such as Bactrim, Septra, and Gantrisin are often prescribed for urinary tract infections. Broad-spectrum antibiotics, such as cephalexin (Keflex), are generally used to treat infections that prove resistant to other medications or in people who are allergic to other drugs. Antibiotic treatment usually lasts from five to fourteen days. The infection may appear to clear earlier, often within a day or two, but the full course of treatment is necessary to eliminate all the infectious organisms. The drugs should be taken on an empty stomach, before meals. Rarely, an antibiotic will need to be given by vein or for a prolonged period of time. For example, bone infections (osteomyelitis) require six weeks of intravenous therapy. Recurrent urinary tract infections or middle ear infections may lead your doctor to prescribe an oral antibiotic for a number of months.

Skin rashes, upset stomach, and diarrhea may occur as side effects of antibiotic use. In such circumstances, an alternative antibiotic is often substituted. The frequency of such reactions in patients taking ampicillin led to the development of a number of ampicillin derivatives, including amoxicillin, which is equivalent in potency but has fewer side effects and can be given with meals three, rather than four, times a day. Although not toxic, tetracycline should not be given to pre-teenagers, as it can stain their teeth and interfere with bone growth and development. Other antibiotics can be substituted and work just as well.

Some people develop allergies to medications, particularly to penicillin and some of its derivatives. An allergic reaction to penicillin can involve hives or, rarely, severe difficulty breathing. If your child is allergic to penicillin or any other drug, make sure that his doctor knows, and that his medical records have been flagged to indicate the nature of the reaction. There are other antibiotics that can be used safely and effectively.

TABLE 19.1 Antibiotics

Generic Name	Trade Name	Common Uses	Preparations	Side Effects
penicillin	Pen-Vee K Pentids	Strep throat, pneumonia, rheumatic fever	T,C,L	upset stomach, rash, allergic reaction
ampicillin	Omnipen Principen Polycillin	middle-ear infection, meningitis, urinary tract infection	C,L	same as penicillin
amoxicillin	Amoxil Wymox Amcill	same as ampicillin	T,C,L	rash, less stomach upset than ampicillin, allergic reaction
cloxacillin	Tegopen Cloxapen	abscesses	C,L	same as penicillin
erythromycin	Erythrocin Pediamycin Ilosone E-Mycin	same as penicillin	C,L	upset stomach
sulfisoxazole	Gantrisin Pediazole	urinary tract infections	C,L	allergic reactions, upset stomach, lower blood count
cephalexin	Keflex	resistant infections	C,L	upset stomach, allergic reactions
tetracycline	Achromycin	acne, mycoplasma, pneumonia	C,L	stains teeth, upset stomach, rash, kidney toxicity
trimethoprim sulfamethoxazole (TMP-SMZ)	Bactrim Septra	urinary tract infections, middle ear infections	C,L	kidney toxicity, decreased blood count, allergic reactions

C = capsules, T = tablets, L = liquid suspension or elixir

SKIN PREPARATIONS

Rashes and skin problems are common in all children, but are even more frequent in children who are wheelchair bound or bed-ridden. Rashes may be symptoms of viral infections such as roseola, measles, or chicken pox, or they can be the result of fungal or bacterial infections. They may also be of noninfectious origin, caused by an allergic reaction, sunburn, or contact with something abrasive. If caused by a virus, the rash will generally disappear when the infection clears up, although your child may need some symptomatic relief in the meantime such as using calamine lotion or the oral antihistamine diphenhydramine (Benadryl). Please note that the combination of calamine lotion and Benadryl (Caladryl) has little benefit over calamine lotion alone and has more side effects.

Certain skin rashes can be protected against. Wearing long-sleeve shirts and jeans can decrease the chance of exposure to poison ivy during hiking. Avoiding contact with foods or chemicals that have previously irritated your child's skin is helpful. Absorbent diapers, frequent diaper changes, and the use of baby powder can decrease the risk of diaper rash.

Finally, applying sunscreen lotion before prolonged sun exposure should prevent sunburn. Sunscreens are labeled according to the amount of protection they provide. For instance, if a sunscreen provides four times as much protection as untreated skin, it would be labeled SPF (Sun Protection Factor) 4. Common over-the-counter sunscreens include Coppertone, Eclipse, and Sundown; each comes in various strengths. They all contain the medication PABA in various concentrations; this is what protects against damaging ultraviolet light from the sun. By trial and error you will find which strength of sun blockage is best for your child. Some people are allergic to PABA products and PABA-free sunscreens are available. In general these lotions need to be reapplied after one hour of swimming.

When a skin rash has developed, a number of medications may be helpful. Topical (rubbed on) skin medications include antibiotics, antifungal agents, steroids, or anesthetics, and come in a variety of forms — powders, creams, ointments, and lotions (Table 19.2). Powders increase drying and are useful in and around body fold areas, such as with diaper rash. Lotions, creams, and ointments are oil and water combinations of varying composition. Lotions are the lightest and most drying of the three, creams somewhat heavier and more "oily," and ointments the heaviest and most penetrating. In addition to these topical medications, some skin problems require treatment with oral medications. The following are common skin conditions and approaches to therapy.

Fungal Infections

Children are often troubled by fungal infections, particularly thrush or monilia, which is caused by a yeast-like fungus called Candida. Other common fungal infections include athlete's foot and ringworm.

Thrush appears as a reddish rash around the genital area or as a white plaque inside the mouth. The antifungal agent nystatin (Mycostatin) is very effective in treating this disorder. Cream and ointment preparations are used for genital infections, liquid for mouth infections.

Fungi that cause ringworm and athlete's foot improve when treated with another antifungal agent, tolnaftate (Tinactin). Tolnaftate is available over the counter (a prescription is not required) in several formulations: cream, ointment, aerosol, and powder. Your doctor can help you decide which formulation will be best. Apply the medication two to four times each day to the affected area. Tolnaftate has few side effects when used for short periods of time. Ringworm can also be treated with clotrimazole (Lotrimin). If it does not completely clear with the topical medication after two weeks, the oral medication griseofulvin (Fulvicin) may be prescribed.

Bacterial Skin Infections

Bacterial skin infections may be treated with either topical or oral antibiotics, depending on the severity and location of the infection. Superficial strep infections may respond to topical neomycin. However, boils, impetigo, or other skin abscesses, in which the bacteria cannot be reached by topical medications, require drainage of the infected area by a physician. This is usu-

TABLE 19.2 Skin Preparations

Generic Name	Trade Name	Common Uses	Preparations	Side Effects
nystatin	Mycostatin	antifungal, yeasts — thrush	cream, ointment, P,L,T	topical-non-toxic oral-diarrhea
tolnaftate †	Tinactin	antifungal, athlete's foot, ringworm	cream, liquid, powder, aerosol	non-toxic
clotrimazole †	Lotrimin	antifungal, ringworm	cream, lotion, solution	peeling, itching, skin irritation
griseofulvin	Fulvicin	antifungal, ringworm	T	skin rash, nausea, headache
lindane	Kwell	scabies, lice	shampoo, lotion, cream	occasionally dizziness or convulsions with lotion
polymyxin B, neomycin, and bacitracin †	Neosporin	prevent infection of cuts	ointment, cream	rash
benzoyl peroxide 5%, 10% †	Clearasil Fostex Oxy	acne	lotion, cream, gel	skin irritation, peeling
clindamycin	Cleocin-T	antibiotic for acne	solution, gel, ointment	diarrhea, colitis, irritated eyes
erythromycin 2%	T-stat	antibiotic for acne	solution	dryness, peeling, irritation of skin
isotretinoin	Accutane	acne	C	cracked lips, conjunctivitis, muscle weakness, headache, light sensitivity, damages fetus
hydrocortisone †	Caldecort Cort-Dome	eczema, dermatitis, poison ivy	P, cream, ointment	skin irritation, dryness, rash
triamcinolone	Kenalog, Aristocort, Kenacort	same as hydrocortisone	P, cream, ointment, lotion	same as hydrocortisone

C = capsules, T = tablets, L = liquid suspension or elixir, S = suppositories, P = powder
† available without a prescription

ally followed by an oral antibiotic such as the antistaphylococcal penicillin derivative cloxacillin (Tegopen).

Acne is also a type of bacterial infection that occurs frequently among adolescents and may last for several years, with periods of improvement and worsening. It is caused by clogged sebaceous glands, or pores, that become infected. Therapy involves keeping the skin clean, removing the dirt, oil, and cell debris that can block the pores, and treating the infection. Frequent washing is important, using a nonirritating soap such as Dove, Dial, Neutrogena, Ivory, or Alpha-Keri. Benzoyl peroxide, the active ingredient in such products as Clearasil and Oxy, has been shown to be helpful in unclogging the skin pores and should be applied twice a day. The topical antibiotics clindamycin (Cleocin-T) and erythromycin (T-Stat) also may be prescribed. For very severe cases, your doctor may suggest an oral vitamin A preparation called isotretinoin (Accutane), which loosens cellular debris around the skin glands. Although effective, it has a number of potential side effects, including cracked lips, severe headache, decreased blood count, and muscle weakness. Significant sunlight exposure should also be avoided during treatment. Although not a problem during childhood, it should be noted that isotretinoin has been associated with birth defects when given to pregnant women.

Allergic Skin Conditions

Many skin problems are caused not by infections, but by allergic reactions. Hives and certain rashes indicate an allergic response and may be treated with oral antihistamines. Another type of skin irritation, called eczema, can appear as a result of contact with a certain type of soap, cosmetic, or other product. Eczema may also occur for unknown reasons, with inflammations appearing as itchy, scaly patches around the elbows, underarms, and neck. Steroid creams such as hydrocortisone or triamcinolone can usually control the irritation. Creams and lotions such as Alpha-Keri, Lubriderm, Nivea, and Aquaphor can be used to treat the dryness and prevent water loss.

Common scalp conditions related to eczema are cradle cap in babies and dandruff among adults. Both manifest as scaliness and flaking. Frequent use of a shampoo that contains selenium sulfide (e.g., Selsun Blue), zinc pyrithione (Head and Shoulders), or salicylic acid-sulfur (Sebulex) can help treat the problem.

Insect-Related Rashes

Intense itching and redness may also be caused by infestation with mites. This condition, known as scabies, may occur anywhere on the body, but most often under the arms or in the groin region. Irritation of the scalp may be caused by infestation with lice, tiny insects that lay their eggs in hair. Both conditions can be treated using lindane (Kwell) preparations. Body lice are treated wtih Kwell cream or lotion rubbed into the affected areas. Head lice are treated with Kwell or A 200 pyrinate shampoo. Usually one application is sufficient. This is a contagious disease since the lice are passed easily at day-care centers or at home when children share towels, brushes, and combs. Therefore, all family members should be checked for the presence of lice or nits (their eggs) on the scalp and usually receive the Kwell treatment.

Topical Anesthetics

Some skin conditions are painful. Anesthetic solutions, such as lidocaine viscous (Xylocaine), can be applied to the mouth and are effective in deadening the pain associated with canker sores, severe sore throats, or herpes lip (cold sores) or throat infection. Anesthetic ointments or sprays are also available for sunburn (Bactine, Solarcaine).

Skin Sores

Skin sores, also called bedsores or decubital ulcers, occur when the skin and underlying tissue break down as a result of pressure, poor nutrition, and/or inactivity. Children who are confined to bed or wheelchairs, such as those with cerebral palsy, muscular dystrophy, or spina bifida, are particularly susceptible. The best approach to treatment is prevention — maintaining good nutrition and hygiene of the skin. Foam or sheepskin can be used to relieve pressure points, and frequent changes of position can reduce prolonged pressure to specific areas — usually bony protuberances such as the hips or backbone. Improved nutrition is also important as it will build up protective tissue under the skin.

If your child develops skin sores, they should be treated immediately. Position your child so that no weight is placed on the ulcer, and treat the wound with wet-to-dry dressings throughout the day. This involves soaking sterile gauze pads in a normal saline (salt) solution and applying them to the wound. Leave them for about ten to fifteen minutes or until they become dry and then replace them with new wet pads. This leads to the gentle removal of dead or diseased tissue. After the soaks, a dense ointment should be applied. Duoderm is one such product; some families even use Maalox. Antibiotics are usually not needed; however, severe ulcerations may require skin grafting. Improvement should be evident in five to seven days although it may take one to

two months for the ulcer to completely heal.

FEVER CONTROL AND PAIN MEDICATIONS

In children, fevers are most frequently associated with viral illnesses such as the flu, measles, or chicken pox. There are only two good reasons to treat fevers. First, very high fevers, above 102° F (38.5° C), are quite uncomfortable. Second, high fevers occurring in children under age four can be associated with convulsions. However, fevers usually do not reach a level that requires intervention. Moreover, some evidence suggests that fever may actually aid the body in fighting off certain infections.

If your child's fever does exceed 102° F, some treatment may be required. You can give him a sponge bath in lukewarm water and cover him lightly in bed. Alcohol rubs should not be used, as the alcohol can be absorbed through the skin and cause intoxication. If high fevers continue for more than a day, consult your pediatrician. Your child may have an infection, for example, of the middle ear or urinary tract, both of which require antibiotics.

Aspirin and acetaminophen are the most common medications used to treat fevers (Table 19.3). Even these commonly used drugs are not without risks. Aspirin has been associated with an increased risk of Reye's syndrome, a rare, viral-related illness of childhood that causes inflammation of the liver and brain and may lead to coma with a 20 percent mortality rate. Aspirin should, therefore, not be used by children with viral illnesses, particularly flu or chicken pox. As aspirin use has been curtailed in children with viral illnesses, the incidence of Reye's syndrome has plummeted. Aspirin may be given safely to chil-

TABLE 19.3   Fever Control and Pain Medication

Generic Name	Trade Name	Common Uses	Preparations	Side Effects
aspirin (acetylsalicylic acid) †	Aspirin	antipyretic, analgesic, anti-inflammatory	T,S	upset stomach, allergic reactions, dizziness, prolonged bleeding time
acetaminophen †	Tylenol, Tempra, Datril, Liquiprim, Panadol	antipyretic, analgesic	T,L,S,C	liver toxicity
ibuprofen †	Advil Motrin Pediaprofen	antipyretic, analgesic, anti-inflammatory	T,C,L	blurred vision, stomach ulcers, abnormal kidney function
codeine preparations	Empirin with codeine Tylenol with codeine	analgesic	T,S	narcotic, dizziness, nausea
oxycodone	Tylox (with acetaminophen)	analgesic	C	narcotic, dizziness, nausea

C = capsules, T = tablets, L = liquid suspension or elixir, S = suppositories
† available without a prescription

dren for other reasons, such as to control pain or inflammation. The principal side effect of aspirin is stomach upset; buffered preparations may be better tolerated. Children's strength aspirin is available as a liquid, pill (both chewable and swallowable), and suppository.

Acetaminophen (Tylenol) has similar effects as aspirin in treating fever and pain but does not reduce inflammation. It is now the most commonly used antifever agent. It has few side effects and is usually easier on the stomach than aspirin. Also, unlike aspirin, it is not associated with an increased risk for Reye's syndrome. However, a toxic overdose (10 to 100 times the normal dose) can lead to severe liver damage. Children's strength acetaminophen is available as a liquid, pill (both chewable and swallowable), or suppository.

Most common childhood pains are associated with headaches, middle ear infections, sore throats, toothaches, and leg pain. The most frequently used pain medications are aspirin, acetaminophen, and ibuprofen (Advil). Aspirin and acetaminophen are described above. They work within about twenty minutes of being taken and the benefits last three to four hours. Children's strength ibuprofen, which requires a prescription, comes in a liquid preparation for children and may give somewhat more pain relief than aspirin or acetaminophen. It can be given at four- to six-hour intervals. These drugs are generally not given in combination.

In the rare instance that a more powerful medication is needed, codeine is the most commonly used powerful analgesic. Oxycodone (in combination with acetaminophen it is called Tylox) is similar in function to codeine and is used for severe pain, such as following surgery.

ANTICONSTIPATION MEDICATIONS

Constipation is a major problem for children with disabilities. Decreased physical activity, a reduced intake of fluids, and uncoordinated bowel contractions and movement all contribute to the problem. Treatment methods differ and are discussed in chapter 16. Medications used to treat constipation are found in Table 19.4.

BEHAVIORAL CONTROL MEDICATIONS

In many cases, behavioral problems in children can be controlled by using behavior-modification techniques (see chapter 15) or by changes in school placement. However, sometimes medication is needed. The most common reasons for using medications in developmentally disabled children are to control hyperactivity, aggressive behavior, and/or self-injurious behavior. All the medications work by altering the neurochemical environment of the brain in regions that affect behavior (Table 19.5).

Hyperactivity is often treated with the stimulants methylphenidate (Ritalin), dextroamphetamine (Dexedrine), or pemoline (Cylert). These all work by increasing brain levels of the neurochemicals norepinephrine and dopamine. These neurochemicals increase attention span and decrease hyperactivity. Among children with normal intelligence, these drugs are about 80 percent effective. For mentally retarded children, there is a lower success rate, about 50 percent. The drugs are usually well tolerated, with side effects occurring in only about 10 percent of children. These include headache, stomachache, decreased appetite, moodiness, and insomnia. There has been some controversy as to whether stimulant medication should be given to children with seizure disorders. Although stimulants can theoretically lead to more frequent seizures, this seems to happen rarely. As a result, many physicians will prescribe stimulants to their hyperactive seizure patients. Long-term therapy with stimulants often results in slowed weight gain, but once the medication is stopped, the child catches up. Ritalin produces fewer side effects than does Dexedrine. Cylert is somewhat less effective than either Ritalin or Dexedrine. There is no evidence

TABLE 19.4   Constipation Medication

Generic Name	Trade Name	Common Uses	Preparations	Side Effects
bisacodyl †	Dulcolax	laxative	T,S	uncommon
docusate †	Colace	stool softener	C,L	rash
senna concentrate †	Senoko T	laxative	T, granules	uncommon
malt soup extract †	Maltsupex	laxative	L, P, T	uncommon

C = capsules, T = tablets, L = liquid suspension or elixir, S = suppositories, P = powder
† available without a prescription

TABLE 19.5   Hyperactivity and Behavior Control Medication

Generic Name	Trade Name	Common Uses	Preparations	Side Effects
methylphenidate	Ritalin	hyperactivity, attention span	T	loss of appetite, upset stomach, irritability, suppression of weight gain, increased heart rate, insomnia
dextroamphet-amine	Dexedrine	hyperactivity, attention span	T,L elixir contains 10% alcohol	same as Ritalin
pemoline	Cylert	hyperactivity	T	liver dysfunction, headache, irritability
clonidine	Catapres	aggressive behavior	T	rash, dry mouth, nausea, fatigue, headache, constipation
chlorpromazine	Thorazine	hyperactivity, aggressive behavior	T,C,L,S injection	weight gain, drowsiness, decreased atten-tion, movement disorder, low blood pressure, lower seizure threshold, liver toxicity
thioridazine	Mellaril	hyperactivity, aggressive behavior	T,L	same as thorazine but less frequent
haloperidol	Haldol	aggressive behavior	T,L	involuntary move-ments, liver toxicity
propranolol	Inderal	aggression, rage reactions	T,C	dizziness, stomach upset, fatigue
imipramine	Tofranil	bed-wetting, hyperactivity, depression	T,C	drowsiness, rapid heart rate, dry mouth, skin rash
nortriptyline	Pamelor	behavior disorder and depression	C,L	same as imi-pramine
alprazolam	Xanax	anti-anxiety	T	same as Valium (Table 19.8)
fluoxetine	Prozac	antidepressant	C	skin rash, insomnia, weight loss, nausea, seizures, fatigue
fenfluramine	Pondimin	behavior disorder	T	drowsiness, diarrhea, dry mouth

C = capsules, T = tablets, L = liquid suspension or elixir, S = suppositories that these drugs are addictive, and they do not commonly lose their effectiveness over time.

Dexedrine and Ritalin are usually given twice a day with breakfast and lunch, or once a day with breakfast in the sustained-release formulation. A third dose may be given in midafternoon if the child has a lot of homework to complete or is a terror at home. The medication takes effect in approximately thirty minutes and its effects last for three to four hours (six hours for the sustained-release pills), thereby providing benefits throughout the school day. Cylert lasts about six hours and may be given once a day. With Ritalin and Dexedrine, improvement may be seen on the first day of therapy. Benefits from therapy with Cylert, however, may not become evident for about three weeks.

Clonidine (Catapres), another neurochemical stimulator, may also be used to control hyperactivity. Though it has been used primarily to control high blood pressure in adults, recent evidence suggests that it can control hyperactivity, particularly if the child has other neurologic abnormalities. Clonidine takes effect within thirty minutes and the effects last for about four hours. Side effects include dry mouth, sedation, and constipation; these effects tend to decrease with continued usage. After long-term therapy, the medication should be discontinued gradually to prevent sudden changes in blood pressure.

Drugs that are used to treat psychiatric disorders may also help control hyperactivity in mentally retarded children. These drugs are called neuroleptics and include haloperidol (Haldol), chlorpromazine (Thorazine), and thioridazine (Mellaril). They have more serious side effects than the stimulants discussed above and may decrease attention while controlling hyperactivity and aggressive behavior. Side ef-

fects include sleepiness, weight gain, and stomach pain. A more serious side effect, seen when these medicines are used over a period of years, is the neurologic disorder tardive dyskinesia, in which the arms and legs move involuntarily. This does not always improve when the medication is withdrawn. In addition, these drugs may increase seizure activity in epileptic children and, in rare instances, will cause liver damage. Thus, neuroleptics should be reserved for severe behavior problems that do not respond to other therapies.

In recent years, the drug propranolol (Inderal) has been used to treat aggressive and rage behaviors. It has been safely used for many years to control high blood pressure and heart disease and is associated with few side effects, although it may worsen asthma. It is unclear by what mechanism propranolol improves behavior, but it is thought to block certain neurochemical receptors. Down syndrome children may need lower than normal doses, as the drug seems to accumulate in their blood. Side effects include light-headedness, stomachache, and fatigue. The anticonvulsant medication carbamazepine (Tegretol) has also been used with some success in treating rage behavior.

Antidepressant medications, called tricyclics, have been used to control behavior problems in adolescents with developmental disabilities. These drugs generally work for children who are depressed and whose behavioral problems are a result of depression. Nortriptyline (Pamelor or Aventyl), imipramine (Tofranil), and desipramine (Norpramin) are the most commonly used of these medications. They begin to improve mood within about one to three weeks. Side effects are rare, but may include dry mouth, stomach pain, sleepiness, and an increased risk of seizures in epileptic children. Finally, anti-anxiety drugs such as alprazolam (Xanax), a drug similar to Valium, have been used to treat behavior disorders in which anxiety seems to precipitate bad behavior. After long-term treatment, the drugs are usually withdrawn gradually over a few weeks to allow the brain to readjust to a new neurochemical environment.

Children who take any of these behavior-control drugs are generally given a drug "holiday" once a year, so the doctor can evaluate whether medication is still needed. Often, medication can be limited to school days, when control of attention, behavior, and activity is most important. Your doctor may ask you and your child's teacher to fill out a behavioral checklist, which will give him objective evidence of the drug's effectiveness.

SLEEP MEDICATIONS

Many disabled children have trouble falling asleep or staying asleep. Treatment differs depending on the problem. Behavioral approaches may work and should be tried first. For instance, if your child has trouble falling asleep, he may benefit from an established nighttime ritual. This might include a bedtime story, quiet games, and so on. The room should be darkened (with a nightlight if your child fears darkness) and household noises should be kept to a minimum. Using this approach, your child should fall asleep within about fifteen minutes.

Children who have difficulty either falling asleep or staying asleep often have not learned to fall asleep on their own. If you allow your child to remain up when he claims not to be sleepy; if he relies on your presence in order to fall asleep (for instance, if he only falls asleep when you rock him); or if you come whenever he

cries or calls out, you are reinforcing his behavior. Often, it is *your* behavior that needs changing! You may want to train him gradually: Start out by allowing him to cry for a few minutes before you respond, then gradually lengthen that time. Be firm in not allowing him to revert to his old reliance on you, including sleeping in your bed.

If your child has a persistent problem falling asleep, a mild sedative may be helpful (Table 19.6). The most commonly used sedative is chloral hydrate (Noctec). One teaspoonful given with juice about thirty minutes before bedtime should lead to at least six hours of sleep. Once your child gets used to this sleep pattern, the medication usually can be gradually withdrawn and sleep improvement will be maintained. There are few side effects other than occasional stomach irritation and pain. This drug is not addictive in the dosage used to treat sleeplessness. Other medications used to treat sleeplessness include antihistamines such as diphenhydramine (Benadryl) or hydroxyzine (Atarax or Vistaril); promethazine (Phenergan), which has antihistamine properties; and anti-anxiety agents such as diazepam (Valium).

Unfortunately no drug is useful in correcting problems with early-morning waking. Most children do not require more than ten hours of sleep. If your child is rising early, that is, at five to six A.M., you may want to move his bedtime to later in the evening.

ANTICONVULSANTS (also see Chapter 8)

Seizures are the result of stimulation of abnormal nerve cells in the brain. Anticonvulsant medications work by a variety of mechanisms to make seizures less likely to occur in susceptible individuals. Different

TABLE 19.6   Sleep Medications

Generic Name	Trade Name	Common Uses	Preparations	Side Effects
chloral hydrate	Noctec	sedation	C,L,S	upset stomach, habit-forming
diphenhydramine †	Benadryl	antihistamine, sedative, treatment of allergic reactions	C,T,L	dry mouth, dizziness, upset stomach, thickens secretions
hydroxyzine	Atarax Vistaril	anti-anxiety, sedation	C,T,L	dry mouth
promethazine	Phenergan Provigan	antihistamine, sedation, allergic reactions	T,L,S	low or high blood pressure, lowers seizure threshold, dry mouth, rash, nausea

C = capsules, T = tablets, L = liquid suspension or elixir, S = suppositories
† available without a prescription

medications are prescribed for different types of seizures (Table 19.7). For example, phenobarbital, phenytoin (Dilantin), and carbamazepine (Tegretol) are the most common medications used to control grand mal seizures. Ethosuximide (Zarontin) is used for petit mal seizures. Primidone (Mysoline) and Tegretol are helpful for temporal lobe seizures, and ACTH, clonazepam (Klonopin), and valproate (Depakene) for minor motor seizures or infantile spasms. Some of these drugs can be used for multiple types of seizures.

Your child's doctor will start with one medication and increase the dose gradually until seizure control is achieved or side effects become prominent. A small proportion of children will require a combination of two drugs. It is rare that more than two drugs are used. Once the condition has stabilized, drug levels in the blood will be tested about twice a year to ensure that they are in the therapeutic range. Blood tests for liver function or other studies may be taken at the same time. Drug levels will be obtained more frequently when the medication dosage is being changed.

Side effects from seizure drugs are varied. Many can cause sleepiness, dizziness, stomach upset, or rash. Some symptoms are specific to one medication. For example, Dilantin causes excessive hair growth and gum swelling. There are few dangerous side effects, the most severe being liver failure reported in rare cases of children treated with Depakene.

ANTIREFLUX MEDICATIONS (also see chapter 16)

Children with cerebral palsy are apt to have problems with food refluxing, or backing up, from the stomach into the esophagus. This can occur when the muscular valve that separates the stomach and food tube doesn't work properly. The acidic stomach contents can then irritate the lower part of the feeding tube. Treatment consists of positioning your child on

TABLE 19.7   Anticonvulsants

Generic Name	Trade Name	Common Uses	Preparations	Side Effects
phenobarbitol	Luminal	grand mal, temporal lobe	L,T elixir contains 14% alcohol	hyperactivity, rash, irritability, sleepiness
phenytoin	Dilantin	grand mal, temporal lobe	C,L,T	rash, dizziness, gum swelling, excessive hair
carbamazepine	Tegretol	grand mal, temporal lobe	T,L	drowsiness, dizziness, urinary retention, rash, low blood count
primidone	Mysoline	grand mal, temporal lobe	T,L	same as phenobarbitol
clonazepam	Klonopin	minor motor, infantile spasms, temporal lobe, grand mal	T	drowsiness, drooling, swallowing problems, dizziness, personality changes
valproate	Depakene, Depakote	grand mal, minor motor, temporal lobe, petit mal, infantile spasms	T,C,L	liver damage, hair loss, weight loss
ethosuximide	Zarontin	petit mal	C,L	liver toxicity, sedation, unsteady walk, stomach upset
ACTH	Cortrophin	infantile spasms	injection	cataracts, brittle bones, diabetes, high blood pressure

C = capsules, T = tablets, L = liquid suspension or elixir

his side, using medications that increase muscle tone (metoclopramide, Reglan) or decrease stomach acidity (cimetidine [Tagamet] or ranitidine [Zantac]), and occasionally performing surgery to tighten the junction. Table 19.8 summarizes the medications commonly used to treat reflux problems.

ANTISPASTICITY MEDICATIONS (also see chapter 9)

Antispasticity medications are used to decrease muscle tone in children with spastic cerebral palsy. Unfortunately, the medications currently available are effective for less than 50 percent of the children who

TABLE 19.8   Antireflux and Antispasticity Medication

Generic Name	Trade Name	Common Uses	Preparations	Side Effects
metoclopramide	Reglan	gastrointestinal reflux	T,L	involuntary movements, drowsiness
cimetidine	Tagamet	ulcers, stomach acidity	T,L	diarrhea, rash, dizziness
diazepam	Valium	decrease muscle tone, anticonvulsant, anti-anxiety	T,L	respiratory depression, drowsiness, drooling, swallowing difficulties
lorazepam	Ativan	similar to Valium	T	same as Valium
baclofen	Lioresal	antispasticity	T	drowsiness, dizziness, low blood pressure, stomach upset
dantrolene	Dantrium	antispasticity	C	liver damage, weakness, diarrhea, drowsiness

C = capsules, T = tablets, L = liquid suspension or elixir

try them and have a high incidence of side effects (see Table 19.8). They must be evaluated to determine if the benefits outweigh the risks. Measures of muscle tone and motor abilities should be made by a physical or occupational therapist before and during treatment. She will look to see whether the treatment makes your child easier to diaper, for example, or if your child can roll over, sit, or stand better.

The medications used either: (1) affect the brain control of muscle tone — for example, diazepam (Valium), lorazepam (Ativan), clonazepam (Klonopin), and baclofen (Lioresal) — or (2) decrease the ability of the muscle to contract, as in the case of dantrolene (Dantrium).

Diazepam, lorazepam, and clonazepam are central nervous system inhibitors and not only decrease muscle tone but may also cause sleepiness and drooling, and interfere with swallowing. Other than those side effects, these medications are generally well tolerated and can be given over a long period of time. If they are going to work, this should become evident within the first week of therapy. Withdrawal should be gradual, as physical dependency can develop.

Baclofen is also a central nervous system inhibitor. It has been used most extensively to treat adults with multiple sclerosis. In addition to sleepiness, side effects include low blood pressure, stomach upset, and feelings of dizziness. About 10 percent of children treated with baclofen have sufficiently unpleasant side effects to discontinue treatment. Effectiveness is similar to Valium.

Dantrolene works directly on muscle cells to inhibit their contraction. Like baclofen, it has been used primarily to treat multiple sclerosis. It has shown limited success in treating children with cerebral palsy. Side effects include a decrease in muscle tone, muscle weakness, and, rarely, severe liver damage.

IMMUNIZATIONS

Vaccinations are used to protect children from contracting infectious diseases. They confer protection by stimulating the child's natural defense system, called the immune system, to prepare itself to attack infectious organisms that the child may come in contact with. During infancy, all children should receive vaccinations against the following diseases: diphtheria, pertussis, and tetanus (these three vaccinations are usually given together as a DPT vaccine), polio (denoted OPV, for oral polio vaccine), measles, mumps, and rubella or German measles (these three given together as the MMR vaccine), and hemophilus influenza type b (called the PRP vaccine) to protect against hemophilus meningitis. The suggested immunization schedule is summarized in Table 19.9. Most of these vaccinations protect your child for life. However, the tetanus vaccine should be repeated every ten years, and a second measles shot is required during the teenaged years. A vaccine for chicken pox should be available soon.

In general, children with disabilities should receive the same immunizations as nonhandicapped children, with one exception. The pertussis (whooping cough) vaccine should not be given to children who have uncontrolled seizures or who have neurologic conditions that predispose them

TABLE 19.9 Recommended Schedule for Active Immunization

Recommended Age	Immunization(s)
2 months	DTP, OPV, HbOC
4 months	DTP, OPV, HbOC
6 months	DTP, HbOC
15 months	MMR, HbOC
18 months	DTP
	OPV
	PRP-D
4–6 years	DTP, OPV
10–12 years	MMR
14–16 years	Td

DTP = diphtheria and tetanus toxoids with pertussis vaccine.
OPV = oral poliovirus vaccine containing attenuated poliovirus types 1, 2, and 3.
HbOC = hepatitis b oligosaccharide conjugate vaccine. An alternate to the HbOC at 2, 4, and 6 months is PRP-OMP (hepatitis b outer membrane protein conjugate vaccine), given at 2, 4, and 12 months.
MMR = live measles, mumps, and rubella viruses in a combined vaccine.
PRP-D = Haemophilus b diphtheria toxoid conjugate vaccine.
Td = adult tetanus toxoid (full dose) and diphtheria toxoid (reduced dose) for adult use.
Source: Committee on Infectious Diseases. *The 1991 Red Book.* American Academy of Pediatrics.

either to seizures or other neurological problems. Some severely disabled children, especially those who are bedridden or who are susceptible to pneumonia, may benefit from additional immunizations. These include vaccines for flu (trivalent influenza) and for pneumococcal pneumonia. Flu vaccination requires two shots at one-month intervals. They must be given each fall, as the specific viral strain, and therefore the vaccine, changes from year to year. The Pneumovax pneumonia vaccine needs to be given only once.

Some disabled children, especially those who are in institutions, may also benefit from receiving the hepatitis (liver infection) vaccine. This vaccine is usually reserved for children who will be in continuous close contact with a child who has a specific type of hepatitis.

Vaccines generally have few side effects. Some children become irritable, develop a low-grade fever after twenty-four to forty-eight hours, or develop pain or swelling at the site of the injection. Acetaminophen can be given for the fever; cold compresses may relieve pain at the injection site. Although some vaccines contain a live virus, there is very little chance of your child contracting the disease. Usually the virus is inactivated or has been altered so as to be harmless. The pertussis vaccine has been very rarely associated with serious side effects, including high fevers, seizures, screaming spells, allergic reactions, and brain damage. However, remember that in the vast majority of cases the vaccine safely protects children from whooping cough, which itself is contagious and can be quite serious. Vaccines are generally not given to children who are febrile or show signs of immunodeficiency. In addition, children who are allergic to eggs may be unable to tolerate certain vaccines that have been produced in eggs. These include the vaccines for measles, mumps, and influenza.

VITAMINS AND MINERALS

Supplemental vitamins and minerals are not usually necessary for children other than in infancy. However, although a normal diet contains sufficient amounts of vitamins, an unbalanced or inadequate diet may be vitamin deficient (Table 19.10). In addition, children who are confined to bed or wheelchair or who are taking the anticonvulsant Dilantin may need supplemental vitamin D. Calcium supplements may also be helpful for nonambulatory children susceptible to serious bone fractures. Complete formulas, such as those used for tube feeding (Sustacal, Complete B, and Isocal), already have sufficient quantities of vitamins and minerals added.

Supplemental vitamins and minerals may be prescribed in certain other situations: Iron supplements, such as Fer-in-sol, are usually recommended after infancy if iron-deficiency anemia is present; other vitamin deficiencies usually appear as a skin condition or hair loss. If you have questions about whether your child needs vitamin or mineral supplements, ask your pediatrician. Little harm will come from giving your child a daily vitamin pill such as Tri-Vi-Sol or Flintstones; excess vitamin

TABLE 19.10 Vitamins and Minerals

Generic Name	Trade Name	Common Uses	Preparations	Side Effects
multivitamins †	Tri-vi-sol Flintstones	vitamins A,C,D	T,L	uncommon
ergocalciferol (vitamin D$_2$) †	Drisdol	prevents rickets	C,L	uncommon
ferrous sulfate †	Fer-In-Sol	prevents iron deficiency	C,L	upset stomach
calcium gluconate †	Calcet	strengthens bone	T	uncommon

C = capsules, T = tablets, L = liquid suspension or elixir
† available without a prescription

will simply be eliminated in the urine. At the same time, there is no evidence to support the use of megavitamin therapy in treating disabled children; none of these treatments has been shown to be effective.

POISONINGS

Children can be poisoned by anything from their own medications to houseplants (Table 19.11). Poisoning can result from an

accidental overdose, mistaking a medication for a piece of candy, or ingesting something not meant for human consumption, such as a drain cleaner or a poisonous plant.

In any event, the best way to deal with poisoning is to prevent it from happening. Medications should be stored in a locked or inaccessible cabinet, out of reach of children. Check the dosages on your child's medication to avoid overdosing, and make a note when he has taken a dose so that he will not forget and take the medication again. Do not increase dosage without first checking with your doctor. More is not always better! As mentioned previously, you may want to keep a week's dosage of medication in a plastic container that has separate compartments for each day of the week. Store medications in their original containers so you retain dosage information and dates of effectiveness. Do not use outdated medications. If you notice new side effects that may have resulted from the medication, have your doctor check the blood level or dosage to see if it needs adjustment.

Kitchen cleaners and other dangerous chemicals should be kept in childproof locations. Discard old medicines and household products. Warn your children not to eat or drink any medications or nonfood items without your permission. Children are most likely to put nonfood items in their mouths during the toddler years. However, in developmentally delayed children, this period may extend for many years.

If your child has ingested a poisonous substance, follow these steps. (It is also wise to keep a standard first-aid chart with step-by-step guidelines on hand for emergency situations.) First, remove any excess from his mouth. The next step you take depends on the type of material ingested.

TABLE 19.11   Toxic and Nontoxic Products

PRODUCTS THAT ARE USUALLY NONTOXIC

Antacids	Cosmetics	Matches
Antibiotics	Crayons	Mercury from
Ball-point pen	Deodorants	a thermometer
inks	Glues and pastes	Modeling clay
Bath soaps	Hair products	Newspapers
Chalk	Hand creams	Pencils
Cigarettes	Latex paint	Shampoos
Colognes	Laxatives	Toilet water
Contraceptive		Toothpaste
pills		

PRODUCTS THAT ARE:

Moderately toxic	*Very toxic*	*Extremely toxic*
Antifreeze	Ammonia	Herbicides
Bleach (sodium	Dishwasher	Insecticides
hypochloride)	granules	Strychnine
Mothballs	Drain cleaners	
Stain remover	Lead paints	
	Petroleum	
	products	

COMMON DRUG INTOXICATIONS

Amphetamines	Barbiturates —	Dilantin
Antihistamines	sleeping pills	Iron prepara-
Aspirin	Digitalis	tions

TOXIC PLANTS

Asparagus fern	Oleander	Some types of
Daffodils	Poinsettia	mushrooms
Dieffenbachia	Rhubarb	Yew
Holly	leaves	Yarrow

Source: M. L. Batshaw and Y. M. Perret, *Children with Handicaps: A Medical Primer.* Second Edition. Baltimore: Paul H. Brookes Publishing, 1986.

United States law requires that labels on containers of hazardous substances include the generic name of the toxic chemical and first-aid instruction in the event of accidental ingestion.

If the instructions tell you to induce vomiting, syrup of ipecac should be used. Ipecac can be obtained in single-dose vials (one ounce) at drugstores without a doctor's prescription and should be kept on hand at all times. For children under one year of age, give only two teaspoons; for older children, give the entire vial. Follow the ipecac with three to six ounces of water. It works most effectively if the ingestion has occurred in the past half-hour. Manual methods of inducing vomiting, such as sticking a finger down the throat, rarely work.

Ipecac should not be used if your child is unconscious or convulsing or the victim of certain types of poisonings. It should not be used if your child has swallowed gasoline or kerosene, as vomiting may lead to aspiration of the toxin into the lungs and the development of a chemical pneumonia. It should also not be used if your child has swallowed a caustic substance, such as oven cleaner, Drāno, or any product containing lye, as the chemical can further injure the esophagus during vomiting.

Caustic material ingestion requires special treatment. First, give a cup of milk to your child to help neutralize the caustic agent and coat the stomach with a protective lining. If caustic materials are spilled on skin, clothing, or eyes, remove the clothes and rinse the areas with cool running water for about five minutes. Then, take your child to the emergency room for further treatment. At the hospital, your child's stomach may be pumped, or activated charcoal or specific antidotes may be administered. Blood and urine tests will often be done to estimate the amount and seriousness of the ingestion. Be sure to bring with you the container of medication or poison ingested by your child and try to estimate the volume or number of pills taken and the time of the ingestion.

If you are not sure whether the substance your child swallowed is poisonous, call a poison control center at a nearby hospital. This should be listed in the front of your telephone directory. For convenience, you may want to keep the number taped to your phone. The people who answer these calls can advise you about emergency treatment and whether your child needs to be brought to the hospital.

In addition to these acute poisonings, you must also be concerned about chronic poisonings, the most common being lead poisoning. Lead poisoning occurs in children who put nonfood items, such as paint chips or plaster, in their mouths. Older homes, particularly those built before World War II and those in inner-city areas, are likely to have been painted in the distant past with lead-based paint. Even if it has been painted over, paint chips can still contain toxic amounts of lead. Symptomatic lead poisoning includes episodes of vomiting, seizures, and coma, with severe brain damage often resulting. However, even in the absence of such symptoms, a child with lead poisoning may experience some speech delay. If you suspect that your child may be susceptible to lead intoxication, have his blood lead level measured. If it is elevated, medications can be given that will lower the lead level quickly.

V Growing Up with a Disability

20 EDUCATIONAL PROGRAMS FOR YOUR CHILD

M. E. B. Lewis, Ed.D., and Robin Gallico, Ed.D.

You will find that one of your major challenges will be to help your child on the path through the school years. All parents hope that this path will lead their children to progressively higher levels of understanding and appreciation of the world around them, and will prepare them for the demands of adulthood. However, if your child has a disability, that path may seem like an obstacle course.

Subtle and not so subtle barriers in society can restrict the educational pursuits of a disabled child. Even educators, who should be sensitive to special-needs children, often fail to notice how some school programs ignore the needs of children who have visual, intellectual, auditory, or motor limitations. Adaptation of school programs is crucial, and many effective measures are quite simple to perform. These include seating a child up front so that he may see and hear the teacher more clearly or using a specially designed desk to accommodate a wheelchair. Other strategies, such as special communication systems or computer-assisted movement devices, call for greater adaptability on the part of the teacher and other students and are

more complex and expensive to implement.

ARIEL, JENNIFER, AND KEVIN

Ariel will be nine years old on her next birthday. She was born eight weeks prematurely after a very difficult pregnancy and weighed under four pounds at birth. She spent four weeks in the neonatal intensive care unit where she had significant respiratory distress and feeding difficulties.

Gradually, Ariel began to stabilize and gain weight and her parents looked forward to bringing her home. At the same time, they were unsure of their ability to care for her. A teacher at her sister's school told Ariel's mother about early-intervention services. Ariel was evaluated and provided with infant stimulation services at home beginning at six months of age.

Ariel entered a special-education pre-school at age three and made wonderful progress. Her program included physical therapy, occupational therapy, speech and language services, and pre-academic and socialization activities. Though her intelligence seemed normal, her physical disabilities, diagnosed as extrapyramidal cerebral palsy, made communication difficult. Her articulation was labored and difficult to understand. Sign language was suggested as a possible alternative to speech, but her fine-motor control was not developed enough to make accurate signs. In addition, she was clumsy and often fell down, and she wore short leg braces. Despite these difficulties, Ariel thrived in the special-education program and learned to read and do simple arithmetic by the end of the first grade. During second grade she continued to defy earlier predictions. As her fine-motor skills improved, she was able to use a total communication system. By the end of the second grade, Ariel's parents felt that she was ready for a more normal educational setting and wanted her to attend their neighborhood school with her older brother.

At the yearly review meeting with school officials, Ariel's parents made their wishes known. The school administration, however, identified several obstacles that were of concern to them. The neighborhood school did not have a nurse, and the physical facility was multilevel with many sets of stairs. In addition, speech and language services were itinerant, which meant that the therapist came to the school only twice a week. Yet, through the persistence of Ariel's parents and the support given to them by the neighborhood school principal, Ariel was transferred to a regular third grade class.

Ariel's teacher worked hard to accommodate her limitations. This positive attitude was communicated to Ariel's classmates, who quickly accepted her, learned how to communicate with her, and acted protectively toward her. It was recommended that Ariel begin to learn to use a computer, as writing would always be slow and laborious and her handwriting illegible to most readers. The school system recommended an evaluation at a nearby university that specialized in adaptive technology and a laptop computer was suggested for school and home use. Ariel learned to type her assignments and a peer tutor was allowed to take notes for her during class. It took Ariel much longer than usual to complete assignments, but her teacher was willing to adapt to this and Ariel was willing to put in the extra time at home. Ariel's parents were very supportive and continued to expect her to do the very best she was capable of. So far this has paid off!

Unlike Ariel, Jennifer's arrival into this world was uneventful. She went home two days after her birth, feeding normally, sleeping well, and rarely fussing. Jenny cooed, babbled, and smiled a bit later than her siblings, but she was so "easy" that her mother had no concerns at her well-baby checkups. When Jenny was six months old, however, her grandmother noticed that she was not acquiring a variety of sounds or attempting to communicate as the other children had. Grandmother wondered if Jenny was hearing what was going on around her. Over time, Jenny began to retreat into a world of her own and did not appear to pay attention to her surroundings or to interact with other family members. At her one-year-old checkup, Jenny's mother confessed to her pediatrician that she feared Jenny was autistic. The pediatrician reassured her that Jenny had developed enough socially to suggest another cause for her apparent language delay. Jenny was referred to a developmental center and received a thorough evaluation. It was determined that she had a severe sensorineural hearing loss in both ears. Hearing aids were fitted and Jenny was referred for early-intervention services through the local public schools. Twice each week she received in-home training from a special educator and a speech pathologist. Jenny's mother was instructed in strategies to facilitate language development.

The whole family became involved in Jenny's program. When Jenny was two and a half, the infant-stimulation teacher, who had been teaching her in her home, suggested that Jenny would benefit from a center-based program. She began attending a preschool communication center once a week and continued to have in-home services one day per week. In addition, Jenny's mother attended a parent support group with parents of other hearing-impaired children. Jenny's mother had become concerned that the once-a-week preschool class was not meeting Jenny's growing communication needs, and through this group she began exploring other options for the hearing-impaired that were within her community. Some of the programs she found taught sign language as the primary form of communication, while others offered a total communication approach that incorporated speech, lip-reading, and sign language (see chapter 11). She is currently trying to determine which programs will be best for Jenny in the long run.

Kevin is sixteen years old and has Down syndrome. His parents have known ever since his birth that he would have special needs. He attended special-education classes throughout elementary school and was transferred to a special center for middle school. After middle school, Kevin's parents began to search for a vocational education program. They felt he could accomplish more than the repetitive assembly tasks that were taught in a sheltered workshop. In fact, Kevin had demonstrated through a summer job at his father's business that he could learn simple filing and

sorting in the mail room. Kevin's parents were interested in a supported employment program they had read about and wanted Kevin to be prepared to live in a supervised alternative-living unit when he finished school.

They were successful in getting Kevin into such a program. Working with job coaches, students in Kevin's program learn the skills involved in light manufacturing and service jobs such as the food industry. Social skills necessary for success on the job are specifically taught through role-playing and on-the-job experience. His day is split between classroom instruction and actual job placement. The job coach works with the employer, school counselor, Kevin's parents, and Kevin himself to build a successful working relationship. In the classroom, Kevin learns to manage his salary and leisure time, as well as other skills required to live independently.

Although Kevin is receiving the best possible training, his parents have been told that the availability of openings in alternative-living units are scarce and Kevin will have to be placed on a waiting list early if a placement is to be available upon completion of his schooling. Over many years Kevin's parents have developed reasonable expectations for him but continue to worry about assuring a meaningful independent life for him when they are no longer around to advocate for him.

LEGAL MANDATES FOR SPECIAL EDUCATION

Whether your child's needs are simple or complex, there are now legal mandates designed to ensure that all children benefit as fully as possible from their school programs. This was not always so. Until relatively recently, disabled children and adults were excluded from many educational programs. This discrimination was finally dealt with through civil rights legislation and the enactment of federal laws beginning in the early 1960s. At that time, Congress provided the means for personnel to be trained and for programs to be developed for disabled children. Through this intervention, programs such as Head Start eventually were made available to disabled children. However, until the enactment of the Education for All Handicapped Children Act of 1975, the necessary political and financial clout to enforce educational equality was lacking. The three pieces of legislation that have the greatest impact on schools are Public Law 94-142, passed in 1975; Public Law 99-457 (part H), passed in 1986; and Section 504 of the Vocational Rehabilitation Act, passed in 1973. These are discussed below.

Public Law 94-142

Public Law 94-142, the Education for All Handicapped Children Act, covers all disabled children between the ages of three and twenty-one. This law addresses six primary issues of educational programming:

1. Zero Reject — *All* children must be provided with a free, appropriate public education, regardless of how severely disabled they are.
2. Evaluation — Each child referred for consideration of special-education services must be evaluated for each area of suspected need by a qualified examiner. These tests must take into account the child's disability and must be appropriate for his or her cultural or linguistic background.
3. Individual Educational Plan (IEP) — Every student receiving special-education services must have his or her individually designed program outlined *in writing*.

4. Least Restrictive Environment (LRE) — Even though a student may have a disability that requires special educational services, whenever possible the student should be with his peers who are not disabled. In other words, children should be placed in as normal an environment as possible.
5. Parents as Partners in Planning — Parents must have access to the educational records of their child, and must receive notification of all decision-making meetings. In addition, parental permission must be obtained in writing before any testing can occur and before a special-education placement can be implemented. In sum, the parent *is part* of the educational team.
6. Due Process — The decision-making process in special education is not always a smooth or agreeable one, and emotions can run high when parents disagree with educational staff over the development and delivery of services for their child. When such disagreements occur and appear to be beyond resolution, legal means are provided for parents and education professionals to have a hearing of their dispute by a qualified, impartial examiner. Each state has a process for hearings and for the appeal of decisions.

Public Law 99-457

Although some states extended the services provided under Public Law 94-142 downward to include infants, the majority did not. The need to provide early-intervention services became more apparent as advances in medical technology provided the means to save premature babies at an ever-increasing rate, thus creating a large group of infants at risk of developing handicapping conditions. In 1986, with the passage of Public Law 99-457 (enactment was mandated for October 1990), the needs of these infants and very young children were recognized and provided for. This legislation mandates services to infants, toddlers, and preschool-aged children through two programs. The first, the Preschool Grants Program, requires that disabled children between three and five years of age receive appropriate *educational* (as distinct from day-care) services designed to lay the foundation for later academic instruction. The programs should provide children with an understanding of language and of the concepts of space and time, and should teach the motor skills necessary to manipulate crayons, scissors, pencils, blocks, puzzles, and toys. They should also emphasize large-muscle activities, such as running and jumping, and should teach the social skills necessary in school — sharing, turn-taking, and cooperating.

The second program mandated under this law is the Handicapped Infants and Toddlers Program. This law differs significantly from previous educationally oriented laws in three important ways. First, it requires collaboration between health, social service, and educational agencies. Second, it is family centered and provides services not only to the disabled child, but to the entire family through its Individual Family Service Plan (IFSP) and needs assessment process. The third difference is that services are extended to children who are *at risk* for developmental delay, not just to those who have already been identified as having a handicapping condition. This law requires each state to make provisions for seeking out children from birth to age three who have conditions such as prematurity that might predispose them to developmental delays. This part of the legislation is an extension of the "Child Find" services already established under 94-142. Under this law each state is required to maintain an office to receive initial inquiries regarding special education. This Child Find service is supposed to identify every disabled child who needs special education. (A listing of the Child Find offices can be found by contacting your State Director of Special Education.)

Just as with Public Law 94-142, 99-457 requires that parents be involved in determining the services needed by their child; that multidisciplinary teams of professionals participate in decision-making and program development; and that certain standards be met. Unlike 94-142, which has been in existence for fifteen years, 99-457 is a new act whose implementation is still in the planning stage in most states. Theoretically, as soon as your child is identified as qualifying for these services, a needs assessment should be done, which forms the basis for the Individual Family Service Plan. The needs assessment will be completed by a qualified professional, who will interview the family to determine specific needs, strengths, and weaknesses. Each state must determine which will be the lead agency overseeing the infants and toddlers program. That lead agency could be the Department of Education, the Health Department, or the Department of Social Services. The services provided may include not only educational services, but also respite care, health services, in-home family support services, and physical, occupational, and speech therapies. Many states are still in the process of establishing regulations for implementing this aspect of the law. In addition, the definition of "at risk" still remains unclear. For specific information about your state's 99-457 program, contact the State Department of Education or the Child Find office.

The Vocational Rehabilitation Act of 1973

The Vocational Rehabilitation Act of 1973 laid the foundation for educational programs that are designed to address the needs of disabled people as they make the transition from childhood to adult life. Several sections of the act, called "titles," deal specifically with issues of employment, independent living, and discrimination against disabled adolescents and young adults. Title I sets forth the basic design of the vocational rehabilitation program, assuring services such as evaluation, testing, provision of adaptive equipment or appliances, medical treatment, counseling, and training. Just as the educational programs outlined above require written documentation to assure adequate provision of services, this legislation also requires written rehabilitative plans with goals and objectives for each area of service. Title V states that discrimination against a handicapped citizen is a federal violation of that person's civil rights and is therefore illegal, just as sex and race discrimination are federally prohibited. Title VII provides for grants to the disabled so that appropriate living arrangements can be made (including adaptations to the home and transportation) in preparation for future employment and independence. This section also encourages the establishment of community-based centers for training disabled citizens. For further information about the legislation mentioned in this chapter, consider reading *Accommodating the Spectrum of Individual Abilities*, a book published by the U.S. Commission on Civil Rights (Clearinghouse Publication #81).

In the ideal model of a lifetime continuum of services, your infant would first be identified as having a disability under Public Law 99-457 and would receive whatever family support services were necessary until he or she reached preschool age. At that time and until the age of twenty-one, Public Law 94-142 would provide special education and related services necessary to prepare your child for as productive and independent a life as possible.* Once your child had completed school, the Vocational Rehabilitation Act would provide training, support, and counseling throughout adult life.

SPECIAL EDUCATION IS A PROCESS

Your child will spend a large portion of his life in an educational setting, and it is critical for you to be well informed about the entire special-education process, including screening, identification, assessment, and placement. If your child's disability is known at birth, you should be directed to the Child Find office during this early period. You may feel that adjusting to the trauma of having a disabled child is all you can handle at the time, and that you would rather put off thinking about how to educate your child for a while. However, parents often find that early-intervention services can offer critical support at a time when they are least in a position to actively seek out these services.

* In 1990, PL 94-142 was reauthorized to provide services to disabled school-aged persons. This reauthorization, called Public Law 101-476, is known as IDEA, Individuals with Disabilities Education Act. The language of the law was expanded to include two conditions not originally mentioned in 94-142 — autism and traumatic brain injury.

Although mandated services are available to deal with your child's special needs, getting these services is not as simple as calling the principal and saying, "My child needs . . ." There are several steps you must take to get the process started:

Request a screening or evaluation

Special-education services are provided for needs that are identified by qualified examiners. Psychologists and special educators evaluate cognitive and instructional needs, while physicians and occupational and physical therapists evaluate specialized physical needs. Needs in the visual and auditory areas are determined by eye specialists and audiologists respectively.

If you notice some area of concern in your child's development, you can request, through your local school, a "screening," which is a quick procedure for determining whether your child needs an in-depth evaluation.

Make your request in writing

Your letter does not have to be lengthy or sophisticated, but serves to document the fact that you made the request. When a screening is requested, the school must complete the evaluation within a set period of time.

You may have already had your child tested prior to the educational screening. This is especially likely if your child has a condition that was evident from infancy, for instance, a physical disability such as cerebral palsy, spina bifida, or other orthopedic conditions; or a genetic abnormality such as Down syndrome. If you have already had your child tested, you should share the testing results with the school staff before the testing begins. This will avoid repeating the same assessments.

Obtain appropriate testing

Testing children with disabilities is neither easy nor exact and must be approached with a degree of flexibility. If your child is inhibited in the presence of a stranger, a familiar adult may need to be included in the testing environment in order to elicit an optimal response. If your child has limited motor or vocal capabilities, steps must be taken to be sure that his or her responses can be properly interpreted. If your child has a hearing or vision impairment, special tests need to be used. Evaluators should have appropriate training and an awareness of the specific disability of each client tested.

Checklists, rating scales, and interviews may be used in conjunction with formal standardized tests to assess and evaluate your child's special needs. In addition, evaluators may systematically observe your child in order to make recommendations. Many evaluators have taught children with similar disabilities. Their knowledge of teaching methods for the disabled means that they may be able to recommend methods, materials, or techniques for training your child in specific skill areas. Request a meeting with the evaluator ahead of time in order to share your concerns and to become as comfortable as possible with the process of evaluation.

Schedule a meeting to review the evaluation results

Your child must be screened within thirty days of the request and evaluated by the appropriate professionals within forty-five days of the screening. After that, the evaluator must discuss the results of the assessment with you within thirty days of the completion of the evaluation. At this meeting you should find out what disabling condition has been identified, the potential impact your child's condition will have on his ability to function in a classroom, and whether further testing is needed. Professionals with expertise in the specialized areas of your child's needs will hear the test reports and formulate a plan for your child's school program. This plan is known as the initial IEP (Individualized Education Plan) and is discussed more fully below.

Identifying Your Child as "Handicapped"

At this evaluation meeting, the team may classify your child as having some "handicapping" condition. This is a sensitive area in special education as it labels your child for the purpose of providing a service. Your child must have a defined disability in order to receive specific services. Many parents and professionals object to this process because they feel it stigmatizes the child and family and creates problems of self-image in a world where being "normal" is important. The label may lead to lowered expectations and may open the door to subtle and sometimes not-so-subtle discrimination. For example, if mentally retarded students are not expected to reach high goals, they may not be sufficiently challenged to reach even reasonable levels of performance. Orthopedically disabled students may not be offered adapted physical education programming because of assumptions that they cannot perform physically. Hearing-impaired or vision-impaired students may become socially isolated within school because they are incorrectly thought to be limited in communication skills.

Perhaps parents' greatest fear is that once placed in special education, their child will be "sentenced" for life to a particular school class situation. In reality, special-education programs are designed to be reviewed at least annually to determine if your child is ready for a change of place-

ment or program. If you do not agree with your child's placement, you can appeal. If you do not feel up to the task of challenging a placement, professional advocates and law offices that specialize in advocacy for the disabled are listed in the telephone directory. Further, each state maintains a system of protection and advocacy services, provided at no cost or low cost to parents in due process (appeals) procedures. The school district is required to provide the names of such persons to you upon request. It is always better to try to settle disputes through open discussion and/or mediation. However, if a due process hearing becomes necessary, the school system will likely have formal, legal representation, and you will want legal representation to assist you as well.

THE INDIVIDUAL EDUCATION PLAN (IEP)

The core of Public Law 94-142 is the Individual Education Plan (IEP). It is through the process of developing and implementing this plan that you can make sure your child receives appropriate educational services. Developing the IEP involves translating the evaluation information into specific special-education directives and formulating a plan for implementation. IEPs should be written with your child in mind, not constructed depending upon what services are readily available or how much any one service will cost.

In each state, designated agencies are required to ensure compliance with IEP requirements. These agencies include the local school districts, but can also include your state's Department of Mental Health, Department of Social Services, or state programs for the deaf and blind.

The IEP represents a commitment by

the school to provide the resources that will enable your child to benefit from her education. A Supreme Court ruling set the standard for determining this educational benefit in a case that involved a hearing-impaired child in a regular classroom (*Rowley* v. *The Board of Education*, decided in 1982). The court ruled that the IEP should be "reasonably calculated to enable the child to achieve passing marks and advance from grade to grade." In other words, the goals set forth in the IEP and the strategies for reaching these goals should be attainable for your child. Although this standard is difficult to apply to severely and profoundly disabled students in highly specialized programs, the program must still meet the standard of "reasonable benefit."

Because some students require more or fewer special services than other students, IEPs vary in length and complexity. For example, a student with an articulation disorder whose only requirement is speech therapy twice per week would have a less involved IEP than a student whose profound mental and physical disabilities require physical therapy, occupational therapy, speech therapy, and nutritional counseling daily in a self-contained educational program.

The Content of an IEP

There is no prescribed IEP form, but the law is very specific about what information must appear within the document, and how the document is created. All IEPs must include the following:

A statement of the child's current level of educational performance

This statement summarizes the results of the previously described evaluations. This includes intelligence test scores, as well as assessments of motor functioning, language and speech abilities, and educational performance (reading, writing, calculating, applying concepts of language and mathematics, and problem-solving). For the development of the IEP to be meaningful, it is a good idea to use information that is fairly recent, that is, obtained within the past year.

A statement of long-term goals and short-term instructional objectives

In each area of educational and related need, there should be a statement that reflects a reasonable expectation of improvement over a period of time, not to exceed twelve months. Long-term goals can be statements such as, "Tom will be functionally independent in dressing and undressing." This long-term goal is further divided into smaller steps, called objectives: "Tom will put on and remove clothing with no fasteners, or with zippers, snaps, buttons, hooks and eyes, or Velcro fasteners." Further objectives might include choosing clothing appropriate for the weather, time of day, and occasion. A good source for such curriculum objectives and activities is a three-volume set entitled *Teaching the Moderately and Severely Handicapped, 2nd edition*, by Michael Bender and Peter Valletutti. A more academically oriented goal might be "Mary will increase her ability to recognize functional signs and vocabulary." The objectives to support this goal might include the skills needed to recognize the signs for the ladies' room, "Do Not Enter," "Exit," "Danger," "Emergency," and so on. Similarly, objectives would address functional consumer skills such as reading advertisements and sale announcements, and differentiating junk mail from bills. A good source for such curriculum objectives and activities is *Teaching Functional Academics: A Curriculum Guide for Adolescents and Adults with Learning Problems*, by Bender and Valletutti.

A statement of specific special-education and related services to be provided and the amount of time the student will spend in regular educational programs

"Special-education services" refers to instructional activities that are specially designed to accommodate the needs of a student. This includes, but is not limited to, instruction provided in a classroom. Some disabled students receive instruction at home or in a hospital. The important point about special education is that the design is "special" and should pertain to the individual student involved. "Related services" are supportive services designed to supplement instruction so that the individual student can benefit from his special-education program. Such services include transportation, speech therapy, audiology, physical therapy, occupational therapy, counseling services, recreation, vocational education, and medical services. Related services are sometimes considered special-education services when they are delivered as instructional strategies in the classroom. An example would be language techniques incorporated into the daily instructional plan through the coordination of the teacher and the speech therapist. Not all related services are delivered outside the classroom. An occupational therapist may come into a classroom to assist a student with a class project involving cutting and pasting. A physical therapist might assist a child with motor difficulties during his physical education class.

An IEP must state how much time each service is offered, such as "90 minutes per week" or "three 30-minute sessions per week." The IEP must also indicate how much of the remaining hours of instruction are spent in exclusively special-education classes. It will also indicate how much time is provided for the student to participate in activities with nonhandicapped students. Although a student may need specialized instruction for some of his daily in-school tasks, he still may be able to eat in the cafeteria with the general school population and attend art, music, and physical education classes with children in the so-called regular educational program. For example, a child with cerebral palsy who has normal intelligence might attend math and English classes with his peers, and then have specialized speech or adaptive physical education services to accommodate for his motor needs.

Projected dates for when services will begin and the duration of service

IEPs are designed to be implemented within a defined time period. That time period cannot exceed twelve months without review. Many IEPs are specifically designed for the period of one school year, and they may state the projected dates as "9/91 to 6/92." However, an IEP can be designed for any time period up to a year, such as a trimester, a quarter, or a semester. Some goals and objectives may have one time line for implementation, such as sixty school days, while others may be designed for a semester or a full school year. The teacher, therapist, or other professional who creates the goals and objectives should specify the expected duration of the service.

Appropriate procedures and criteria for evaluating success in meeting the goals and objectives

Special-education services are delivered in a variety of ways. Some services are delivered through specialized techniques, such as sensory integration training for motor development (see chapter 18), or Bliss symbols for communication (see chapter 11). If special methods are to be used, they must be specified on the IEP. Sometimes several strategies are used to accomplish the same objective. For example, a certain reading objective might use both the "language experience approach" and "phonics." In this case, both techniques would be listed for that objective.

Once the method for addressing an objective is determined, the criterion for deciding when the objective has been met must be stated. For some tasks, the criteria might be that the child successfully completes the task a certain number of times, such as "four times out of five." For other tasks, a percentage correct would be a better determination of mastery. In this case, the criteria might be: "The student will attain a score of 80 percent on weekly math drills." Some tasks require total mastery and cannot be fractionalized. "Susan will walk ten feet unassisted" is one such example. She cannot be said to have mastered the objective unless the full distance is accomplished. It is important that the means of delivering services and measuring success are clear to all who are expected to share in the implementation of the IEP.

Developing the IEP

The IEP is developed, reviewed, and/or revised through the input of a team of people who bring their expertise and perspective on your child to the IEP meeting. The initial IEP is formulated for the purpose of placing your child in a special-education program. This IEP is written when the team that evaluated your child meets to review the evaluation and identify your child's disability. According to law, parents must be included in this process.

The IEP meetings should include as many of the following individuals as possible: (1) a representative of the public agency involved with your child's program who is authorized to commit resources on behalf of the agency, (2) your child's teacher or teachers, (3) you and your spouse, (4) your child, when that is deemed appropriate, and (5) any other individual who you or the agency feels can contribute to the development of your child's educational plan. This might include anyone who has recently evaluated your child, or a professional currently offering a service, such as a private physical therapist, speech therapist, or behavioral psychologist.

At the IEP meeting, each person has an opportunity to share his or her perspective on your child's needs, including recent testing information. A written plan emerges from this sharing. Sometimes your child's current teacher or someone else from the school will have drafted an IEP before the meeting. The meeting then provides the opportunity for everyone to review and revise the draft IEP and eventually to generate the final and formal copy. **You are entitled to a copy of your child's IEP.**

Parents are usually asked to sign the yearly IEP to show that they had an opportunity to participate in its development, but federal law does not require parent signatures for the yearly IEP to be implemented. However, parent signatures are required on the initial IEP, which leads to your child's placement in a special-education program. Although not required, it is always wise to review and sign the yearly IEP, as an assurance of your role as a fully participating decision-maker on behalf of your child. If for any reason you do not agree with the goals and objectives or services offered in an IEP, it is wise *not to sign* the document until there is agreement. It is perfectly acceptable to ask for additional time to review the document before signing.

FINDING PROGRAMS THAT FULFILL THE GOALS OF THE IEP

After the multidisciplinary team meets with you, and you agree on the goals and objectives of the IEP, you and the team must determine which available school programs meet these goals. A whole range of programming should be examined, including early-intervention services for pre-schoolers and both public and private school services for older children.

Early-Intervention Services

It is logical to assume that the earlier specialized services are provided, the sooner your child will benefit. Early-intervention services are designed to stimulate the development of the disabled infant and provide training and support for the family. At a time when your family is most vulnerable and adjusting to the realities of raising a disabled youngster, the early-intervention team can help shift your focus from concentration on the stresses of daily life to facilitating your child's development. As parents, you are equal partners in early-intervention services, and will probably provide the day-to-day follow-up to the therapeutic interventions offered. As described earlier, special-education early-intervention services still fall under the auspices of 94-142 and the local departments of education. The extension of these services to include infants and toddlers falls under the auspices of 99-457 and is interagency in design. These services are usually offered in three models: home-based programs, center-based programs, and combination home- and center-based programs.

Each school system has an office called the Office of Child Find, which is set up to identify children with special needs. Your pediatrician can help you determine when such a contact should be made. Programs start in infancy for children who have significant needs. Once your child is identified as in need of early-intervention services, a needs assessment will determine the type and extent of services needed. In a home-based program, a team will be identified, usually consisting of a case manager, home teacher, and whatever therapists will be working with your child (physical therapist, occupational therapist, speech therapist). The team will visit your child in the home on a regular schedule, usually weekly. A program will be developed and you will be trained to supplement the program between team visits. For example, if one of the goals is to increase your child's ability to sit independently, you would receive instruction on how to position him appropriately. The home-based teacher may design activities to stimulate your child's cognitive and sensory development, for example, by offering suggestions about appropriate toys and mobiles. The speech therapist will train you to help in the development of language skills.

The next logical step in the progression of early-intervention services is a combination of home-based and center-based services. This approach will encourage socialization as your child gets older. Such a program usually involves your child coming into the center two to three days per week for structured activities with other children of similar needs. The program is coordinated by a special-education teacher, who may be assisted by a physical, occupational, or speech therapist. On the days that your child is not attending the center, you will be asked to continue the home-based program to maintain skills already learned and to facilitate the learning of new skills. These programs also offer you the opportunity to interact with other parents and share your successes and frustrations with others who are in a similar situation.

Most school systems have either a chronological or developmental age minimum for full-time attendance in center-based programs, which usually operate five half-days per week, although full-day programs are increasingly available. A full-day program has two advantages. First, if both you and your spouse have jobs, you may need a full-day program to provide child-care as well as education. Second, many disabled youngsters require a variety of therapies in addition to educational programming, which may be difficult to accommodate in a half-day session. For instance, a physically disabled four-year-old may need physical, occupational, and speech therapy as part of the daily school program in order to facilitate school readiness and socialization skills. Full-day sessions also allow the program to be spread out over a longer time and be interspersed with relaxation and rest periods. This approach may help your child avoid exhaustion from the physical and mental activities of the learning program. On the other hand, a full-day program itself may be exhausting for a young child and he may find it difficult to be separated from you for such a prolonged period of time. These advantages and disadvantages need to be weighed before you decide on which program is best for your child.

Programs for the School-aged Child

In choosing a program for your school-aged child, the available resources within the public schools of the community or district are the first to be reviewed. If the placement team concludes that your child's needs cannot be met in a public school, a rare occurrence, the law then allows for your child's placement in certain private or "nonpublic" schools that offer special-education programs. These schools must meet certain standards to be approved for use by public school systems. Disabled students still have IEPs in these "nonpublic" schools, and these plans are implemented the same way IEPs are carried out in public schools. When private schools are deemed necessary for services, the public school district is required to pay for these services. However, placement in private special-education programs must be approved for funding prior to placement. If you place your child in such a private school unilaterally, you will have to go through a due process hearing in order to establish the need for such a placement; otherwise, you will be responsible for paying the tuition.

Representatives of the school district have information about which specific schools among the district's offerings have the services necessary for your child. You should investigate these programs by calling them for information or visiting them to see the programs in action. The more you know about what is available, the better informed you will be when it comes time to agree to a placement.

There is a continuum of special-education programs that ranges from remedial help in a regular classroom to distant residential schools (Figure 20.1). Children are entitled to receive services in the *least restrictive environment* that is appropriate for them (see the discussion of "mainstreaming," below). This usually means finding a placement in a neighborhood school. However, some children will need to be transported to schools outside their neighborhoods to get services. Very special-

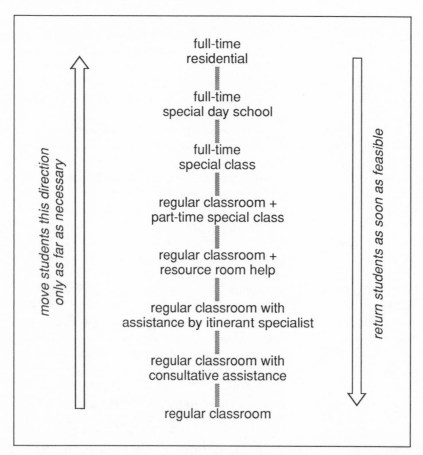

full-time
residential

full-time
special day school

full-time
special class

regular classroom +
part-time special class

regular classroom +
resource room help

regular classroom with
assistance by itinerant specialist

regular classroom with
consultative assistance

regular classroom

move students this direction
only as far as necessary

return students as soon as feasible

Figure 20.1. *These is a continuum of special-education programs that ranges from remedial help in a regular classroom to distant residential schools. Your child should be moved up this continuum only as far as necessary and should be returned to a more regular program as soon as feasible.*

ized services, such as monitoring care of students with tracheostomies (breathing tubes), or specialized behavior-management systems for students who injure themselves, may require placement in schools that are away from your community. The important thing to remember is that if your child must be moved away from a regular school program, he should be returned to as normal a program as possible as soon as this is feasible.

Each child's special-education program needs to be periodically reevaluated to be sure that it is still appropriate for her. Remember: special education is a *service* not a *sentence*. It is the vigilance of parents and professionals together that keeps chil-

dren from getting lost in the system of services. Even fairly restrictive settings do not necessarily indicate that a child is forever "condemned" to special education.

MONITORING YOUR CHILD'S PROGRAM

Once you agree to a placement for your child, let the school staff know that you are an interested and knowledgeable parent. Communicate with them regularly. Tell them how you feel about your child's progress. Relay your concerns but also compliment them if you are happy with the program. Teachers and therapists, like everyone else, need reinforcement and are excited when your child makes significant progress.

When your child first enters the program, the teacher will not know him well. Share information about your child, so the teacher can avoid wasting a lot of time experimenting with systems of communication and management. She will then know ahead of time which approaches work best and what situations present the greatest difficulty. The home and school are a team, and the players must learn to trust each other and communicate effectively. This can be accomplished with a system of daily or weekly notes, or by monthly telephone conferences. You should also consider making periodic visits. You may wish to review the IEP with your child's teacher; feel free to do so. It is from this periodic review of the written plan that a new plan emerges for future services. Although special-education placements must be reviewed *at least* annually, the review meeting can occur at any time you, or the professionals involved in your child's program, call for one. This is particularly true in the case of a new placement, or when some new technique or method is being introduced. The review may occur after a designated number of school days, such as a sixty-day review after initial placement, or a midterm review of part or all of your child's IEP. This approach prevents time being wasted on parts of the program that are not successful or need adjustment.

ADVOCATE FOR YOUR CHILD

The process of getting educational services for your child may be complicated, but it doesn't have to be unpleasant or adversarial. Although no one knows your child as well as you do, educators do have expertise and knowledge about children with special needs. Working together, you, the teacher,

and therapists can develop an optimal program for your child. However, if you do not feel comfortable in dealing with the large numbers of professional staff that become involved in the educational planning for your child, you can engage a *professional advocate*. Local, state, and national chapters of special-interest groups for various disabling conditions may assist you in finding such an individual. The local school district, your state's department of education, or your Legal Aid Society can also provide the names of advocates.

If you find yourself in disagreement with the school staff over the diagnosis, placement, or services provided for your child, you are entitled to a hearing of your concerns by an impartial person. This individual can mediate or decide the issues in a formal setting. This exercise of your "due process rights" is mandated by the special-education law, and information on the procedure for accessing this right is available from your local school district.

GETTING INTO THE MAINSTREAM

"Mainstreaming" is a concept that is as old as the original legislation for the disabled student. The idea of placement in the "least restrictive environment" provides opportunities for your disabled child to spend as much time as possible working and socializing with students who are not disabled. As part of this initiative, children with milder levels of disabling conditions (for example, learning disabilities or moderate hearing impairment) have been mainstreamed. It is likely that, in the future, some children with moderate or even severe disabilities also will be integrated into the mainstreaming process. This is based on studies that have shown that mildly mentally retarded children left in regular classes achieve a higher academic level than do their counterparts in special classes. On the other hand, there are some social and emotional advantages to the child's remaining in special education classes. The advantages and disadvantages of mainstreaming need to be balanced in making decisions for your child.

There are a variety of strategies for mainstreaming a student with disabilities into a regular educational setting. These include:

- creative scheduling, for example, adjusting the length of time spent on written assignments and on homework;
- peer coaching and peer tutoring, in which the student is assisted by a classmate who has skills in the area covered by the assignment;
- team teaching by regular and special educators, allowing specialized techniques to be used in combination with traditional curriculum strategies;
- cross-age or cross-grade grouping, i.e., placing students with classmates of a different age who have similar levels of physical skills or intellectual achievement;
- diagnostic/prescriptive teaching, in which the special-education teacher works to assist the classroom teacher in identifying areas of need;
- mastery learning, in which the student paces herself by achieving work goals rather than by completing assignments on time. The objective is to achieve a level of mastery using as many tries and as much time as it takes.

There is a good deal of controversy surrounding mainstreaming. We believe that mainstreaming is not necessarily the right choice for all children, especially for those with severe or multiple disabilities. It can be a disadvantage to your child if the proper special-education services are not then available. Remember that special-education programming is considerably more expensive than regular education. The school system may be only too happy to agree to mainstream your child, since it will save money. It is important to realize that these financial considerations may have an impact on program decisions for your child. Carefully weigh the advantages and disadvantages for your child and then make a decision.

A vital element in the successful incorporation of a disabled child into a regular classroom is the acceptance of the special student by "regular students." All individuals with disabilities are susceptible to myths and stereotyping by those who do not have handicaps. On top of this, children are at times insensitive or even cruel, which can lead to victimization of the disabled student. Education of the "able" students about the needs and abilities of the child with a disability is a critical feature of mainstreaming.

EDUCATING THE CHILD WITH SEVERE DISABILITIES

Low-incidence disabilities are rather severe conditions that occur infrequently in the general population. They include five categories:

- vision impaired (chapter 13)
- hearing impaired (chapter 10)
- mentally retarded (chapter 6)
- orthopedically or physically handicapped (chapters 9 and 14)
- multiply handicapped

Students with these disabilities often need intensive specialized services, adaptive systems of communication, behavior-management systems, and/or physical management that frequently cannot be provided in a regular school setting. Whether such a disabled student should be integrated into a mainstream classroom or attend a self-contained program depends on how readily the child can participate in the learning activities that make up the instructional day. These activities include participating in oral discussions, taking notes or copying information and assignments from a blackboard, using workbooks or study sheets, taking tests and quizzes, organizing a notebook, and working with peers in small group learning activities or on study teams. If a student can manage to gain information and relay it appropriately within the classroom, the integration is smoother and the independence of the student is fostered. We will indicate below each of these handicapping conditions and some educational strategies that have been found to be successful in helping these children. These are strategies that can be used in self-contained classrooms or in regular classes.

It should be noted that specific methods and materials are not mandated under law and their availability and use will vary with the specific professionals involved. Rarely will any one student receive all or even most of the adaptations listed below. However, you should be assertive in getting specific adaptations included in your child's IEP or made available to the school.

Vision-Impaired Students

Your vision-impaired child, for example, may benefit from the following adaptations:

- placement at the front of the classroom to allow for optimal viewing of assignments
- enhanced lighting at the child's seat
- use of a Perkins Brailler, a slate and stylus system for taking notes

- use of an Optacon, a reading device that turns a printed image into a tactile stimulus of vibrating "pins" for the reader to interpret by use of Braille
- use of a Kurzweil Reading Machine, which converts print into speech
- use of a Braille Recorder, which tapes information for later translation into Braille
- use of a Talking Calculator, which reacts with spoken numbers as calculations are performed, also providing feedback on correct and incorrect answers
- use of an Interactive Classroom Television System, which places a camera and monitor at both the teacher's and student's desks, bringing the image closer
- use of mobility devices such as human guides, guide dogs, Hoover canes, laser canes, Sonicguide glasses, Canterbury Child's Aid, or other sound-emitting devices for detecting obstacles

Hearing-Impaired Students

Adaptations for the hearing-impaired student depend on the degree and type of hearing loss. Severely impaired children, especially if deaf from birth, may have inadequate communication skills to function in a regular classroom. On the other hand, students with milder forms of impairment, or those who lost hearing later in childhood, may have the language skills needed for participation in the regular education classroom.

Mainstreaming is particularly recommended if your child has a mild hearing loss. By sitting near the teacher, your child will be able to use her hearing abilities optimally, though she may require the use of amplification. The hearing-impaired child can learn best if the teaching method does not rely on sound. For example, phonetics-based reading approaches do not work well, but "language experience" and "structural analytic" or "whole word" approaches are generally successful. Language experience capitalizes on your child's own words to describe day-to-day experiences or to write stories. Structural analysis emphasizes breaking down words into their component elements such as roots, prefixes, suffixes, and endings. Whole-word approaches require memorizing the whole word rather than analyzing its components.

If your child has a moderate hearing loss, he will require more complex alterations of the classroom environment. However, these can often be implemented without major disruptions to the classroom. Hearing aids will help, but may not solve the problem of filtering out distracting sounds in the learning environment. For this reason, your child's ability to read lips and the teacher's ability to speak distinctly during instruction will influence learning. The teacher may also use an FM microphone that projects her voice directly to your child's hearing aid without interference from outside noise. Mainstreaming may be a part-time arrangement, with specialized tutorial services or speech/language therapy incorporated into the school day.

As much as possible, information that is presented orally should be reinforced with a printed version or summary. There also needs to be good communication between the regular classroom teacher and the special-education teacher or therapist so that each is aware of the material being covered by the other. Such reinforcement strategies are time consuming and may result in delays in the completion of tasks. Creative and flexible scheduling of assignments and tests can address this issue. An important factor in the mainstreaming of the hearing-impaired student is *the will-*

ingness of the regular classroom teacher to make modifications in the presentation of the curriculum, such as:

- standing in your child's visual field so he or she can lip-read
- speaking clearly and using a microphone if necessary
- providing printed summaries and pictures of material that will be covered in a lecture format
- using visual aids, such as overhead projectors, to highlight key points of a lesson
- giving an advance "agenda" of new material so your child can organize note-taking
- if necessary, learning and using a brief repertoire of signs

The regular classroom teacher should be reminded not to slow down or otherwise alter her speech for the hearing-impaired student, as this tends to foster the stereotype that all hearing-impaired individuals are retarded.

If your child has a severe or profound hearing loss, the adaptation needed in the mainstream environment is more involved. This may include time with deaf education specialists in learning to apply manual methods (signing, finger spelling or cued speech), oralism (with an emphasis on lip-reading and speech training rather than signing), and total communication (blending oral and manual systems). The better the support systems in the regular classroom environment, the greater the likelihood of success. However, some of these children will need to remain in a self-contained special-education setting.

Mentally Retarded Students

Schools are designed to make the greatest demands in the two areas in which the mentally retarded student is most delayed:

cognitive development and social functioning. Therefore, classroom modifications for the mentally retarded student must reflect an understanding of the learning process and the particular limitations of the student. All school programs are organized according to curricula that involve developing gradually increasing levels of skills, arranged in a specific order of presentation. Curricula for the intellectually limited must include, in addition to some academics, the teaching of independent-living skills and social functioning.

If your child is mildly retarded, she should be involved in an academic program designed to promote independence within the home, school, and community. During elementary school, she will learn similar academic skills (reading, math, social studies, and science) as those taught to non-retarded children, but at a rate and level of complexity appropriate to her cognitive functioning. In addition, she should receive instruction that will form the basis for vocational education when she is older, such as skills in organization and getting along in a work environment. For a teenager, a good functional academic program should stress the learning of practical skills. Examples would include learning to clip coupons from the advertisement supplement of the Sunday paper in order to be a more frugal consumer or reading and ordering from a menu.

As adults, most intellectually limited individuals will be employed in some way, either independently or in a supported program. Therefore, their educational program should include pre-vocational and vocational skill-building. If resource help is to be part of your child's school program, ongoing and effective planning and communication between special-education and regular classroom teachers is vital.

Educational planning for moderately re-tarded children will differ from a program designed for mildly retarded students. The moderately retarded student will concentrate on mastery of independent-living skills rather than on academics.

Regardless of the level of retardation, teachers must appreciate that mentally impaired students will be slower to remember, organize, and retrieve information, and will have greater difficulty applying what they learn. Lessons and classroom organization should include the following:

- clear step-by-step directions for tasks
- routines for the accomplishment of tasks
- periodic checking of work and immediate feedback to students on their work
- hands-on applications to reinforce abstract concepts — for example, using cooking to teach the sequential processing skills of reading and math
- step-by-step presentation of tasks, so your child is not overwhelmed by large or complicated assignments
- continual repetition of skills learned, such as continuation of assignments at home
- use of visual aids, such as underlining, circling in color, or using arrows to direct the student's eye to various parts of a task
- use of a notebook so you can know about assignments that your child may have forgotten
- encouragement of the student to describe aloud what he or she is doing
- assistance with daily routines such as riding a bus, using a telephone, or finding the correct classroom, until your child is familiar with and can accomplish the routine on his own
- expectation that your child will be as independent as possible in all tasks, including self-care skills

- classroom activities appropriate to your child's age — for example, an adolescent student should not be asked to memorize nursery rhymes
- teaching in small groups whenever possible
- use of typewriters, computers, tape recorders, and other devices for a multisensory approach
- use of functional examples and materials from daily life (such as the newspaper or television) whenever possible to reinforce skills. This fosters later independence.

Orthopedically and/or Physically Impaired Students

Students with physical, but not mental, handicaps can often function in a regular classroom with some modifications of the physical space. Some students, such as those with spina bifida or cerebral palsy, may need medical or nursing services such as urinary catheterization or tube feeding during their educational program. According to a 1984 Supreme Court decision (*Irving Independent School District* v. *Tatro*), it is the responsibility of the school system to arrange for such services if they are necessary for the student to attend school. Your child cannot be excluded from attending a neighborhood school simply because he needs the services of a health professional.

Adaptations include the following adjustments in the physical space of the school and in the implementation of the curriculum:

- making sure your child has access to the school via elevators and ramps and that the school has accessible fountains, lavatories, and telephones — *this is mandated by law*

- availability of lapboards, clipboards, chalkboards, specially adjusted desks, and storage areas that can accommodate wheelchairs or other equipment in the classroom, library, computer lab, and auditorium
- availability of word processors or other specialized communication systems for students who cannot offer vocal or traditional written responses in a timely or clear manner
- availability of adapted keyboards, head wands, light-activated, or breath-activated computer systems
- adapted seating and positioning devices for students with cerebral palsy, spina bifida, or muscular dystrophy — these might include adjustable seats, wedges, sandbags, or simply periodic changes of position
- adjusted trays or tables to assist in control of arm movement
- adapted pencils, pens, and scissors with grips for control while writing and cutting
- creative and flexible formatting and scheduling of tests, quizzes, and assignments
- adaptation of note-taking to allow for taping

Multiply Handicapped Students

If your child has a combination of handicaps, he is considered multiply handicapped. The educational definition states that a multiply handicapped child must have a number of handicaps of equal importance, which makes placement into a program for any one of the individual handicaps alone inappropriate. For example, if your child has both cerebral palsy and mental retardation, a program designed for a mentally retarded child would not be appropriate if it did not take into account his physical disabilities. What is important here is that school personnel pay attention to *all* of your child's needs. The program will require more integrated and comprehensive planning by all the professionals involved. When the handicapping condition also creates medical and/or health needs, this coordination is especially vital. However, the existence of more than one handicapping condition does not necessarily eliminate the possibility of mainstreaming.

INTERACTION WITH PEERS

When a disabled individual enters a regular school, he may face rejection from peers who harbor misconceptions about the disabled. Educators, counselors, therapists, and parents can work together to break down these stereotypes, by arranging frank and open discussions about the variety of developmental disabilities that able-bodied students will see. Questions about seizures, speech disorders, mental retardation, the random movements made by those with cerebral palsy, and the physical needs and capabilities of the physically disabled person should be answered fully. Rumor and conjecture should be dispelled. Whenever possible, the disabled student should be part of these sessions.

Schools are social places, and the educational program of all students, able or disabled, must allow for social development. Dances, parties, assemblies, sports, and field trips should be accessible to your child.

All people love and hate, are motivated and bored, have friends and enemies, and have opinions and appetites. This must be recognized whether the individual is restricted to a wheelchair, must use a hearing aid, is accompanied by a guide dog, or

is limited in understanding the world in which he or she lives. Educators and parents must keep this in mind when they plan for the school experiences a student will have.

CAREER EDUCATION AND VOCATIONAL EDUCATION

All students with disabilities, whether they are instructed in special-education programs or in regular educational settings, need *career education.* This is not a concept to be confused with *vocational education,* which prepares students for specific job skills. Career education focuses on the skills necessary for adult living. These skills are sometimes called "functional" or "survival" skills, and include the following: managing money, caring for a home and for personal possessions, participating as a citizen (obeying laws), using time wisely for work and play, communicating needs to others (such as to store clerks, doctors, employers), following a schedule, keeping a job, participating in recreational activities, and a host of other daily habits and procedures needed for independent living. These skills and a suggested educational curriculum for gaining them are outlined in *Career Education for Handicapped Individuals,* 2nd edition, by C. J. Kokasha and D. E. Brolin.

Such "survival" skills can and should be introduced as early as possible into your child's educational program. Practice in these areas will help your child learn how to think on his own, solve problems, and make good choices.

Vocational education actually prepares students for specific jobs, recognizing that a student with physical or mental limitations can still learn the skills necessary to succeed in a job. Many secondary schools offer programs to train disabled students for employment. These are often transitional programs, in which skills are first learned in the classroom, and then "practiced" in actual job settings, supervised by special educators or specially trained staff members of the school and/or the workplace. The goal is to give on-the-job experience to the disabled individual so he or she can learn the routines required to perform the skills learned in the classroom. Over time, the disabled individual learns to use his skills and to deal with the people and the demands that will be faced on a daily basis.

The assisting staff member gradually "fades" in importance as the prospective employee gains independence in the work setting. The student learns how to use career-education skills to manage a salary and to plan a living arrangement. These employment-training strategies are often combined with sheltered living arrangements, where the disabled individual lives in an apartment or house with others who are also learning independent skills. Such living programs are supervised by professionals trained in special education and/or vocational rehabilitation. If your child is approaching the last years of special-educational programming and you are looking for ideas for future employment and training, you should contact the Vocational Rehabilitation Administration of your community for information about sheltered employment and living programs. Another source is the guidance counselor or special-education chairperson at the school your child currently attends.

SOME QUESTIONS ANSWERED

If I have a private evaluation done on my child, can I give that to the school for my child's record and will such an evaluation be considered "legitimate"? Will they want to do their own?

You should share private evaluations with the school system, for it will assist them in making the best educational plan for your child. The school system should consider any information you present to them; however, they are not bound by the recommendations of an outside specialist. Most school systems will want to do at least some assessment of their own so that they are not making decisions solely on the recommendation of outside persons.

I disagree with the amount of services being recommended for our daughter. The school proposes therapy twice a week, but we think every day would help our daughter improve more quickly. Can we insist on this?

You can request additional services if there is documentation to support the need for more. For instance, if your child is seen privately, and the private therapist makes a recommendation that exceeds what the school is providing, you can request a meeting to discuss the additional recommendations. However, more is not always better. Some skills will improve only as your child's nervous system matures and is ready to master them.

I am considering requesting a special hearing regarding the placement of my daughter. What happens during a special-education hearing?

Although the actual hearing process may vary from state to state, the general procedure is outlined by law. First, you need to request in writing a due process hearing regarding the delivery of special-education services. You should engage a professional advocate to assist you in this process. Next, a hearing will be scheduled and each side will submit a set of documents and a witness list at least five days prior to the hearing to allow for disclosure to all parties. At the hearing either a single impartial hearing officer or a panel of officers will allow each side to present its case with cross-examination and questioning. Finally, a written decision will be issued by the hearing officer and given to all parties.

On a local talk show I heard a discussion of "REI," which I understand is the regular education initiative. Is this required by law and how is it different from mainstreaming?

The movement called the Regular Education Initiative is not specified under Public Law 94-142. All that the law requires is that, to the extent that it is appropriate, disabled children be educated with their nonhandicapped peers. REI has been promoted by national, state, and local special-interest groups that believe all children should be integrated into regular education. It is not the same as mainstreaming, which allows for a continuum of services from special schools to regular classes.

Do I have a choice about whether or not my child will be mainstreamed?

You certainly will have input into the decision and your feelings will carry a lot of weight with the school system. However, the final decision will rest with the school system. Remember that if you disagree, your right to an appeal hearing is guaranteed.

My five-year-old is physically handicapped and uses canes to walk. My neighborhood school does not have an elevator, and even though the kindergarten is on the ground level, the children must go upstairs to use the other facilities. Will my child be assigned to a different school that is accessible instead of attending our neighborhood school?

The law does not require that every school be made accessible to the disabled. Each school system must make available some renovated buildings with handicapped access, and all new schools built must be accessible. Your child, therefore, would be assigned to the closest accessible school to your neighborhood.

WHAT THE FUTURE HOLDS

Adadot Hayes, M.D.

Mentally retarded and other developmentally disabled adults have a wide range of needs and capabilities. At the age of twenty-one, though your son or daughter may function at a pre-adolescent level, he or she is more than a "large child." But unfortunately, there are few mandated programs for adults in the area of education, medical care, housing, or recreation. There are also few well-trained service providers, since most adult programs do not require workers to have any sort of certification, and generally lack adequate funding. As your disabled child reaches adulthood, legal issues regarding guardianship, marriage, sterilization, and institutionalization also become confusing. Added to all these difficulties is the fact that individuals with disabilities, like the population in general, are living longer than ever before and thus have increasing medical, financial, and social needs. These issues, combined with the changing attitudes and resources of society, often leave adults with disabilities out in the cold.

Though there are few formal programs for adults, the Americans with Disabilities Act does regulate services that encourage independence, productivity, and integration into the community. In addition, disabled and needy adults are eligible to collect Supplemental Security Income (SSI), which includes cash benefits and Medicaid coverage. Individuals with disabilities who may have been ineligible for the benefits as children because of their parents' income become eligible on their own at age eighteen, regardless of their parents' income. Recent special amendments have been passed to allow adults with disabilities to supplement this income with work earnings without jeopardizing cash or Medicaid benefits.

JOHN, LINDA, AND RICHARD

John was born to a mentally retarded teen-aged mother and raised in a series of foster homes. He has an IQ of 55. As a young adult, he earned minimum wage working as a driver. At age twenty-two, he married a woman who had an IQ of 61. John and his wife had a son, Christopher, and although they began parenting classes, their attendance was poor and the baby was taken from them at two months of age because of neglect. At that time Christopher weighed only eight pounds. He was placed in a foster home and at the age of two his maternal grandmother obtained legal guardianship. Now seven years old, Christopher is moderately mentally retarded. John has quit his job and is often drunk and abusive. By court order, he is no longer allowed to see Christopher.

On the other hand, Linda, born with Down syndrome, lived at home until the age of eighteen. She then moved into a group home, where she continues to live with two other developmentally disabled women in their mid-twenties. She completed a vocational training school program at age twenty-one and now, at age twenty-three, earns a regular paycheck in a sheltered workshop. Linda has her own room, decorated with posters of movie stars, and has a stereo she bought for herself. Her favorite leisure activity is formal dancing. She goes often enough that she owns a beautiful formal gown and cuts quite a figure on the dance floor. She continues to go home on many weekends, and her family helps chaperon many of the social functions she attends.

Richard is currently thirty-seven years old and mildly mentally retarded. At the age of seven he was admitted to a state facility for the retarded because of behavior problems. There he had no formal education. As a result of the de-institutionalization movement of the 1980s, Richard was discharged to the community at the age of thirty-one and went to live in a group home with two other young men. Though he had problems adjusting to the formal programming and demands of the living arrangement, he has adapted. He moved into a board-and-care home and later to his own apartment, where he currently lives with intermittent supervision. He has chosen not to continue in a formal day program, but volunteers at a local nursing home.

John, Linda, and Richard are but three examples of the range of possibilities that may await your mentally retarded/developmentally disabled (MR/DD) child. You can maximize your child's chances for a positive future by planning carefully and early. This chapter outlines the services that are available for disabled individuals and discusses the transition from childhood to adulthood.

TRANSITIONS

Although transitions between programs, schools, and doctors may be familiar to your family, the jump from childhood to adulthood and the associated separation from school are significant milestones. The normal transitions to adult life — establishing an adult identity, launching a career, and creating a family — are difficult tasks for anybody. For people with disabilities, transitions may be even more imposing. They may include changes in residence (from parents' home to a group home), day program (entry into a sheltered workshop), and leisure-time activities.

Planning ahead for these transitions will give you more time to explore various options. In addition, you may be able to avoid delays that might otherwise cause your child to lose financial entitlements, or that would place him at the end of a long waiting list for services. Plan early, because decisions made when there is no pressure or crisis are usually better decisions.

MAKING DECISIONS

Planning for the future is important, but it is also frightening. It is difficult to imagine who could possibly take care of and love your child when she leaves home. No one can replace you as the parent, but if you begin early to plan and make decisions about the future, you can ensure that your child will be well taken care of.

Letting go of any child is difficult, whether on the first day of school, at high school graduation, or when your child is married. Allowing a handicapped child to have a life of his own is doubly hard. But each individual has a right to try — to succeed or fail. This does not mean that you simply hold your breath, close your eyes, and let go. Instead you plan, dream, hope, advocate, get as much information as possible, and consider all the options.

Families make decisions differently, and each family must work within its own framework. However, the goal of planning is the same for all: a quality life that provides the opportunity to live, work, and play in the community, and to have meaningful personal relationships. Over time, you will have to make decisions about many aspects of your child's life — social, sexual, leisure, residential, and vocational. Decision-making involves a number of steps: you must recognize a problem or need, think of as many options as possible and then choose one, discuss the decision with your child, implement it, and finally evaluate the outcome.

As with other decisions, the needs of the whole family should be considered. The individual for whom the decision is being made should be included to the extent that he is capable. When your child is young, you can begin involving him in decision-making by confronting small issues, such as which movie to go see. As he gets older, include him in making important decisions such as where he will live and work, how he will handle money, and when he will establish sexual relationships.

In some instances, the disabled adult is not competent to make decisions on his own and must rely on someone else — a legal guardian. In order to determine whether this applies to your child, we must first discuss the concepts of competence and guardianship.

Mental Competence in Decision-making

While the law allows parents to make decisions for children, once a child reaches adulthood he or she is presumed to be competent. The age at which a minor becomes an adult varies from state to state. In forty-three states, adulthood is reached at age eighteen; in the other states it ranges from age nineteen to twenty-one. Although the law presumes adults to be mentally competent, this presumption can be set aside when a legal writ finds an adult to be incompetent.

An individual may be retarded but still competent if the person is able to make and communicate decisions. Most law currently recognizes that disabled individuals may be competent enough to make some decisions, but not others. Three categories of competence are usually recognized: complete competence, partial competence, and incompetence.

You can assess competence in your child by using the criteria for decision-making noted above, beginning with identifying a need and ending with implementing the decision. An additional factor in competence is the importance of the decision. For example, a decision to sterilize an individual as a means of birth control is not lightly made. On the other hand, decisions about spending earnings from a sheltered workshop involve little risk. Your child might be incompetent to make the former decision but competent to make the latter.

Consent and Legal Guardianship

While competence refers to the ability to make decisions, consent is the act of actually making the decision. Normally consent is given by the person directly affected. However, consent may be given by a third party if the affected person is deemed incompetent; this is called substitute or indirect consent. Or, if a person is considered partially competent, a third party may help make the decision; this is called concurrent consent. Take the thorny issue of sterilization. If a person is competent, she can decide for herself whether or not to consent to the procedure. However, if she is declared incompetent, someone else must decide for her.

When a person is declared incompetent, a guardian is appointed who is able to give consent. Parents are natural guardians until their child reaches legal age. After that, if you wish to retain guardianship, you will need a lawyer. Guardianship is effective only after a court proceeding determines that the individual is truly incompetent (partially or completely). The guardian is then appointed by the court to serve either broad or limited functions. A guardianship can be plenary, in which case the guardian has full authority; or it may be limited, which recognizes that the individual has some competence in decision-making. Guardianship may be personal, financial, or general. A personal guardian has power over lifestyle decisions. A financial guardian has power to give consent for financial matters. A general guardian has both powers. Most states impose some limits on the power of guardianship. For example, the guardian is generally not allowed to draft the ward's will, make decisions about marriage, decide for whom the ward will vote, or terminate a ward's life support system.

The guardian must report to the court on a regular basis.

Having a guardian does not always guarantee optimum decision-making. Professional financial guardians charge fees, and there may be delays in disbursement of funds. Personal guardianship does not always ensure that the guardian will act in the best interests of the ward or make decisions the ward would have made had he or she been competent. Thus, decisions about guardianship must be made with care.

Individuals or agencies (both public and private) may serve as guardians. There may be an individual guardian (e.g., a sister or brother) or joint guardians (e.g., parents for a child). Collective guardianship (a corporation organized to serve several individuals) and public guardianship (where the individual does not have a responsible relative or friend) also exist in most states.

There are alternatives to guardianship for providing substitute consent. These include implied consent, representative payee, and trusts. The doctrine of implied consent assumes that the person would consent to services if competent to do so. An example of this would be emergency care of an individual who is unconscious after an automobile accident. A representative payee is someone who can receive checks issued on behalf of a disabled person. A trust, where a donor may give property to the trustee for the benefit of a disabled individual, may be used to supplement governmental benefits.

MEDICAL CARE AND LIFE SPAN

Finding good medical care for an MR/DD adult can be much more difficult than for a disabled child. One reason for this is that while pediatrics has a subspecialty to care for developmentally disabled children (developmental pediatrics), few internists or family practitioners are trained to take care of developmentally disabled adults. While an internist is quite capable of treating hypertension in a normal individual, his lack of understanding of the MR/DD individual's disability can render him either incapable or unwilling to take care of, say, a hypertensive man with spina bifida. Generally speaking, the subject of developmental disabilities is poorly covered in medical school and residency training. This has been slowly changing but remains a problem. In addition, many severely handicapped individuals who need complex medical care may have uncommon diagnoses. Often, you may know more about your child's disease than does the doctor. This can create friction when you need to rely on the doctor's expertise for treatment. This problem occurs not only in doctors' offices but also in emergency rooms, health departments, and insurance offices.

Another roadblock to finding good medical care is that, often, the nature of the disability requires a team approach. While medical personnel are used to treating medical problems, many are neither trained in nor accustomed to "care by committee."

And finally, some health-care providers, like some people in all parts of our society, reject or feel uncomfortable around impaired individuals. While this is less acceptable in the health-care profession than in society at large, it unfortunately is still true.

Added to the problem of finding good medical care is the fact that medical technology has led to a prolonging of life among MR/DD individuals. Antibiotics have resulted in a significant decrease in death from pneumonia; orthopedic surgery

to correct contractures and scoliosis has improved the overall well-being of disabled people; and advances in the care of the newborn have increased the survival of premature infants and those born with defects that previously were lethal.

Changes in attitudes and ethics, and increased funding, have also contributed to both quality of life and life span. More advanced care is now available for people with disabilities including surgical procedures for the correction of scoliosis, gastrostomy tube placement, and insertion of shunts to treat hydrocephalus. This trend has been amplified by the "Baby Doe Laws," which require equal hospital treatment for disabled patients. Although these laws do not mandate extraordinary care, as they have often been mistakenly interpreted, they have certainly increased the availability of care to disabled people.

Though it used to be thought that Down syndrome children would not reach adulthood, now we know that, barring a severe medical complication, they often live into their sixties. Textbook descriptions of trisomy 13 note that these children rarely live through infancy, but in fact, many now live into their teens. In addition to the specific advances in medical care, disabled people who live in residential programs are usually required to have regular, preventive, medical checkups. This gives them an advantage over noninstitutionalized adults, including "normal" people. So, the odds are heavily stacked in favor of your child's outliving you, in spite of her disabilities.

As these advances have led to a longer life span, the medical problems of elderly disabled people have become a new concern. We now know that some (but not as many as previously thought) Down syndrome adults will develop Alzheimer's disease. Also, up to 10 percent of severely to profoundly retarded individuals develop recurrent aspiration of food into the lungs, leading to pneumonia. This is often associated with problems of reflux and secondary esophageal ulcers (see chapter 16). In addition, adults with choreoathetoid cerebral palsy may develop spinal cord injuries as they grow older.

Many disabled individuals experience premature aging. As a result, age fifty-five in the mentally retarded population is considered to be "aged." This population has specific needs that may not be met by currently available services. In addition, it may be difficult to tell when a disabled adult becomes aged and begins to lose skills and decline.

Those who stay at home often become aged at the same time as their parents, and it is difficult to determine whose needs are greater. The MR/DD individual may be without siblings to care for him or her, and rarely has children. Thus, this person may have no other option than institutionalization, either with other MR/DD individuals with similar skill levels but different ages (age integration) or with the general elderly population (generic integration). Both options may present problems. A disabled adult who is losing skills may not fit into an age-integrated group for long. And generically integrated groups may not meet the special programming standards mandated for MR/DD individuals.

Funding for Medical Care

Obtaining adequate medical care is further complicated by financial concerns. On the one hand, increases in funding have contributed to improved medical care, and medical insurance has become more readily available for disabled individuals as well as the general population. A disabled child over eighteen can usually stay on his or her parents' insurance if proper proce-

dures are followed. As noted above, all disabled adults may receive SSI (Supplemental Security Income) benefits irrespective of parents' income. They are also eligible for Medicaid coverage. On the other hand, Medicaid reimbursement for physician fees and hospital bills is far below customary charges. This, combined with the fact that MR/DD patients take longer than average to examine, means that many physicians limit the number of disabled Medicaid patients they will treat. In addition, even when insurance or Medicaid coverage is available, there are some areas of need that are not covered. For instance, insurance often does not cover necessary equipment such as wheelchairs; therapy services, such as physical, occupational, and speech therapy; or social work or behavioral therapy services. Yet, among disabled individuals, these are often the keys to good health care.

Another problem with insurance coverage is that some insurers refuse to pay for pre-existing diseases and some Health Maintenance Organizations (HMOs) limit services. This can restrict the freedom of some families to change jobs, move, and get insurance for other family members. Thus, early planning for medical coverage may increase the quality of your child's life and improve the flexibility of your family.

However, there are some exciting programs cropping up around the country that have been designed to bypass these funding problems. One example is the Morristown Model, a developmental disabilities center that is staffed with developmental pediatricians, nurse practitioners, a consultant in internal medicine, a genetics counselor, and a dentist. Patients both from group homes and those still living at home are served. Outpatient visits and hospital stays are available to treat both medical and behavioral problems. It has also provided a valuable setting for training. We hope that this model will be utilized to develop other programs throughout the country.

EDUCATION

Until your child reaches the age of twenty-one, the federal government mandates that he or she receives a free and appropriate education (Public Law 94-142; see chapter 20). Yet after that cutoff, few educational services are mandated. Moreover, the special-educational services provided often fail to address all the needs of disabled people. Too often, curricula are designed to teach the "three R's" rather than to teach the survival skills that the MR/DD adult will need to function independently in society. Education should focus on aids to daily living, work skills, and vocational training. You should start looking toward adulthood while your child is still in elementary school.

A PLACE TO LIVE

Most children leave home by their late teens or early twenties. They become independent, and their parents enter a new period of increased freedom. This may not be the case with a disabled child. Although legally an adult, your child may be incapable of caring for himself, and you will have to decide how and where he will continue to receive appropriate care. Some parents choose to keep their child at home. Others feel that their child will function better and more happily with some degree of independence.

When aging parents continue to care for a grown child, several problems can arise for both parents and child. First, the parents may feel somewhat resentful about spending their retirement years caring for

their child. Meanwhile, the child misses the experience of living outside the shelter of home and may experience major problems in transition after the death of the parents.

Many parents feel the only alternative to care at home is having their adult child "put away" in a large state institution. In reality, federal legislation and state regulations now severely limit the number of individuals who are institutionalized. However, there are many other options available, ranging from home care to private residential care.

The 1980s have seen the principles of de-institutionalization and normalization markedly change the availability of adult living sites for MR/DD individuals. Normalization, first proposed in 1959 in Denmark, is a concept that encourages people with disabilities to achieve an existence as close to normal as possible. This philosophy has led to the development of programs that keep disabled adults in the community. There have been problems, such as lack of community services and discrimination in housing, but progress has been steady. Many individuals who, in the past, would have resided in large, isolated institutions, now lead productive and rewarding lives.

Out-of-Home Placement

As a result of de-institutionalization, many large public institutions have been closed and replaced by small community programs. Unfortunately, these community facilities are too few in number to satisfy the demand and often are filled with people who were placed there under court order when state institutions closed. Even if space in a group home is secured, the demand for other community services, such as medical care, sheltered workshops, leisure activities, and counseling services, often outstrips the supply. The result may be long waiting lists and little choice. In sum, planning for transition is not easy and you will need to develop your own approach.

Current policy is to keep all individuals, no matter what their abilities or disabilities, in a setting as close as possible to what they might have experienced had they not been disabled. For living sites, this has resulted in a range of options that includes, but is not limited to: (1) living at home with support services or respite care; (2) living independently with the support of a caseworker/adviser for supervision and protection; (3) living independently with partial services, for example in a cluster of apartments with overnight staff; (4) living in board-and-care homes or adult foster homes; (5) living in a small (usually three to six persons) group home, or a small (usually eight to fifteen persons) facility; and, rarely, (6) living in a large private or public facility.

Although many options are available, you may have difficulty looking to the future to make these plans. You may feel either that it is your burden to care for your child "till death" or that no one else is capable enough or loving enough to care for your child. While it is true that you have certain obligations toward your children and that you are their best advocate, separation of parent and disabled child when the child becomes an adult is often advantageous to both. It allows your child to develop independence in pursuing age- and developmentally appropriate activities. The majority of these programs require that young adults maintain or develop skills. It also allows you to have more freedom to enjoy your own lives. It does not mean a complete separation. Your child is still free (and encouraged) to go home for holidays and visits. You may visit as often as you

like and are encouraged to be part of decision-making and program-planning.

These programs also allow some relief from financial responsibility. Once your child is over eighteen years of age, he will be eligible for SSI funds and have his own income. This can be coupled with other entitlements such as Medicaid and food stamps. You are rarely financially responsible for these programs unless you choose private services. This is also the case for most residential facilities that are funded by the state and/or federal government.

In order to prepare your child for the transition to living away from home, you may wish to consider the use of respite care. Respite care most commonly involves having your child stay in one of a variety of settings outside the home, where your child is cared for by trained individuals. Most respite care is for a period of one week or less. It permits you to take a vacation or do something special with your spouse and other children that may not be possible with your disabled child. Many parents underutilize or don't use respite care at all, again thinking that they should bear the burden alone. You may also worry that your child will feel rejected. However, when viewed from your child's perspective, respite care offers many benefits and can assume a new importance. It allows your child to experience new caregivers and new experiences in a situation that he or she knows is only temporary. It also allows you to evaluate a variety of settings and caregivers for consideration as a future permanent placement.

Despite the presence of community placements, there still may be times or situations when an adult needs a residential placement in a large facility. This may be temporary, as in the case of vocational training or treatment of behavior problems, or permanent, as in the case of the MR/DD individual who has complex medical problems or who is elderly. In addition, there exist intermediate care facilities for the mentally retarded, which provide residential and other services to individuals who require twenty-four-hour care. These facilities are funded by the government. Parental assets or income are not considered in determining eligibility.

Since the referral process and available programs vary from state to state, you will need to seek local information and guidance in making these decisions. To access these services, begin with the community service section of the phone book, talk to other parents, and call local services such as special education, sheltered workshops, and early-intervention programs. Having done this, you probably will be pleasantly surprised by advances in medical care, rehabilitation planning, and normalization in these programs. You will be relieved to find that your child has the opportunity to develop in as normal and as stimulating a setting as possible.

OCCUPATIONS

The three primary activities of people's lives are education, work, and leisure. This is also true for MR/DD adults. Thanks to Public Law 94-142, education takes up a major part of the day until your child reaches age twenty-one, but after that period day programming is still necessary. In fact, most residential programs include or require a day program. These programs may vary, depending on the abilities of the individual, and can range from day-care to independent employment.

Unfortunately, programs for adults with disabilities are rarely mandatory and vary significantly in quantity and substance from one location to another. They may be structured or informal, often combine skill

development and recreational activities, and can be similar to previous schooling. Most programs relate to some sort of work or training for work. Some professionals feel that all individuals, regardless of their level of disability, are employable. Indeed, there are a few programs that employ even severely and profoundly retarded individuals.

Most regions of the country have some sort of a sheltered work service system. Work may include both pre-vocational activities such as sorting, and simple work station activities such as folding napkins, assembling parts, packaging, and pasting on labels. Handicapped adults are usually paid by the piece and work at their own pace. These programs generally depend on contracts from businesses and often there is a lack of suitable work. Though these programs are the first step on the continuum of work projects available, the disadvantages are: (1) a lack of integration into normal work environments; (2) the variable quantity of work available because of the lack of contracts; and (3) the limited training options. However, some programs flourish and are very productive. The repetitive nature of the tasks is often suitable to lower levels of functioning, and quality is often high, because mentally handicapped adults may not become easily bored with the work. My first experience with a sheltered workshop was a setting where moderately retarded individuals were folding parachutes. They rarely made mistakes with this repetitive task. I was surprised to learn of the high number of mistakes made by people with normal intelligence who were presumably bored with the task.

More MR/DD individuals could function effectively in the competitive workplace, but in order to do so, they must overcome a number of barriers: (1) they will lose their Social Security checks, (2) employers often fear that they will incur increased liability, (3) families worry about their child's ability to perform adequately and without being ostracized, (4) other employees are often unfamiliar and untrained in working with disabled persons, (5) the disabled individual may not have received adequate training, (6) transportation to and from work may be difficult, and (7) the disabled person may be discouraged by those around him.

Where available, vocational rehabilitation services can be the key to a worthwhile occupational experience. Vocational rehabilitation was mandated by the Vocational Rehabilitation Act. To be eligible, one must have a physical or mental disability that results in substantial obstacles to employment. One must also have a reasonable expectation of benefit from the program in terms of potential for employment. An applicant is evaluated and, if found qualified, trained. Training can range from vocational training to college, and involves the development of an Individual Written Rehabilitation Program (IWRP). Vocational rehabilitation services include evaluation, counseling and guidance, physical restoration services (surgery, dental work, assistive devices, speech therapy), training (vocational and other, such as work attitudes), maintenance (basic hiring expenses), transportation, services to family members, interpreter services for persons with hearing disabilities, reader services for people with vision impairments, aids and devices (e.g., reading machines, voice-command wheelchairs), recruitment and training services, job placement, post-employment services, occupational licenses, and other services. In order to have your child evaluated, you should contact the vocational rehabilitation representative in your child's high school or directly contact the Department of Vocational Rehabilitation, which is listed in telephone books under government agencies.

A fairly recent development in the work area for disabled adults has involved integrated employment. In this situation the individual works in a regular work setting. There are two options for integrated employment, supported and competitive. With competitive employment, a disabled adult obtains the job by being qualified for the position. With supported employment, the individual has outside supports, often in the form of a job coach from the Department of Vocational Rehabilitation. This is someone who helps with training and assistance and may act as a liaison among the client, family, and employer.

There are, of course, other options besides integrated employment. One is volunteer work, in which the individual learns job-related and other skills such as adhering to a schedule.

Finally, when the individual ages and production rate decreases and skills deteriorate, retirement should be considered. The older MR/DD individual should have the right to retire just as anyone else, and is eligible to receive Social Security benefits.

LEISURE TIME

As mentioned above, life is divided among education, work, and leisure time. Since adults with disabilities are out of school and may have limited work opportunities, they are often left with a lot of leisure time. Many people in this country regard leisure time as unimportant, but for disabled children and adults, not only is leisure time a potential source of enjoyment, it may also contribute to skill development. However, as with other activities, evaluation and training may be necessary to gain the greatest benefit from leisure time.

Recreation may be viewed as productive and relaxing, or just a means of filling in time. It can include simple activities such as watching TV or coloring, or more complicated activities such as hobbies, sports and games, reading, and even religion. Disabled adults have the right to choose and experience a wide variety of activities, either formally or informally. They may take part in and observe family activities, or participate in formal leisure programs for the disabled.

Disabled individuals often also can participate in "regular" programs, designed for nondisabled individuals, the advantage being their abundance. However, there may be barriers to participation. For example, local bowling leagues, church programs, and excursion bus trips are under no obligation to accept everyone. Yet, with some persistence, planning, and flexibility, a variety of recreation and leisure activities can be pursued.

There are also many therapeutic recreation programs, which use recreation to help disabled people enjoy leisure lifestyles as independently as possible. They strive to minimize the effects of the disability and maximize the quality of life and can be provided in many settings: hospital, rehabilitation center, activity center, and so on. Individuals can participate at all levels of functioning. Services may include leisure counseling, leisure skill development, or adaptation of existing skills.

Religion is a crucial part of life for many families. Certain major religious events, such as First Communion or Bar/Bat Mitzvah, have been denied to disabled individuals in the past. Many churches and synagogues now have special programs adapted to accommodate impaired individuals.

Leisure time should not be looked upon as idle activity. For many individuals, it is a great source of satisfaction and may contribute significantly to growth, development, and emotional stability.

SEXUALITY, LOVE, AND MARRIAGE

Most parents are reluctant to discuss sex with their disabled child. Yet, it is a myth that sexual development in disabled individuals is different from normal. Disabled adolescents have similar sexual development, confusion, and drives as the rest of the adolescent population. And, they are exposed to as much sexual stimulation as other teenagers. What they usually lack is adequate knowledge and education about the implications of sexuality. Normal urges (sexual curiosity, masturbation) are often misinterpreted as sexual perversion. Further, they often receive conflicting messages from society, television, family, teachers, and peers.

Some parents seek sterilization of their child (especially a female child) as a way of protecting her from the consequences of sex. However, while sterilization will prevent pregnancy, it does nothing to protect her from the other consequences of sex, including psychological trauma and sexually transmitted diseases. Only education, with an understanding and appreciation of privacy and personal rights, can do that. Most people capable of engaging in a sexual union are also capable of learning how to refuse this opportunity.

Most states require that the person to be sterilized give informed consent. This means that she must be capable of giving consent, understand the procedure and its effects, and give consent voluntarily. In most cases, parents cannot decide for their child, and court permission is usually difficult to obtain.

You may also struggle over the issue of whether your child should be allowed to marry and bear children. The right to marry is protected under the Fourteenth Amendment. However, laws vary from state to state, and marriage can be prevented if it may harm an individual who is incapable of providing informed consent. While some state laws limit marriage of adults with certain disabilities and forbid sexual activity, this is usually unenforceable. Education and attention to personal respect have a much greater possibility of meeting both society's and the individual's needs.

Many people find it difficult to accept the normal sexual urges of disabled persons, but they are entitled to full, responsible sexual expression. This includes masturbation, having relationships that may include sexual activity, the right to have sex education, the right to obtain birth control, and the right to bear children.

Sex education is often denied to mentally retarded people on the grounds that they lack good judgment or on the mythical assumption that it is sexually stimulating. There is no evidence that sex education stimulates sexual activity. More likely, lack of education will lead to poor judgment. Birth control is often denied to these individuals because it is felt they are unable to utilize it. They can be taught. Similarly, they can learn that masturbation is an activity that should be practiced in private. There is also fear that retarded individuals would bear retarded children. This is generally not the case, but if you have concerns, seek genetic counseling (see chapter 4).

The right to bear children involves more than just engaging in sex. There are some disabled individuals who have the capacity to be good parents. However, children of retarded parents are at greater risk of psychosocial deprivation and retardation, as in the case of John and Christopher. Customary personal support networks (in-laws, friends, and co-workers) are often missing. The chief problems with children born to and raised by retarded parents are abuse and neglect. About 50 percent of these children end up being removed from the home. Parent-training programs have had mixed effectiveness and variable outcomes.

BEHAVIORAL AND EMOTIONAL PROBLEMS

Unfortunately, in addition to the inherent difficulties of raising a child with developmental problems, current trends present additional stresses. De-institutionalization, while laudable in theory, often lacks the network of community-based services necessary to promote a smooth transition. Current approaches to mainstreaming in schools may not allow for effective transition, appropriate education, and the provision of associated services such as occupational, speech, and physical therapies. These shortcomings may be magnified for individuals who have spent many years in an institution and are then discharged by court order to be confronted with a community-living situation for which they may not be prepared. Such was the case with Richard at the beginning of this chapter.

As a result, there may be times when your child needs mental health services. These services can involve counseling, medication, or both. Until the 1970s, a high percentage of individuals in institutions received psychotropic drugs. Because of abuses in this area, use of such medications became unpopular and has been heavily regulated. Behavior-modification programs then became the usual mode of treatment. Currently the pendulum has swung to a more balanced position, and the judicious use of both medication and behavioral programs is recognized as being the most effective approach (see chapters 15 and 19). Research has confirmed advantages and drawbacks of various treatment methods. It is now recognized that disabled individuals can be depressed, psychotic, and so forth, and can benefit from traditional psychiatric treatment, including medication.

SOME LEGAL ISSUES

There are several legal issues which need to be mentioned. However, specific details should be discussed with your lawyer.

1. *Wills* — Adults with disabilities can make a valid will if they are of sound mind. Wills made by parents with proceeds to their disabled children should be carefully discussed with a lawyer. If they are not clearly written as trusts, there can be loss of assets set aside to provide support and maintain services.
2. *Voting* — About forty states have limitations on voting rights for persons with mental disabilities. These laws have rarely been challenged.
3. *Criminal prosecution* — Most prosecutions are based on the issue of competence, that is, for the individual to have understood what he did, so mental limitation is a crucial issue in any court proceeding. Also, if convicted, protection and special placement are usually necessary if mentally retarded adults are put in prison.

ADVOCACY

You have concerns about your child's life and may be compelled to advocate for ser-

vices. This can be frustrating. Each parent has his or her own way of dealing with these issues, ranging from writing letters and joining parent organizations to creating programs. First, you need to educate yourself and define the problem you want to address. Then, develop alternatives and choose a course of action. It is a long and difficult process, but there are many support systems, including neighbors and local, state, and national organizations. Most of the major changes in services for the disabled have come about through advocacy by parents.

SOME QUESTIONS ANSWERED

I want to provide for my child after I die. Should I will my house to him?

All disabled adults over eighteen are eligible for a variety of entitlements if they have financial need. This means they cannot have a lot of assets. If your child inherits property, his or her assets will be used for medical care, residential fees, and so on, until they drop to a level where your child again qualifies for entitlements. Therefore, assets that you have carefully accumulated to ensure your child's well-being will be used for services to which he would have been entitled anyway.

It might be more prudent to set up a trust so your child would not be a direct beneficiary but would benefit from the assets. This must be done through a lawyer. Lawyers with expertise in this area can usually be found through local advocacy groups or the Association for Retarded Citizens.

I want my child to work but I am afraid he will lose benefits.

Since many benefits are based on financial need, this must be carefully planned. However, work contributes not only financially to a person's life, but to his or her health and self-image as well. Because this is recognized, there are provisions to allow disabled adults to earn some income and still keep benefits. This can be discussed with the benefit agency (for example, Social Security or Medicaid). Another area to consider is total assets. Some entitlements (e.g., Supplemental Security Income) require that recipient's assets not exceed maximum levels (usually $1,500–$2,000). This means, for instance, that if your child has a savings account and accumulates above the limit, his check may be reduced. In some cases, therefore, it may be wise not to build up funds.

Suggested Readings and Resources

Chapter One: Your Child Has a Handicap

Blodgett, H. E. *Mentally Retarded Children: What Parents and Others Should Know.* Ann Arbor: Books on Demand, 1976.

Breslau, N., M. Weitzman, and K. Messenger. "Psychological Functioning of Siblings of Disabled Children." *Pediatrics* 67 (1981): 344–353.

Buscaglia, L. *The Disabled and Their Parents: A Counseling Challenge.* Thorofare, NJ: Slack, 1983.

Carson, M. *A Guide for Friends, Neighbors and Relatives of Retarded Children.* Chicago: Claretian Publishing, 1991.

Darling, R. B. *Families Against Society.* Newbury Park, CA: Sage Publications, 1979.

Darling, R. B., and J. Darling. *Children Who Are Different.* St. Louis: C. V. Mosby Co., 1982.

Ellifritt, J. *"Life with My Sister — Guilt No More." Exceptional Parent* 14 (1984): 16–21.

Featherstone, H. *A Difference in the Family: Living with a Disabled Child.* New York: Penguin Books, 1981.

Glendinning, C. *Unshared Care: Parents and Their Disabled Children.* New York: Routledge Chapman & Hall, 1983.

Goldfarb L. A., M. J. Brotherson, J. A. Summers, et al. *Meeting the Challenge of Disability or Chronic Illness: A Family Guide.* Baltimore: Paul H. Brookes Publishing, 1986.

Greenfeld, J. *A Child Called Noah.* New York: Holt, Rinehart and Winston, 1972.

Heisler, V. *A Handicapped Child in the Family. A Guide for Parents.* New York: Grune and Stratton, 1972.

Kupfer, F. *Before and After Zachariah.* New York: Delacorte Press, 1982.

Kushner, H. *When Bad Things Happen to Good People.* New York: Avon, 1983.

Lonsdale, G. "Family Life with a Handicapped Child: The Parents Speak." *Child Care, Health and Development* 4 (1978): 99–120.

Mantle, M. *Some Just Clap Their Hands.* New York: Adama Books, 1985.

Maryland State Planning Council on Developmental Disabilities. *An Update to: A Reader's Guide for Parents of Children with Mental, Physical, or Emotional Disabilities.* Baltimore: MSPCDD, 1983.

Meyer, D. J., et al. *Living with a Brother or Sister with Special Needs: A Book for Sibs.* Seattle: University of Washington Press, 1985.

Moore, C. B., and K. G. Morton. *A Reader's Guide for Parents of Children with Mental, Physical, or Emotional Disabilities.* U.S. Department of Health, Education and Welfare. DHEW Publication No. (HSA) 77-5290, 1976.

Pader, O. F. *A Guide and Handbook for Parents of Mentally Retarded Children.* Springfield, IL: C. C. Thomas, 1981.

Pearlman, L., and K. A. Scott. *Raising the Handicapped Child.* New York: Prentice-Hall, 1981.

Perske, R. *Hope for the Families: New Directions for Parents of Persons with Retardation or Other Disabilities.* Nashville, TN: Abingdon Press, 1981.

Powell, T. H., and P. A. Ogle. *Brothers and Sisters — A Special Part of Exceptional Families.* Baltimore: Paul H. Brookes Publishing, 1985.

Schleifer, M. J., and S. D. Klein, eds. *The Disabled Child and the Family: An Exceptional Parent Reader.* Boston: The Exceptional Parent Press, 1985.

Seligman, M., ed. *The Family with a Handicapped Child: Understanding and Treatment.* New York: Grune and Stratton, 1983.

Strauss, S. *Is It Well with the Child? A Parent's Guide to Raising a Mentally Handicapped Child.* New York: Doubleday, 1975.

Thompson, C. E., M.D. *Raising Handicapped Children.* New York: William Morrow, 1986.

Turnbull, A. P., and H. R. Turnbull, III. *Parents Speak Out: Then and Now.* Columbus, OH: Charles E. Merrill, 1985.

Wright, L. *Parent Power: A Guide to Responsible Childrearing.* New York: Psychological Dimensions, 1978.

Exceptional Parent, 605 Commonwealth Ave., Boston, MA 02215.

Parentele, 5538 N. Pennsylvania, Indianapolis, IN 46220.

Chapter Two: Finding a Doctor

Easterbrook, E. "The Revolution in Medicine," *Newsweek* (Jan. 26, 1987): 40–74.

Jones, M. L. *Home Care for the Chronically Ill or Disabled Child.* New York: Harper & Row, 1985.

American Academy of Cerebral Palsy and Developmental Medicine (AACPDM), 2315 Westwood Ave., PO Box 11083, Richmond, VA 23230.

American Academy of Pediatrics, 141 Northwest Point Rd., PO Box 927, Elk Grove Village, IL 60007.

American Association of University Affiliated Programs for Persons with Developmental Disabilities (AAUAP), 8605 Cameron St., #406, Silver Spring, MD 20910.

Children's Seashore House, 3405 Civic Center Blvd., Philadelphia, PA 19104.

Society for Developmental Pediatrics, Kennedy Inst., 707 N. Broadway, Baltimore, MD 21205.

Chapter Three: Why My Child?

Ballard, J. L., K. K. Novak, and M. Driver. "A Simplified Score for Assessment of Fetal Maturation of Newly Born Infants." *Journal of Pediatrics* 95 (1979): 769–774.

Bennett, F. C., N. M. Robinson, and C. J. Sells. "Growth and Development of Infants Weighing Less than 800 Grams at Birth." *Pediatrics* 71 (1983): 319–323.

Franco, S., and B. F. Andrews. "Reduction of Cerebral Palsy by Neonatal Intensive Care." *Pediatric Clinics of North America* 24 (1977): 639–649.

Chapter Four: What About Our Next Child?

Apgar, V., and J. Beck. *Is My Baby All Right?* New York: Pocket Books, 1973.

Fraser, F. C., and J. J. Nora. *Genetics of Man.* 2nd ed. Philadelphia: Lea and Febiger, 1986.

McKusick, V. A. *Mendelian Inheritance in Man: Catalogs of Autosomal Dominant, Autosomal Recessive and X-linked Disorders.* 7th edition. Baltimore: Johns Hopkins University Press, 1988.

Milunsky, A. *Choices, Not Chances: An Essential Guide to Your Heredity and Health.* Boston: Little, Brown, 1989.

Smith, D. *Recognizable Patterns of Human Malformation. Genetic, Embryologic and Clinical Aspects.* 3rd ed. Philadelphia: W. B. Saunders Co., 1982.

March of Dimes Birth Defects Foundation, 1275 Mamaroneck Ave., White Plains, NY 10605.

National Genetics Foundation, 555 W. 57th St., New York, NY 10019.

National Society of Genetic Counselors, Department of Pediatrics, University of California, Irvine Medical Center, 101 City Dr., Orange, CA 92668.

Chapter Five: The Development of a Young Child

Caplan, F., ed. *The First Twelve Months of Life.* New York: Bantam Books, 1984.

Caplan, F., and T. Caplan. *The Second Twelve*

Months of Life. New York: Bantam Books, 1977.

Caplan, T., and F. Caplan. *The Early Childhood Years: The Two to Six Year Old.* New York: Bantam Books, 1984.

Cowan, P. A. *Piaget with Feeling: Cognitive, Social and Emotional Dimensions.* New York: Holt, Rinehart and Winston, 1978.

Fraiberg, S. H. *Magic Years: Understanding and Handling the Problems of Early Childhood.* New York: Charles Scribner's Sons, 1984.

Frankenburg, W., J. Dobbs, and A. W. Fandal. *Denver Developmental Screening Test Manual.* Denver: University of Colorado Medical Center, 1970.

Gesell, A. L., and F. L. Ilg. *Child Development: An Introduction to the Study of Human Growth.* New York: Harper & Row, 1949.

Illingworth, R. S. *The Development of the Infant and Young Child: Normal and Abnormal.* 9th ed. New York: Churchill Livingstone, 1987.

Kennedy, Joseph P., Jr. Foundation. *Let's Play to Learn.* Washington, 1986.

Knobloch, H., and B. Pasamanick, eds. *Gesell and Amatruda's Developmental Diagnosis.* 3rd ed. Philadelphia: Lippincott, 1974.

Noback, C. R. *The Human Nervous System: Basic Principles of Neurobiology.* 3rd ed. New York: McGraw-Hill, 1980.

Piaget, J. *The Origins of Intelligence in Children.* Madison, CT: International University Press, 1966.

Thain, W. S., et al. *Normal and Handicapped Children: A Growth and Development Primer for Parents and Professionals.* Littleton, MA: PSG Publishing, 1980.

Chapter Six: Mental Retardation

Bayley, N. "Value and Limitations of Infant Testing." *Children* 5 (1958): 129–133.

Edgerton, R. B. *Mental Retardation.* Cambridge: Harvard University Press, 1979.

Frankenberger, W. "A Survey of State Guidelines for Identification of Mental Retardation." *Mental Retardation* 22 (1984): 17–20.

Illingworth, R. S. *The Development of the Infant and Young Child: Normal and Abnor-*

mal. 9th ed. New York: Churchill Livingstone, 1987.

Jablow, M. M. *Cara: Growing with a Retarded Child.* Philadelphia: Temple University Press, 1982.

Pader, O. F. *A Guide and Handbook for Parents of Mentally Retarded Children.* Springfield, IL: Charles C. Thomas, 1981.

Scheerenberger, R. C. *A History of Mental Retardation.* Baltimore: Paul H. Brookes Publishing, 1983.

Wodrich, D. L. *Children's Psychological Testing: A Guide for Nonpsychologists.* Baltimore: Paul H. Brookes Publishing, 1984.

Zimmerman, R. L., and G. T. Heistad. "Studies of the Long Term Efficacy of Antipsychotic Drugs in Controlling the Behavior of Institutionalized Retardates." *Journal of the American Academy of Child Psychiatry* 21 (1982): 136–143.

American Association on Mental Deficiency, 1719 Kalorama Rd. NW, Washington, DC 20009.

Association of Retarded Citizens of the United States, 2501 Avenue J, Arlington, TX 76011.

National Association of Developmental Disabilities Councils, 1234 Massachusetts Ave. NW, Washington, DC 20057.

Chapter Seven: Down Syndrome and Other Chromosomal Disorders

Antonarahis, S. E., and the Down Syndrome Collaborate Group. "Parental Origin of the Extra Chromosome in Trisomy 21 as Indicated by Analysis of DNA Polymorphisms." *New England Journal of Medicine* 327 (1991): 872–876.

Bender, B., E. Fry, B. Pennington, et al. "Speech and Language Development in 41 Children with Sex Chromosome Anomalies." *Pediatrics* 71 (1983): 262–267.

Brown, W. T., E. C. Jenkins, E. Friedman, et al. "Folic Acid Therapy in the Fragile X Syndrome." *American Journal of Medical Genetics* 17 (1984): 289–297.

Caldwell, P. D., and D. W. Smith. "The XXY (Klinefelter's) Syndrome in Childhood: Detection and Treatment." *Journal of Pediatrics* 80 (1972): 250–258.

Cunningham, C. *Down's Syndrome: An Introduction for Parents.* Cambridge, MA: Brookline Books, 1982.

Cronk, C., A. C. Crocker, S. M. Pueschel, et al. "Growth Charts for Children with Down Syndrome: One Month to Eighteen Years of Age." *Pediatrics* 81 (1988): 102–110.

DiMaio, M. S., A. Baumgarten, R. M. Greenstein, et al. "Screening for Fetal Down Syndrome in Pregnancy by Measuring Maternal Serum Alphafetoprotein Levels." *New England Journal of Medicine* 317 (1987): 376–378.

Edwards, J. P., and D. Dawson. *My Friend David. A Source Book about Down Syndrome.* Austin, TX: PRO-ED, 1983.

Fishler, K., R. Koch, and G. N. Donnell. "Comparison of Mental Development in Individuals with Mosaic and Trisomy 21 Down's Syndrome." *Pediatrics* 58 (1976): 744–748.

Hagerman, R. J., and P. M. McBogg, eds. *The Fragile X Syndrome.* Dillon, CO: Spectra Publishing, 1983.

Hanson, M. J. *Teaching Your Down Syndrome Infant: A Guide for Parents.* 2nd ed. Austin, TX: PRO-ED, 1986.

Hodes, M. E., J. Cole, C. G. Palmer, et al. "Clinical Experience with Trisomies 18 and 13." *Journal of Medical Genetics* 15 (1978): 48–60.

Hook, E. B., and J. J. Fabia. "Frequency of Down Syndrome in Live Births by Single-year Maternal Age Interval: Results of a Massachusetts Study." *Teratology* 17 (1978): 223–228.

Niebuhr, E. "The Cri-du-chat Syndrome: Epidemiology, Cytogenetics, and Clinical Features." *Human Genetics* 44 (1978): 227–275.

Palmer, C. G., and A. Reichmann. "Chromosomal and Clinical Findings in 110 Females with Turner Syndrome." *Human Genetics* 35 (1976): 35–49.

Pueschel, S. M. *Down Syndrome: Towards a Better Future.* Baltimore: Paul H. Brookes Publishing, 1990.

Pueschel, S. M., ed. *The Young Person with Down Syndrome: Transition from Adolescence to Adulthood.* Baltimore: Paul H. Brookes Publishing, 1988.

Pueschel, S. M. "Facial Plastic Surgery for Children with Down Syndrome." *Developmental Medicine and Child Neurology* 30 (1988): 540–543.

Pueschel, S. M., and J. C. Pezzullo. "Thyroid Dysfunction in Down Syndrome." *American Journal of Diseases of Children* 139 (1985): 636–639.

Pueschel, S. M., and F. H. Scola. "Atlantoaxial Instability in Individuals with Down Syndrome: Epidemiologic, Radiologic and Clinical Studies." *Pediatrics* 80 (1987): 555–560.

Pueschel, S. M., C. Tingey, J. E. Rynders, et al. *New Perspectives on Down Syndrome.* Baltimore: Paul H. Brookes Publishing, 1987.

Seigfried, F. R., and S. M. Pueschel, eds. *Down Syndrome: Growing and Learning.* Kansas City, MO: Andrews and McMeel, 1978.

Smith, D. *Recognizable Patterns of Human Malformation: Genetic, Embryologic and Clinical Aspects.* 3rd ed. Philadelphia: W. B. Saunders, 1982.

Smith, D. W., and A. C. Wilson. *The Child with Down's Syndrome.* Philadelphia: W. B. Saunders, 1973.

Stay-Gundersen, K., ed. *Babies with Down Syndrome: A New Parent's Guide.* Rockville, MD: Woodbine House, 1986.

National Down Syndrome Society, 70 W. 40th St., New York, NY 10018.

National Down Syndrome Congress, 1800 Dempster St., Park Ridge, IL 60068.

Sharing Our Caring: A Journal on Down's Syndrome. PO Box 400, Milton, WA 98354.

Chapter Eight: Seizure Disorders

Ferry, P. C., W. Banner, and R. A. Wolf. *Seizure Disorders in Children.* Philadelphia: J. B. Lippincott, 1985.

Holmes, G. L. *Diagnosis and Management of Seizures in Childhood.* Philadelphia: W. B. Saunders, 1987.

Jan, J. E., R. G. Ziegler, and G. Erba. *Does Your Child Have Epilepsy?* Austin, TX: PRO-ED, 1983.

Niedermeyer, E. *Epilepsy Guide: Diagnosis and Treatment of Epileptic Seizure Disorders.* Baltimore: Urban and Schwarzenberg, 1983.

Epilepsy Foundation of America, 4351 Garden City Dr., Suite 406, Landover, MD 20785.

Chapter Nine: Cerebral Palsy

Cooper, I. S., M. Riklan, I. Amin, et al. "Chronic Cerebellar Stimulation in Cerebral Palsy." *Neurology* 26 (1976): 744–753.

Freeman, J. M., and K. B. Nelson. "Intrapartum Asphyxia and Cerebral Palsy." *Pediatrics* 82 (1988): 240–249.

Harris, S. R., and A. H. Purdy. "Drooling and Its Management in Cerebral Palsy." *Developmental Medicine and Child Neurology* 29 (1987): 807–811.

Hirst, M. "Patterns of Impairment and Disability Related to Social Handicap in Young People with Cerebral Palsy and Spina Bifida." *Journal of Biosocial Science* 21 (1989): 1–12.

Matthews, D. J. "Controversial Therapies in the Management of Cerebral Palsy." *Pediatric Annals* 17 (1988): 762–764.

Nelson, K. B., and J. H. Ellenberg. "Antecedents of Cerebral Palsy." *American Journal of Diseases of Children* 139 (1985): 1031–1038.

Neveille, B. G. "Selective Dorsal Rhizotomy for Spastic Cerebral Palsy." *Developmental Medicine and Child Neurology* 30 (1988): 395–398.

Robinson, R. O. "The Frequency of Other Handicaps in Children with Cerebral Palsy." *Developmental Medicine and Child Neurology* 15 (1973): 305–312.

Russman, B. S., and J. R. Gage. "Cerebral Palsy." *Current Problems in Pediatrics* 19 (1989): 65–111.

Thompson, G. H., I. L. Rubin, and R. M. Bilenker. *Comprehensive Management of Cerebral Palsy.* Orlando: Grune and Stratton, 1983.

United Cerebral Palsy Inc., 66 E. 34th St., New York, NY 10016.

Chapter Ten: Hearing Impairment

Berg, F. S. *Facilitating Classroom Listening. A Handbook for Teachers of Normal & Hard of Hearing Students.* Boston: College-Hill Press, 1987.

Bess, F., ed. *Hearing Impairment in Children.* York, PA: York Press, 1988.

Calvert, D. *Parent's Guide to Speech and Deafness.* Washington, DC: Alexander Graham Bell Association, 1984.

Freeman, R. D., C. F. Carbin, and R. J. Boese. *Can't Your Child Hear? A Guide for Those Who Care about Deaf Children.* Baltimore: University Park Press, 1981.

Grundfast, K., and C. J. Carney. *Ear Infections in Your Child. The Comprehensive Parental Guide to Causes and Treatments.* Hollywood, FL: Compact Books, 1987.

Harris, G. A. *Broken Ears, Wounded Hearts.* Washington, DC: Gallaudet College Press, 1983.

McArthur, S. H. *Raising Your Hearing Impaired Child: Guideline for Parents.* Washington, DC: Alexander Graham Bell Association, 1982.

National Center for Law and the Deaf. *Legal Rights of Hearing-Impaired People.* 3rd ed. Washington, DC: Gallaudet University Press, 1986.

Northern, J., and M. Downs. *Hearing in Children.* 3rd ed. Baltimore: Williams & Wilkins, 1984.

Ross, M. *Hard of Hearing Children in Regular Schools.* Englewood Cliffs, NJ: Prentice-Hall, 1982.

Turnbull, A. P. *Parents Speak Out: Views from the Other Side of the Two-Way Mirror.* 2nd ed. Columbus, OH: Charles E. Merrill, 1985.

American Speech-Language-Hearing Association, 10801 Rockville Pike, Rockville, MD 20852.

American Hearing Research Foundation, 55 E. Washington St., Chicago, IL 60602.

Self Help for Hard of Hearing People, Inc., 7800 Wisconsin Ave., Bethesda, MD 20814.

The National Information Center on Deafness, Gallaudet College, Washington, DC 20002.

The National Association of the Deaf, Suite 301, 814 Thayer Ave., Silver Spring, MD 20910.

Alexander Graham Bell Association for the Deaf, 3417 Volta Pl. N.W., Washington, DC 20007.

Chapter Eleven: Communication Disorders

Barach, C. *Help Me Say It — A Parent's Guide to Speech Problems.* New York: Harper & Row, 1984.

Blank, M., S. Rose, and L. Berlin. *The Language of Learning: The Preschool Years.* Orlando, FL: Grune and Stratton, 1978.

Isaacson, R. *The Retarded Child: A Guide for Parents and Friends.* Allen, TX: Argus Communications, 1974.

Murphy, K. *Special Children, Special Parents.* Englewood Cliffs, NJ: Prentice-Hall, 1981.

Shanin, S. *Songs for Language Learning.* Tucson, AZ: Communication Skill Builders, 1987.

White, B. *The First Three Years of Life.* Englewood Cliffs, NJ: Prentice-Hall, 1984.

National Easter Seals Society, 2023 W. Ogden Ave., Chicago, IL 60612.

American Speech-Language-Hearing Association, 10801 Rockville Pike, Rockville, MD 20852.

American Cleft Palate Association and Educational Foundation, 331 Salk Hall, University of Pittsburgh, Pittsburgh, PA 15261.

Chapter Twelve: Autism

American Psychiatric Association. *Diagnostic and Statistical Manual of Mental Disorders.* 3rd ed., revised. Washington, DC: American Psychiatric Association, 1987.

Campbell, M., L. T. Anderson, S. I. Deutsch, et al. "Psychopharmacological Treatment of Children with the Syndrome of Autism." *Pediatric Annals* 13 (1984): 309–316.

Cohen, D. J., A. M. Donnellan, and R. Paul, eds. *Handbook of Autism and Pervasive Developmental Disorders.* New York: John Wiley & Sons, 1987.

Courchesne, E., R. Yeung-Courchesne, G. A. Press, et al. "Hypoplasia of Cerebellar Vermal Lobules VI and VII in Autism." *New England Journal of Medicine* 318 (1988): 1349–1354.

Folstein, S., and M. Rutter. "Infantile Autism: A Genetic Study of 21 Twin Pairs." *Journal of Child Psychology and Psychiatry* 18 (1977): 297–321.

Hagberg, B., J. Aicardi, K. Dias, et al. "A Progressive Syndrome of Autism, Dementia, Ataxia, and Loss of Purposeful Hand Use in Girls: Rett's Syndrome: Report of 35 Cases." *Annals of Neurology* 14 (1983): 471–479.

Hagerman, R. J. "Fragile X Syndrome." *Current Problems in Pediatrics* 17 (1987): 621–674.

Minshew, N. J., and J. B. Payton. "New Perspectives in Autism." *Current Problems in Pediatrics* 18 (1988): 561–694.

Percy, A. K., H. Y. Zoghbi, K. R. Lewis, et al. "Rett Syndrome: Motor and Behavioral Differentiation from Autism." *Neurology* 37 (1987): 220–221.

Ritvo, E. R., ed. *Autism: Diagnosis, Current Research and Management.* New York: Spectrum, 1976.

Rutter, M. "Autistic Children: Infancy to Adulthood." *Seminars in Psychiatry* 2 (1970): 435–450.

Rutter, M. "The Treatment of Autistic Children." *Journal of Child Psychology and Psychiatry* 26 (1985): 193–214.

Rutter, M., and E. Schopler, eds. *Autism: A Reappraisal of Concepts and Treatment.* New York: Plenum Publishing, 1978.

Szatmari, P., G. Bartolucci, and R. Bremner. "Asperger's Syndrome and Autism: Comparison of Early History and Outcome." *Developmental Medicine and Child Neurology* 31 (1989): 709–720.

Wing, L. *Autistic Children, A Guide for Parents.* New York: Brunner-Mazel, 1985.

Autism Clinic (Director: Susan Folstein, M.D.), Johns Hopkins Hospital, Meyer 2-181, 600 N. Wolfe St., Baltimore, MD 21205.

Autism Clinic (Director: Edward Ritvo, M.D.), University of California, 760 Westwood Plaza, Los Angeles, CA 90024.

Autism Clinic (Director: Lee Marcus, M.D.), University of North Carolina, 7180 Medical School Wing E, Chapel Hill, NC 27599-7180.

Autism and Social Disabilities Clinic (Director: Nancy Minshew, M.D.), Western Psychiatric Institute, 208 Iroquois Building, 3811 O'Hara St., Pittsburgh, PA 15213.

Autism Services Center, 101 Richmond St., Huntington, WV 25702.

Autism Society of America (ASA), formerly National Society for Autistic Adults and Children (NSAAC), 8601 Georgia Ave., Suite 503, Silver Spring, MD 20910.

Institute for Child Behavior Research, 4182 Adams Ave., San Diego, CA 92116.

TEACCH Group (Director: Eric Schopler, M.D.), University of North Carolina, Chapel Hill, runs periodic training sessions for parents and teachers working with autistic children.

Chapter Thirteen: Vision and Its Disorders

Adams, R. J., D. Maurer, and M. Davis. "Newborns' Discrimination of Chromatic from Achromatic Stimuli." *Journal of Experimental and Child Psychology* 41 (1986): 267–281.

Ferrell, K. A. *Reach Out and Teach: Parent Handbook & Reachbook.* New York: American Foundation for the Blind, 1985.

Fraiberg, S. *Insights from the Blind.* New York: New American Library, 1979.

Freeman, R. D., E. Goetz, D. P. Richards, et al. "Blind Children's Early Emotional Development: Do We Know Enough to Help?" *Child Care Health and Development* 15 (1989): 3–28.

Greenwald, M. J. "Visual Development in Infancy and Childhood." *Pediatric Clinics of North America* 30 (1983): 977–993.

Heiner, D. *Learning to Look. A Handbook for Parents of Low Vision Infants and Young Children.* East Lansing, MI: International Institute for Visually Impaired, 1986.

Isenberg, S. J. *The Eye in Infancy.* Chicago: Year Book Medical Publishers, 1989.

Kastein, S., I. Spaulding, and B. Scharf. *Raising the Young Blind Child.* New York: Human Sciences Press, 1980.

Krents, H. *To Race the Wind.* New York: Bantam Books, 1972.

Scott, E. P., J. E. Jan, and R. D. Freeman. *Can't Your Child See?* 2nd ed. Austin, TX: PRO-ED, 1985.

Teplin, S. W. "Development of Blind Infants and Children with Retrolental Fibroplasia." *Pediatrics* 71 (1983): 6–12.

Williamson, W. D., M. M. Desmond, L. P. Andrew, and R. N. Hicks. "Visually Impaired Infants in the 1980s." *Clinical Pediatrics* 26 (1987): 241–244.

American Foundation for the Blind, 15 W. 16th St., New York, NY 10011.

Associated Services for the Blind, 919 Walnut St., Philadelphia, PA 19107.

Association for Education and Rehabilitation of the Blind and Visually Impaired, 206 N. Washington, St., Alexandria, VA 22314.

International Institute for Visually Impaired, 1975 Rutgers, East Lansing, MI 48823.

National Association for Visually Handicapped, 22 W. 21st St., 6th Floor, New York, NY 10010.

National Society to Prevent Blindness, 79 Madison Ave., New York, NY 10016.

Chapter Fourteen: Spina Bifida and Muscular Dystrophy

Backman, E., E. Nylander, I. Johansson, et al. "Selenium and Vitamin E Treatment of Duchenne Muscular Dystrophy: No Effect on Muscle Function." *Acta Neurologica Scandinavica* 78 (1988): 429–435.

Barohn, R. J., E. J. Levine, J. O. Olson, et al. "Gastric Hypomotility in Duchenne's Muscular Dystrophy." *New England Journal of Medicine* 319 (1988): 15–18.

Bertorini, T. E., G. M. Palmieri, J. Griffin, et al. "Chronic Allopurinol and Adenine Therapy in Duchenne Muscular Dystrophy." *Neurology* 35 (1985): 61–65.

Brooke, M. H. *A Clinician's View of Neuromuscular Disease.* 2nd ed. Baltimore: Williams and Wilkins, 1986.

Charney, E. B. "Myelomeningocele." In

Schwartz, M. W., E. B. Charney, T. A. Curry, and S. Ludwig, eds. *Primary Pediatric Care: A Problem Oriented Approach.* 2nd ed. Chicago: Yearbook Publishers, 1986.

Charney, E. B.: "Social and Developmental Outcome of Myelomeningocele in Spinal Dysraphism." In T. S. Park, ed. *Contemporary Issues in Neurological Surgery.* Blackwell Scientific Publications, New York (in press).

Cole, C. G., A. Walker, A. Coyne, et al. "Prenatal Testing for Duchenne and Becker Muscular Dystrophy." *Lancet* 1 (1988): 262–266.

Curran, F. J., and A. P. Colbert. "Ventilator Management in Duchenne Muscular Dystrophy and Postpoliomyelitis Syndrome." *Archives of Physical Medicine and Rehabilitation* 70 (1989): 180–185.

Dorman, C., A. D. Hurley, and J. D'Avignon. "Language and Learning Disorders of Older Boys with Duchenne Muscular Dystrophy." *Developmental Medicine and Child Neurology* 30 (1988): 316–327.

Dubowitz, V. *Muscle Disorders in Childhood.* Philadelphia: W. B. Saunders, 1978.

Fitzpatrick, C., C. Barry, and C. Garvey. "Psychiatric Disorder among Boys with Duchenne Muscular Dystrophy." *Developmental Medicine and Child Neurology* 28 (1986): 589–595.

Hoffman, E. P., K. H. Fischbeck, R. H. Brown, et al. "Characterization of Dystrophin in Muscle-biopsy Specimens from Patients with Duchenne's or Becker's Muscular Dystrophy." *New England Journal of Medicine* 318 (1988): 1363–1368.

Hyser, C. L., and J. R. Mendell. "Recent Advances in Duchenne and Becker Muscular Dystrophy." *Neurologic Clinics* 6 (1988): 429–453.

Mendell, J. R., R. T. Moxley, R. C. Griggs, et al. "Randomized, Double-blind Six-month Trial of Prednisone in Duchenne's Muscular Dystrophy." *New England Journal of Medicine* 320 (1989): 1592–1597.

Shurtleff, D. B. *Myelodysphasias and Extrophies: Significance, Prevention and Treatment.* New York: Grune & Stratton, 1986.

Sussman, M. D. "Treatment of Scoliosis in Duchenne Muscular Dystrophy." *Developmental Medicine and Child Neurology* 27 (1985): 522–524.

Williamson, G. G. *Children with Spina Bifida: Early Intervention and Preschool Programming.* Baltimore: Paul H. Brookes Publishing, 1987.

Muscular Dystrophy Association. 810 Seventh Ave., New York, NY 10019.

Spina Bifida Association of America, 1700 Rockville Pike, Suite 540, Rockville, MD 20852.

Chapter Fifteen: Love and Discipline

Anderson, D. R., G. D. Hodson, and W. G. Jones. *Instructional Programming for the Handicapped Student.* Springfield, IL: Charles C. Thomas, 1975.

Baker, B. L., A. J. Brightman, L. J. Heifetz, and D. M. Murphy. *Behavior Problems.* Champaign, IL: Research Press, 1990.

Becker, W. C. *Parents Are Teachers: A Child Management Program.* Champaign, IL: Research Press, 1990.

Blechman, E. A. *Solving Child Behavior Problems at Home and at School.* Champaign, IL: Research Press, 1985.

Christophersen, E. R. *Little People: Guidelines for Common Sense Child Rearing.* 2nd ed. Austin, TX: PRO-ED, 1982.

Miller, L. K. *Principles of Everyday Behavior Analysis.* 2nd ed. Monterey, CA: Brooks-Cole Publishing, 1980.

Patterson, G. R. *Families: Applications of Social Learning to Family Life.* Champaign, IL: Research Press, 1990.

American Association for the Mentally Retarded (AAMR), 1719 Kalorama Road NW, Washington, DC 20009 (800-424-3688).

Association for the Advancement of Behavior Therapy (AABT), 15 W. 36th St., New York, NY 10018 (212-279-7970).

Association for Behavior Analysis (ABA), Department of Psychology, Western Michigan University, Kalamazoo, MI 49008 (616-387-4494).

American Psychological Association (APA), 1200 17th St. NW, Washington, DC 20036 (202-955-7600).

Chapter Sixteen: Nutrition and Dental Care

American Academy of Pediatrics Committee on Nutrition. *Pediatric Nutrition Handbook.* 2nd ed. Elk Grove Village, IL: American Academy of Pediatrics, 1985.

Dietz, W. H., and L. Bandini. "Nutritional Assessment of the Handicapped Child." *Pediatrics in Review* 11 (1989): 109–115.

Fomon, S. M. *Infant Nutrition.* 2nd ed. Philadelphia: W. B. Saunders, 1974.

Palmer, S., and S. Ekrall. *Pediatric Nutrition in Developmental Disorders.* Springfield, IL: C. C. Thomas, 1978.

Robson, J. R., J. E. Konlande, F. A. Larkin, et al. "Zen Macrobiotic Dietary Problems in Infancy." *Pediatrics* 53 (1974): 326–329.

National Foundation of Dentistry for the Handicapped, 1250 14th St., Suite 610, Rockville, MD 20852.

National Nutrition Consortium, 24 Third St. NE, Washington, DC 20002.

Chapter Seventeen: Physical Therapy

Finnie, N. R. *Handling the Young Cerebral Palsied Child at Home.* 3rd ed. New York: E. P. Dutton, 1990.

Hale, G. *The Source Book for the Disabled.* London: Imprint Books Ltd., 1979.

Harrison, H., and A. Kositsky. *The Premature Baby Book: A Parent's Guide to Coping and Caring in the First Years.* New York: St. Martin's Press, 1983.

Jaeger, D. L. *Transferring and Lifting Children & Adolescents: Home Instruction Sheets.* Tucson, AZ: Communication & Therapy Skill Builders, 1989.

Jaeger, D. L. *Home Program Instruction Sheets for Infants and Young Children.* Tucson, AZ: Communication & Therapy Skill Builders, 1987.

Levy, J. *The Baby Exercise Book.* New York: Pantheon Books, 1974.

Schleichkorn, J. *Coping with Cerebral Palsy.* Austin, TX: PRO-ED, 1983.

Tingey-Michaelis, C. *Handicapped Infants and Children: A Handbook for Parents & Professionals.* Baltimore: University Park Press, 1983.

American Physical Therapy Association, 1111 N. Fairfax St., Alexandria, VA 22314.

Spina Bifida Association of America, "Insights," 343 S. Dearborn, Suite 317, Chicago, IL 60604.

Sports & Spokes Magazine, 5201 N. 19th Ave., Suite 111, Phoenix, AZ 85015.

Chapter Eighteen: Occupational Therapy

Ayres, A. J. *Sensory Integration and the Child.* Los Angeles: Western Psychological Services, 1979.

Finnie, N. R. *Handling the Young Cerebral Palsied Child at Home.* 3rd ed. New York: E. P. Dutton, 1990.

Hotte, E. B. *Self-Help Clothing for Children Who Have Physical Disabilities.* Chicago: National Easter Seals Society for Crippled Children and Adults, 1979.

Jones, M. L. *Home Care for the Chronically Ill or Disabled Child.* New York: Harper & Row Publishers, 1985.

Klein, M. D. *Dressing Techniques for Children Who Have Cerebral Palsy.* Tucson, AZ: Communication & Therapy Skill Builders, 1988.

Nelson, D. L. *Children with Autism and Other Pervasive Disorders of Development and Behavior: Therapy Through Activities.* Thorofare, NJ: Slack, 1984.

Pratt, P. N., and A. S. Allen. *Occupational Therapy for Children.* 2nd ed. St. Louis: C. V. Mosby, 1989.

Stern, F. M., and D. G. Gorga. "Neurodevelopmental Treatment (NDT): Therapeutic Intervention and Its Efficacy." *Infants and Young Children* 1(1) (1988): 22–32. Aspen Publishers Inc.

Trombly, C. A., ed. *Occupational Therapy for Physical Dysfunction.* 2nd ed. Baltimore: Williams & Wilkins, 1983.

American Occupational Therapy Association,

Inc., 1383 Piccard Dr., PO Box 1725, Rockville, MD 20850.

Neurodevelopmental Therapy Association, Inc., PO Box 70, Oak Park, IL 60303.

Sensory Integration International, 1402 Cravens Ave., Torrance, CA 90501.

Adaptive Equipment Center, Newington Children's Hospital, 181 E. Cedar Street, Newington, CT 06111.

Cleo, Inc. (Self-Help), 3957 Mayfield Road, Cleveland, OH 44121.

Discovery Toys, 2530 Arnold Drive, Suite 400, Martnex, CA 94553.

Fred Sammons, Inc. (Self-Help), Box 32, Brookfield, IL 60513.

Kapable Kids (Toys), PO Box 250, Bohemia, NY 11716.

Chapter Nineteen: Commonly Used Medicines

American National Red Cross. *Standard First Aid and Personal Safety.* Garden City, NY: Doubleday, 1987.

Gilman, A. G., L. S. Goodman, and A. Gilman. *The Pharmacological Basis of Therapeutics.* 6th ed. New York: Macmillan, 1980.

Physicians' Desk Reference. 44th ed. Oradell, NJ: Medical Economics Co., 1990.

Chapter Twenty: Educational Programs for Your Child

Aserlind, L., and E. R. Browning. *Minds into the Mainstream.* Dubuque, IA: Kendall/Hunt, 1987.

Bailey, D., and M. Wolery. *Teaching Infants and Preschoolers with Handicaps.* Columbus, OH: Charles E. Merrill, 1984.

Bender, M., and P. Valletutti. *Teaching Functional Academics: A Curriculum Guide for Adolescents and Adults with Learning Problems.* Baltimore: University Park Press, 1982.

Bender, M., and P. Valletutti. *Teaching the Moderately and Severely Handicapped.* Vols. 1–3. Austin, TX: PRO-ED, 1985.

Cain, E., and F. Taber. *Educating Disabled People for the Twenty-first Century.* Boston: College-Hill, 1987.

Gearheart, B. R., M. W. Weishahn, and C. J. Gearheart. *The Exceptional Student in the Regular Classroom.* 4th ed. Columbus, OH: Charles E. Merrill, 1988.

Kirk, S. A., and J. J. Gallagher. *Educating Exceptional Children.* 6th ed. Boston: Houghton Mifflin, 1989.

Kokasha, C. J., and D. E. Brolin. *Career Education for Handicapped Individuals.* 2nd ed. Columbus, OH: Charles E. Merrill, 1985.

Muklewicz, C., and M. Bender. *Competitive Job-finding Guide for Persons with Handicaps.* Boston: Little, Brown, 1988.

United States Commission on Civil Rights. *Accommodating the Spectrum of Individual Abilities.* Washington, DC: Clearinghouse Publication 81, 1983.

Center for Innovation in Teaching the Handicapped, 2805 E. 10th St., Room 150, Bloomington, IN 47405.

Council for Exceptional Children, 1920 Association Ave., Reston, VA 22091.

National Association of Private Schools for Exceptional Children, 2021 K. St. NW, Suite 315, Washington, DC 20006.

TASH: The Association for Persons with Severe Handicaps, 7010 Roosevelt Way NE, Seattle, WA 98115.

Chapter Twenty-one: What the Future Holds

Buscaglia, L. *The Disabled and Their Parents.* Rev. ed. New York: Henry Holt, 1983.

Ludlow, B. L., A. P. Turnbull, and R. Luckasson. *Transitions to Adult Life for People with Mental Retardation — Principles and Practices.* Baltimore: Paul H. Brookes Publishing, 1988.

Rubin, I. L., and A. C. Crocker. *Developmental Disabilities, Delivery of Medical Care for Children & Adults.* Philadelphia: Lea & Febiger, 1989.

Schulman, E. D. *Focus on the Retarded Adult, Programs & Services.* St. Louis: C. V. Mosby, 1990.

Seltzer, M. M., and J. W. Krauss. *Aging and Mental Retardation.* AAMR Monographs #9. Washington, DC: AAMR, 1987.

Thomas, A. P., M. C. O. Bax, and D. P. Smyth.

The Health and Social Needs of Young Adults with Physical Disabilities. Philadelphia: J. B. Lippincott, 1989.

Turnbull, H., III, et al. *Disability and the Family: A Guide to Decisions for Adulthood.* Baltimore: Paul H. Brookes Publishing, 1988.

Whitman, B. Y., and P. J. Accardo. *When a Parent Is Mentally Retarded.* Baltimore: Paul H. Brookes Publishing, 1990.

ACCENT on Living, P.O. Box 700, Bloomington, IL 61701.

American Coalition of Citizens with Disabilities, 1012 14th St. NW, Suite 901, Washington, DC 20005.

Boy Scouts of America, Scouting for the Handicapped Division, 1325 Walnut Hill Lane, Irving, TX 75038.

Center on Human Policy, Syracuse University, 406 Huntington Hall, Syracuse, NY 13210.

Children's Defense Fund, 122 C St. NW, Washington, DC 20001.

Coalition on Sexuality and Disability, 853 Broadway, Room 611, New York, NY 10003.

Council for Disability Rights, 343 S. Dearborn, #318, Chicago, IL 60604.

Girl Scouts of the USA, 830 Third Ave., New York, NY 10022.

The Sibling Information Network, Department of Educational Psychology, Box U-64, University of Connecticut, Storrs, CT 06268.

Special Olympics, 1350 New York Ave. NW, Suite 500, Washington, DC 20005.

Team of Advocates for Special Kids (TASK), 1800 E. La Veta, Orange, CA 92666.

Index